Splendid Pages

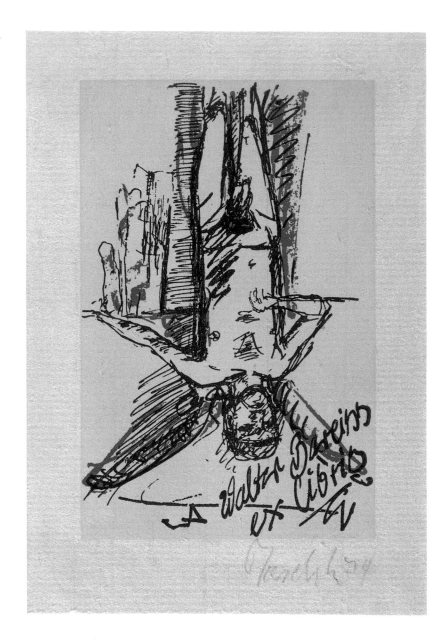

THE MOLLY AND WALTER BAREISS
COLLECTION OF
MODERN ILLUSTRATED BOOKS

Splendid Pages

JULIE MELLBY

WITH CONTRIBUTIONS BY

WALTER BAREISS
MEI-MEI BERSSENBRUGGE
MAY CASTLEBERRY
RIVA CASTLEMAN
JOHANNA DRUCKER
ELEANOR M. GARVEY
MICHAEL SEMFF
KIKI SMITH

HUDSON HILLS PRESS, NEW YORK AND MANCHESTER
IN ASSOCIATION WITH THE
TOLEDO MUSEUM OF ART

All illustrations, unless otherwise noted, are from the Molly and Walter Bareiss Collection of Modern Illustrated Books at the Toledo Museum of Art, Toledo, Ohio. Gift of Molly and Walter Bareiss.

This book is issued in conjunction with the exhibition *Splendid Pages: The Molly and Walter Bareiss Collection of Modern Illustrated Books,* held at the Toledo Museum of Art, from February 14 to May 11, 2003.

This book was published with the assistance of The Andrew W. Mellon Foundation.

FIRST EDITION
© 2003 Toledo Museum of Art

Published in the United States by Hudson Hills Press LLC, 74-2 Union Street, Manchester, Vermont 05254. Distributed in the United States, its territories and possessions, and Canada by National Book Network, Inc. Distributed in the United Kingdom, Eire, and Europe by Windsor Books International.

Founding Publisher: Paul Anbinder
Executive Directors: Randall Perkins and Leslie van Breen

Publication Supervisor: Sandra E. Knudsen
Curator of Works on Paper: Julie Mellby
Conservation Technician-Graphic Arts Assistant: Thomas Loeffler
Graphic Arts Cataloguer: Paula Reich
Editor: Monica S. Rumsey
Designer: Katy Homans
Manufactured in Japan by Toppan Printing Co.

Toledo Museum of Art
2445 Monroe Street, P. O. Box 1013, Toledo, Ohio 43697-1013
Telephone (419) 255-8000; fax (419) 255-5638; internet www.toledomuseum.org

Frontispiece: Fig. 1. Georg Baselitz, *Walter Bareiss Ex Libris* (1974). Etching. Edition: unnumbered/2,000.
Fig. 153 on page 224: Max Ernst from *La ballade du soldat.* Text by Georges Ribemont-Dessaignes (Vence: Pierre Chave, 1972). Color lithograph. Edition: 47/199.

Library of Congress Cataloging-in-Publication Data

Mellby, Julie.
 Splendid pages : the Molly and Walter Bareiss collection of modern illustrated books / Julie Mellby : with contributions by Walter Bareiss ... [et al.]. — 1st ed.
  p. cm.
Includes bibliographical references and index.
 ISBN 1-55595-209-7 (alk. paper)
 1. Artists' illustrated books — Catalogs. 2. Bareiss, Molly — Art collections — Catalogs. 3. Bareiss, Walter — Art collections — Catalogs. 4. Artists' illustrated books — Private collections — Ohio — Toledo — Catalogs. 5. Artists' illustrated books — Ohio — Toledo — Catalogs. 6. Toledo Museum of Art — Catalogs. I. Bareiss, Molly. II. Bareiss, Walter. III. Toledo Museum of Art. IV. Title.
 NE890 .M45 2003
 769'.074'77113 — dc21
                    2002011598

Contents

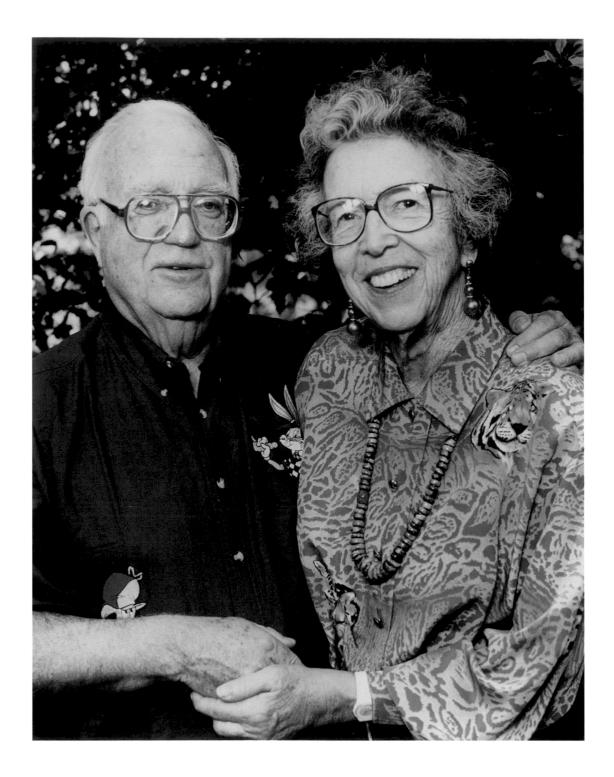

Fig. 2. *Molly and Walter Bareiss*, 2001. Photograph.

Courtesy of Molly and Walter Bareiss.

Director's Foreword

When I became the seventh director of the Toledo Museum of Art in January 1999, high on my agenda was to re-acquaint myself with Molly and Walter Bareiss of Greenwich, Connecticut, and to promote completion of the catalogue of their modern book collection, which they so generously donated to the Museum in 1984.

The wonders of Molly and Walter Bareiss's collection have been enlightening visitors to our Museum, as well as my predecessors, Roger Mandle and David W. Steadman. The collection has further served as unparalleled inspiration to graphic arts curators Roberta Waddell, Marilyn F. Symmes, Christine Swenson, and especially to Julie Mellby. Ms. Mellby has enthusiastically shared the dreams of a catalogue and exhibition to celebrate this treasure trove of modern illustrated books.

It has been my honor, my responsibility, and indeed my great pleasure to see this catalogue to its publication. Among the rewards of any museum project is sharing great works of art with the public. Our Museum has the unique opportunity to heighten public appreciation of a choice selection in words and images of the vast and various books that were assembled by Molly and Walter Bareiss. Art collected by individuals has the distinct advantage over that acquired by an institution in being both personal and private. In the case of the Bareiss book collection, each volume was pursued, examined, researched, and, in the end, purchased only when it brought pleasure to these two judicious and passionate collectors. Like Shakespeare, who wrote, "No profit grows where is no pleasure ta'en; In brief, sir, study what you most affect," the Bareiss Collection is the product of one couple's enormous pleasure. It is intensely personal and idiosyncratic, both wonderful and mysterious, with surprises inside every cover.

It is the Bareisses' delight and enthusiasm for books that we most wish to convey through this catalogue. One finds in these creative collaborations the interaction of words and images, of literature and poetry with the visual arts, to form a hybrid particularly revealing of modern artists. It is both a picture *and* a thousand words: the best of all possible worlds. Each page resonates in a different way—here classical elegance, there wild abandon—until one simply must give in to the amazing variety in this vast collection and resolve never to completely understand it, but rather to love it all the more for its tremendous scope.

How does one properly thank these two remarkable people? Where do we find the words to express our appreciation, not only for the works of art but also for the patience and support they have shown our Museum over the years? We hope this book will inspire art lovers, bibliophiles, scholars, and novices to the genre. For only through a multitude of voices will a message of sufficient power reach our friends in Connecticut.

ROGER M. BERKOWITZ

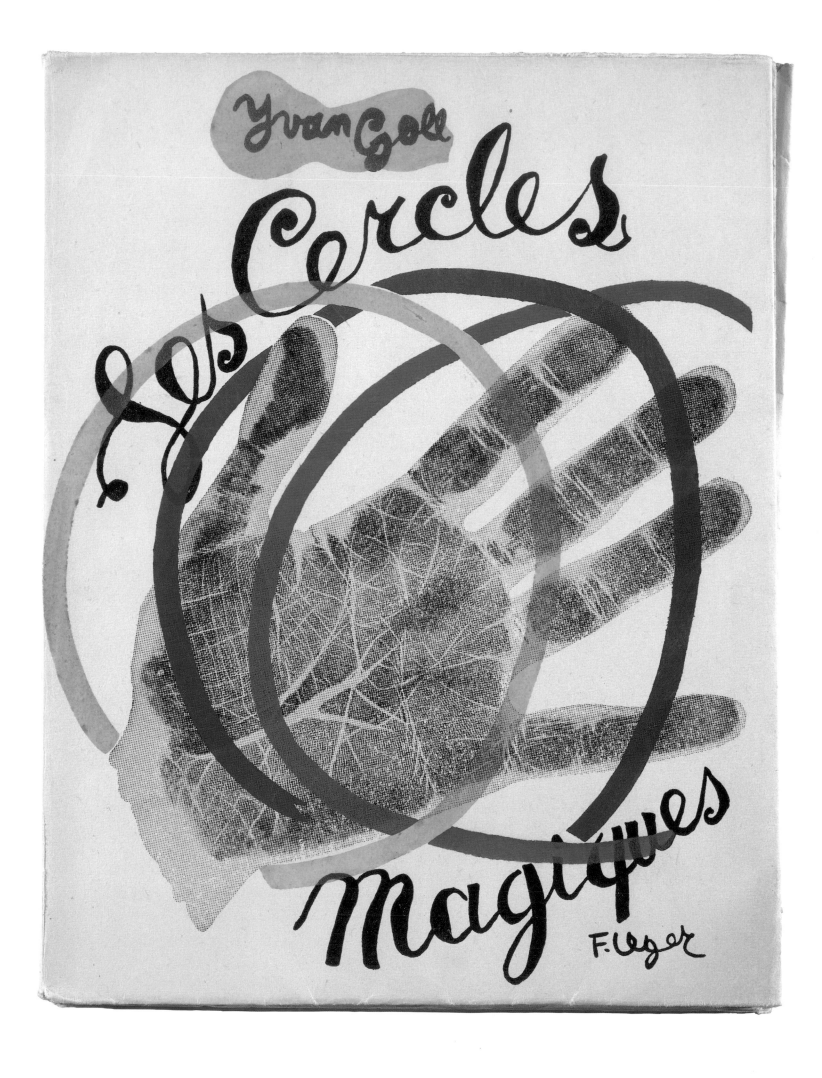

Yvan Goll

Les Cercles

Magiques

F. Léger

Acknowledgments

Any project nearly twenty years in the making must acknowledge the help of a great many people. These few words of thanks cannot adequately express my gratitude and admiration for all the work that has been focused on the Bareiss Collection—in the past, in the present, and for the future.

First and foremost, this catalogue celebrates a stunning gift by Molly and Walter Bareiss to the Toledo Museum of Art: more than 1,400 modern illustrated books collected individually with great love and devotion. Through their gift, these two generous donors have transformed the graphic arts department at the Toledo Museum. I can only hope this catalogue of the Bareiss Collection will offer the world a sense of the great beauty and historical significance found inside these volumes.

Three directors have shared the responsibility for this project, beginning with Roger Mandle in the 1980s. At that time, few directors had the foresight and courage to make such an acquisition happen. David W. Steadman followed, making sure the cataloguing of the Bareiss Collection continued even when times were hard. Finally, Roger M. Berkowitz, current director of the Toledo Museum, understood the importance of the collection and brought it to the forefront of Museum activities. He re-energized stalled momentum, found the appropriate funding, and galvanized commitment from every corner of the Museum. Without his support and infectious enthusiasm, this catalogue would not have been published.

Several generations of Toledo Museum curators of graphic arts have also contributed to the success of this project, and I wish to acknowledge each of them. Roberta Waddell, currently curator of prints for the New York Public Library, worked tirelessly with Roger Mandle to convince the Bareisses that Toledo would be the perfect home for their books. Marilyn F. Symmes, now curator of drawings and prints at the Cooper-Hewitt, National Design Museum, was responsible not only for initially receiving, housing, and inventorying the collection but also for organizing the first exhibitions and publications interpreting this material. She wrote the first essays, gave the first tours, and arranged the first loan exhibitions. We continue to rely heavily on her scholarship and wish to express our gratitude for her enormous accomplishments. Christine Swenson joined the Museum in the 1990s and continued to integrate the Bareiss Collection with the Toledo Museum's own books and prints through exhibitions and tours. Under her management the detailed cataloguing for this vast collection was nearly completed and preparations for a major exhibition began.

Roberta Waddell and Marilyn Symmes served as invaluable readers, providing historical details as well as editorial direction. I am most grateful to them for delving into their past, offering both guidance and support. In fact, we challenged the memories of many former staff members, and it is a testament to the friendship

Fig. 3. Fernand Léger from *Les cercles magiques.* Text by Yvan Goll (Paris: Éditions Falaize, 1951). Photomechanical reproduction with added pochoir color.

and generosity of Molly and Walter Bareiss that people immediately came to our assistance when they learned the nature of the project.

The Toledo Museum's graphic arts area of expertise has been ably assisted by a variety of staff members, interns, and volunteers over the last twenty years, including Loviah E. Aldinger, Sarah Black, Suzanne Guinivere, Danis Houser, Mary Mosing-Kruger, Thomas Loeffler, Carol Orser, Paula Reich, and Amy Timar. I fear several names may have fallen between the cracks as we attempt to recognize each one individually and hope they know how grateful we are for their contributions, their understanding, and their dedication to making this catalogue a reality.

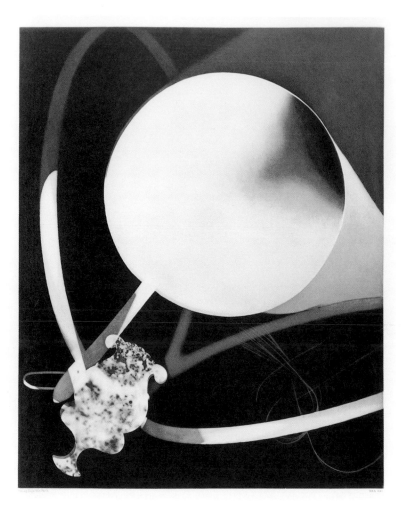

Fig. 4. Man Ray from *L'ange Heurtebise.* Text by Jean Cocteau (Paris: Librairie Stock, 1925). Photogravure of a rayogram. Edition: 73/300.

This catalogue was supervised by Sandra E. Knudsen, coordinator of publications at the Toledo Museum. Her attention to detail, long-term planning, and ceaseless good humor have made working with her a pleasure. Editorial direction was provided by Monica S. Rumsey, who remained sensitive to each author's voice while managing to lead a diverse group in a common direction. Caryl Avery assisted in the organization and editing of Mr. Bareiss's own essay, and John Gabriel provided a thoughtful English translation for Michael Semff's contribution.

Our publisher, Paul Anbinder at Hudson Hills Press, allowed us the freedom to develop this very personal project while still providing the necessary support and guidance. Katy Homans, one of the great masters of book design, created a beautiful framework in which the diverse words and images of the Bareiss Collection could live harmoniously. We are indeed fortunate that artist Kiki Smith and poet Mei-mei Berssenbrugge agreed to contribute an essay to the catalogue and to collaborate with Katy on the design of their pages.

When looking for authors to contribute to this catalogue, we approached artists, writers, publishers, editors, designers, curators, collectors, and historians in the hope that each might shed important light on the collaborative nature of this dynamic art form. Each was asked to share a personal story or develop a personal interest, and we are grateful for their compelling essays, which illuminate not only the Bareiss Collection but also the marvelous art form it represents. Walter Bareiss, Mei-mei Berssenbrugge, May Castleberry, Riva Castleman, Johanna Drucker, Eleanor M. Garvey, Michael Semff, and Kiki Smith are each experts in their field who took time to share their knowledge with our readers. We are honored to publish their work in this catalogue.

Funding for this catalogue comes from the Andrew W. Mellon Foundation, and we wish to express our sincere gratitude for its continuing support of the Toledo Museum of Art's publication program.

I owe an enormous debt to the staff of the Toledo Museum of Art, none of whom refused requests for assistance with this publication. Our registrars, Patricia J. Whitesides, Karen Serota, and Nicole Rivette, along with Lee Mooney, were responsible for the accessioning of the books and for the continued maintenance of their documentation. Our tremendous exhibitions team, past and present, includes Teresa Beamsley, Charlene Bettencourt, Cathy Brindley, Claude Fixler, Julia Habrecht, Mary Plouffe, and Carolyn M. Putney. These colleagues worked to prepare the collection for publication and for the accompanying exhibition.

Research assistance was provided by our archivist Julie McMaster and our librarians Anne O. Morris and Heidi Yeager. Additional research came from Bernice Parent at Yale University and Rebecca Stickney at Bennington College.

Photography for the catalogue was beautifully accomplished by Mark Oberst of Image Source, Toledo, with additional work by the Museum's talented photographer, Kathy Gee. Several institutions helped to supply complementary illustrations for the essays and we wish to acknowledge their prompt assistance: Dr. Margrit Brehm, Staatliche Kunsthalle, Baden-Baden, Germany; Lee McLaird, Bowling Green State University Libraries, Center for Archival Collections, Bowling Green, Ohio; Tom Ford, Houghton Library of the Harvard College Library, Cambridge, Massachusetts; Yale University Art Gallery, New Haven, Connecticut; The New York Public Library Humanities Division, New York City; François and Sophie Mairé, Iliazd-Club, Paris; Mary Ellen Brezovsky, COBAR Management, Stamford, Connecticut; National Gallery of Art, Washington, D.C.; and Larissa Goldston, Universal Limited Art Editions, West Islip, New York. In addition, numerous rights and reproductions agencies worked with our publications team to allow us the opportunity to publish these beautiful images.

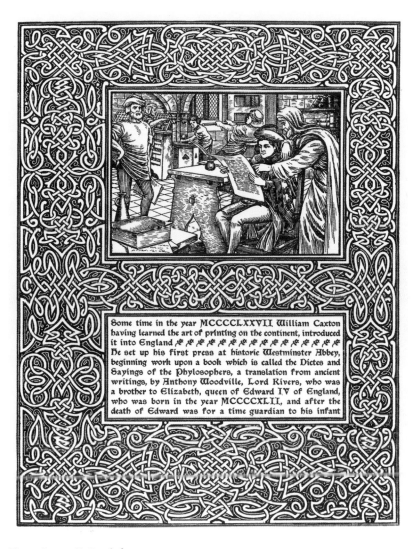

Fig. 5. George G. Booth from *The Dictes and Sayings of the Philosophers* (Detroit: Cranbrook Press, 1901). Wood-engraving. Edition: 141/244.

Finally, I wish to recognize the current graphic arts team who worked tirelessly to bring this catalogue and the accompanying exhibition to fruition: Thomas Loeffler, Paula Reich, and our volunteers Carol Orser and Suzanne Guinivere. No element of this project went unattended by these wonderful people. Carol helped to unpack the Bareiss Collection when the books first arrived at the Museum in the 1980s and was still hard at work, together with Sue, when the last book was photographed in 2002. Paula patiently checked every detail of the cataloguing, not once or twice but countless times to assure the accuracy of the entries. Tom assisted Marilyn Symmes and Christine Swenson, and continues to manage the care and display of our collections with sensitivity and imagination. Each one contributed ideas, research, organizational planning, and valued friendship. They are the reason this book is complete, and they deserve my heartfelt thanks.

JULIE MELLBY

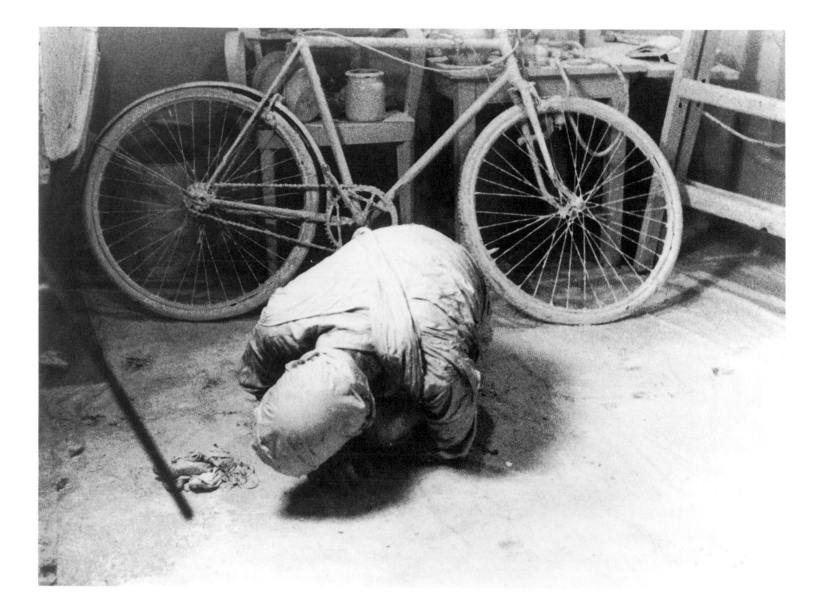

Fig. 6. Günter Brus from *Ana: 1. Aktion, 1964*
([Wien]: Galerie Heike Curtze, Galerie Krinziner,
[1984?]). Gelatin silver print. Edition: 17/35.

JULIE MELLBY

Introduction

What is the use of a book, thought Alice, without pictures or conversations?
—LEWIS CARROLL, *Alice's Adventures in Wonderland* (1864)

From its earliest days, the Toledo Museum of Art had a mandate to collect, exhibit, and interpret the history of the written and printed word. From rolled papyrus scrolls to illuminated vellum leaves, from carved clay tablets to carved blockbooks, from Johannes Gutenberg to William Morris, the history of the book has an important presence in the Museum's galleries. The interest in rare and illustrated books began with George W. Stevens, the Museum's director from 1903 to 1926. Stevens established a noteworthy collection of the book arts from their earliest forms through the contemporary work of his day, at the beginning of the twentieth century. He purchased such treasures as the *Liber Chronicarum (The Nuremberg Chronicle)* printed by Anton Koberger (1493); pages from *The Apocalypse of Saint John* (ca. 1450) and *Biblia pauperum* (1430–40); an English horn book from the seventeenth century; and a Hebrew scroll of the Book of Esther, written on vellum and rolled into an etched silver cylinder.

   In 1907 Stevens mounted the collection in a small exhibit alongside the painting galleries. It was so popular that when the closing day came, rather than being de-installed, the exhibition was successively moved wherever space was available. When the Museum's new building was opened in 1912, an exhibition gallery (affectionately known as the "book room") was permanently devoted to the book arts. Stevens wrote the following mission statement:

> *It is the aim of our Museum some day to tell perfectly the story of printing, engraving, and illustrating, from the ancient days of the clay tablet, down through papyri, vellum, the handwritten books, incunabula, the early engraving on wood and copper, etching, printing and book making in all its steps.*[1]

Stevens not only built a collection but also built the audience to appreciate it. In 1923 he instigated a campaign to have every member of the Museum give one dollar toward the purchase of a seventeenth-century second folio of the works of William Shakespeare. This and many other campaigns succeeded in nurturing several generations of book lovers in the Toledo area.

   Stevens was succeeded by Blake-More Godwin, director from 1926 through 1958, who greatly expanded the Museum building, including the amount of gallery space available for exhibitions. From 1959 to 1976 director Otto Wittmann built the reputation of the institution through significant acquisitions and renowned

1. *Toledo Museum of Art Museum News,* no. 40 (December 1921).

exhibitions. Clearly in tune with the development of art museums in the United States, he began a graphic arts program in the early 1970s, hiring May Davis Hill as a part-time curatorial consultant to oversee the opening of the Grace J. Hitchcock Print Study Room in 1972. Curatorial intern Patrick Noon was hired to assist students who could now study art history through original prints and rare books.

When Roger Mandle became director in 1977, he brought with him the same enthusiasm and commitment to books held by George Stevens. It was Mandle who made the momentous decision to create the position of curator of graphic arts, along with acquisition funds to develop the collection of prints and photographs and to revitalize the book collection. Print specialist Roberta Waddell joined the Museum and, with Mandle's support, expanded the collection to include modern illustrated books. She purchased fine-press, limited-edition volumes containing original prints by celebrated artists, beginning with Jasper Johns's important new publication *Foirades / Fizzles* (1976) [Fig. 63]. Her timing was impeccable, and in 1979 the Museum acquired artist illustrated books from the personal library of the renowned New York dealer and publisher, George Wittenborn. The collection included an astonishing selection of Dada and Surrealist books and ephemera, as well as such masterpieces as Pablo Picasso's *Le chant des morts* by Pierre Reverdy (1948), Joan Miró's *Ubu Roi* by Alfred Jarry (1966), Aristide Maillol's *Eclogues* in Virgil's original Latin (1927), Henry van de Velde's *Also sprach Zarathustra* by Friedrich Nietzsche (1908), and *Solidarité* by Paul Éluard (1938), with etchings by Picasso, Miró, Tanguy, and others.

In a department known for its old master prints, drawings, and illuminated manuscripts, Waddell gave equal exhibition space to the art of the modern book with such exhibitions as *Dada and Surrealist Prints and Books, Brooke Alexander, Russian Books and Prints,* and *Matisse Prints and Illustrated Books.* The latter illustrates Waddell's effort to incorporate books into print shows, reflecting the painter-printmaker's ongoing involvement in bookmaking. In 1984 *The Book: A Celebration of the Museum's Collection* marked the opening of the newly renovated George W. Stevens Gallery, featuring such cornerstones of printing as *The Nuremberg Chronicle* and pages from the *Gutenberg Bible,* along with twentieth-century *livres d'artistes.* Among the visitors to the Museum in these years were Molly and Walter Bareiss of Greenwich, Connecticut, and Munich, Germany.

Friendship was the main impetus for the Bareisses' trips to Toledo. Since her Bennington College days, Molly (Stimson) Bareiss had kept in touch with her two roommates: Carol Channing (who became the well-known Broadway and Hollywood actress) and Barbara K. Kirchmeier, an art history student. When they graduated in 1941, "Bobbie" Kirchmeier returned to Ohio, where she volunteered at the Toledo Museum's library and soon married William G. Sutherland, settling in the nearby town of Perrysburg. Molly was swept away to New York City by her new husband, Walter Bareiss, but in spite of the distance, the couples maintained a close friendship (each raising one daughter and four sons). Over the years, a visit to Perrysburg would often include a trip to the Toledo Museum of Art, where the Sutherlands introduced their friends to its marvelous collections and to members of the staff.

Although it was Molly's close ties with a former roommate that brought the Bareisses to the area, it was Walter's great love for the arts that made the Museum visits inevitable. There are few collectors who are as well acquainted with the museums of Europe and the United States as Walter Bareiss. A graduate of Yale University (class of 1940), Barciss majored in industrial engineering and economics but also took classes in the history of art. In remembering those early years, he wrote, "I couldn't stand that [course of study] without there being a balancing force of fine arts."[2] In particular, George Heard Hamilton, professor and trustee of The Museum of Modern Art, became a mentor and, later, a friend. After serving in the army, Bareiss moved to New York City, where he was a regular visitor to the art galleries. He may have been the youngest client many dealers saw in those days; this was certainly true for Paul Rosenberg, whose gallery had just opened in 1940.[3]

Bareiss mixed a busy career in the textile industry with the pursuit of modern painting, African sculpture, Greek vases, Asian ceramics, prints, drawings, and surprisingly, artist illustrated books. Writing for *The New York Times*, William Zimmer called Bareiss "one of the rare breed of successful businessmen whose studies in art history kept pace with his studies in economics."[4] In a 1984 interview with Jacqueline Brody, Bareiss speaks of being re-energized by art:

> *To me, it's the most peaceful, relaxing activity. It's aesthetic beauty—let's face it, that's a bad word, not politically correct—but it's aesthetics, and that's something. For instance, when I had a very difficult week in the textile business I was in, and a lot of complications which were not easily resolved, and then I go look at my pictures or I go out and visit a gallery or several galleries, I have a feeling my blood pressure goes down twenty points, and I feel newborn.*[5]

However, this was more than a Sunday afternoon hobby. Bareiss practiced great connoisseurship in the arts, studying the history, provenance, condition, and aesthetics of a work of art before adding it to one of his diverse collections. A good example in the Bareiss book collection is the *Antitête* series [Fig. 18].

> *I purchased one little print by Miró and then researched where it came from, finally located the series and successfully bought the series of three books [Max Ernst's* Monsieur Aa l'antiphilosophe, *Yves Tanguy's* Minuits pour géants, *and Joan Miró's* Le désespéranto] *for less than the single print. That was in 1949 in Europe.*[6]

In 1956 Bareiss sold his business in New York City. When his father died unexpectedly two years later, he moved to Munich and ran his father's company for another twenty-five years. During this time, he chaired the Munich Gallery Association for many years and worked with many German dealers, patronizing Galerie Fred Jahn in particular, from its earliest days. He was invited to join committees at art institutions worldwide and eventually came to sit on the boards of The Metropolitan Museum of Art and The Museum of Modern Art in New York City, the Yale University Art Gallery in New Haven, and the Bavarian State Museum in Munich, among many others. By the 1980s Molly and Walter Bareiss were also members of the Toledo Museum of Art's Council on the Collection.

Bareiss's love of antiquities found a kindred spirit in Toledo's curator of ancient art, Kurt T. Luckner. (The J. Paul Getty Museum later purchased the magnificent Bareiss collection of Greek vases.[7]) Roberta Waddell remembered that it was through Luckner that the Bareisses first made their way to the graphic arts galleries and were introduced to her. In 1981 she was invited to visit the Bareiss home in Connecticut and allowed to see, firsthand, the amazing array of paintings, sculpture,

2. Paul Cummings, "Interview: Walter Bareiss Talks with Paul Cummings," *Drawing* 6, no. 4 (November–December 1984): 84.

3. Jacqueline Brody, "Focus on Collecting: Walter Bareiss," *Print Collector's Newsletter* 25, no. 2 (May–June 1994): 50.

4. William Zimmer, "Dramatic Neuberger Show of Artist-Illustrated Books," *The New York Times* (October 9, 1988): 38.

5. Brody, op. cit. (note 3): 56.

6. Correspondence from Walter Bareiss to Marilyn F. Symmes, August 8, 1985.

7. *Corpus Vasorum Antiquorum, The J. Paul Getty Museum, Molly and Walter Bareiss Collection* (Malibu, California: The J. Paul Getty Museum, 1988–1998), fasc. 1, Andrew J. Clark (1988); fasc. 2, Andrew J. Clark (1990); fasc. 5, Marit R. Jentoft-Nilsen in collaboration with A. D. Trendall (1994); fasc. 7, Richard T. Neer (1997); fasc. 8, Mary B. Moore (1998).

and, most important, the stunning selection of books collected by this adventure-some couple. Walter Bareiss, a man of endless graciousness and hospitality, marked her visit with a donation of two books to the Toledo Museum: Jean Dubuffet's *La fleur de barbe* (1960) and A. R. Penck's *Standarts* (1970).

In 1984 Walter Bareiss sold his father's business and, as the year came to an end, he and Molly made the magnanimous donation of their entire collection of more than 1,400 modern illustrated books to the Toledo Museum of Art. Among them, seventy-three volumes with original prints by Pablo Picasso were specifically donated in honor of Barbara Sutherland who, sadly, did not live to see the collection installed at the Museum. When deciding where to place their book collection, Mr. and Mrs. Bareiss considered a number of institutions. In the end, it was the Toledo Museum's long-standing commitment to the art of the book, along with the personal friendships developed here, that made it a perfect fit.

Marilyn F. Symmes, curator of graphic arts from September 1984 to 1991, had just arrived at the Museum when Roger Mandle announced the exciting news that the Bareiss Collection of Modern Illustrated Books was coming to Toledo. Before the boxes were unpacked, preparations had already begun for an exhibition featuring highlights of this extraordinary collection. *The Bareiss Collection of Modern Illustrated Books from Toulouse-Lautrec to Kiefer* opened on September 22, 1985. A handsome catalogue was published documenting the eighty-eight volumes chosen for the exhibition.[8]

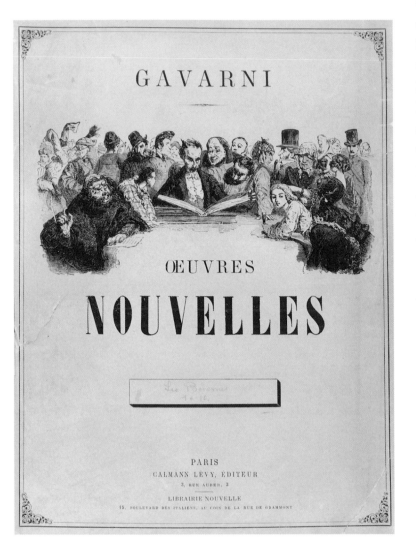

Fig. 7. After Paul Gavarni from *Oeuvres nouvelles: Les bohèmes* (Paris: Librairie Nouvelle, 1853). Wood-engraving.

Throughout the 1980s and 1990s, the Bareiss Collection provided the inspiration for regular exhibitions, scholarly programs, and individual research in the Museum's print study room. *Prints and Books Illustrated by Jean Dubuffet* was mounted in 1986, and *Picasso as an Illustrator* (with catalogue) followed in 1988, as well as the loan exhibition entitled *Bonnard to Kiefer: 20th-Century Artist-Illustrated Books from the Bareiss Collection at the Toledo Museum of Art* shown at the Neuberger Museum of Art (at SUNY Purchase, New York) later that year. In 1992 Christine Swenson became curator of graphic arts and for the next seven years continued the tradition of organizing exhibitions to feature the book collection, culminating in 1997 with a yearlong "celebration of the book."

When I joined the Toledo Museum in late 1999, director Roger M. Berkowitz had begun work toward a major publication that would both document and celebrate the Bareiss Collection of Modern Illustrated Books. The detailed cataloguing of each volume was nearly complete. To showcase the spectacular scope of the Bareiss Collection, *Splendid Pages*—the exhibition and the book—was conceived. To build momentum toward the 2003 grand opening, annual exhibitions featuring aspects of the collection were planned for the spring of 2000, 2001, and 2002.[9]

Once I got to know the collection, I found Walter Bareiss to be an adventurous and daring collector, eager to learn and enthusiastically seeking out the most

8. Marilyn F. Symmes, *The Bareiss Collection of Modern Illustrated Books from Toulouse-Lautrec to Kiefer* (Toledo: Toledo Museum of Art, 1985). 9. *Classically Modern: Classical Texts with Modern Prints from the Bareiss Collection of Modern Illustrated Books* with an essay by Andrew Szegedy-Maszak (Toledo: Toledo Museum of Art, 2000); *Don't Feed the Books: Birds, Bugs, and Bestiaries Featuring the Bareiss Collection* with an essay by Teresa Nevins (Toledo: Toledo Museum of Art, 2001); and *Embracing the Page: Images of Love and Romance Featuring the Bareiss Collection* [no catalogue], 2002.

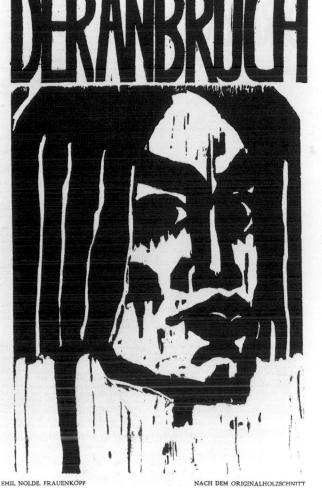

EMIL NOLDE, FRAUENKÖPF   NACH DEM ORIGINALHOLZSCHNITT

Fig. 8. Emil Nolde from *Der Anbruch* Oct. 1919, [no.] 6/7. Texts by various authors, edited by Otto Schneider and J. B. Neumann (Berlin: J. B. Neumann, 1919). Photomechanical reproduction. Listed in Checklist under Various Artists.

10. Note that many books have more than one artist and, therefore, this is not meant to be a precise accounting of each volume but, rather, a general view of the collection's scope.
11. For a good explanation of these terms, see Robert Rainwater's eloquent introduction to *The American Livre de Peintre,* catalogue by Elizabeth Phillips and Tony Zwicker (New York: Grolier Club, 1993).

avantgarde of contemporary artists. He is a connoisseur with the self-confidence to stray outside the norm. The rewards of this assuredness can be found throughout his book collection, which is filled with treasures of many nationalities and artistic periods; with books containing uncommon mediums by young, talented artists side by side with the great classics of the genre.

It is helpful to look at statistics when trying to grasp the breadth of this collection. There are 328 books containing work by French artists, 257 feature the work of American artists, and 252 the work of German artists.[10] Artists from Austria, Belgium, Chile, Cuba, Czechoslovakia, Denmark, Great Britain, Hungary, Iceland, Italy, Japan, Mexico, the Netherlands, Norway, Poland, Romania, Russia, Spain, and Switzerland can also be found. The poets and authors represented in these books include a similar range of nationalities with texts that date as far back as Sappho, about 610–about 580 B.C.E.

The earliest publications in the collection are two volumes of Paul Gavarni's *Oeuvres nouvelles: Les bohèmes* [Fig. 7], published in 1853. Several books illustrated by Jean-Louis Forain and J.-F. Raffaëlli, Wilhelm Busch, and Amédée Lynen date from the 1880s, along with an unillustrated, fine-press edition of Émile Zola's *Mon salon.* But the collection really begins with the 1890s, when we see the birth of what we now know as the *livre de peintre* or *livre d'artiste.*[11] *La damnation de l'artiste* (1890), *Flambeaux noirs* (1891), and *La passante* (1892) each contain dark and magical prints by Odilon Redon. Pierre Bonnard, Maurice Denis, Henry van de Velde, Édouard Vuillard, Henri de Toulouse-Lautrec, Auguste Donnay, Alfred Jarry, Louis Legrand, and Théo van Rysselberghe are some of the other artists represented in magnificent, late-nineteenth-century limited editions.

It is difficult to single out individual treasures within such a rich collection. There are the classics of modern artist illustrated books such as Pierre Bonnard's monumental *Parallèlement* (purchased from the German dealer Richard Zinser, in 1944) [Fig. 17], Joan Miró's *À toute épreuve* with text by Paul Éluard [Fig. 9], Antoni Tàpies's *Air* with text by André du Bouchet [Fig. 12], and Anselm Kiefer's marvelous *Brünhilde schläft* [Fig. 131]. Unquestionably a major strength of the collection is the extraordinary gathering of books containing original prints by Picasso. It is a remarkable achievement to have collected the work of this seminal artist in such depth—seventy-three volumes containing more than eight hundred prints. They are a tremendous resource for the exhibition and study of twentieth-century art at the Toledo Museum of Art.

Walter Bareiss also championed the work of modern German and Austrian artists, such as Horst Antes, Georg Baselitz, Joseph Beuys, Wolfram Erber, Franz Hitzler, Jörg Immendorff, Anselm Kiefer, Hermann Nitsch, A. R. Penck, Arnulf Rainer, and Dieter Roth. Illustrated journals such as *Der Anbruch* [Fig. 8], *Der Bildermann, Interfunktionen, Die Schaströmmel,* and *SPUR: Die Verfolgung der Künstler* were also collected.

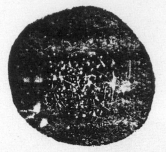

Peut-il se reposer celui qui dort

Il ne voit pas la nuit ne voit pas l'invisible

Il a de grandes couvertures

Et des coussins de sang sur des coussins de boue

Sa tête est sous les toits et ses mains sont fermées

Sur les outils de la fatigue

Il dort pour éprouver sa force

La honte d'être aveugle dans un si grand silence.

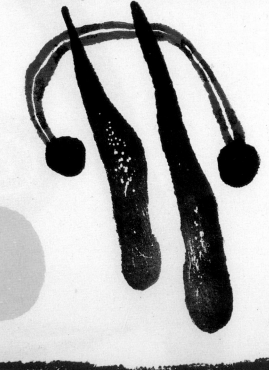

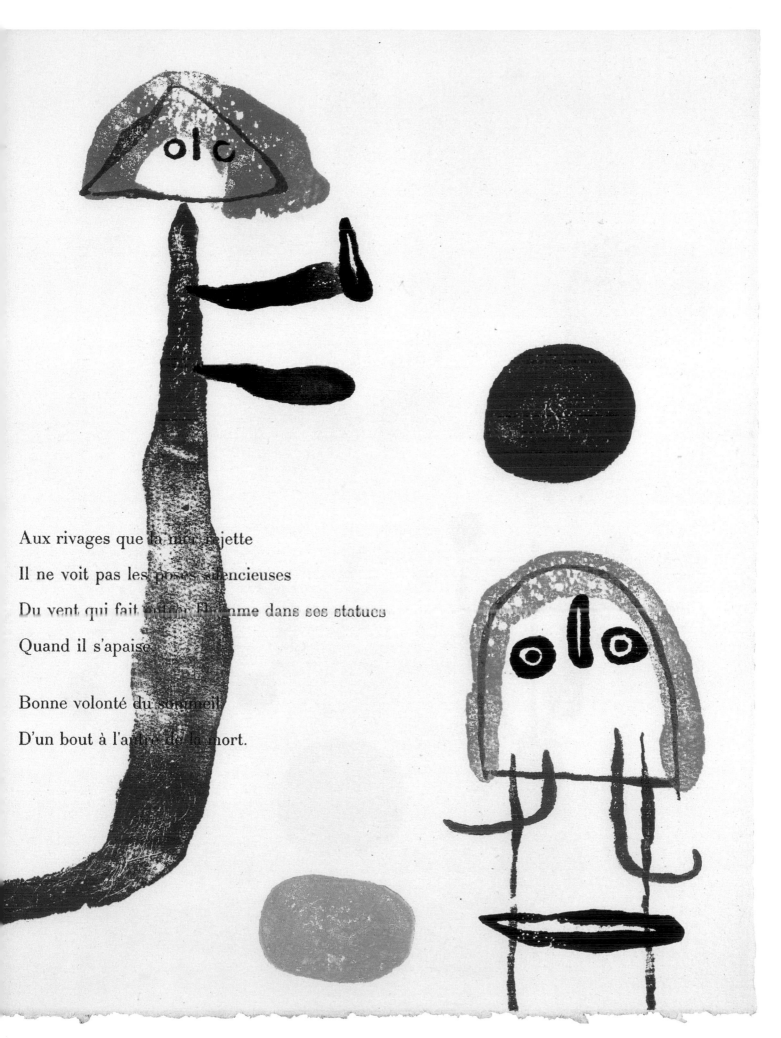

Aux rivages que la mer rejette

Il ne voit pas les poses silencieuses

Du vent qui fait comme dans ses statues

Quand il s'apaise.

Bonne volonté du sommeil

D'un bout à l'autre de la mort.

Fig. 9. Joan Miró from *À toute épreuve*. Text
by Paul Éluard (Genève: Gérald Cramer, 1958).
Color woodcuts. Edition: 25/106.

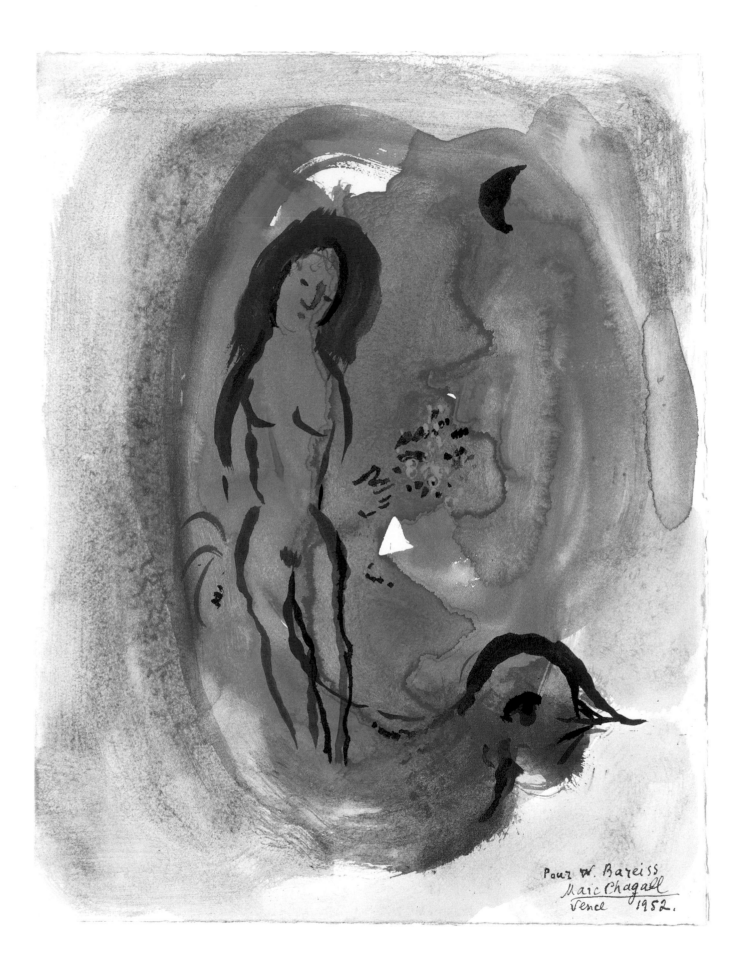

Fig. 10. Marc Chagall from *Fables*. Text by
Jean de La Fontaine (Paris: Tériade, 1952).
Watercolor drawing in this copy only, inscribed
"Pour W. Bareiss, Marc Chagall, Vence 1952."
Edition: 126/185.

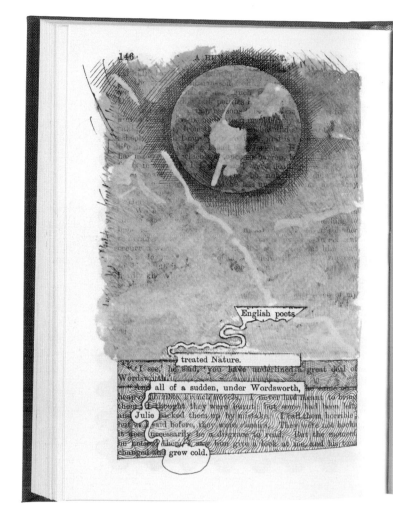

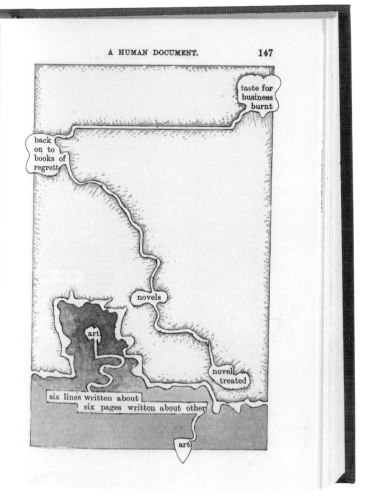

Fig. 11. Tom Phillips from
*A Humument: A Treated
Victorian Novel* (London:
Thames and Hudson, 1980).
Photomechanical reproduction.

The Bareiss Collection also holds a number of books and catalogues extra-illustrated with drawings and prints often added specifically for Molly and Walter Bareiss, such as *Fables* by Jean de La Fontaine (1952), which includes an original Chagall drawing as well as the traditional prints [Fig. 10]. No fewer than thirty four volumes carry personal inscriptions from the artists. Also added to each book in the collection is the personal Bareiss bookplate, designed by Georg Baselitz [Fig. 1]. It is telling that in 1974, when the bookplate was commissioned, the Bareiss Collection was already substantial enough and enthusiasm was such that a print run of two thousand bookplates was considered necessary.

In addition to the classic *livre d'artiste,* the Bareiss Collection includes many examples of mass produced artists' books beginning in the 1960s, exemplified by Edward Ruscha's *Every Building on the Sunset Strip.* There are unique book-objects, collections of visual poetry and innovative typographic design, altered novels such as Tom Phillips's *Humument* [Fig. 11], and portfolios of prints that may or may not fall under the auspices of the "book." Günter Brus's *Ana: 1. Aktion, 1964* [Fig. 6] is a clearly sequential group of photographs documenting an early work of performance art. Richard Long's broadside *Kicking Stones* is the conceptual product of a walk from Cork to Sligo, Ireland, in 1989.

This later work came to the Toledo Museum in the 1990s, thanks to the continuing generosity of Walter Bareiss. Not only was an acquisition fund established but also the ever-vigilant eye of the collector made sure that the most innovative projects found their way into the Toledo Museum's collection. In 1987 a large shipment including work by Lothar Baumgarten, Eric Fischl, Timothy Ely [Fig. 142], and Per Kirkeby was offered and quickly accepted. The files are filled with

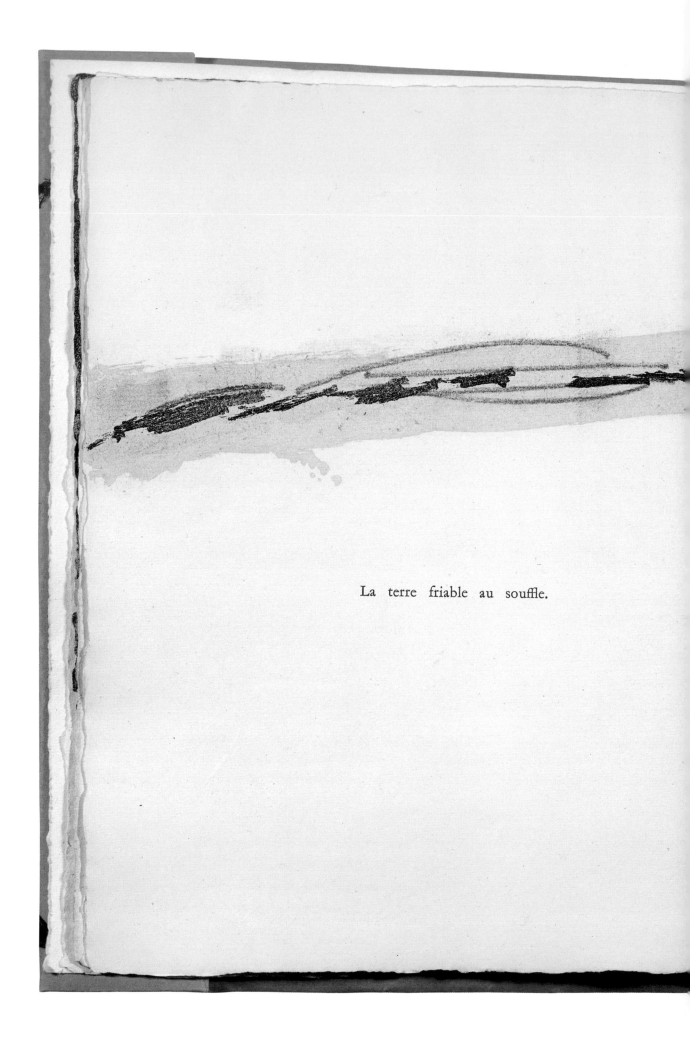

La terre friable au souffle.

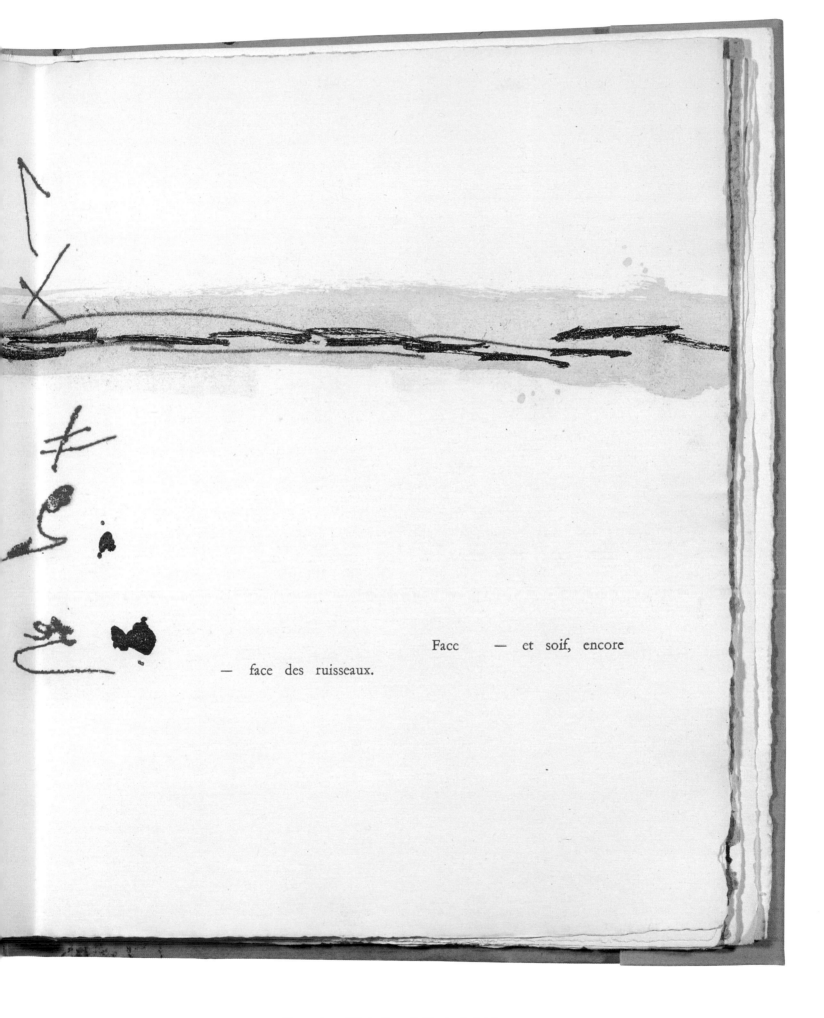

Facc   — et soif, encore

— face des ruisseaux.

Fig. 12. Antoni Tàpies from *Air*. Text by André du Bouchet (Paris: Maeght éditeur, 1971). Color soft-ground etching. Edition: 78/150.

memos, such as a 1986 note from Marilyn Symmes that reads, "Walter Bareiss has arranged for Galerie Fred Jahn, Munich, to send us two "hot-off-the-press" books by A. R. Penck. . . ."[12]

Thanks to the Bareiss fund, Martin Kippenberger's *Hotel-Hotel* (1992) [Fig. 13] came to the Museum soon after publication. A large group of broadsides, Fluxus objects, and multiples by Ian Hamilton Finlay came in 1997. *Endocrinology* [Fig. 68] by Kiki Smith and Mei-mei Berssenbrugge was published in 1997 and acquired the following year. Bareiss commented on this in a 1992 interview:

I still have some very interesting books that I keep, but I think I should eventually give them. Normally, it's easier to give current things immediately, because I don't have any evaluation problems. I just give the museum the money and they buy as I've negotiated it. I call Riva [Castleman] or Dick Field[13] and say, "Are you interested? Do you like it? I've reserved one, and I'll give you the money if you want it." I did that with the marvelous little [John] Chamberlain book that Pace just brought out [Conversations with Myself, 1992]. I gave one to Toledo, and one to the Modern, and one I bought for myself.[14]

When considering which experts to select as guest authors for this catalogue, I was influenced by the untimely death of Tony Zwicker, a dealer who enthusiastically promoted the work of contemporary book artists. The event reminds us of the necessity to document (while still possible) the stories of those who have been personally involved with the book arts, whether collectors, artists, editors, publishers, or historians. Each author was invited to write about his or her personal experiences with this art form and to provide a unique historical perspective concerning the collaborative nature of the genre, whether between words and images or among artist, printer, and publisher.

Obviously, Walter Bareiss is the best source for insights into why he acquired the art and books he chose. Riva Castleman, chief curator emerita of prints and printed books at The Museum of Modern Art, has written extensively on prints and illustrated books. Her essay recounts a trip through Germany, expertly guided by Walter Bareiss, who introduced her to German artists and scholars. Eleanor M. Garvey, as former curator of the Department of Printing and Graphic Arts at Harvard's Houghton Library, is the best authority to write about Philip Hofer's instrumental role in pioneering the scholarship of the history of book arts in this country. Hofer began collecting only slightly before Walter Bareiss, and it is fascinating to contrast his collection at Harvard with the Bareiss Collection now at the Toledo Museum.

May Castleberry was editor of the Whitney Museum's Artists and Writers Series from 1982 to 2000 and is now editor of the Library Council of The Museum of Modern Art. Her publications have revitalized the *livre d'artiste* with a new breed

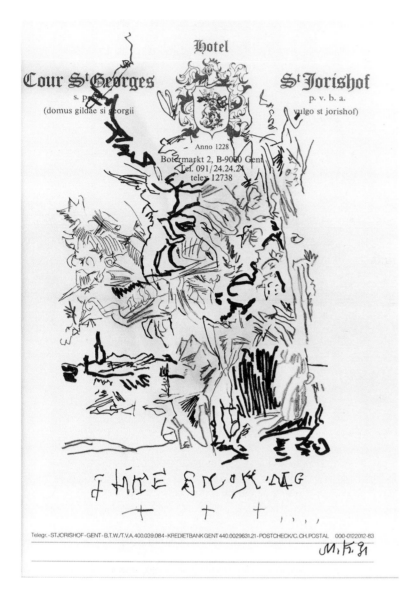

Fig. 13. Martin Kippenberger from *Hotel-Hotel* (Köln: Verlag der Buchhandlung Walther König, 1992). Photomechanical reproduction. Edition: 238/950.

12. Memo from Marilyn F. Symmes to Roger Mandle, October 31, 1986, Toledo Museum curatorial files.
13. At that time, Riva Castleman was print curator of The Museum of Modern Art and Richard Field, print curator of the Yale University Art Gallery.
14. Brody, op. cit. (note 3): 53.

of contemporary artists and writers who closely collaborate on the composition, design, and content of the work. Michael Semff, director of the Staatliche Graphische Sammlung in Munich, explores the crossover between three-dimensional sculpture and the traditionally two-dimensional medium of prints offered by the book format. Johanna Drucker, Robertson Professor of Media Studies at the University of Virginia, has been a forceful scholar and champion of the work of modern and contemporary book artists. Her essay examines the collaborative book projects of Iliazd, the innovative Russian book artist and designer — a preview of her major scholarly publication on Iliazd in progress.

Finally, artist Kiki Smith and poet Mei-mei Berssenbrugge have come together once again to write about the creative process behind their 1997 collaboration, *Endocrinology*. They worked with our designer, Katy Homans, to provide an innovative presentation for this material.

We at the Toledo Museum of Art are fortunate to count ourselves among the friends of Molly and Walter Bareiss. We are extremely grateful for their generosity and unending kindnesses. They are tireless collectors who love great art wherever they find it. Our Museum visitors can now experience the joy and enchantment the Bareisses found on each splendid page of each book in their collection.

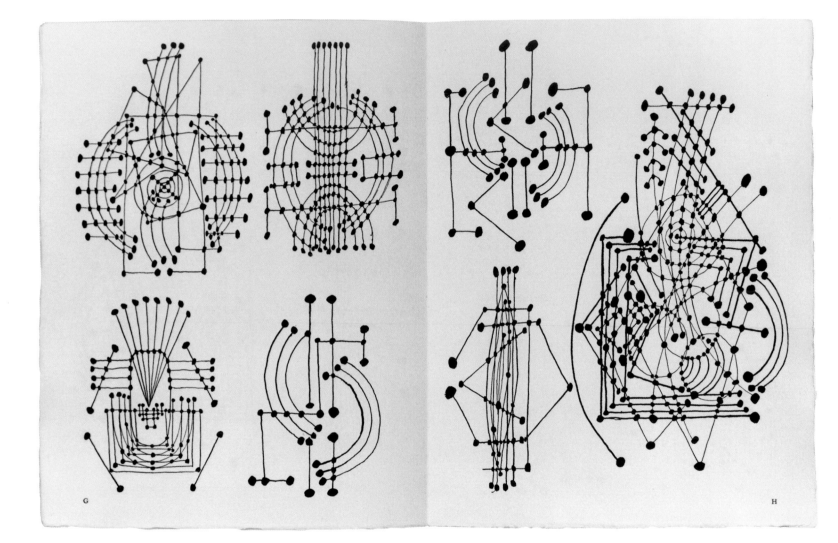

G

H

Fig. 14. Pablo Picasso from *Le chef-d'oeuvre inconnu*. Text by Honoré de Balzac (Paris: Ambroise Vollard, 1931). Wood-engraving. Toledo Museum of Art, Mrs. George W. Stevens Fund. Listed in Checklist under Additional Books.

Recollections of a Book Addict

People often ask me how I became a collector. I never gave it much thought until I sat down to write this essay and then was surprised that the answer came so quickly: How could I *not* become a collector!

My mother, born in Germany, was always interested in the arts, especially in paintings and antiques of the seventeenth and eighteenth centuries, since that was what surrounded her in the castle in Württemberg where she grew up. My father, born in Chicago, had no great passion for art until, as an engineering student in Zurich and Berlin, he began visiting art dealers and became enamored of British and French paintings of pretty women. So while my appreciation of beautiful things might not have been, strictly speaking, genetic, it was surely bred in the bone.

When I came along in 1919, my parents—both of whom were now American citizens—were living in Salach, Württemberg, near the family-owned textile mill that my father ran. With the exception of a trip to Chicago in 1921 (so that I could be properly admired by my father's family) and several months in Zurich, we remained in Germany until the summer of 1931. It was during these boyhood years that I was bitten by the collecting bug: Fascinated by everything that went on in my father's office, I began assisting with the mail on Sundays, opening letters and handing them to my father for processing. I soon became an ardent stamp collector, part of which collection I have to this very day.

It was also as a young boy that I started going to museums—both art and science. My father by this time had developed a great interest in museums, but rarely had the time to go. Consequently, when his German friend Richard Zinser—who later became a well-known art and jewelry dealer in New York—would show up to sell him some of his wares or take him to a particularly exceptional exhibition, my father would inevitably say, "Richard, I'm too busy, take my son." From the age of eight until my parents sent me to college at Yale to escape the Nazi threat, I was the fortunate beneficiary of "take my son." Mr. Zinser was probably the one who gave me the first push toward becoming a collector of art, rather than of stamps or the scientific paraphernalia I also admired.

Already distrusting Hitler, my father moved the family again to Zurich in 1931, but that didn't stop me from accompanying Mr. Zinser to museums in both Switzerland and Germany. A trip we took in 1932 to the famous Berlin museums made a particular impression on me.

The real epiphany, however, came at the Picasso retrospective of the same year in Zurich. My father and I went any number of times to see this show, but on one occasion, Mr. Zinser accompanied us, explaining to me not only the prints and drawings in which he was particularly interested but also Picasso's first illustrated books. I was hooked. Shortly thereafter, I asked my father to buy me for my birthday a Picasso print, *Salomé* [Fig. 15], that I'd seen at a small gallery near my school. It turned out to be the first piece I selected purely by myself, from a choice of many.

The next fortuitous event occurred the following year, when I was fourteen: I was sent to a boarding school near Munich. The Swiss curriculum, we'd discovered, was considerably different from the German one, and since I was not a very good student, my parents thought I had a better chance of being promoted if I went to a German school. This turned out to be correct; private schools in Germany still had obligatory courses in drawing, printmaking, and carpentry! But a second piece of luck had an even greater impact on my future: My drawing teacher, Mr. Gollwitzer, decided to devote one hour a week to art history and to indoctrinate us in the art of collecting.

A passionate collector himself, Mr. Gollwitzer took our class to Munich every other Sunday to visit art museums and private galleries. After feasting our eyes, we would feast on Weisswurst, then head to the open-air art and magazine stalls where we were each handed fifty German pennies (about twelve cents) to purchase an original work of art. I still own several small woodcuts by Maillol from *Daphnis et Chloé* that I bought with a little negotiating for the equivalent of five cents each.

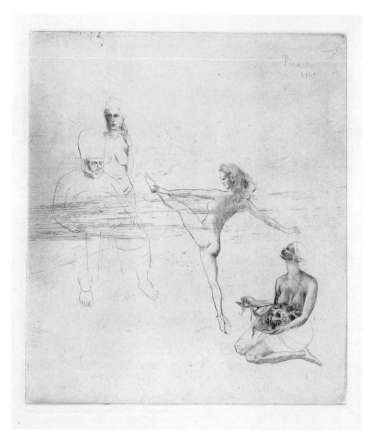

Fig. 15. Pablo Picasso, *Salomé*, from the *Saltimbanques* suite, 1905. Drypoint. Courtesy of the Yale University Art Gallery, Gift of Molly and Walter Bareiss, B.S. 1940s.

I finally graduated in 1937—an A student, at least in Latin, art history, drawing, and photography. And a budding collector as well.

That summer, I moved to the United States, not, fortunately, as an immigrant, but as an American citizen by birth. In the fall, I entered Yale University as a sophomore in the Class of 1940. There I had another great piece of luck. Although I was majoring in industrial engineering and economics, I had vowed to myself that I would take one art history course a year, and the first happened to be with George Heard Hamilton, then an assistant professor and nine years my senior. He became a real inspiration to me, and a friend for over sixty years. Almost every Saturday he would say to a group of students, "Who has a car?" And we would pile in and head for a museum in New York, Hartford, or Providence. I can't remember how many museums he introduced me to. But I do remember that he began almost every hour he taught with a slide—usually a detail—of a work of art we had to identify and write a few words about. It was an incredibly good education in learning how to look.

My senior year at Yale, I began to think seriously about collecting. I purchased my first Japanese woodcuts and illustrated books of the fifteenth through nineteenth centuries—works by Hiroshige, Hokusai, Utamaro, Harunobu, and Sharaku. (Most of this collection was eventually given to the Yale University Art Gallery, which has an excellent Far Eastern Department.) At the same time, I started collecting single-color Chinese ceramics, mostly of the Tang through Sung dynasties. Then came prints (a continuation of my high school interest) of the eighteenth, nineteenth, and twentieth centuries. Before graduating, I purchased a beautiful landscape painting by Courbet and, shortly after, a Crespi da Bologna, which I still own.

While still at Yale, I began collecting drawings, primarily by Picasso, and also bought my first illustrated books: *Livret de folastries* by Maillol and *Le chef-d'oeuvre inconnu* by Picasso [Fig. 14]. The latter I bought for $200 from my father's friend Richard Zinser, who, along with Curt Valentin, a New York dealer, became one of my major suppliers until I was able to begin going to Paris.

Paris only increased my enthusiasm for original illustrated books. I quickly discovered Alexandre Loewy's gallery on the rue de Seine, and in 1948 I serendipitously met Heinz Berggruen at the first Ketterer auction in Stuttgart, where alphabetically arranged reserved seats placed me—a "Ba"—next to him—a "Be." Heinz invited me to the gallery he had recently opened in Paris, and the rest, as they say, is history. I not only bought many books and other works of art from him over the years but also benefited from his extensive knowledge of the illustrated book market in France, Italy, and Switzerland. We became good friends and to this day I have the greatest admiration for him—not least because he has the most beautiful collection of Cubist art I have ever seen!

This is not to say that I bought all my illustrated books in Paris. Indeed, most were purchased in the United States, quite often directly from German, French, or Belgian refugees. I also found great resources in New York, including Peter Deitsch, Lucien Goldschmidt, Monica Straus, and E. Weyhe, as well as Brooke Alexander for American illustrated books.

Why books—as opposed to simply prints—is a question I am often asked, and the answer is easy. First, I "inherited" a taste for artists' books from my father, who collected them, though not seriously. You could say my own collection started with the copy of Voltaire's *Kandide*, illustrated with pen-and-ink drawings by Paul Klee, that he gave me for my eleventh birthday. (I still have it.) Even when I received the Picasso *Salomé* a few years later, I remember thinking, "Why aren't there any books by Picasso that illustrate such stories?"

Second, books, in my opinion, are more intellectually stimulating, because you see the artwork in a context. I spent considerable time reading and studying Picasso's *Les métamorphoses* [Fig. 16], as I had read Ovid in the original Latin in my junior and senior years at boarding school. Even if you don't read the entire text, however, you can read selectively, or at least appreciate the relationship between the printed or handwritten word and the illustrations—for example, in Bonnard's *Parallèlement* [Fig. 17] or Dubuffet's *La métromanie*. In addition, the very choice of text the artist has illustrated tells you something about him or her (although occasionally an artist is pressured by a publisher to illustrate a work of its choosing—a practice I am against). To me, nothing beats pulling a book out of the bookcase on a rainy afternoon and enjoying it as a total object—text, illustrations, layout, paper, binding. And so much easier than taking a print off the wall!

Third, illustrated books provide insight into the artistic process that prints cannot. It's often possible to purchase drawings, color sketches, collages, or trial

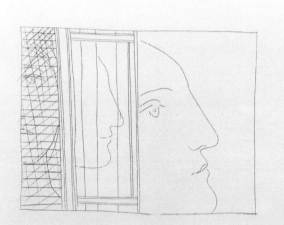

LIVRE NEUVIÈME

L E héros, fils de Neptune, demande au dieu quelle est la cause de ses gémissements et de la mutilation que son front a subie; alors le fleuve de Calydon, ses cheveux flottant sans apprêt sous une couronne de roseaux, commence ainsi : « Tu me demandes une faveur qui me coûte; quel est le vaincu qui voudrait rappeler ses combats? Pourtant je te raconterai tout fidèlement; il y eut moins de honte à être vaincu que de gloire à lutter et c'est pour moi une grande consolation que d'avoir trouvé mon vainqueur dans un

213

Fig. 16. Pablo Picasso from *Les métamorphoses*. Text by Ovid, translation by Georges Lafaye (Lausanne: Albert Skira, 1931). Etching. Edition: "maquette."

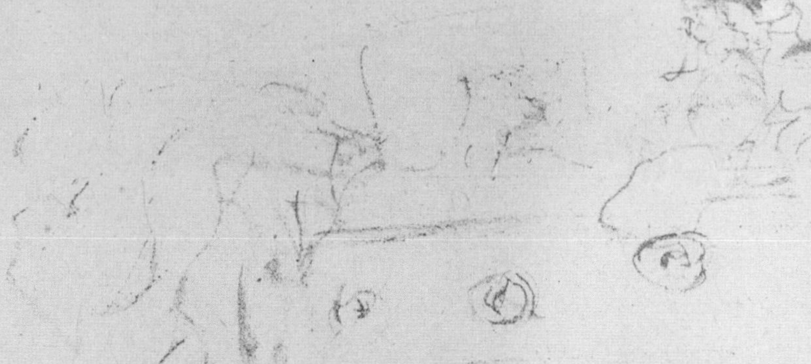

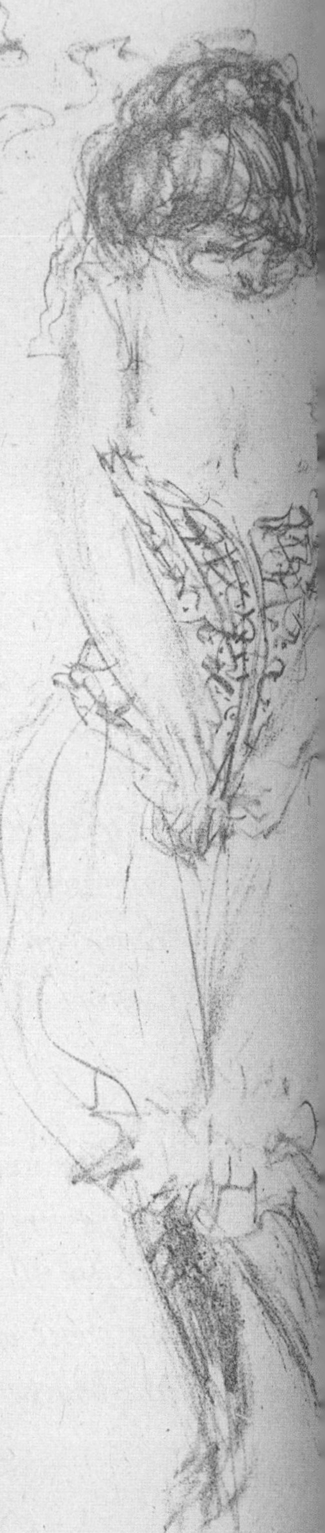

Je te veux trop rieuse
Et très impérieuse,
Méchante & mauvaise &
Pire s'il te plaisait,
Mais si luxurieuse!

Ah, ton corps noir & rose
Et clair de lune! Ah, pose
Ton coude sur mon cœur.
Et tout ton corps vainqueur,
Tout ton corps que j'adore!

Ah, ton corps, qu'il repose
Sur mon âme morose
Et l'étouffe s'il peut,
Si ton caprice veut!
Encore, encore, encore!

28

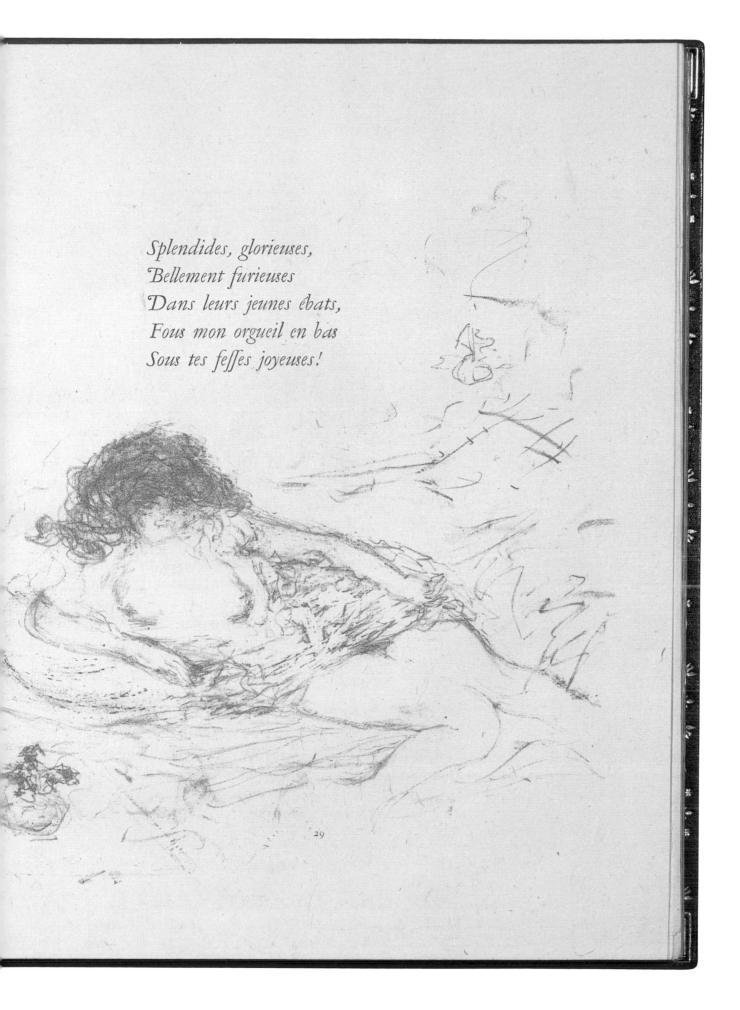

Splendides, glorieuses,
Bellement furieuses
Dans leurs jeunes ébats,
Fous mon orgueil en bas
Sous tes fesses joyeuses!

29

Fig. 17. Pierre Bonnard from *Parallèlement*.
Text by Paul Verlaine (Paris: Ambroise Vollard,
1900). Color lithograph. Edition: 5/200.

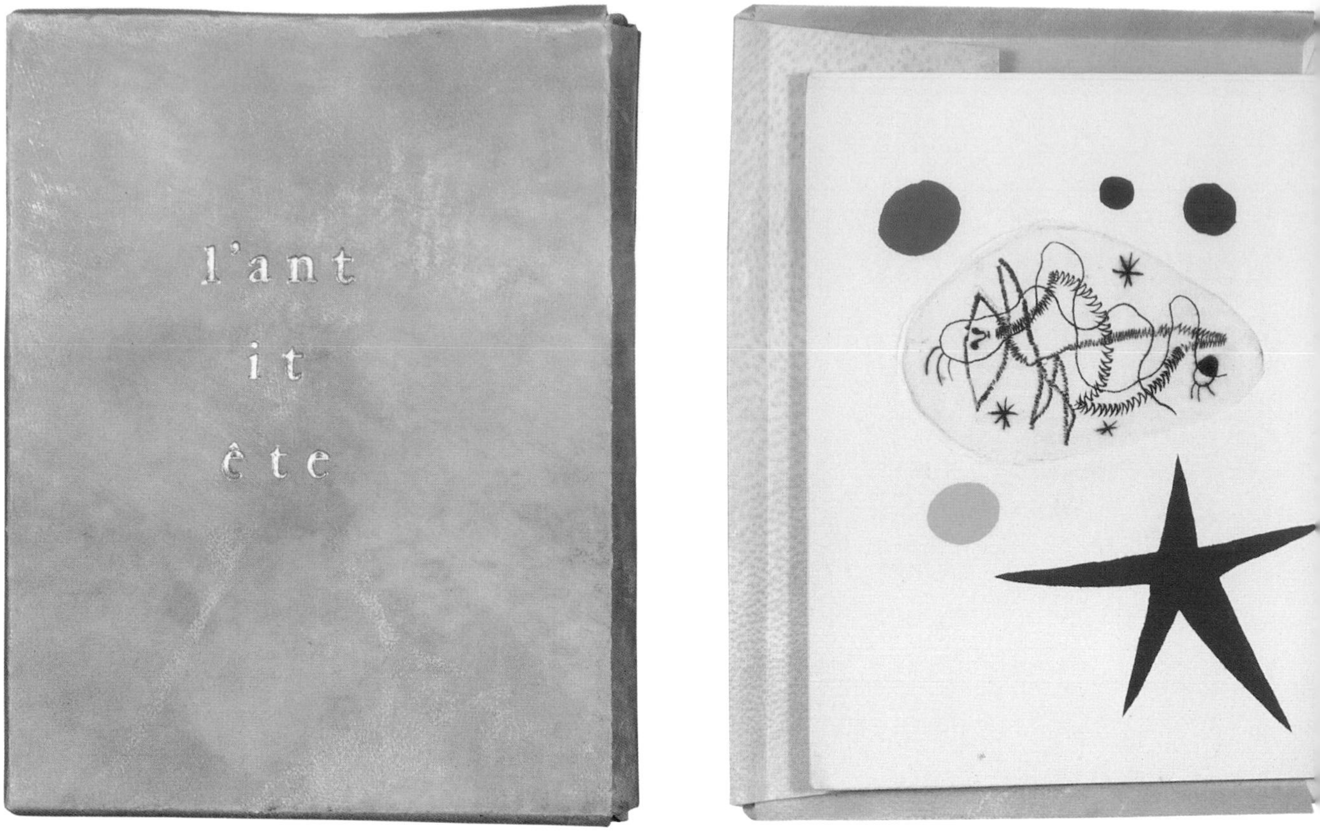

Fig. 18. Joan Miró from
L'antitête. Text by Tristan Tzara
([Paris]: Bordas, 1949). Etching
with added pochoir color.
Edition: 20/200. Listed in
Checklist under Ernst.

proofs produced before a book is issued that reveal how the book developed. And sometimes they are better than the final versions. Trial proofs I had collected of Delacroix illustrations to Goethe's *Faust,* for instance, turned out to be far superior to the prints that ultimately appeared in the commercial edition. The separate suites in *éditions de tête* or deluxe editions often give the artist the ability to express himself more fully and personally, frequently through the use of marginal *rémarques* that do not appear in the regular edition. Deluxe editions that are particularly interesting because of their *rémarques* include Bonnard's *Parallèlement,* Dalí's *Les chants de Maldoror,* Picasso's *Les métamorphoses,* and *L'antitête* [Fig. 18], illustrated by Miró, Ernst, and Tanguy. The deluxe edition of this last book is so different that it can hardly be recognized as an outgrowth of the regular edition.

Finally, when I started collecting, books—except for deluxe editions—were considerably less expensive than prints, because the individual lithographs or etchings they contained generally were not signed. Plus, for the price you might pay for a single print, you got several, even hundreds, in a book—and of comparable quality to individual prints. The affordability of artists' books, together with the fact that I simply found them easier to enjoy, made them my indulgence of choice.

What I bought over the years was determined solely by aesthetics, although my desires were sometimes limited by the status of my pocketbook. Whenever possible, I would choose the *édition de tête* over the regular edition of a book. (Later in my collecting years, my interest in *éditions de tête* diminished somewhat because too many of them showed up on the market. If they were not outstanding, I would pass them up, even if I could afford them.) Often I would go for a very small edition with something special in it, such as Miró's *À toute épreuve* [Fig. 9], which included a woodcut with added gouache. What I didn't do is buy a book based on whether it would become more valuable. I never sold a book, so I wasn't interested

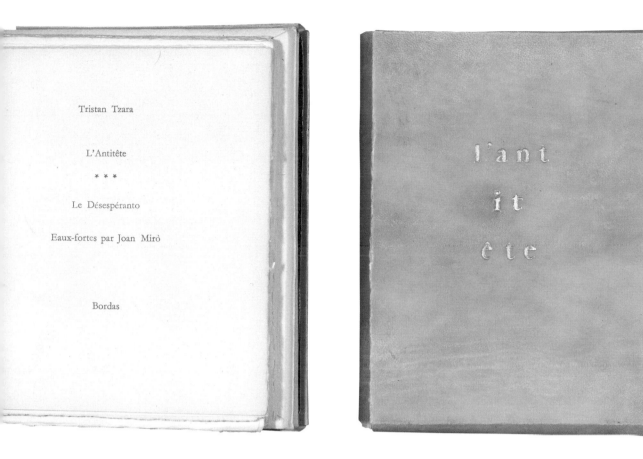

in what it might become worth. Only occasionally did I trade a book—usually a regular edition (plus some additional money) for a deluxe edition.

In putting together my collection, I eliminated from the beginning so-called coffee-table books, as well as art history books. I also had no interest in collecting first editions or specially bound books (although occasionally I was forced to buy one—for example, Bonnard's *Parallèlement*—if that was the only way to acquire a particular work).

I expanded the definition of "artists' books," however, to include not only limited editions with original prints but also facsimile editions of books not otherwise available: Gauguin's beautiful Tahitian diary, *Noa Noa;* Delacroix's Moroccan sketchbook; Manet's *Lettres illustrées,* among others. Although I would not assemble a collection solely of such books, I felt they were worthy of inclusion because of the quality of the reproductions and because they occupy a significant place in the artists' oeuvres.

Also fair game were books with reproductions of original drawings, watercolors, or collages created specifically to illustrate a particular literary work. James Joyce's *Dubliners,* for example, inspired an exceptional series of illustrations by the German artist Erwin Pfrang. (I happen to have collected the original watercolors and collages.) Other first-class books in this category are David Hockney's *Six Fairy Tales,* a number of books illustrated with reproductions of overpaintings by Arnulf Rainer [Fig. 20], and Georg Baselitz's *Die Gesänge des Maldoror* [Fig. 26]. To my mind, this book, with its photomechanical reproductions, is no less worthy of inclusion than Dalí's *Les chants de Maldoror* [Fig. 32], with its original etchings. Although these books are generally not published in limited editions, but often in editions of a thousand or more, this does not detract from their artistic merit, which depends solely on the quality of the illustrations and the overall design and production of each book.

While these parameters informed my decision making, the most important factor in any collection is personal taste. And when it comes to taste, I am a firm believer in flexibility and evolving development. Among other things, that's what keeps collecting fresh and fun.

Because I have always been interested in the close relationship between art and text, to a great extent I concentrated my collecting on Picasso, whose books exemplify a similar interest: He searched out writers like Max Jacob, or old mythologies, or even wrote text himself—and illustrated them all seamlessly. But that doesn't mean I overlooked Matisse, for whom the written word was incidental, as in *Jazz* [Fig. 35], or Laboureur, who, in illustrating Wilde's *Picture of Dorian Gray* [Fig. 22], let the text decidedly dominate.

Although I've tended to value the art in a book over the content (being more of a visual than a literary or musical person), I tried to be open to artists who used the book as a medium to disseminate their ideas. Consequently, I collected numerous books by Rainer and A. R. Penck. (I must admit I actually found Penck's *Standarts* to make very good reading.) And, of course, I didn't turn my nose up at Bonnard's *Petit solfège illustré* [Fig. 21] or Braque's *Le piège de Méduse* [Fig. 24], with text by Érik Satie.

I was also always open to being seduced by new publishers, and a great number of them came into existence during the 1940s, '50s, and '60s. One of the most charming was P. A. Benoit (PAB, Paris). He published mostly small books in small editions and I loved them! I tried to collect all of them and succeeded in snagging some wonderful ones—Jean Dubuffet's *Oreilles gardées,* Marcel Duchamp's *Tiré à 4 épingles,* many Picassos, including *Pierres*—but my goal eluded me. If only fifty copies of a book had been produced, sometimes they would all have been sold before I had a chance.

Not that there was a shortage of marvelous presses: Éditions du Livres, Paris, which produced Dubuffet's *Les murs* [Fig. 25]; Tériade, Paris, publisher of Chagall's *Fables* [Fig. 10] and Léger's *Cirque* [Fig. 150]); Éditions du dragon, Paris, publisher of a number of books by my close friend Enrique Zañartu, including *La rose séparée;* Erker-Presse, St. Gallen, publisher of Chillida's *Die Kunst und der Raum* [Fig. 23]; Petersburg Press in London, publisher of Jim Dine's *The Picture of Dorian Gray;* Eremiten-Presse, Stierstadt im Taunus; Berggruen, Iliazd, and Maeght Éditeur in Paris; Ernst Beyeler, Basel; Fred Jahn, Munich; Brooke Alexander, New York; Pratt Adlib Press, Brooklyn; Arion Press, San Francisco. But that didn't stop my good friend George Hamilton and me from starting our own: Readymade Press, New Haven, Connecticut. The name of our press came from Duchamp's *From the Green Box,* which we published in 1957. It was followed a year later by Josef Albers's *Poems and Drawings.*

In addition to the fun of finding, buying, and studying these books for over sixty years, collecting them led to innumerable adventures, produced myriad friendships, and yielded immense satisfactions.

On the adventure front, none surpassed meeting Picasso in 1971. As chairman of the Acquisitions Committee of The Museum of Modern Art, I was asked to call on Picasso in the south of France to try to persuade him to accept a painting of

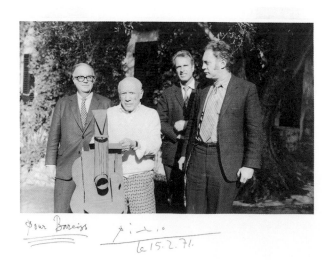

Fig. 19. Jacqueline Roque, *Walter Bareiss with Pablo Picasso, Ernst Beyeler, and William Rubin,* 1971. Photograph. Yale University Art Gallery, Gift of Molly and Walter Bareiss, B.S. 1940s.

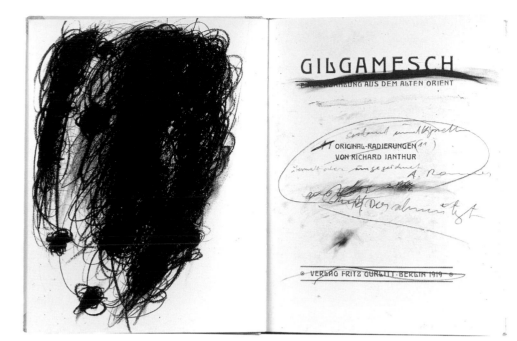

Fig. 20. Arnulf Rainer from *Gilgamesch: Eine Erzählung aus dem alten Orient* (Unna, Deutschland: Ceresit-Werke, [after 1960]). Photomechanical reproduction. Edition: 185/1,000.

Fig. 21. Pierre Bonnard from *Petit solfège illustré*. Music by Claude Terrasse (Paris: Ancienne maison Quantin, Librairies-imprimeries réunies, [1893]). Relief etching. Edition: unnumbered/2,000.

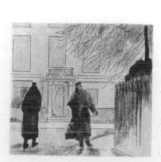

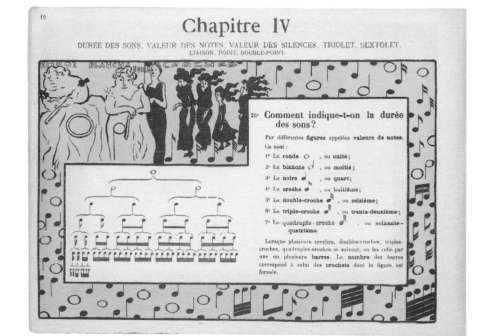

Fig. 22. Jean-Émile Laboureur from *Le portrait de Dorian Gray*. Text by Oscar Wilde (Paris: Société d'édition "Le livre," 1928). Engraving. Edition: 137/250.

Fig. 23. Eduardo Chillida from *Die Kunst und der Raum*. Text by Martin Heidegger (St. Gallen, Schweiz: Erker-Presse, 1969). Collaged lithograph. Edition: 6/150.

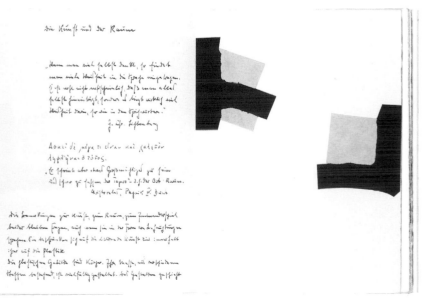

L'Estaque by Cézanne (we knew he owned several good Cézannes) in exchange for one of his own Cubist metal sculptures. There were none on the market (because Picasso rarely parted with them), and the Museum wanted one badly. During the four hours we spent at his home on a Saturday night, Picasso showed us monotypes by Degas he had recently purchased, parts of sculptures from the 1930s that he had never completed, paintings he had never signed. (He generally never signed a painting until he was ready to sell it.) When I mentioned my interest in his illustrated books, he pulled out proofs of prints published in some of his Cubist works—the best Cubist books ever produced. Then, without addressing the issue at hand, he suggested we go to our hotel and return Monday morning. We did. After taking photographs with Picasso that morning (with him still holding onto the sculpture) [Fig. 19], my wife Molly and I and Bill Rubin of MoMA drove off in our Renault with the prized possession. Picasso had declined the swap, but gave the *Guitar* (1912–13)[1] outright. To this day I remember locking it in a closet in our hotel room until the shipping agents arrived the next day!

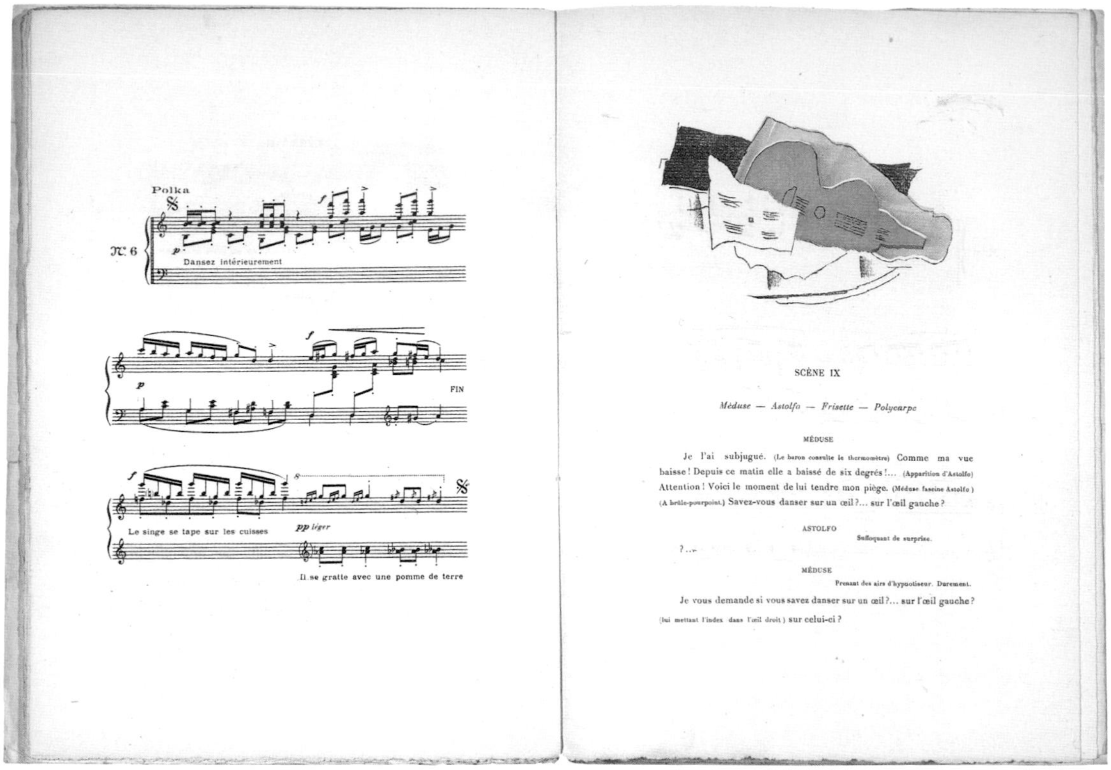

In addition to Picasso, I met a great number of artists through my collecting. Some I know quite well, including Tony Bevan, Franz Hitzler, and Hermann Nitsch. Molly and I would often visit Robert Motherwell, who produced one of my favorite books, *El Negro* [Fig. 136], and lived in Greenwich toward the end of his life. Fairfield Porter, who painted portraits first of our eldest son Henry and then of Molly and me, spent several weekends with us. (I had wanted all our children to sit for portraits, but they had other ideas!) Other artists I knew more casually: Matisse, Chagall (who inscribed an original watercolor to me in my copy of his *Fables* [Fig. 10]), Miró, Max Beckmann, Lyonel Feininger, Patrick Procktor, Jim Dine, Robert Rauschenberg. Georg Baselitz, whom we saw often in Munich or at his home near Hildesheim, not only created the wonderful *ex libris* that Molly commissioned for my fifty-fifth birthday but insisted on signing all two thousand copies [Fig. 1]!

Our enjoyment of these adventures and friendships has been matched by our delight in knowing that our collection of illustrated books has found an excellent home in the Toledo Museum of Art. In 1984 Molly and I decided that we wanted to donate the collection to an institution that had an interest in artists' books, as well as an excellent print department. We felt strongly that it should go to an area of the country where there was no large library of nineteenth- and twentieth-

Fig. 24. Georges Braque from *Le piège de Méduse.* Text and music by Érik Satie (Paris: Éditions de la Galerie Simon, 1921). Color woodcut. Edition: 22/100.

1. Pablo Picasso, *Guitar,* construction of sheet metal and wire, winter 1912–13. The Museum of Modern Art, gift of the artist, 94.71.

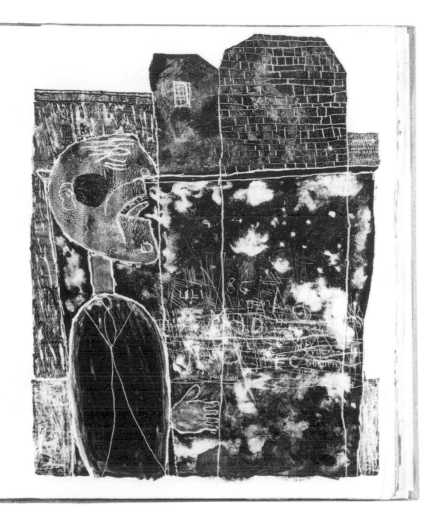

**C'est dans les murs
Que sont les portes
Par où l'on peut entrer**

**Et par l'une
Arriver.**

Fig. 25. Jean Dubuffet from *Les murs*. Text by Eugène Guillevic ([Paris]: Éditions du livre, 1950). Lithograph. Edition: 67/160.

century books. That eliminated The Museum of Modern Art in New York, the Museum of Fine Arts in Boston, the National Gallery of Art in Washington, D.C., and the Yale University Art Gallery. I also knew that a former classmate of mine, one of the most important friends of the Minneapolis Institute of Arts, planned to include illustrated books in his program of giving. Therefore, when Barbara (Bobbie) Sutherland, Molly's former roommate at Bennington, suggested Toledo, it seemed like a perfect match. (Sadly, Bobbie died of cancer that same year. All of the books by Picasso were donated in her honor.)

And it has proven to be a perfect match. We are delighted with the interest the Toledo Museum of Art has continued to show in modern illustrated books in general and in our collection in particular. Certainly art historians and the viewing public will benefit from the care, energy, and professionalism with which curator Julie Mellby and her staff have mounted this exhibition. Molly and I appreciate their efforts and enthusiasm. Finally, I would like to thank Caryl Avery, who worked with me to prepare this essay.

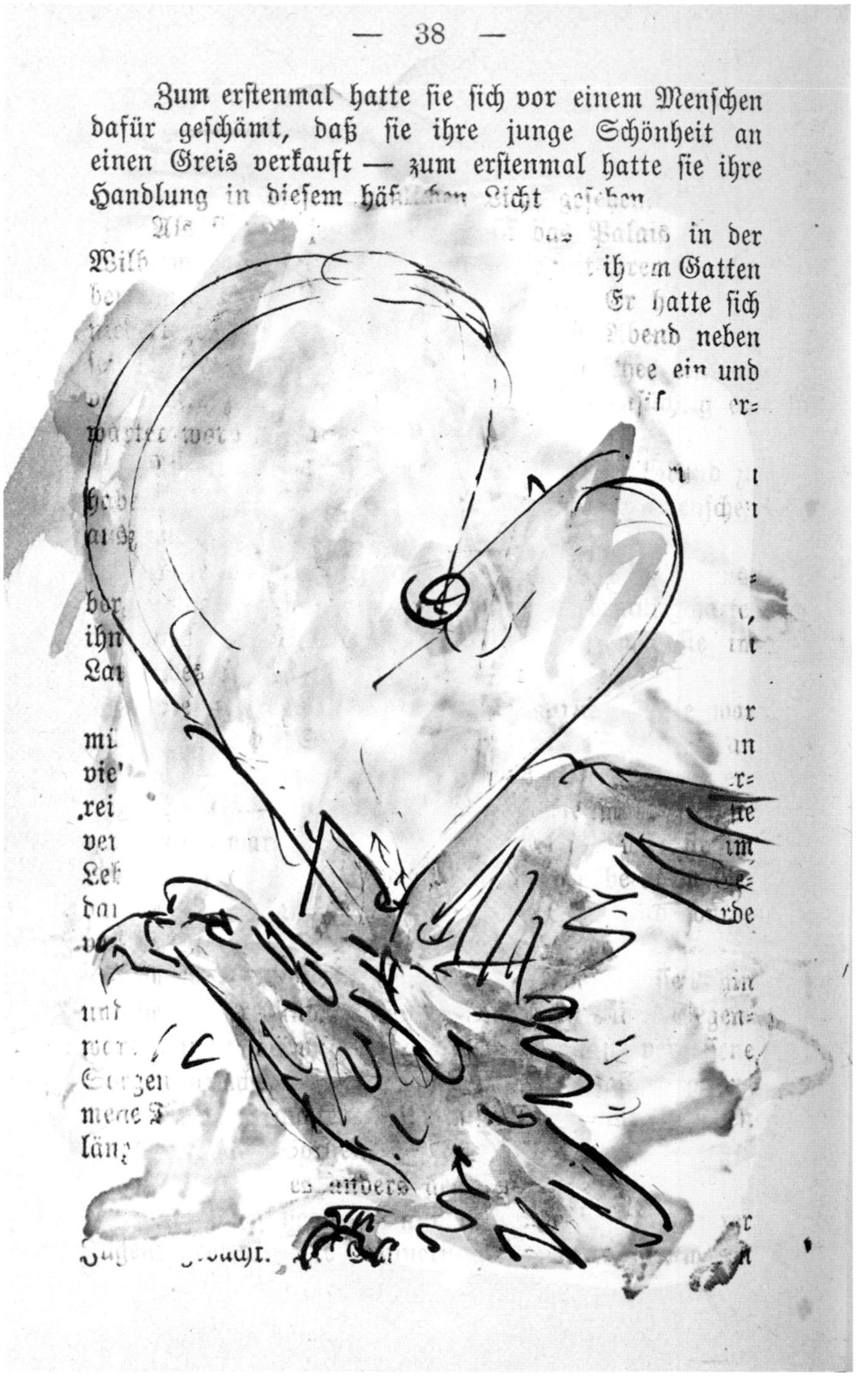

Fig. 26. Georg Baselitz from *Die Gesänge des Maldoror*. Text by Comte de Lautréamont (München: Rogner & Bernhard, 1976). Photomechanical reproduction.

RIVA CASTLEMAN

On the Road with W. B.

A little more than twenty years after the executors of the estate of Louis E. Stern bestowed his illustrious collection of modern illustrated books on The Museum of Modern Art (MoMA) in New York, Walter and Molly Bareiss presented their splendid and far larger collection to the Toledo Museum of Art. Between those two events I was to study the Stern books, catalogue many of them,[1] exhibit some of them, and discuss them numerous times with Walter Bareiss. He invited me to lecture on his collection at its Greenwich Library exhibition in January 1983, and at the opening of its inaugural exhibition in Toledo in 1985. The commitment made by MoMA in 1963 to organize a major exhibition of Stern's collection had to be fulfilled before my retirement in 1995. In 1991 it was decided to hold the exhibition in October 1994. It would be called *A Century of Artists Books.*

As the most influential and knowledgeable member of the acquisitions committee of MoMA's Department of Prints and Illustrated Books, Bareiss was not only superbly qualified but more than welcome to offer advice on the content of the exhibition, and he was as eager as I was to promote its importance. Each time we discussed the exhibition more ideas surfaced as I recounted my ongoing search to unearth original maquettes, notes, and proofs for the masterpieces of twentieth-century *livres d'artiste.* Based on visits to Geneva, Paris, and major American collections, as well as studies resulting from a visiting fellowship at the Getty Research Institute in California, I had identified some crucial works that had to be borrowed, including some from the Bareiss Collection. Over lunches at Christers restaurant near the Museum, Walter and I made plans for finding even more sources. The exact moment that we decided to hunt together in Germany has disappeared into oblivion, but the trip itself remains indelible.

More than a few times I had traveled to Munich for openings of museums and exhibitions that, in one way or another, involved Walter. His many positions in the world of culture over the decades that I have known him have ranged from being a Trustee and, in 1969–70, Acting Director of The Museum of Modern Art, to Chairman of the Governing Board of the Yale University Art Gallery; he also was a founding member and chairman of the acquisition committee of the Münchner Galerie-Verein and a founder and Vice President of Save Venice, Inc. Most importantly for me, he had been an active member of MoMA's Committee on Prints and Illustrated Books since 1973. When I visited him in Munich he would often introduce me to the works of a new artist, show me proof copies of a new book by an artist not yet represented in MoMA's collection, run through stacks of new prints

1. *Illustrated Books from the Collection of The Museum of Modern Art, New York,* ed. Carol Smith and Audrey Isselbacher (New York: The Museum of Modern Art, 1994). CD-ROM catalogue of the entire Stern Collection and other illustrated books in the Prints and Illustrated Books Department (1,264 titles), distributed without cost to public collections throughout the world.

at Galerie Fred Jahn, or send me off to the latest exhibition of drawings at the gallery of his niece, Margaret Biederman. Inevitably, Walter would always know the who and what of the local art situation, despite the fact that he spent less than a third of each year in Munich. I doubt if many curators had such a direct line to the culture of that German city. Walter and I would visit in his cramped office off Maximillianstrasse, amid the company of many African masks and figures. Once, to my amazement, he handed me a catalogue from the Getty Museum in Malibu, California, of yet another of his collections, this time Greek vases. Even the hotels he recommended seemed to lead to a rewarding surprise. Once, on my way to Vienna, he sent me to the modest Beethoven Hotel. It was on the same street as the spectacular Otto Wagner buildings and, more important, it was across from the market where he urged me to have a quick lunch of some delicious sausage on peasant bread. The surprise was that my hotel room was opposite the famous Theater an der Wien, where, in 1953, I had seen and heard Beethoven's *Fidelio* on the same stage as its first performance in 1805.

Walter worked out a perfect itinerary when we decided we had to see the Herzog August Bibliothek in Wolfenbüttel for the first time. He also hoped to show me the Otto Shaeffer Foundation in Schweinfurt, but problems of various kinds made that collection inaccessible. Another modest hotel, this time in Berlin, was our meeting place. On April 17, 1993, we went out to the Gemäldegalerie in Dahlem to bid farewell to the wonderful old master paintings there. Only four years after the Wall came down in Berlin, the need for more space to unite the collections had resulted in a new building next to Mies van der Rohe's Neue Nationalgalerie near Potsdamer Platz. In the afternoon we met with Alexander Duckers, Curator of Drawings and Prints, in the new Kupferstichkabinett located in one wing of the yet-to-be-completed building. A marvelous study and storage facility for prints and the library were the first elements to be opened. An inaugural display of master drawings, including some Botticellis, provided more evidence of the impressive treasury of the revived capital.

In the evening we dined with an extraordinary couple, Walter's good friends Wolfgang and Birgitte Wolters, in their apartment. It was located next to a small park where Mrs. Wolters grew plants for her pharmacological research. In the apartment itself were some wonderful German Expressionist paintings, but the conversation over dinner had more to do with Venice. Mr. Wolters, an architectural historian, had worked for years in the German institutes in Florence and Venice. His brother, Christian, together with Walter Bareiss and some other foreign lovers of Venice, had founded Save Venice, Inc. not only to create worldwide awareness of the dire physical situation of the city but also to arrest the deterioration of its artistic monuments. A few years later, Wolfgang began to coordinate the restoration of works that Save Venice funds.

The next day, in a soaking rain, Walter and I went to the Bauhaus-Archiv Museum für Gestaltung to see the Henry van de Velde retrospective exhibition. We were both captivated by the Belgian artist's ravishing *Also sprach Zarathustra* (1908) by Friedrich Nietzsche, which I had seen reproduced but never given the consideration it deserved because its pages appeared, in black and white, more as graphic design than illustration. Walter and I agreed that the aesthetic impact of its maroon and gold pages was comparable, for its time, to that of books by El Lissitzky fifteen years later, making it a worthy candidate for the MoMA exhibition. In 1902 Count

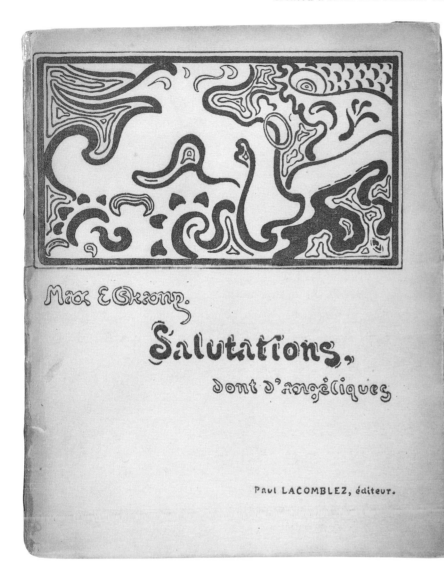

Harry Kessler had become closely involved with the Nietzsche archive in Weimar. He asked van de Velde to design the writer's *Ecce Homo* and *Also sprach Zarathustra* shortly thereafter. Although the artist designed only a title page for *Ecce Homo,* he created a total and brilliant environment for Nietzsche's *Zarathustra.* It would be the earliest book to represent Count Kessler's importance in the publication of artists books. It was also part of his productive relationship with van de Velde, whom he brought to Weimar. There, from 1906 to 1914, the Belgian taught at the Kunstgewerbeschule for which he designed the building that later became the Bauhaus.

In the process of looking back on our visit to the Berlin exhibition, I found that Walter had in his collection one of Henry van de Velde's earliest books, *Salutations, dont d'angéliques* (1893) [Fig. 27], with decorations which the author, Max Elskamp, hoped would be a "glos linéaire" and "équation symbolique" to his poems.[2] By the time of its publication, van de Velde, one of the artists known as "Les Vingt" who showed in Brussels during the late 1880s and early 1890s, had turned to graphic design, decorative arts, and architecture. For a while he and Aristide Maillol seemed to follow parallel paths, influenced by Japanese prints and their wave motifs that both put into graphics and pictorial tapestry. By the late 1890s Maillol had turned to sculpture. In 1908, during van de Velde's Weimar years, Kessler had taken Maillol on a trip to Greece in the hope that the artist would illustrate some classic text for him. In 1926 Kessler's Cranach Presse finally published Maillol's version of Virgil's *Eclogues.* Earlier, Maillol was to contribute a sculpture to a Nietzsche memorial project, a stadium in Weimar designed by van de Velde. Coincidental with my realization of a van de Velde–Maillol connection was the revelation that Walter's earliest collecting efforts were of single woodcuts from Maillol's *Daphnis et Chloé,* soon after its 1937 publication. Had he more than the few pennies that he paid for these prints, I am sure the eighteen year old would have acquired then and there his first illustrated book. Not too long afterward, his father gave him a copy of Maillol's Virgil.

To return to our journey, immediately after we emerged from the van de Velde exhibition, we entered Walter's splendid chariot (a.k.a. Volkswagen bus). It was still pouring as we set out on the fairly dilapidated roads of the former East Germany that would take us to Braunschweig and toward our goal, the famous library in Wolfenbüttel. Selections from the modern collection of the Herzog August Bibliothek in Wolfenbüttel had been shown for the first time at Documenta in Kassel in 1959. Catalogues sent to MoMA of further exhibitions in Hannover (1989) and Weimar (1991) brought the collection to my attention. One of a series of well-illustrated -

Fig. 27. Henry van de Velde from *Salutations, dont d'angéliques.* Text by Max Elskamp (Bruxelles: Paul Lacomblez, 1893). Color relief print. Edition: 120/200.

2. Klaus Weber, "Der Dämon der Linie," in *Henry van de Velde, Ein europaischer Künstler seiner Zeit,* ed. Klaus Jurgen Sembach and Birgit Schulte (Köln: Weinand Verlag, 1992): 128. From a letter from Elskamp to van de Velde postmarked 13.3.1892.

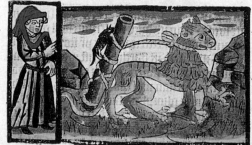

ym folt fey brait·Vmb fey ftolze clugkeit·An yn
wart fchlahen nit gefpart·Schemlichē er herauß
getreiben wart·welch thore des begere·Das ir na-
tur nit mag benueren·Der mag des wol engelten·
Darzu fol man in wol fchelte·Der fich dick ding
nymet an·Das fein gefchlecht noch nye gewan·
Des mag der mēfch nit wider ftreben·was die na-
tur hat gegeben·Den hūtlein ftund an fein fpil
wol·Der efel leck tragen fol·

18 Eins mals ein leo ficher ging·In einem wald
do er ving·Ein mauß die wolt er getot han·
Hie fprach leo las mich gan·Es zrupt nit dein
wirdikeit·Nach deiner arbeit·wider lob nach er
leit daran·Ob du mich toteft laß mich gan·was

Fig. 28. Albrecht Pfister,
printer, from *Der Edelstein.*
Text by Ulrich Boner
(Bamberg, Deutschland,
1461). Hand-colored
woodcut. Courtesy of the
Herzog August Bibliothek,
Wolfenbüttel.

3. *A Treasure House of Books: The Library of Duke
August of Brunswick-Wolfenbüttel,* ed. Helwig
Schmidt Glintzer (Wolfenbüttel: Herzog August
Bibliothek, 1998): 11–12, 22, 26, 49. Exhibition
catalogue of the Grolier Club, New York.

catalogues of artists books, *Paul Éluard und Joan Miró, À toute épreuve: leuchtend
klare Metamorphosen* (1990), edited by Sabine Solf and Harriet Watts, an American
working at the library, reminded me of Walter's contribution of a copy of *À toute
épreuve* to MoMA so that it could appear in the large Miró retrospective exhibition
some few months after its publication in 1958. With interests so close to ours, we
looked forward to meeting Dr. Watts. The library became the primary
objective of our three-day trip that also would include Stuttgart and
conclude in Walter's sometime hometown, Munich.

We arrived in Braunschweig in the late afternoon that gloomy
Sunday. To cheer us up, Walter decided that we had to see the bronzes
in the cathedral of Hildesheim before we dined in a restaurant he knew
there. In college, when I studied medieval sculpture, Hildesheim's
Ottonian treasures were in the upper tier of major monuments, but
I had never visited them. The famous metal doors with their reliefs of
man's fall and redemption, the bronze column covered with reliefs
of the life of Christ, and the baptismal font were difficult to see in the
dim, barely lit church. However, in such an atmosphere, the murky
visual experience was transformed into a profoundly mystical one,
enchantingly accentuated by Walter's recollections of his earlier visits to
these marvels of the eleventh century. Closing time sent us back out
into the April showers and quickly into the warm Gemütlichkeit of a
typical German restaurant. There, with glasses of wine and good food,
we traded stories of travel, art, and books.

The sun appeared for our early journey to Wolfenbüttel. Settled
into comfortable, executive-style, swivel seats in the back of our moving
office, we were guided with quiet expertise by Walter's Silesian driver,
Mr. Opalla. He was so adept at this sort of tour, having worked for
the Bareiss company for twenty-five years, that it almost seemed like
the bus drove itself. What delight, then, to arrive in the midst of
Wolfenbüttel's core of lovely buildings, some former palaces and the rebuilt library,
almost all housing nearly half a million books, mostly printed before 1850, and
twelve thousand manuscripts. Many other royal collections in Europe had famous
librarians, but none more distinguished than two of Wolfenbüttel's, Gottfried
Wilhelm Leibniz in the seventeenth century and Gotthold Ephraim Lessing in
the eighteenth.[3]

We first met with Dr. Watts, who showed us the modern illustrated book collection, stored in two large rooms. Most of the books were unbound and in their
own solander boxes, just the way they are most useful for exhibition purposes.
However, it was the boxes themselves that were quite memorable: many were covered with identical printed paper, the image of which was very much like one of
Jean Dubuffet's *Phénomènes* prints. The color of the pattern differed according to
the country of each book's origin. The largest ones lay flat on shelves. Later, when
we compared our impressions, I remembered the pattern, but Walter, the typical
collector who has never had enough room for everything he loves, remembered that
most were stacked only three books high, a practical method but a truly luxurious
waste of space.

As we went through some of the modern illustrated books, many looking as if
they had just been delivered from the printer, we enjoyed our time with a number

of familiar friends. We were actually enjoying the legacy of the library's vigorous librarian, Erhart Kästner. From 1950 to 1968 he restored the library's older buildings and was the first to build a collection of modern illustrated books. The most recent book we were shown was a unique one made up of large, awkward pages filled with collages of prints, leaves, and feathers by a young artist who had also been commissioned to make another for the collection. Unfortunately, there was too little time to view other, very contemporary books in the collection.

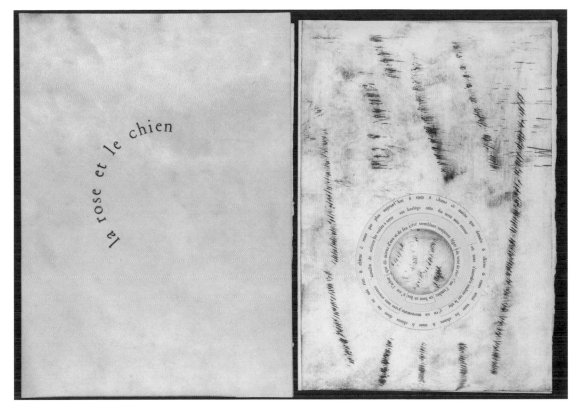

The best, and certainly unexpected, part of our visit was still to come. After lunch with Dr. Solf, we visited the Conservator, Heinrich Grau, in his workrooms. There, in a kind of alchemist's garret, hardly the sterile modern laboratory of newer institutions, we examined some of the library's treasures that had recently been repaired or were undergoing a periodic check-up. Among them was a small,

Fig. 29. Pablo Picasso from *La rose et le chien: poème perpétuel.* Text by Tristan Tzara (Alès, France: PAB, [1958]). Drypoint with engraving. Courtesy of the Spencer Collection, The New York Public Library, Astor, Lenox, and Tilden Foundations.

hand-colored book, *Der Edelstein* by Ulrich Boner, printed by Albrecht Pfister in Bamberg in 1461 [Fig. 28]. This gem, the only copy known, combines woodcut with movable type and is the first dated printed illustrated book.[4] We also paged through a magnificent volume with dozens of brilliantly hand-colored movable discs or astrolabes, *Astronomicum caesareum* (1540) by Petrus Apianus. This book was a tactile and visual adventure, which reminded both Walter and me of one of Pierre A. Benoit's (PAB) always inventive books illustrated by Picasso, *La rose et le chien: poème perpetuel* (1958) [Fig. 29], which has Tristan Tzara's text on similarly movable discs. As the shape of MoMA's exhibition was evolving, the Apianus stimulated my search for forerunners of modern books. Ultimately, the Picasso would be shown in the MoMA exhibition in a section on unusual formats, and its historical model would be an earlier, less sumptuous study of the movement of celestial bodies, Johannes Regiomontanus's *Calendrium* (1476).

A day's visit to a great book collection could offer only a small taste of any library's mostly hidden riches. Naturally, comparisons between the Bibliothek's and the two collections Walter and I cared about happened more in our minds than in conversation. But our unforeseen visit to the conservation studio had been a unique and exciting adventure. It was the conservator who gave the spark of life to very old objects, both through his work on them and his presentation of them to us. We left still wanting more. After our privileged hands-on experience, new ideas about presenting the essence of books while keeping them secure in exhibition cases filled the air as our Volkswagen bus carried us away from Wolfenbüttel.

4. Ibid., 10; James C. Thomas. "Die Undatierung eines Wolfenbütteler Fruhdruckes des 'Ackermann aus Bohmen.'. . . ," *Wolffenbütteler Notizien zur Buchgeschichte* 13 (1988): 106–24.

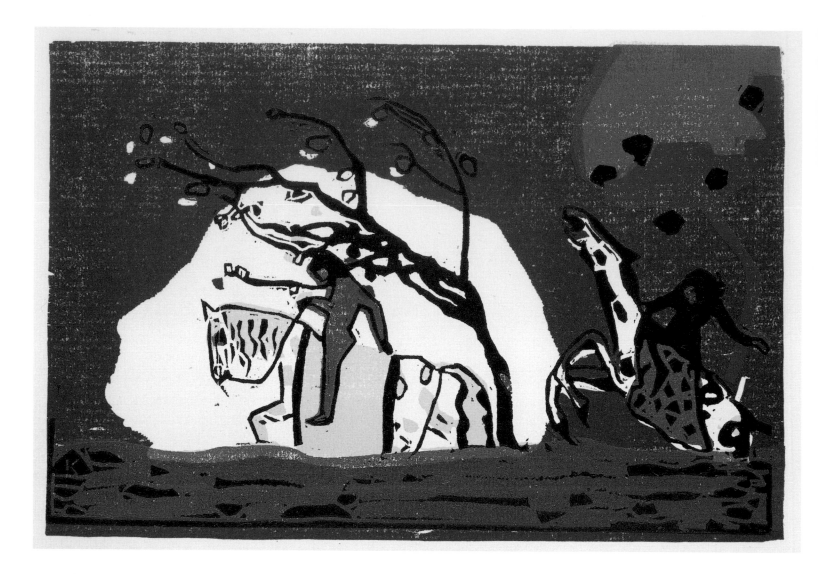

Fig. 30. Wassily Kandinsky
from *Klänge*. Text by Wassily
Kandinsky (München: R.
Piper & Co., [1913]). Color
woodcut. Edition: 131/300.

The next event of the day was a late afternoon visit to the castle home of the
artist Georg Baselitz in Derneburg. Walter had collected Baselitz's work for years,
and his interest in German artists of Baselitz's generation was invaluable to MoMA
as we added contemporary prints to the collection. I have also treasured one of
Walter's bookplates by Baselitz, commissioned by Mrs. Bareiss. The artist's younger
son, Anton Kern, was currently interning in the print department at MoMA.
Anton would directly participate in my exhibition, by reciting in German some
of Wassily Kandinsky's *Klänge* poems on the videotape we presented of the entire
book [Fig. 30].

On arrival at Derneburg we crossed a sort of moat, went through the entryway
hung with the artist's huge paintings, and entered his baronial home. After looking
at a studio filled with new paintings, we sat around in a room the size of a hotel
lobby, chatting away. Walter had purchased his first painting by Baselitz only a few
years after the artist had moved from East to West Berlin, and changed his name
from Kern to that of his birthplace, Deutschbaselitz. Walter had met Baselitz about
1965 through Heiner Friederich, an art dealer in Munich who had taken on a group
of Berlin artists with roots in East Germany. Fred Jahn, Friederich's associate, spe-
cialized in Baselitz's graphics. After Friederich left Munich, Jahn opened his own
gallery and offered Walter first choice of the artist's new work. Among many enter-
prises he undertook, Jahn directed the publication of Baselitz's gouaches for the
famous text *Les chants de Maldoror* by Comte de Lautréamont (Isidore Ducasse),
in a soft-cover book, *Die Gesänge des Maldoror* (1976) [Fig. 26].

Before we sat down to tea with Baselitz's wife, Elke, we toured the upper floors. Baselitz's woodcuts were normally printed in one area where there was a printing press, stacks of paper, and storage cabinets. We were shown a few of his recent prints as well as some much older engravings in his collection. In addition to African sculpture, this artist, whose literary interests have infused his work, also had a mammoth collection of books, which seemed to hold up the walls everywhere. They also filled the library, another grand room on the main floor, where we finished our visit. As we left, Baselitz gave me a copy of his Lautréamont book, signing it, and misdating it "April 19, 1994."

We returned to our hotel in Braunschweig and set out early the next day for the long trip to Stuttgart. There would be a stop on the way meant for convenience, as well as pleasure. Walter knew that there was an exhibition of Richard Tuttle's work at the famous spa of Baden-Baden, so on a pleasantly balmy day we found our way there. While we had no intention of gambling, we did have a very luxurious bite at the Brenner's Park Hotel before crossing the town's old-fashioned promenade garden to the art gallery. There we exercised (after all, we were at a spa) all the kinks out of muscles atrophied from long hours of seated travel by looking at Tuttle's exhibition, *CHAOS THE/DIE FORM* [Fig. 31]. Every small drawing was installed as the artist planned, just above the baseboard, about seven inches from the floor. Walter is a long-time admirer of Tuttle, and he happily went through the several rooms of the exhibition, bending down to nearly every drawing! I tried to do the same, but every few minutes he would call me over to see one he thought was special. Afterward, I realized that inserting a bit of discussion about a work now and then allowed both of us to stand up and stretch. Tuttle's drawings were fascinating and well worth the stopover, but the physical aspects of Tuttle's exhibition were equally memorable.

That evening we arrived in Stuttgart, where both Walter and I were looking forward to seeing important books from the L'Oncle Collection, catalogued as a school project in 1965. Ulrike Gauss, the curator of prints and drawings of the Staatsgalerie, had already discussed possible loans to my exhibition in New York. However, Ulrike had prepared other works that led to an important decision about its content. Rainer Michael Mason, curator of the Cabinet des Estampes in Geneva, had recently published information on Salvador Dalí's work on *Les*

Fig. 32. Salvador Dalí from
Les chants de Maldoror. Text by
Comte de Lautréamont (Paris:
Albert Skira, 1934). Etching.
Edition: 18/200.

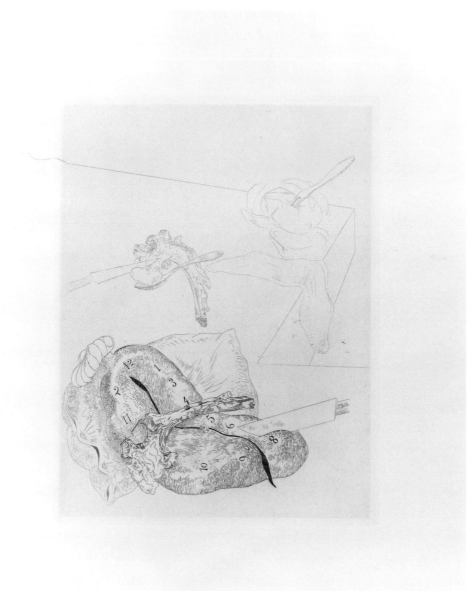

chants de Maldoror [Fig. 32] that examined Dalí's involvement with the actual etchings.[5] It was a good moment to discuss this with Ulrike who was ready with two drawings by Dalí for the book. Walter and I both recalled the commercial exhibition in New York of "original" copper plates for Dalí's book. Mason had concluded that the plates were predominantly photo-etchings of drawings, some of which had possibly been enhanced by Dalí and/or a skilled printer. After seeing some of the trial proofs in Geneva, and now the drawings, Walter and I were convinced that American scholars and collectors would find the juxtaposition of Dalí's famous illustrated book with these drawings an illuminating element in MoMA's exhibition.

❧

Because *Les chants de Maldoror* had established itself as a leitmotif of our trip, I thought I might insert a pause into this account of our travels and take a detour into the Bareiss Collection itself, to compare three versions there: the two we had seen on our trip and one by René Magritte [Fig. 33]. Did Baselitz's twenty gouaches, so wild and full of youthful passion, Dalí's refined Surrealist visions, and Magritte's less publicized edition have more in common than Lautréamont's story? There have been countless numbers of words written about Dalí's version, how he was asked to illustrate the text, and how he was thrilled to follow Picasso's Ovid and Matisse's Mallarmé as one of the publisher Skira's anointed triumvirate of important artist-illustrators. The Surrealists considered Lautréamont's text of the late 1860s a foundation of their movement, when André Breton issued the movement's manifesto in 1924 (the date, coincidentally, of the first English translation of Lautréamont). When Dalí made his drawings for his book in 1933 he perpetuated an irrational, dream-like imagery in what he called his "paranoiac critical method." He occasionally "illustrated" incidents in the text. He also produced variants of earlier images that were to become icons in his own history, such as the limp watch, best known in the painting *The Persistence of Memory* (1931).[6] Its placement in Chant 2 in the book is near a text that repeatedly refers to time: "Minute by minute I observed the vicissitudes of their last agonies. . . . Every quarter of an hour or so. . . ."[7] Here the limp watch is made of bread or meat. An ink drawing of the same period, *The Cannibalism of Objects* (1933), depicts various objects made of meat, including a meat watch.[8]

5. Rainer Michael Mason, *vrai Dalí / fausse Gravure: l'oeuvre imprimé 1930–1934* (Genève: Cabinet des Estampes du Musée d'art et d'histoire, 1992).

6. Salvador Dalí, *The Persistence of Memory,* 1931. Oil on canvas. The Museum of Modern Art, New York. Given anonymously.

7. Comte de Lautréamont (Isidore Ducasse), *Lautréamont's Maldoror,* trans. Alexis Lykiard (New York: Thomas Y. Crowell Company, 1971): 73.

8. Robert Descharnes and Gilles Neret, *Salvador Dalí 1904–1989,* v. I (Köln: Benedikt Taschen, 1994), cat. 467. *The Cannibalism of Objects,* 1933. Pen and ink. Private collection.

Fig. 33. René Magritte from *Les chants de Maldoror*. Text by Comte de Lautréamont (Bruxelles: Éditions "La Boëtie," 1948). Line block reproduction. Edition: 443/4,100.

The first Chant of Lautréamont's text was printed in Belgium in 1868, and its excessive immorality led to its exclusion from France. The complete text of *Les chants de Maldoror* was published in Belgium a year later, shortly before the author's death in 1870. The Belgian Surrealist René Magritte was an obvious choice to illustrate a new publication of the exploits of Maldoror, possibly meant to commemorate the centennial in 1946 of Lautréamont's birth. Although Magritte made his ink drawings for the text in 1945, the year they were exhibited, the book itself was not published until 1948.[9] His full-page illustrations combine his well-developed double entendre imagery of unexpected forms with a new infusion of Expressionist sketches for initials and inserted vignettes. These latter seem to have reflected the reviving interest in another Belgian, James Ensor, manifested by several younger artists who took the name COBRA (after their origins in COpenhagen, BRussels, and Amsterdam). Magritte's full-page drawings include images that, like Dalí's, were already famous in Magritte's pictorial vocabulary, such as the fish-headed human figure he drew in 1934 and then painted in 1935, titled *Collective Invention*.[10] The image in the book recalls the extraordinary beings of the underworld painted centuries earlier by two other Lowland artists, Hieronymus Bosch and Pieter Bruegel the Elder. It is placed in Chant 1 where the author, in a series of stanzas that begin "Old ocean," alternately hails and berates the mighty seas, finally asking, "Tell me, ocean . . . tell me if Satan's breath creates the storms that hurl your salty waters up to the clouds. This you must tell me because I would rejoice at knowing hell so close to man."[11]

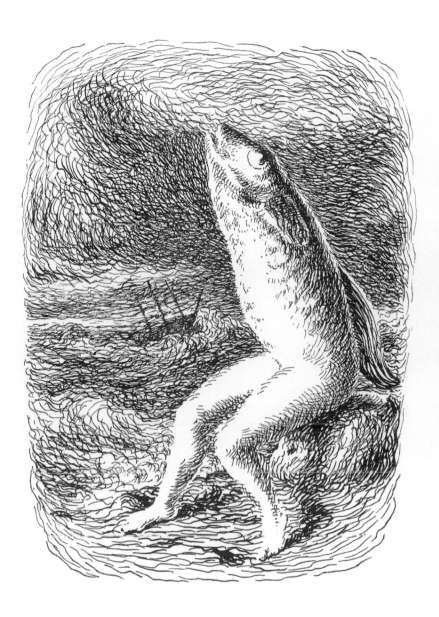

In an appendix of Baselitz's book, a history of the text notes that the first translation into German of the complete *Les chants de Maldoror* was published in 1954. One can imagine the impact such a book might have had on the teenaged Baselitz. After his move to West Berlin in 1956, his artistic point of view was significantly catalyzed. Baselitz wrote and decorated two manifestos with his friend Eugen Schönebeck: *Pandämonium* in 1961 and *Pandämonium II* the following year. The radical language and imagery simulated that of Lautréamont and Dalí, as in the second manifesto, "Paranoia, on to paranoia, in the outspread fingers, the knuckles that leave the gentle rhythms of paranoia on the wall."[12] In 1961 Baselitz began a series of gouaches, inspired by the Maldoror text, which he completed in 1965.

As with Dalí's and Magritte's versions, Baselitz's illustrations did not specifically hew to the text, though their motifs were suitably horrific. In the 1976 publication

9. David Sylvester, *René Magritte Catalogue Raisonné,* v. II (London: Philip Wilson Publishers, 1994): 110–11.

10. Ibid., cat. 360, *Collective Invention,* 1935. Oil on canvas. Private collection; v. IV, cat. 1109, *Collective Invention,* 1934. Gouache and china ink. Private collection, Düsseldorf.

11. *Lautréamont's Maldoror,* op. cit. (note 7): 17.

12. *Georg Baselitz: Paintings 1964–1983,* ed. Nicholas Serota and Mark Francis, trans. David Britt (London: Whitechapel Art Gallery, 1983): 25.

the gouache chosen for the cover was one of an eagle, a subject that had become closely identified with the artist after his series of paintings and prints during the early 1970s.[13] The illustration appears again within the book in the midst of a passage in Chant 4, in which the ever-heinous Maldoror asks for martyrdom. However not much earlier, in Chant 3, Maldoror turns himself into an eagle and kills a dragon, emerging from the battle "redder than a lake of blood."[14] Lautréamont's battle between good and evil cast Maldoror in the role of the dragon-slayer, traditionally St. George. Georg Baselitz's early portrayal of the eagle may have been a mixed symbol, both of his country and, in this context, of his namesake.

cs

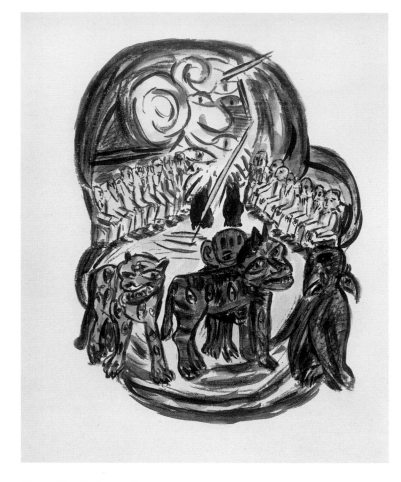

Fig. 34. Max Beckmann from *Apokalypse* (Frankfurt am Main: Bauerschen Giesserei, 1943). Color lithograph. Gift of Mrs. Max Beckmann. Photograph © Board of Trustees, National Gallery of Art, Washington, D.C.

Continuing our visit in Stuttgart, Walter and I emerged from the storerooms of the Staatsgalerie's classical-style building into the energized rooms of James Stirling's wing, with its Kelly green floor covering. We saw Oskar Schlemmer's works for his *Triadic Ballet* and some special paintings by Paul Klee and Jackson Pollock that resided among a number of well-known German Expressionists. We talked about German art, both old and new, and Walter suggested that we go up a few blocks to the Galerie der Stadt, which I had never visited, to see more German Expressionist paintings. We found a pivotal Otto Dix painting, *Man's Head* (1919), that I had searched for years before, thinking it was at the other museum. Thanks, as always, to my cicerone, more than a few holes in my education were filled on our trip.

While it is usually sad to come to the end of the road, arriving in Munich was quite the opposite. For the first time I visited the Bareiss apartment, where I was entertained by, among many things, *Hercules and the Lion,* painted by Peter Paul Rubens, beautiful pieces of Italian majolica, and some of Walter's extensive Japanese contemporary ceramic collection, another part of which I had often admired in his home in Connecticut. To complete our journey, Walter was to introduce me to Dr. Michael Semff, the new Curator of Prints at the Staatliche Graphische Sammlung. During a short visit Dr. Semff enthusiastically showed us his most recent print acquisitions. As we left the print collection I remembered what it was like to be a new curator, and now Semff would also flourish with Walter's guidance and support. Before our next appointment we savored our farewell lunch at the Franziskaner restaurant opposite Munich's Opera. Walter had to leave later that afternoon for Frankfurt to discuss a forthcoming exhibition of his African sculpture.

After lunch we spent some valuable time with Dr. Elmar Heterich, the Librarian at the Bayerische Staatsbibliothek, and Dr. Karl Dachs, Curator of Collections, discussing which books from the library we should consider. A major exhibition of modern books, *Papiergesänge,* had been organized there in 1992, and I was to meet one of the authors of its catalogue and see some of the selections. Of particular interest was Max Beckmann's *Apokalypse* of the early 1940s [Fig. 34]. It had been featured in his retrospective exhibition in St. Louis in 1984, but I had never looked

13. Kevin Power, "Existential Ornament," in *Georg Baselitz,* ed. Maria Corral (Barcelona: Fundacion Caja de Pensiones, 1992): 42, "Lautréamont's identification with the animal kingdom . . . led him to what would become one of Baselitz's family of images: the eagle. For the poet it was . . . the symbol of man's cruelty to man; for the painter, it has assumed other connotations that give additional weight to his symbolical meaning."

14. *Lautréamont's Maldoror,* op. cit. (note 7): 97.

through it. After he left Germany in 1937 and set up in Holland, Beckmann was commissioned by Georg Hartmann to create transfer drawings for an illustrated Apocalypse. They were privately printed as lithographs at Hartmann's Bauerschen Giesserei in Frankfurt am Main. After the plates were hand-colored (some by Beckmann), the book was issued in 1943 ("the fourth year of the Second World War . . . ," according to the colophon). The copy we saw in Munich came directly from the Bauerschen Giesserei. As the book contained some of Beckmann's strongest compositions during that period of exile, Walter and I agreed that a book with such an extraordinary history had to be added to the MoMA exhibition.

My second mission at the library was to look at fifteenth-century blockbooks, one of which I was determined to use as model for the woodcut books of the early twentieth century. The next day, although Walter Bareiss and I were no longer "on the road" together, this odyssey ended at the Staatsbibliothek with a feast of eight thin, bound blockbooks, some of the *Apocalypse,* others of the *Dance of Death, Ars Moriendi,* and *Canticum Canticorum.* After studying this book form in depth for the first time, I searched other troves. Eventually, a blockbook from the J. Pierpont Morgan Library in New York was added to the MoMA exhibition. Going beyond a book's original issue date enhances its meaning. At the end of the twentieth century, our trip suggested several possibilities of doing just that.

Traveling with W. B. persuaded me that something sure to elicit the joy of discovery might often be just around the corner. Walter's enthusiasm for artistic achievement, in fields as far apart as ancient Greek vases, African tribal sculpture, contemporary German art, and modern artist's books, is contagious. Our trip of five days was a mini-version of Walter's numerous, longer campaigns to locate elusive potters or obscure sites of great art. On these trips, he has shared his generosity of spirit with other art lovers, rewarding us all with wonder and enlightenment.

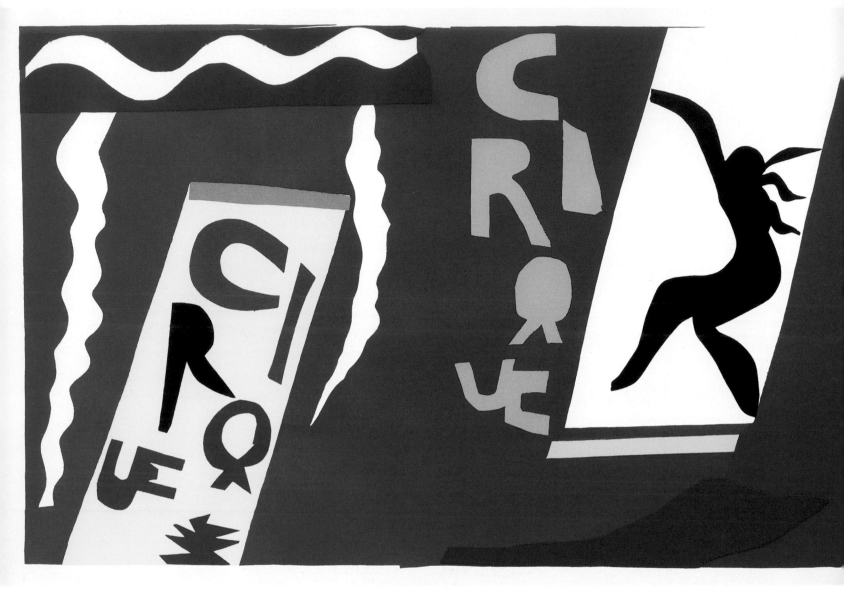

Fig. 35. Henri Matisse from *Jazz* [portfolio]
(Paris: Tériade, 1947). Color pochoir print.
Edition: 53/100.

MICHAEL SEMFF

"L'ordonnance d'un labyrinthe": Sculptors' Contributions to the Illustrated Artist's Book

When we speak of twentieth-century illustrated artists' books like those so devotedly and knowledgeably collected by Molly and Walter Bareiss, we generally mean bibliophile editions illustrated with original prints, of the type that experienced an unprecedented heyday, especially in France, from the 1930s onward. By way of introduction, let us take a brief look at the development of this genre and its continuing vitality since the nineteenth century, in order better to understand the illustrated book as an aesthetic phenomenon.

Great French artists of the nineteenth century, from Eugène Delacroix through Édouard Manet and Henri de Toulouse-Lautrec down to the Nabis who gathered around the journal *La Revue Blanche*—above all Maurice Denis, Pierre Bonnard, and Aristide Maillol—made pioneering contributions to the emancipation of a new art of the book. Diverging from eighteenth-century tradition, they developed a new form of illustration that evocatively paralleled, rather than directly related to, the text. To this end a promising new medium was available—lithography, invented by the German printer Aloys Senefelder in 1798. Nevertheless, the traditional wood-engraving process for reproducing illustrations continued to dominate throughout the nineteenth century.

Yet lithography did provide an early stimulus to the collaboration of author and illustrator. This "daringly pioneering work in the transition to the Romantic Era"[1] was an 1828 edition of Goethe's *Faust*, illustrated with full-page lithographs by Delacroix [Fig. 45]. The marvel of this attempt was not destined to be matched until 1875, with Manet's folio publication of Edgar Allan Poe's *The Raven,* in the translation by Stéphane Mallarmé. It was a brilliant, interdisciplinary work of art in which the contributions of author, translator, and artist jointly invoked the atmospheric, suggestive power of word and image. Thanks to a complex lithographic transfer process, Manet achieved an effect of fleetingness and gestural spontaneity, which translated Poe's mysterious nocturnal scene into congenial imagery. Such achievements found a direct continuation in Toulouse-Lautrec's book designs of the 1890s, in which the legacy of the French printmaker Honoré Daumier also bore fruit. Toulouse-Lautrec's illustrated albums were marked not only by his phenomenal ability to evoke character but also by an absolute interaction of typography and image, a field in which the artist made daring advances.

1. Karin von Maur, "Tendenzen der Buchkunst im zwanzigsten Jahrhundert," in *Papiergesänge – Buchkunst im 20. Jahrhundert* (München: Bayerische Staatsbibliothek München, 1992): 12. The present author owes important insights and quotations to this exemplary overview of the topic.

In regard to the decorative unity of the illustrated book page, a goal toward which William Blake successfully strove prior to 1800, Maurice Denis achieved a compelling synthesis that combined Symbolism with elements of Japonisme. Denis defined his approach as the decoration of a book "sans servitude du texte, sans exacte correspondance de sujet avec l'écriture . . ." [without slavery to the text, without exact relation between subject and writing . . .].[2]

No review of historically and aesthetically significant nineteenth-century artists' books that paved the way for the next hundred years can afford to overlook one outstanding chef-d'oeuvre: Bonnard and Vollard's epoch-making edition of Verlaine's poetry volume *Parallèlement,* published in 1900 [Fig. 17]. The audacity of this deluxe edition lay in its subtle, leitmotif-based structure, in which Bonnard's more than one hundred lithographs, printed in a delicate rose tint, played around the limpid rhythms of Verlaine's erotic verses. Here, the page layout was revolutionized by an unprecedented interaction between illustration and typography, setting a standard that retained its influence all the way down to Picasso's brief *rémarques* on Luis de Góngora's poems of nearly fifty years later.

In the present essay I shall address an issue that has tended to be overlooked until now. Can we find illustrated books of the twentieth century whose aesthetic structure clearly indicates the hand of a sculptor at work? Can we define the criteria with which the characteristic approaches of painters and sculptors to this highly refined genre can be clearly distinguished?

☙

In 1925 Julius Rodenberg characterized the illustrated book as the result of an interplay between two arts, a "reciprocal effect between the temporal configurations of the poet and the spatial configurations of the artist."[3] Karin von Maur has termed the deluxe edition "a space-time *Gesamtkunstwerk* 'in miniature' " and, in describing the diverse sensory stimuli it provides to the reader-viewer's mind and eye, she pointed out its tangible character, the "substantial qualities of binding and paper, or the relief structure of the print."[4] Such statements strikingly emphasize the haptic—tactile—and three-dimensional nature of the book, as opposed to the graphic or two-dimensional nature of illustration. In this light, let us look into the question of whether and how artists reflected upon these specifically sculptural aspects, and describe a few examples in which sculptural ideas found a special and individual expression.

It should come as no surprise that some of the most fruitful forays into book design were undertaken by precisely those sculptors in whose oeuvres plastic and graphic forms of expression were inseparable. Not only were these sculptors outstanding draftsmen, but they also treated volume and its translation into a pure, planar, linear art as synonymous. In each medium with its characteristic means, they pursued the same abstract, creative essence.

A number of major twentieth-century sculptors represented by key works in the Bareiss Collection—such as Ernst Barlach, Marino Marini, Henry Moore, Alberto Giacometti, Germaine Richier, or Fritz Wotruba—were also masters of drawing, although the importance of drawings in the context of their sculptural work may have differed from case to case. Strikingly, all of these artists worked in a figurative vein, in which drawing—generally serving the preparation or paraphrasing of a sculpture—revolved around the definition of an existential human image

2. Quoted in Günther Thiem, "Introduction" to *Französische Maler illustrieren Bücher* (Stuttgart: Staatsgalerie, 1965): 12.
3. Julius Rodenberg, *Deutsche Pressen. Eine Bibliographie* (Zürich: Amalthea-Verlag, 1925): 19.
4. Von Maur, op. cit. (note 1): 11.

that, concentrated and self-contained, never deviated into mere decor or ornamental paraphrase.

Let us turn to an Expressionist artist, such as Barlach. The approach and tangible character of his 1919 work *Der Kopf,* with ten woodcuts designed to accompany a poem by the Baltic author Reinhold von Walter, immediately reveal the hand of a sculptor and woodcarver.

> *[Von Walter's poem] invokes poverty, need, hunger, and oppression, but also compassion and despairing piety—all of which Barlach translates into monumental figures and scenes of primal power. The deep channels cut by the knife into the block transform the entire pictorial field into a surging primeval ground out of which the figures struggle to emerge and in which they will remain captured for life.*[5]

Avoiding decorative design in the sense of the polyphonal, refined aesthetic of the illustrated artist's book, Barlach the sculptor transmuted the existential content of von Walter's text into imagery of lapidary sculptural power.

A quite unexpected parallel in French art is found in the early woodcuts of the painter and sculptor André Derain. His first essay into the bibliophile book, an edition of Guillaume Apollinaire's prose novelette *L'enchanteur pourrissant,* was published in 1909 under the typographical direction of Daniel-Henry Kahnweiler.[6] Paralleling the greatest achievements in Die Brücke printmaking, which Derain may well have known through Kahnweiler, the thirty-one woodcuts possess a forceful directness that makes them incunabula of Expressionism. In the twelve full-page and eleven partial and half-page vignettes, some of the "elementary magic of Gauguin's woodcuts" lives on.[7] The evocative, plastic vitality of the angular contours and precise black-white contrasts in the interior articulation immediately convey the attack of a sculptor's hand, which is also reflected in the figures' rhythmical placement.

❧

A spare, undecorative approach to the figure may have been the essential reason why artists like Moore, Giacometti, or Wotruba nearly always favored full-page, non-integrative illustrations or separate suites of individual prints. This underscored their character as autonomous images which, rather than illustrating a text, merely alluded to its content or accompanied it. Moore's late etchings on the *Elephant Skull,*[8] or Wotruba's graphic legacy *Zehn Radierungen,*[9] are discrete portfolios in which no attempt was made to create an interplay of content and form, in the sense of text, page, sequence, or typography conceived in a structured, aesthetic polyphony of unity.

In the case of Giacometti's illustrated books, too, the classical division of text page and adjacent full-page etching or lithograph dominates,[10] and no conscious attempt was made to create a dialogue with the typeset text. However, such a dialogue would miraculously come about posthumously in 1967, a year after Giacometti's death, when Jean Hugues edited *L'inhabité* with a text by André du Bouchet. The etched images are extremely diaphanous, seemingly on the point of dissolving in space. Some are mere suggestions of landscape, which correspond nicely with the typography set sparingly in the space of the book. Giacometti's etchings for *Vivant cendres, innommées,* a text by the fatally ill Michel Leiris, are dominated by an inward, spiritual mood, perhaps because instead of an interaction

5. Von Maur, op. cit. (note 1): 28

6. Guillaume Apollinaire, *L'enchanteur pourrissant* (Paris: Kahnweiler, 1909). This small-format book, printed in an edition of 100, is owned by the Toledo Museum of Art but not as a part of the Barciss Collection. See von Maur, op. cit. (note 1): 19–20, fig. 3.

7. Von Maur, op. cit. (note 1): 20.

8. Henry Moore, *Catalogue of Graphic Work 1931–1972* (Genève: G. Cramer, 1973–86): cat. nos. 109–46.

9. *Fritz Wotruba, Druckgraphik 1950–1975* (Wien: Graphische Sammlung Albertina, 1989): cat. nos. 63–69.

10. As in the editions *Dans la chaleur vacante* (1961), *L'épervier* (1960), and *Pomme endormie* (1961).

with the typographic page, the artist focused on the sheer effect of lines circling around the ultimate questions of life. Giacometti was apparently not interested in determining, or even influencing, the structure and rhythm between text and images. He merely supplied the required illustrations and let the editor arrange them as he saw fit. This assumption is supported by the fact that even in Paris in the 1930s, at the height of his experimental Surrealist phase, Giacometti undertook no book project with any of the many illustrious publishers active at the time.

☙

In regard to sculptors beholden to the classical French ideal, such as Despiau, similar tendencies to the strictly figurative sculptors mentioned above can be detected. Still, the sequence and rhythm of Despiau's lithographs of nudes for the exquisite edition of the *Poèmes de Baudelaire* (1933), some of which are delicately superimposed on the text, reflect not only the personality of the book designer but also the ordering hand of the sculptor and sensitive draftsman.

When it comes to the classic Maillol, we are confronted by a genuine book artist, because his illustrations are not three-dimensional paraphrases of his sculpted figures but purely linear projections that stand in sensitive equilibrium with typography and printed page. The extreme sensitivity of the placement of the delicate imagery, often playing with slight shifts away from the type area, reflects a sovereign, classical employment of the art of line. Here the idea of female corporeality, which dominated Maillol's drawings from the turn of the century and through all phases of his development, entirely recedes.[11] Nor is there much sense of that tactile, sensuous attack of knife on wood seen in the work of Barlach or Derain. In Maillol's hands the book woodcut experiences an ascetic reduction that excludes every Expressionist element, and whose abbreviated touch tends more to recall the straightforward, contour-emphasizing wood-engravings prevalent in the 1920s. In addition to the edition of *Les géorgiques,* Virgil's *Eclogues* [Fig. 49], with their forty-three woodcuts, embody this style most compellingly.

This illustrious artist's book, printed at the Cranach Presse in 1926, is a culmination of the genre in the twentieth century. A truly European *Gesamtkunstwerk,* it was produced by Count Harry Kessler in collaboration with the best professionals (e.g., in typography and paper) he could find from various nations.[12] The plan had already taken shape on the famous trip to Greece to which Kessler had invited Maillol and Hugo von Hofmannsthal in April–May 1908. There can be no doubt that the echoes of the ancient Greek spirit found in Maillol's finely incised contours, reminiscent of Attic Greek vase paintings, are owed to this journey. The trip to Greece was probably as much of a revelation for Maillol as Klee's Tunis journey had been for him.

A similar spirit informs Henri Laurens's art for the book. Three of his major works — *Les idylles, Loukios ou l'âne,* and *Dialogues*[13] — were based on texts by the great ancient poets Lucian of Samosata and Theocritus [Fig. 36]. The thirty-eight reddish brown color woodcuts to *Les idylles,* executed in 1945 by Théo Schmied after Laurens's designs, immediately recall Attic red-figure vase painting, especially because of the fine incised lines on the opaque interior areas. In Tériade's layout, the woodcuts are either placed full-page, opposite the text, or used as vignettes. Some derive their effect from an extreme distance from the text, while others form an interplay with the white of an empty page. Occasionally Laurens's figurations,

11. In addition to the genre of plastically modeled drawings, however, Maillol's oeuvre also contains pure contour drawings in which he tested the effects of composition and silhouettes.

12. Such as Edward Prince for his font based on Nicolas Jenson's Venetian antiqua, Eric Gill for titles and initials, and Gaspar Maillol, the sculptor's nephew, for the hand-laid paper.

13. Lucian of Samosata, *Loukios ou l'âne, bois originaux de Henri Laurens* (Paris: Tériade, 1947). *Loukios ou l'âne* still remains a desideratum for the Toledo Museum of Art.

LES CHANTEURS BUCOLIQUES

Le charmant Daphnis faisant paître ses bœufs se rencontra, dit-on, avec Ménalcas qui paissait ses ouailles sur les hautes montagnes. Ils étaient blonds tous les deux, tous les deux encore enfants, tous les deux instruits à jouer de la syrinx, tous les deux instruits à chanter. Ménalcas, regardant Daphnis, lui adressa le premier la parole :
« Pasteur de vaches mugissantes, Daphnis, veux-tu chanter contre moi ? Je prétends te vaincre, en chantant aussi longtemps qu'il me plaira. » Daphnis lui répondit en ces termes : « Pasteur de brebis laineuses, joueur de syrinx, Ménalcas, jamais tu ne me vaincras, quand même tu te tuerais à force de chanter. »

MÉNALCAS
Eh bien ! veux-tu l'essayer ? Veux-tu déposer un enjeu ?

DAPHNIS
Je veux l'essayer, je veux déposer un enjeu.

MÉNALCAS
Mais quel enjeu mettrons-nous qui corresponde à nos moyens ?

DAPHNIS
Moi, je mettrai un veau ; toi, mets un agneau déjà grand comme sa mère.

MÉNALCAS
Jamais je ne mettrai un agneau ; car mon père est sévère, et ma mère aussi, et, le soir, ils comptent tous leurs moutons.

DAPHNIS
Alors que mettras-tu ? Qu'est-ce que gagnera le vainqueur ?

MÉNALCAS
Une belle syrinx à neuf voix, que j'ai faite moi-même et que j'ai enduite de cire blanche en bas et en haut. Celle-là, je peux l'engager ; mais ce qui appartient à mon père, je ne l'engagerai pas.

DAPHNIS
Eh bien ! moi aussi, j'ai une syrinx à neuf voix, enduite de cire blanche en

46

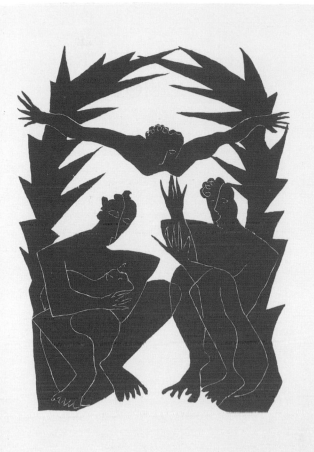

Fig. 36. Henri Laurens from *Les idylles.* Text by Theocritus (Paris: Éditions de la revue Verve, 1945). Color wood-engraving. Edition: 168/200.

with their repeatedly interrupted planes and razor-sharp silhouettes against a light ground, create the impression of cutouts or flat reliefs. This would seem to reflect the sculptural ideas of Laurens, who, after Cubist beginnings, developed a masterful command of the relief medium. It is no coincidence that this marked the first appearance of the woodcut in Laurens's oeuvre, for he never used this technique to produce individual images.[14] Two years later he created one of his bibliophile masterpieces, *Loukios ou l'âne.* Its sixty-eight color woodcuts included fourteen full-page depictions, which are overlaid with a strange, hatched form that looks like an interior shadow of the figure. This dark, nuclear shape, found in many of his drawings and prints since the 1930s, seems to have been a quite original invention of Laurens's. Christa Lichtenstern's report (based on a 1973 conversation with the sculptor's son, Claude) that Laurens would cut out such a "parafigure" and "move it around the figure until the desired relation to it was established," reflects clear links with the planar Cubist collages prior to 1920. This is an indication of that organic harmonization, paralleling the development of his sculptures that gradually suffused Laurens's graphic art. In the thirty-four color woodcuts to the four *Dialogues* of Lucian (1951), Laurens again played with the Cubist principle of additively staggering planes as in a low relief, as if overtly returning to the devices so effectively employed in his early collages.

Laurens's drawings of the 1930s and 1940s, in their complete dependence on pure line and plane, are among the most congenial correspondences to the plastic configurations of any sculptor in the twentieth century. The tense vitality of volume and rhythmical resiliency of line are virtually synonymous. This approach was truly predestined for adaptation to the aesthetic of the illustrated artist's book.

14. See the Laurens catalogue raisonné by Brigitte Völker, "Oeuvrekatalog der Druckgraphik und illustrierten Bücher," in *Henri Laurens* (Hannover: Edition Brusberg, 1985): 244.

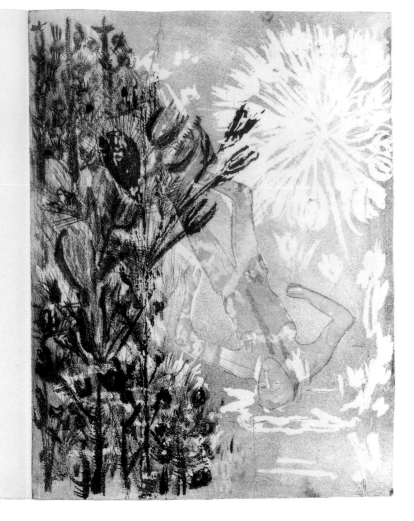

C'est elle, la petite morte, derrière les rosiers. — La jeune maman trépassée descend le perron. — La calèche du cousin crie sur le sable. — Le petit frère — (il est au Indes!) là, devant le couchant, sur le pré d'œillets. — Les vieux qu'on a enterrés tout droits dans le rempart aux giroflées.

L'essaim des feuilles d'or entoure la maison du général. Ils sont dans le midi. — On suit la route rouge pour arriver à l'auberge vide. Le château est à vendre; les persiennes sont détachées. — Le curé aura emporté la clef de l'église. — Autour du parc, les loges des gardes sont inhabitées. Les palissades sont si hautes qu'on ne voit que les cimes bruissantes. D'ailleurs, il n'y a rien à voir là-dedans.

Les prés remontent aux hameaux sans coqs, sans enclumes. L'écluse est levée. O les calvaires et les moulins du désert, les îles et les meules!

Des fleurs magiques bourdonnaient. Les talus le berçaient. Des bêtes d'une élégance fabuleuse circulaient. Les nuées s'amassaient sur la haute mer faite d'une éternité de chaudes larmes.

66

Fig. 37. Germaine Richier from *Une saison en enfer. Les déserts de l'amour. Les illuminations.* Texts by Arthur Rimbaud (Lausanne: André Gonin, 1951). Etching with aquatint. Edition: 77/118.

In ten of the *Loukios* woodcuts, the hatched shadow shape appears doubled, as if it were an echo or reflection. This is the only time that the interior shadow frees itself from the figure, and that the abstract core of the figure takes on the character of an autonomous, hovering biomorphic shape. Associations with Arp's organic forms immediately come to mind.

This device opens an exciting range of possibilities for illustration. The laying bare of the plastic core in the hatched area, in immediate proximity to the linear contour indicating form, visualizes a fundamental artistic problem that exists between sculpture and drawing. Here, spatial interpenetration and linear projection prove to be inseparable sides of the same coin. Doubtless the genuinely French love of the playful and wittily decorative is at work here, too, something found neither in Wotruba, Moore, nor Giacometti. There is a revealing statement that sheds light on Laurens's secret as a book artist: "For me, Laurens's sculpture, more than any other, is a true projection . . . into space, a bit like a shadow with three dimensions."

⁊

A fundamentally different attitude, contrary to Maillol's or Laurens's noble esprit, is reflected in the remarkable book illustrations of the French sculptor Germaine Richier. In *Une saison en enfer* of 1951 [Fig. 37], based on texts by Arthur Rimbaud, a nearly Baroque abundance of sensory stimuli is evoked by a technical and material variety of graphic configuration and presentation. It is as if the enigmatic, surreal interweaving of Richier's hybrid figure-animals took place in a very specific, gestural graphic idiom. The pages, in which full-page images alternate with

Fig. 38. Jean (Hans) Arp
from *La sphère du sable*.
Text by Georges Hugnet
(Paris: Robert-J. Godet,
1943). Line block repro-
ductions. Edition: 161/176.

Fig. 39. Jean (Hans) Arp
from *Cinéma calendrier du
coeur abstrait: maisons*. Text
by Tristan Tzara (Paris:
Au sans pareil, 1920).
Woodcut. Edition: 78/150.

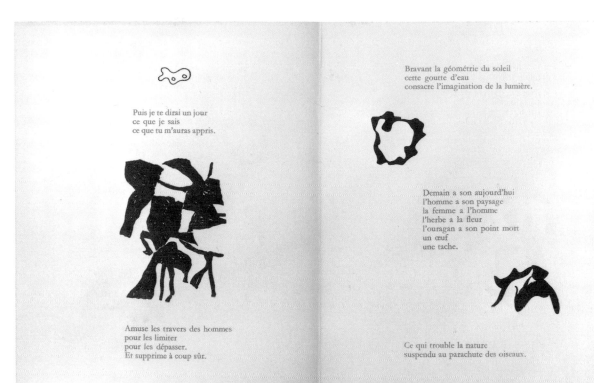

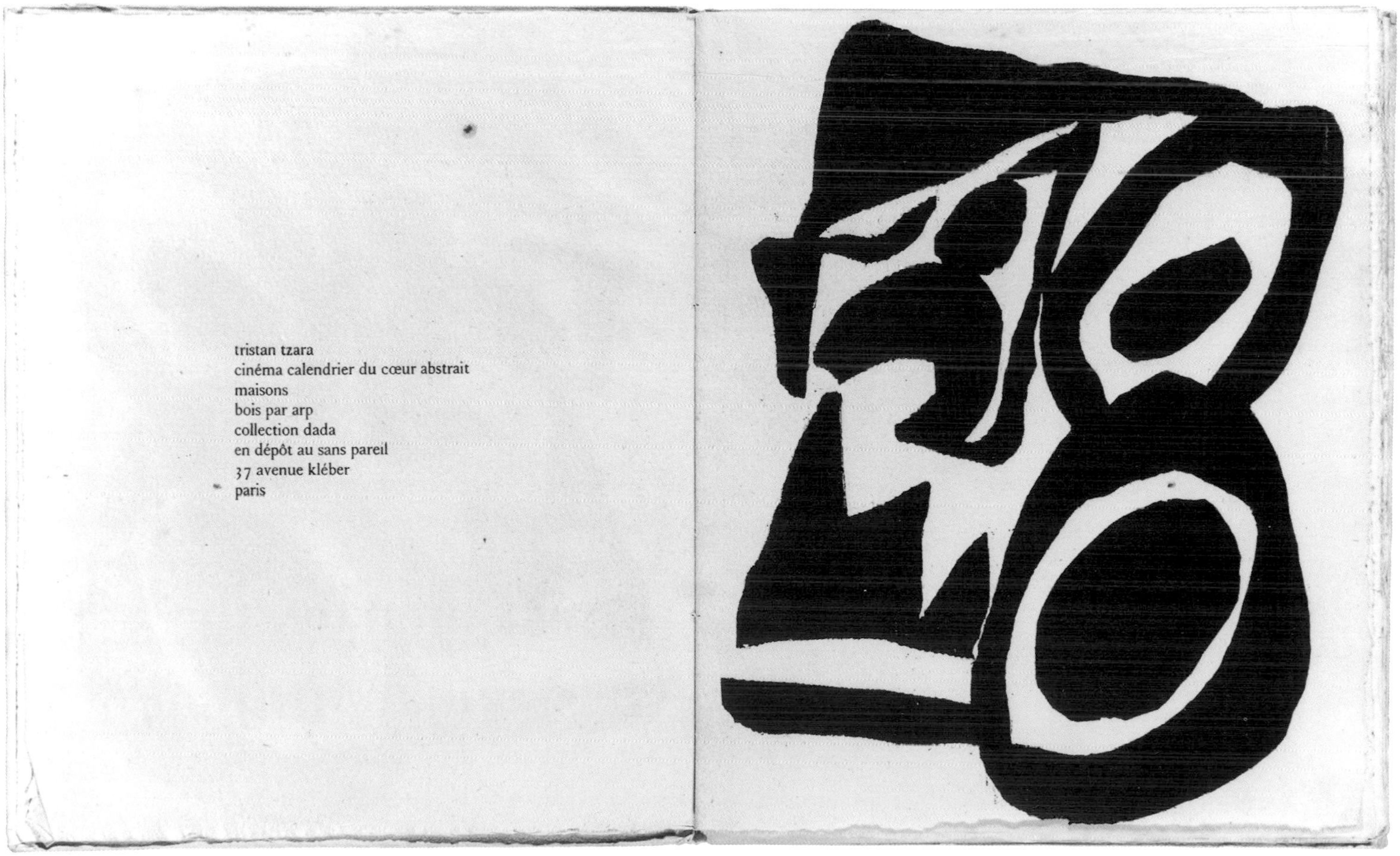

Puis je te dirai un jour
ce que je sais
ce que tu m'auras appris.

Amuse les travers des hommes
pour les limiter
pour les dépasser.
Et supprime à coup sûr.

Bravant la géométrie du soleil
cette goutte d'eau
consacre l'imagination de la lumière.

Demain a son aujourd'hui
l'homme a son paysage
la femme a l'homme
l'herbe a la fleur
l'ouragan a son point mort
un œuf
une tache.

Ce qui trouble la nature
suspendu au parachute des oiseaux.

14

15

tristan tzara
cinéma calendrier du cœur abstrait
maisons
bois par arp
collection dada
en dépôt au sans pareil
37 avenue kléber
paris

occasional gestural vignettes, are like a poetic echo of the evocative verbal imagery. More than any other sculptor's illustrated book, this one confronts us with a truly painterly handling of the material, which employs etching, aquatint, and roulette work to evoke a delicate range of values.

Incomparably more radical in approach and completely denying an aestheticism of surfaces is the work of a solitary giant among book artists: the Alsatian sculptor, painter, draftsman, and poet Jean (Hans) Arp. In 1951 Arp revealed his extraordinary sensibility for the synaesthetic work of art in book form in an enthusiastic echo of Kandinsky's *Klänge* [Fig. 30].[15] The Bareiss Collection includes a remarkable number of major books by Arp. As an example, let us take *La sphère du sable* [Fig. 38], with a text by Georges Hugnet. In a masterful rhythm between text blocks and woodcut miniatures, some of them full shapes, others reduced to contours, a veritable spatial play of positive and negative occurs. Similarly, the cover of *Le voilier dans la forêt* contains three forms animated by the rhythms of silhouette and an interplay between solid and empty, an ambivalent effect that is augmented by the thin, beige translucent Japan paper. By contrast, in Arp's late *Vers le blanc infini*, full-page etchings with abstract, linear contours are set opposite empty pages, with no attempt at rhythmical integration.[16]

One of the most compelling book creations of Arp's early period is certainly *Cinéma calendrier du coeur abstrait: maisons* [Fig. 39], based on a text by Tristan Tzara. The slight diagonal shift of the woodcut on the first page, which seems almost to explode off the sheet, evokes an amazing unfolding of space within the image plane. As the book goes on, Arp plays with variations on a metamorphosis of highly diverse size relations, all the way down to the miniature. His abstract-biomorphic woodcut configurations sit solidly on the page like immovable blocks, like haptic monuments. In this juxtaposition of pictorial blocks with blocks of type, the woodcut once again proves to be the most immediately sculptural graphic medium of all.

In connection with *Cinéma*, which appeared in 1920 as part of the *Collection Dada*, we should recall another published only four years later. This was a modest brochure done by Arp's artist-poet friend and fellow Dadaist Kurt Schwitters, in collaboration with Käte Steinitz, titled *Die Märchen vom Paradies*. Here each page was composed in various type sizes and fonts, and a different typography interspersed with collage-like imagery.[17] Encouraged by Theo van Doesburg, Arp immediately produced another typographical book consisting solely of printed elements. This genre had existed since shortly after 1900, and had been used in highly creative ways even by leading architects such as Henry van de Velde and Peter Behrens.[18] In 1925 Arp produced the fairy-tale *Die Scheuche*, whose tradition-breaking typography of "unleashed letters"[19] was apparently inspired by a "book construction" published two years previously in Berlin. In El Lissitzky's *Dlia golosa* [Fig. 40], with thirteen poems by Vladimir Mayakovsky, typography experimentally emancipated itself for the first time "from the line inextricably chained to syntactic sequence, and conquered the 'book space'."[20] With the vision of a sculptor and architect who thought in terms of large spatial dimensions, Lissitzky invoked "the shaping of the book space by means of typographical material"[21] and anticipated a future "plastic-representative form of book."[22]

Let us return to a master of the art of the book in the twentieth century, Henri Matisse. The great painter and draftsman, whose sculptural oeuvre, though small, placed him among the major sculptors of the century, once said something that

15. Hans Arp, "Der Dichter Kandinsky," in Max Bill, *Wassily Kandinsky* (Paris: Maeght, 1951): 147.
16. See Arp's *Mondsand* (Pfullingen: G. Neske, 1959).
17. Von Maur, op. cit. (note 1): 31f.
18. Ibid., 17.
19. Ibid., 32.
20. Ibid., 33.
21. Quoted in Camilla Gray, "El Lissitsky's Typographical Principles," in *El Lissitzky* (Hannover: Kestner Gesellschaft, 1965–66): 20.
22. Ibid., 50.

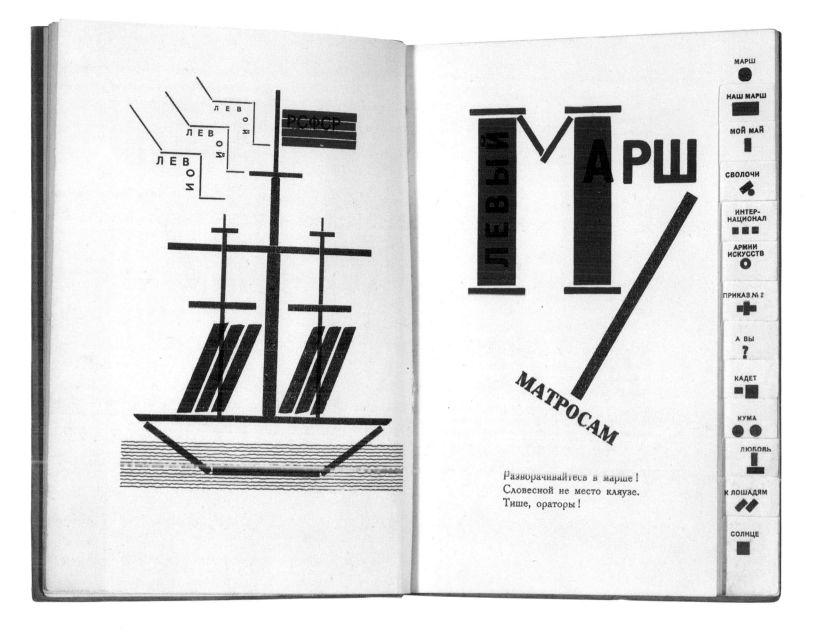

Fig. 40. El Lissitzky from *Dlia golosa*. Text
by Vladimir Mayakovsky (Berlin: R.S.F.S.R.
Gosiudarstvennoe Izdatel'stvo, 1923). Typographic
designs. Edition: unnumbered/3,000.

sheds a marvelous light on the subject of our essay. This statement is found in the handwritten texts accompanying Matisse's magisterial opus, *Jazz* [Fig. 35], published in 1947 by Tériade. It can be read as a key to the creative audacity of the book, in its interplay of written text pages and painting-like two-page spreads, collages of paper painted with gouache and cut out with scissors: "Dessiner avec des ciseaux — Découper à vif dans la couleur me rappelle la taille directe des sculpteurs. Ce livre a été conçu dans cet esprit" (Drawing with scissors — Cutting straight into the color, reminds me of the direct carving of the sculptor on stone. My book has emerged from this spirit).[23]

Matisse's mental association is a rare witness to deeper levels of the aesthetic process that usually remain unconscious. It refers specifically to the mentality of the material and its imaginative transcendence.[24] Three years prior to the publication of *Jazz*, Matisse had already used a cutting process that reminded him of chiseling in stone, in his five linoleum cuts for Henri de Montherlant's *Pasiphaé, chant de Minos*. Here, unlike the *Poésies* of 1932, we find not black lines on a white ground but vice versa, negative white lines on black, illuminating the surface like bright bands of light.

Prior to 1943, *gouache découpée* was merely a technical aid for Matisse rather than an aesthetic process in its own right. It was not until he began making maquettes for the twenty gouache cutouts later used in *Jazz* that he discovered methods that led to a new, autonomous means of expression. Matisse continued to work at perfecting this process until his death in 1954.[25] Perhaps he invoked the spirit of sculpture in his note to *Jazz* because he rightly feared that it would be lost in the translation of the *gouaches découpées* into color reproductions. Only the original cutouts convey the tactile quality of the shapes, the way they overlap with the background and appear "more like flat reliefs than paintings."[26] The fact that the paper shapes were usually attached with pins or thumbtacks, which in some cases were left standing in the final versions, lends these gouache cutouts the character of "objects projecting into space."[27]

While Matisse was working on his cutouts and developing an almost somnambulistic mastery of the interplay of line, plane, and space, a twenty-five-year-old Spaniard, Eduardo Chillida, gave up his architectural studies in order to devote himself entirely to sculpture and drawing. Chillida has continued to draw intensively throughout his career. His drawings, especially the extensive series of prints begun in 1959, correspond beautifully with his work in sculpture. His graphic work is characterized by an abstract projection of spatial relations onto the two-dimensional plane. Reinhold Hohl has aptly spoken of "ideographs that write two-dimensional 'space.'"[28] At the start of Chillida's career in the late 1940s, linear drawing predominated. By comparison to the French ballads of a Matisse or Laurens, Chillida's pure contour drawings have a sparser, cooler, and harsher touch that is like a posthumous evocation of Brancusi's absolute lines. It is typical for the Spaniard that, when characterizing a basic element such as line, he immediately refers to philosophical dimensions such as motion, time, and space.[29] It would seem surprising that Chillida devoted himself to the illustrated artist's book only sporadically, since he, like few other sculptors, would appear predestined to fulfill Rodenberg's definition, quoted above, of finding creative equivalents in the "reciprocal effect between the temporal configuration of the poet and the spatial configuration of the visual artist."[30]

23. Quoted in Henri Matisse, "Jazz, 1947," in *Henri Matisse, Farbe und Gleichnis, Gesammelte Schriften* (Zürich: Arche, 1955): 96.

24. If there were earlier sources of this kind relating to past art, back to the medieval period and antiquity, one would probably be surprised at what unexpected, illuminating insights they would provide.

25. On this topic, see Andreas Stolzenburg, "Henri Matisse, Das Buch Jazz und der Beginn der Gouaches découpées," in *Henri Matisse, Zeichnungen und Gouaches découpées* (Stuttgart: Graphische Sammlung, Staatsgalerie Stuttgart, 1993): 227–39.

26. Ibid., 227.

27. Ibid.

28. Reinhold Hohl, "Zweidimensionaler Raum, Zum Graphischen Werk von Eduardo Chillida," in *Eduardo Chillida* (München: Studio Bruckmann, 1975): 20.

29. Kosme de Baranano, *Chillida, Dibujos* (Bilbao: Guggenheim Museum, 1999): 28.

30. Rodenberg, op. cit. (note 3): 19.

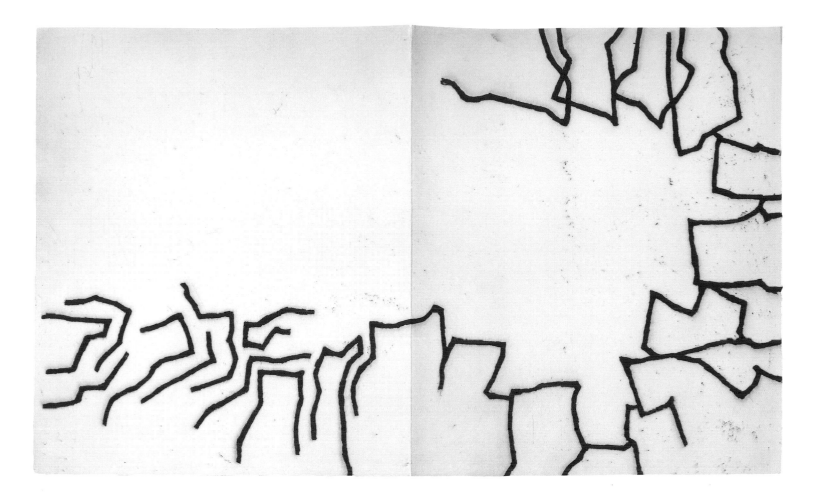

Entrainé hors du chemin, tu ne le quittes pas.
Les maisons abandonnées, il les porte avec toi,
les clôtures défaites, le jardin recouvert,
l'odeur de l'âtre, ancienne, dans la salle voûtée,
le figuier au travers du moulin à huile.

L'enclos précieux sous les ombrages retirés,
les essences venues d'ailleurs, l'ordonnance d'un labyrinthe,

Figs. 41 a & b. Eduardo Chillida from *Le chemin
des devins, suivi de Ménerbes*. Text by André
Frénaud (Paris: Maeght éditeur, 1966). Embossed
etching (Side A and Side B). Edition: 8/175.

With Aimé Maeght in Paris and Franz Larese and Jürg Janett in St. Gallen, Chillida had first-class publishers at his disposal. His collaboration with Martin Heidegger in 1969 on the famous St. Gallen edition of *Die Kunst und der Raum* [Fig. 23] was a significant event. Still, in terms of concise, poetic expression, the crown must go to Chillida's first publication in this field—apart from *Derrière le miroir* editions with original prints—which appeared three years earlier. This was *Le chemin des devins, suivi de Ménerbes* [Fig. 41], with a text by the poet André Frénaud and nine etchings by the artist. Among the superb full-page etchings that dominate the page, much like the imagery in many of Arp's books, there is a sequence of pages in which the text was purposely printed on the back of the etchings, creating deep embossings with a negative relief effect. Again and again, the book space is dynamically activated by continuous etchings spread across two pages. The heavy lines, with dark haloes resulting from the drypoint technique, run across the gray plate tone like veins in rock. Embossing, etching, and typography work together to engender a pictorial space which—precisely due to the absence of spatial illusion—holds the shifting border between exterior and interior in equilibrium through a purely planar articulation. Hohl's description of a 1975 Chillida woodcut applies as well to the general effect of this illustrated book:

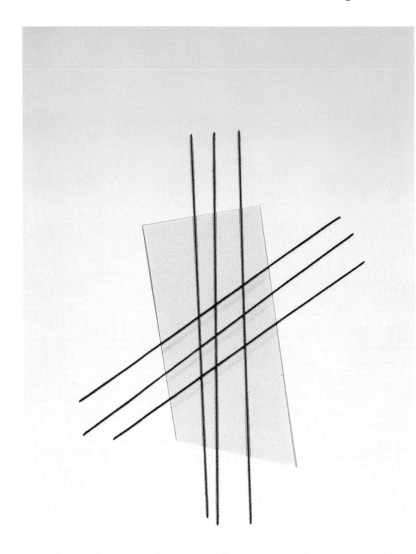

What we . . . sense in terms of volumetric force and spatial effect is the result of . . . the interior edges, the . . . course of the labyrinth, the distribution of masses, and the paper ground penetrating into the overall form.[31]

A profound correspondence between text and form becomes apparent, as confirmed by Frénaud: "L'enclos précieux sous les ombrages retirés, les essences venues d'ailleurs, l'ordonnance d'un labyrinthe. . . ." Chillida's book pages, on which two-dimensional space is inscribed, deal with nothing else but the intellectual order of those hidden labyrinths between fullness and void, those enigmatic spaces between volume and plane, to the visualization of which the artist has devoted a lifetime of sculptural and graphic work.

ട

In conclusion, no essay on the topic of the illustrated artist's book in the twentieth century would be complete without the name of the most brilliant and protean practitioner in the field—Pablo Picasso. Over a period of nearly seventy years, in collaboration with the most significant authors and publishers of the day, Picasso invested the range of his art in no fewer than 156 projects. The books jointly produced with Iliazd and Pierre André Benoit count especially among the masterpieces in the field. Iliazd's typographic genius, paired with his striving for

Fig. 42. Pablo Picasso from *L'escalier de Flore.* Text by René Char (Alès, France: PAB, 1958). Collage with string and die cut. Edition: 7/36.

31. Hohl, op. cit. (note 28): 16.

aesthetic perfection and his vision of the architecture of the book, led to publications of unsurpassed unity. Books of comparable artistry, whose structure and execution reflected specific affinities to sculpture and occasionally bore the mark of the experimental, could be inspired only by the extraordinary poet, publisher, and typographer Benoit (PAB), from Alès in southern France. Benoit was the book designer who entered Picasso's circle at the latest point, completing his first project with the artist in 1956, when Picasso was over seventy-five years old. Benoit sent the artist a piece of celluloid only a few centimeters in size, and the artist immediately scratched a face onto it with a few rapid strokes. The celluloid engraving provided the nucleus for *Nuit,* based on an early poem by René Crevel.[32] This method, in which the publisher fanned a spark provided by the artist rather than requiring the artist to fulfill certain conditions, led to a whole series of rare books and, occasionally, miniatures of a playful lyricism. These included *Autre chose* and *Picasso derrière le masque.*[33] Here, for the first time, Picasso used the burin to incise right through the soft plate in places, creating holes that printed as white, negative forms.

Out of the many and extraordinary fruits of Benoit and Picasso's collaboration, mention should be made of Pindar's *VIIIᵉ pythique,* of 1960.[34] From the second celluloid sheet depicting "The Athlete on the Way to the Contest," Picasso cut three irregular pieces, then incised two figures and a face on them. These served Benoit as the point of departure for three further books.[35] At the same time, Picasso used the negative shapes in the background of the image to evoke the tactile, relief effect of an antique *opus interrasile.*

Iliazd and Benoit, those unmatched masters of twentieth-century book design, joined forces with Picasso to produce a self-contained universe in which the book was sufficient unto itself, a highly refined *l'art pour l'art* whose poetry was accessible only to a few initiates. In this sense, a symbolic meaning attaches to the cover designed in 1958 by PAB and Picasso for René Char's *L'escalier de Flore* [Fig. 42]. A grid of red and black threads across the cover creates the ambiguous impression that the book is accessible while remaining strangely hermetic. This is a discreet yet immediately tangible visual translation of allusions made in a poem by Benoit, published in the catalogue raisonné of Picasso's illustrated books in 1983. Here Benoit compares books to "rare blossoms" that retain their "mystery" and are "often kept concealed in the herbariums of ardent connoisseurs. . . . The book—flower full of secrets—Even open, it is closed."

Translated from the German by John William Gabriel

32. Sebastian Goeppert, Herma Goeppert-Frank, and Patrick Cramer, *Pablo Picasso, catalogue raisonné des livres illustrés* (Genève: Cramer, 1983): cat. no. 74.
33. Ibid., cat. nos. 79 and 83.
34. Ibid., 108.
35. Ibid., 105, 106, 114.

Le Lion.

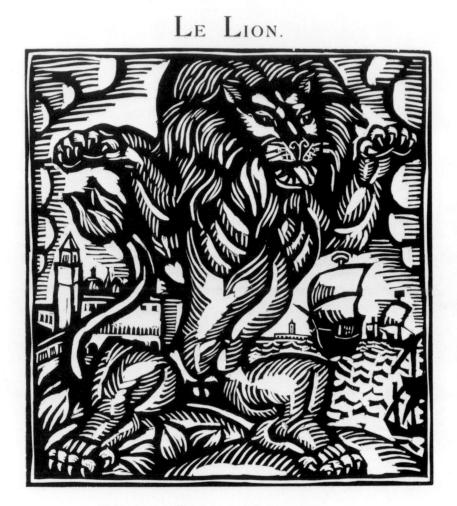

O lion, malheureuse image
Des rois chus lamentablement,
Tu ne nais maintenant qu'en cage
A Hambourg, chez les Allemands.

Fig. 43. Raoul Dufy from *Le bestiaire, ou cortège d'Orphée*. Text by Guillaume Apollinaire (Paris: Deplanche, 1911). Woodcut. Edition: 23/120. Toledo Museum of Art, purchased with funds from the William J. Hitchcock Fund in memory of Grace J. Hitchcock and the Libbey Endowment, Gift of Edward Drummond Libbey.

ELEANOR M. GARVEY

The Whole Picture:
Philip Hofer and the Arts of the Book

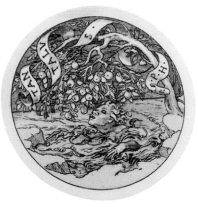

Fig. 44. Rudolph Ruzicka, after
Hans Holbein, *Tantalus* (1937).
Color wood-engraved bookplate.
Courtesy of the Department of
Printing and Graphic Arts,
Houghton Library of the Harvard
College Library.

The dilemma of Tantalus is familiar to all collectors. So vivid was it to Philip Hofer
that he acquired Hans Holbein's little watercolor of this subject (now in the
Division of Prints, Drawings and Photographs at the National Gallery of Art,
Washington, D.C.) and commissioned the artist Rudolph Ruzicka to make a color
wood-engraving as a book label [Fig. 44]. It appears as the frontispiece in a 1937
booklet, *Tantalus*,[1] with a foreword by Hofer and the imprint of the Cygnet Press,
which he had founded in the late twenties with George Parker Winship, the
Harvard librarian whose teaching influenced a generation of young collectors.
For Walter Bareiss's bookplate, a contemporary artist was also chosen — Georg
Baselitz — who has depicted one of his characteristic solitary, inverted figures, this
time winged and touched with red in the color printing [Fig. 1]. It is interesting
to compare the collecting of Hofer and Bareiss, who both began to appreciate the
livre de peintre well before the general public. Just as publishers and booksellers
have influenced the field, so also have collectors of these works of graphic art. It
has been their selection and connoisseurship that in many cases determine what
we now view as the classics of this medium.

Hofer felt that no true collector ever stops; only death can intervene. The
interests of this collector were wide-ranging and constantly expanding. He was
born in Cincinnati in 1898, in the decade that saw Ambroise Vollard's first modern
French publications, and he died in 1984, as artists' books were shaping a new
graphic idiom. Until his death, he continued to collect and to maintain a study
in the Houghton Library, where he was a vital presence — an *éminence rouge* rather
than *grise*.

The traditions of Vollard, modern graphic art, and the *livre de peintre* are well
represented in the Hofer Collection and first documented in *The Artist & the Book*,[2]
the exhibition and catalogue of 1961. That revealed the range of Hofer's interest
in this area — forerunners and contemporary examples of the genre — which he
had begun to acquire many years earlier. In 1936 he was not only a lender to The
Museum of Modern Art's seminal exhibition *Modern Painters and Sculptors as
Illustrators*,[3] but he was also one of five people specially thanked by Monroe Wheeler
on the acknowledgments page for "encouragement and counsel." The others in that
distinguished company were Edith Wetmore, Ambroise Vollard, A. Hyatt Mayor,
and J. B. Neumann. In her essay on Wheeler in the publication *Grolier 2000*,[4]
Riva Castleman notes that Philip Hofer, as a member of the Museum's Library

1. *Tantalus*, illustrated by Rudolph Ruzicka after
Hans Holbein the Younger (Cambridge,
Massachusetts: Cygnet Press, 1937).
2. *The Artist & the Book, 1860–1960 in Western
Europe and the United States*, compiled by Eleanor
M. Garvey, introduction by Philip Hofer (Boston:
Museum of Fine Arts; Cambridge: Harvard College
Library, 1961).
3. Monroe Wheeler, *Modern Painters and Sculptors
as Illustrators* (New York: The Museum of Modern
Art, 1936).
4. *Grolier 2000: A Further Grolier Club Biographical
Retrospective in Celebration of the Millennium* (New
York: Grolier Club, 2000): 388.

Committee, played a critical role in persuading the Trustees to approve that influential exhibition. He lent some thirty items—books and drawings—ranging from Goethe's *Faust* (1828) with lithographs by Eugène Delacroix [Fig. 45] to Ivan Bilibin's Russian folk and fairy tales entitled *Vol'ga* (1904) and Aleksandr Blok's *Dvenadtsat'* (1918), illustrated by Yury Annenko, to Guillaume Apollinaire's *Le bestiaire* with woodcuts by Raoul Dufy [Fig. 43].[5] At the time, Hofer was Assistant Director of the Pierpont Morgan Library (1934–37), following four years as Adviser to the Spencer Collection at the New York Public Library (1930–34). In 1938 he founded and became the first Curator of the Department of Printing and Graphic Arts in the Harvard College Library, which in 1942 was established in the newly built Houghton Library, named for Arthur A. Houghton, Jr., of the Harvard class of 1929.

It was in Cambridge and Boston that Hofer had begun his collecting. As a Harvard undergraduate in the class of 1921, he frequented the old Boston bookshops, then so numerous. His first purchase was a copy of the 1895 London edition of *The Surprising Adventures of Baron Munchausen,*[6] illustrated by William Strang, which he bought for eight dollars. Years later, when his interests had broadened, he was able to acquire the original Strang drawings.

Because Hofer collected simultaneously in many periods and many media, it is difficult to trace the evolution of his collecting and impossible to wall off his interests, which intersected and reveal unexpected connections. His personal and his institutional collecting went hand in hand, for almost everything he acquired was designated for the Houghton Library, as an immediate or future gift or bequest. So identified in Hofer's mind was his personal collection with the Department of Printing and Graphic Arts that labels and loans always referred only to the collection, never to the collector. This led to the occasional *bella confusione.* For example, of the 304 items in *The Artist & the Book,* 165 were pre-1960 Hofer gifts to the Houghton Library, and 25, listed anonymously, were his personal loans from "a lender who wished to remain anonymous," as he noted in the introduction.

This brought a chuckle to friends and colleagues (and some grief to researchers) who knew that he had originated and organized the show. From the beginning of this project, Hofer had enlisted the cooperation of the Museum of Fine Arts, Boston, of which he was a Trustee and a member of the Visiting Committee of the Department of Prints and Drawings; for reasons of space, the exhibition was mounted there. The Museum and the Department of Printing and Graphic Arts in the Harvard College Library were co-sponsors and co-publishers of the catalogue.

This nineteenth- and twentieth-century material points to the unique character of the Hofer Collections (the word must be plural, for the range is from illuminated and calligraphic manuscripts to Renaissance, Baroque, and Modern books and includes binding, lettering, typography, and type specimens: all the arts of the book). Goaded by Tantalus, Hofer was guided not only by his own taste and perceptive eye but also by academic concerns to form a teaching collection. Serving for many years as Curator of Printing and Graphic Arts in the Houghton Library, as

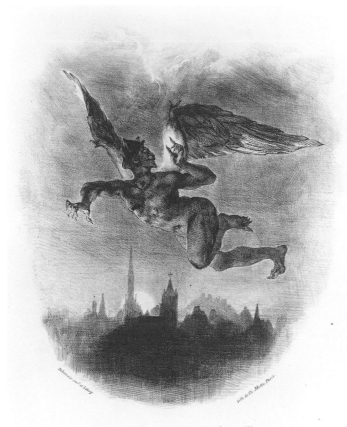

Fig. 45. Eugène Delacroix from *Faust, tragédie de M. de Goethe.* Text by Johann Wolfgang von Goethe (Paris: C. Motte [etc.], 1828). Lithograph. Courtesy of the Department of Printing and Graphic Arts, Houghton Library of the Harvard College Library.

5. Johann Wolfgang von Goethe, *Faust* (Paris: Motte et Sautelet, 1828); *Vol'ga* (Petrograd: Bilibin, 1904); Aleksandr Aleksandrovich Blok, *Dvenadtsat',* 3rd ed. (Peterburg: "Alkonost," 1918); Guillaume Apollinaire, *Le bestiaire, ou, Cortège d'Orphée* (Paris: Deplanche, 1911).
6. *The Surprising Adventures of Baron Munchausen* (London: Lawrence and Bullen, 1895).

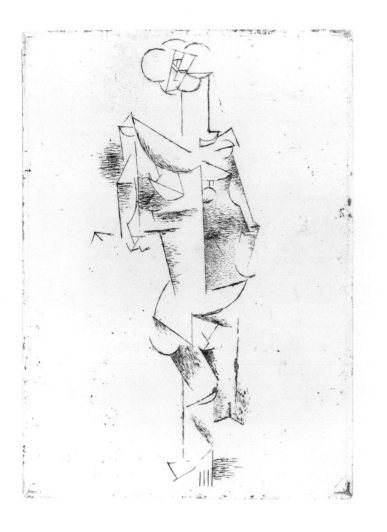

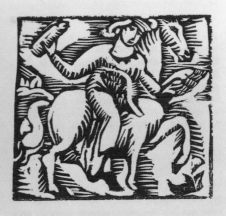

POÈMES PERSANS

Plus légers que des plumes, les arbustes en
forme d'aigrette dans l'obscurité.

Le vase d'albâtre, aux mille personnages n'est
qu'un fantôme, et les deux roses du bouquet
pourrissent comme des mondes: où se posera
l'oiseau du ciel ?

Fig. 46. Pablo Picasso from
Saint Matorel. Text by Max
Jacob (Paris: [Daniel-]Henry
Kahnweiler, 1911). Etching.
Edition: 69/100.

Fig. 47. André Derain from
*Les oeuvres burlesques et
mystiques de Frère Matorel.*
Text by Max Jacob (Paris:
[Daniel-]Henry Kahnweiler,
1912). Woodcut. Edition: 77/100.
Toledo Museum of Art, Mrs.
George W. Stevens Fund.

7. Max Jacob, *Saint Matorel* (Paris: Henry
Kahnweiler, 1911).

8. Max Jacob, *Les oeuvres burlesques et mystiques de
Frère Matorel* (Paris: Henry Kahnweiler, 1912); Max
Jacob, *Le siège de Jérusalem* (Paris: Henry
Kahnweiler, 1914).

Secretary of the Fogg Art Museum, and as a lecturer in both departments, he introduced many a Fogg student to the range and variety of the graphic arts and to the
book as a medium of graphic expression. As a Trustee of the Museum of Fine Arts,
Boston, the Institute of Contemporary Art, and the Boston Athenaeum, he maintained close contacts with the worlds of collecting, exhibiting, and educating and
was in a position to guide young collectors and curators. At his most persuasive
when showing and discussing his books, he captivated viewers and listeners and
helped to shape a collecting path for those who followed.

There were lessons to be learned at a time when prints of the Modern "old
masters" were becoming popular and commercially successful, and loose plates
began to circulate and to lose their identity. Even sophisticated collectors could be
unaware of the sources of these images. *Mlle. Léonie* [Fig. 46], for example, one
of Picasso's rare early Cubist etchings, is a plate from his friend Max Jacob's *Saint
Matorel* of 1911[7] and is meant to be an integral part of the book. *Saint Matorel,*
in turn, is the first volume of Jacob's trilogy, followed by *Les oeuvres burlesques et
mystiques de Frère Matorel* with woodcuts by André Derain (1912) [Fig. 47] and *Le
siège de Jérusalem* (1914) with additional Cubist etchings by Picasso.[8] This trio of
young artist and author friends in the same avantgarde circles, brought into the
Paris book world by the German-born publisher Daniel-Henry Kahnweiler, is part
of the experimental approach to the new twentieth-century aesthetic. Their presence in the Hofer Collection demonstrates his interest in representing the full
graphic oeuvre of major artists who were often better known for painting and

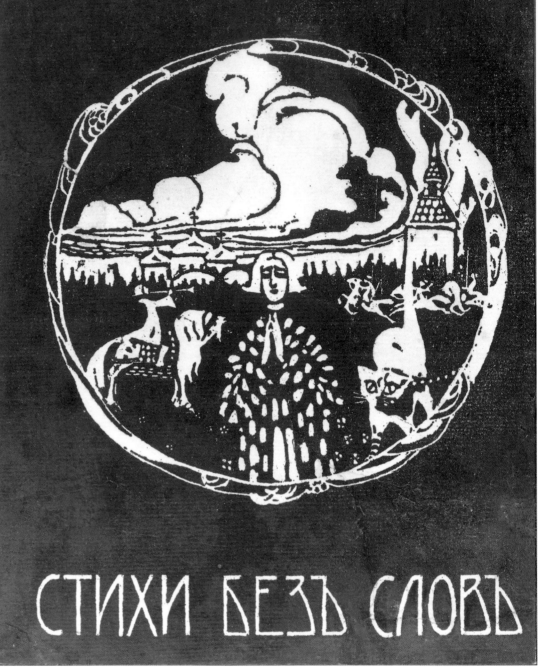

9. Vittorio Benacci, *Descrittione de gli apparati fatti in Bologna per la venuta di n.s. Papa Clemente VIII* (Bologna: Vittorio Benacci, 1599); Jan Six, *Medea* (Amsterdam: Jacob Lescailje, 1679); Wassily Kandinsky, *Stikhi bez Slov* (Moscow: Akademii Stroganova, 1903); *Theater und Kabarett Fledermaus,* [Programmheft] 1.2 (Wien: Wiener Werkstätte, 1907).

sculpture. In choosing the title *The Artist & the Book* for the 1961 exhibition, Hofer was expressing this concept, which had guided his collecting in earlier periods. From the sixteenth century, etchings by Guido Reni illustrate a festival book — Vittorio Benacci's *Descrittione de gli apparati fatti in Bologna per la venuta di n.s. Papa Clemente VIII* (1599); from the seventeenth century, little-known etchings by Rembrandt illustrate Jan Six's *Medea* (1679). From the twentieth century, there are early examples of Wassily Kandinsky — *Stikhi bez Slov* (1903) [Fig. 48] — and Oskar Kokoschka — *Theater und Kabarett Fledermaus* (1907).[9]

Drawings for book illustration represent another genre collected by Hofer, demonstrating an interest in process and in the necessary steps from the artist's original conception to the printed page. Nineteenth- and twentieth-century

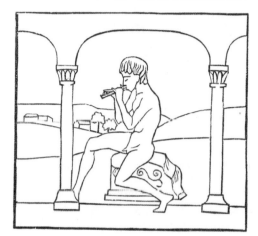

DIE ECLOGEN VERGILS
IN DER URSPRACHE UND DEUTSCH
ÜBERSETZT VON RUDOLF ALEXANDER
SCHROEDER : MIT ILLUSTRATIONEN

GEZEICHNET UND GESCHNITTEN
VON ARISTIDE MAILLOL

drawings include two Eugène Delacroix ink drawings for Goethe's *Faust* (1828); a Théodore Chassériau graphite and red chalk drawing for his set of *Othello* etchings (Paris, 1844); the Gustave Courbet charcoal drawing for the frontispiece of Champfleury's *Les amis de la nature,* etched by Félix Bracquemond (Paris, 1859); an Henri de Toulouse-Lautrec graphite drawing for Jules Renard's *Histoires naturelles* (Paris, 1899); and four Alexander Calder pen and ink drawings for *Fables of Aesop* (Paris, 1931).[10]

Special copies with drawings and proofs can reveal the evolution of the artist's ideas and the influence of process on style. One of the Hofer loans to The Museum of Modern Art 1936 exhibition was a portion of the three-volume set of Guillaume Apollinaire's *Le bestiaire, ou cortège d'Orphée* (1911), illustrated with woodcuts by

10. Théodore Chassériau, *Othello* (Paris: Au bureau de la revue [Mensuelle], 1844); Champfleury, *Les amis de la nature [par] Champfleury* (Paris: Poulet-Malassis et De Broise, 1859); Jules Renard, *Histoires naturelles* (Paris: 1899); Aesop, *Fables of Aesop according to Sir Roger L'Estrange* (Paris: Harrison; New York: Minton, Balch, and Company, 1931).

Raoul Dufy [Fig. 43]. This monumental example of the early-twentieth-century *livre de peintre* demonstrates the evolution and strength of Dufy's early Fauve style.

Another special item is the Cranach Presse's edition of Virgil's *Eclogae* [Fig. 49], begun in 1912 but not published until 1926, in a Latin and German edition, and in 1927 in a Latin and English edition.[11] Illustrated with wood-engravings by the sculptor Aristide Maillol, this copy contains two sets of proofs and three sheets of preliminary drawings. The Latin-German edition is further distinguished by a white pigskin binding specially commissioned by Hofer from the German binder Ignaz Wiemeler, whose work Monroe Wheeler had celebrated in a 1935 Museum of Modern Art exhibition and catalogue. A comparable special copy is *The Four Gospels* of 1931 from The Golden Cockerell Press, with drawings and proofs by Eric Gill.[12] The latter two items indicate something of the range of Hofer's collecting in the twentieth century, for they carry on the English tradition of fine printing led by William Morris, whose Kelmscott Press influenced Count Harry Kessler's Cranach Presse. Equal attention was given to type, paper, layout, and binding as to illustration, all of which remain in harmonious balance.

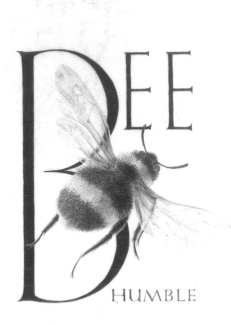

Fig. 50. Marie Angel from *An Animated Alphabet*, 1971. Drawing. Courtesy of the Department of Printing and Graphic Arts, Houghton Library of the Harvard College Library.

Friendships with artists, typographers, printers, designers, publishers, and booksellers played an important part in Philip Hofer's life. In reminiscing, he recalled that he could not exaggerate his excitement as a young collector in London, entering for the first time the quarters of Bernard Quaritch, then at 11 Grafton Street, and thinking: I am about to enter the most attractive and exciting book shop in the world. The green baize covers over the cases, the dusty curtains, and the slightly musty atmosphere (his words) only added to his satisfaction. As the years passed, distinguished booksellers in many parts of the world (including Japan) would welcome a Hofer visit as a great event, at the same time marveling at his bargaining skills.

Quite the opposite reaction was elicited by a visit in the early thirties to a Soviet-sympathizing Russian bookseller in New York, in cramped upstairs quarters piled with pre-Revolutionary titles scorned by the bookseller. Hofer bought abundantly, especially children's books. He was a romantic at heart, and he cherished as association copies the Bilibin *Vol'ga*, which is inscribed in Russian, "to darling Alexei," and an Alexander Benois *Alphabet*[13] with the childish signature "Anastasia" and the date 1905. He was convinced that the books had come from the children's library at Tsarskoe Selo and had belonged to the Tsarevich and his sister.

Hofer's professional and collecting friendships led to rich and complex collections and commissions, generally of a traditional character emphasizing book design and fine printing. At the same time, he was also collecting Picasso, Matisse, Cubism, Expressionism, Futurism, and Surrealism. However, he was less likely to know these artists, and few commissions transpired.

One of the strongest of his artist friendships was with Rudolph Ruzicka, the Czech-born artist, type and book designer, whose color wood-engravings in his

11. Virgil, *Die Eclogen Vergils in der Ursprache und Deutsch* (Weimar: Cranach Presse, 1926).
12. Eric Gill, *The Four Gospels of the Lord Jesus Christ* (Waltham Saint Lawrence, Berkshire: Golden Cockerel Press, 1931).
13. Alexandr Benois, *Azbuka v kartinakh* (St. Petersburg: Ekspeditsiia zagot. gos. Bumag, 1905).

books of New York and Newark in 1915 and 1917 first brought him to the notice of collectors.[14] For over fifty years this friendship flourished, and Hofer commissioned Ruzicka to design alphabets and broadsides that were reproduced for sale in the Houghton Library. At the other end of the stylistic spectrum, Leonard Baskin and Philip Hofer were warm friends and fellow collectors, who swapped books and prints and inspired each other's collecting. Hofer lent the artist some small woodblocks engraved by Thomas Bewick for *Select Fables.* Baskin printed and published them in 1967 at his Gehenna Press in Northampton, Massachusetts, under the title *Aesopic,* with an afterword by Hofer and couplets by Anthony Hecht.[15] Hofer had acquired the blocks in 1944 from the estate of the great printer Daniel Berkeley Updike.

The best known of the Hofer commissions introduced the English artist Marie Angel to an American audience. When he first saw her fine miniature work on bookplates and bookmarks, he recognized a potential for development. From this encounter came the series of small alphabets and bestiaries that evolved from emblematic drawings commissioned for the Hofer family. They were reproduced in little keepsake volumes: *Bestiary* (1960), *New Bestiary* (1964), *Animated Alphabet* (1971) [Fig. 50], and others.[16] They were always printed by the Meriden Gravure Company and the Stinehour Press (now Meriden-Stinehour), whose proprietors Harold Hugo and Roderick Stinehour became Hofer's friends and typographic guides.

A sure eye, serious study, opportunity, impulse, determination, connections, and the sheer joy of the hunt all played a part in Hofer's collecting. He liked to borrow a phrase from the late revered and redoubtable William M. Ivins, Curator of Prints at The Metropolitan Museum of Art from 1916 to 1946, whom Hofer greatly admired: always try to see the whole picture.

14. *New York: A Series of Wood Engravings in Colour and a Note on Colour Printing by Rudolph Ruzicka* (New York: The Grolier Club, 1915); *Newark: A Series of Engravings on Wood by Rudolph Ruzicka* (Newark, New Jersey: Carteret Book Club, 1917).
15. *Aesopic: Twenty Four Couplets by Anthony Hecht to Accompany the Thomas Bewick Wood Engravings for Select Fables, with an Afterword on the Blocks by Philip Hofer* (Northampton, Massachusetts: The Gehenna Press, 1967).
16. Marie Angel and Philip Hofer, *A Bestiary* (Cambridge, Massachusetts: Houghton Library, Harvard College Library, 1960); Marie Angel, *New Bestiary* (Cambridge, Massachusetts: Harvard College Library, 1964); Marie Angel, *Animated Alphabet* (Cambridge, Massachusetts: Harvard College Library, 1971).

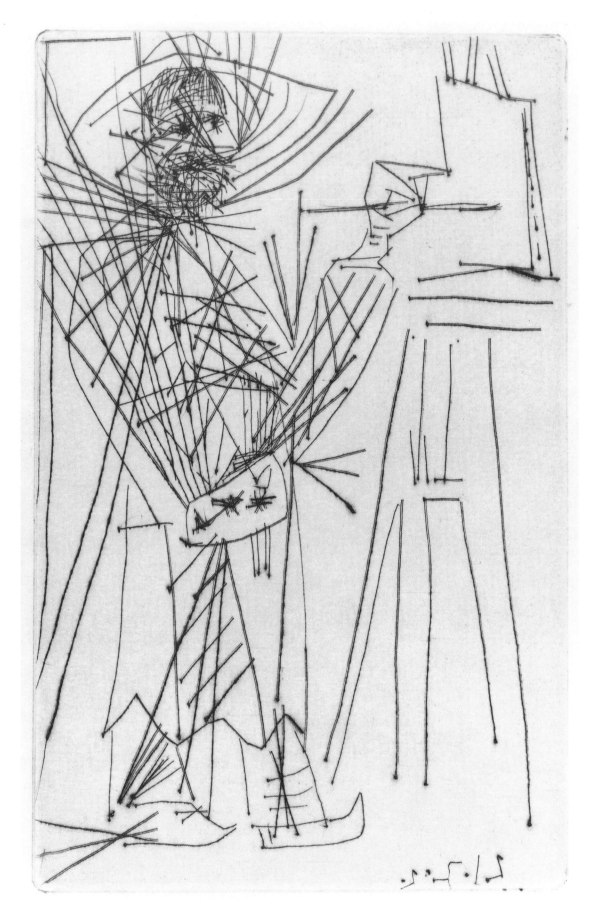

Fig. 51. Pablo Picasso from *Pirosmanachvili 1914*.
Text by Iliazd (Paris: Le degré quarante et un
(Iliazd), 1972). Drypoint. Edition: 13/78. Picasso's
frontispiece of the artist at his easel can be read as
a portrait of Pirosmanasvili, the Georgian painter
who is the subject of the essay. But it also suggests
the aging Iliazd or even Picasso himself, thus
creating a point of intersection among all three
men whose identities figure in this work.

JOHANNA DRUCKER

Iliazd and the Art of the Book

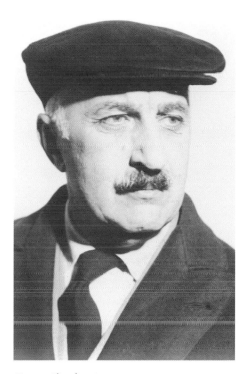

Fig. 52. *Iliazd*, 1960.
Photograph. Courtesy of
Fonds Iliazd, Paris.

The books of Iliazd have found an appreciative audience among a knowledgeable handful of collectors and curators, but they deserve more attention than the size of their limited editions and this constrained circulation have afforded. Iliazd's works will probably never be as well known as those of his justly famous counterparts, such as the editor-publishers Ambroise Vollard, Albert Skira, and Daniel-Henry Kahnweiler. But amid this company, Iliazd deserves recognition for his unique aesthetic contribution to twentieth-century *livres d'artiste*—specifically, a highly personal investment in every volume of the nearly three dozen works he brought into being. Iliazd's work was created in two distinct periods of activity: an early phase in the late 1910s through 1923 that belongs to the era of Russian Futurism and avantgarde innovation, and a later period of production after mid-century, when he was fully established in the international artistic circles of Paris. The compellingly autobiographical lens through which Iliazd focused his editorial role is what distinguishes his vision as an artistic—rather than merely, strictly, professional—undertaking. Iliazd made books first and foremost as the unique expression of deeply held beliefs, because they were the single medium in which he could give form to the many aspects of his intellectual and aesthetic interests. Among the volumes in the Bareiss Collection, several are outstanding instances of this distinctive sensibility.

Pirosmanachvili, finished in 1972, when Iliazd was in his late seventies, is one of the singular achievements of this individual approach. Though not the final book Iliazd completed before his death in 1975, it was, like *Boustrophédon au miroir* (completed a year earlier), deliberately calculated as a concluding work to his life and career. Each echoes the ideals of Iliazd's youth while touching on various themes with which he had been concerned throughout his lifetime. They interweave personal references and aesthetic precepts, loyal attention to the avantgarde, an almost romantic faith in artistic imagination and creativity and, within this, a respect for classical form—its clarity, equilibrium, proportion.

In the drypoint by Pablo Picasso that provides a frontispiece for the work, the Georgian artist Niko Pirosmanasvili appears as a dynamic figure poised in mid-stroke in front of his canvas [Fig. 51]. The image is of an aging artist, his body thick, his hat shielding a pouched, lined countenance, while his facial expression displays rapt attention to the process of creation. But the painter's action is suspended. Why? So that he may consider the progress of the work? Or because he has been caught up in awareness of his own mortality? Is this Picasso, autobiographical as ever, producing a self-portrait? Or is this a metaphoric image of Iliazd, the long-time friend of the distinguished modern painter? Or is it the image of the artist as an old man, a trope in which the figures of all three individuals combine to produce a larger symbolic image that aims to be universal as well as historical and specific? In this regard, the frontispiece signals the extent to which the creation of *Pirosmanachvili* provided a closing parenthesis to a long career for Iliazd, the Georgian-born émigré poet and publisher.

Any book embodies a complex thread of narratives, the intertwined lives and circumstances that contribute to its production. Even the most banal object of trade publishing emerges from such a context. But nowhere is this process more compellingly clear than in the productions of Ilia Zdanevich, who used a contracted form of his name, Iliazd, and the imprint 41 Degrees, as his professional rubrics.[1] Perhaps I am more sensitive to these stories than I am to those that attach to the works of many other publisher-editors of fine editions, having had the opportunity to piece them together through the intimate process of archival research and anecdotal evidence.[2] But I cannot look at any single volume of Iliazd's without finding the pages almost disappear from my mind's eye, replaced by a swarming wealth of biographical information. These stories cannot simply be recovered by handling the books. No amount of careful study of the finely wrought proportions of typography or of considered relations of text and image ever releases the hidden history of their production. And yet, the works could not exist if they had not come into being through that complex nexus of intricate arrangements.

In the case of *Pirosmanachvili,* for instance, the frontispiece not only embodies multiple projections of identity and identification which for Iliazd have become combined in the figures of Picasso and Pirosmanasvili, but also exemplifies the interlocked narratives of their individual lives. Iliazd had become aware of the work of the Georgian painter as a teenager, a young student spending a summer interval in his native Tiflis. His intellect was charged with ideas gleaned from his first seasons of exposure to the revolutionary aesthetic activities of Moscow and St. Petersburg. In company with his brother Kyril and their companion Michel Ledentu (who, like Kyril, was an art student), Iliazd "discovered" the sign-painter's "naïve" canvases. Vernacular images, folk and traditional sources, an unschooled, non-academic approach to composition, thematics, and finish were all striking and attractive features of Pirosmanasvili's work. And the man himself provided strong attraction. In 1912 he was an outsider, living on the margins of society in the provincial capital, roaming fields and woods, earning barely enough money through his work for drink and sustenance. A romantic figure, to be sure. His paintings, like those of his French counterpart the Douanier Rousseau, came to be much valued and collected in later decades. For Iliazd, the thrill of discovery was intensified by the conviction that by curating an end-of-summer exhibition of the artist's work, he was also fulfilling the aesthetic imperatives important to the cosmopolitan couple, Natalia Gontcharova and Mikhail Larionov, whose protégé he had become.

The 1912 encounter with Pirosmanasvili was a crucial moment for Iliazd. Still in his formative years, he wrote the critical study of Pirosmanasvili's work that forms the text of this 1972 book. In almost the same breath, in the season of 1913, he had crafted another essay—this one on the work of Larionov and Gontcharova for the occasion of a large exhibition of their paintings. The links forged between

1. The first use of the imprint occurred in the 1920 publication of *Zga,* the last work Zdanevich produced in Tiflis, and in publicizing *Ledentu as Beacon,* in 1923, he initiated use of the contracted form of his name for this work, the final of the five dramas that constitute his Futurist plays. This volume was produced in Paris, a year after Iliazd's arrival for what was to have been a brief visit. Iliazd had received funding from a Georgian cultural agency to spend a year in the French capital to immerse himself in its aesthetic climate. Iliazd's own financial circumstances delayed his return to either Tiflis or Russia, which by then had become the Soviet Union. News from his friends in Moscow and St. Petersburg grew increasingly discouraging as the decade of the 1920s passed, and Iliazd remained in Paris. He married, had children, became involved in textile work with the French fashion designer Coco Chanel, and then took up books as his primary focus again in the late 1940s, fully immersed in the international artistic community of Modern art.

2. No artist or writer works in isolation, but the book publisher–printer, more than a painter or poet, creates through an elaborate context of social relations. I had the rare privilege of being able to glimpse some of the complexities of the life and world in which Iliazd produced his books because of the connection I made with his widow, Hélène Zdanevich, in the mid-1980s. Working with her I met a group of other scholars, artists, critics, historians, and individuals who had played active parts in Iliazd's productions and could provide some information about the process specific to his projects. I had hardly any *impersonal* acquaintance with his books in advance of this investigation and so never perceived them as simply autonomous and fixed objects. This insight seems so significant, yet so obvious, that I cannot imagine any book outside of such living networks. Should I ever rework my unfinished study of Iliazd for publication, I would at least rewrite it with attention to this understanding—and to the stories of individuals and circumstances encountered in my research. In its current form (written more than a decade ago) that project, mistakenly I now see, conformed to the conventions of scholarly writing, eliminating all that is relevant and compelling about Iliazd, his work, the processes of book production, an era, and the work of scholarship itself.

these Georgian origins, folk roots, and the authentic strains of an indigenous aesthetic and the world of self-conscious high art—with its inflammatory avant-gardism—would remain in place throughout Iliazd's life. Fundamental loyalties to the underdog, to the undiscovered, obscure, and unrecognized artist-poet, and a conviction that innovative form was an essential component of artistic imagination became unshakable tenets of Iliazd's belief system. Pirosmanasvili, for all the attachment to naïve tradition that his work displayed, was resolutely an outsider, an artist for whom the imaginative temperament was a driving force, not a surface conceit or convenient social posture. These character traits provide the locus of identification for Iliazd. From the very first, in his early years as a young cadet within the avantgarde circles of the Russian Futurist movement, he was attached to this vision of the romantic artist, whose imagination he believed freed the human spirit from the crushing formulae of convention and the repressive norms of bourgeois culture.

Pirosmanasvili's image meshes with that of Picasso, toward whom Iliazd had feelings of fraternal affection as well as artistic identification. Iliazd had met Picasso soon after his arrival in Paris in 1922 and the two men remained friends and collaborators even as differences in success and stature separated their circumstances. Iliazd took vacations in Golfe-Juan, on the south coast of France, where he and Picasso were recorded in photographs that amply testify to their affectionate connection. Very similar in build and age, the two men exhibited the same robustness, energetic physicality, direct engagement with the moment, and high spirits. Iliazd collaborated with Picasso on nine books—nearly a fifth of the volumes he produced under his imprint 41 Degrees. The relationship was important symbolically as well as materially, and as surely as Picasso came to represent Modern art, so Iliazd came to see himself, and not without good cause, as the modern artist of the book—or the artist of the modern book. As Modernism matured in the twentieth century, synthesizing relations between innovation and classicism, so did Picasso and Iliazd, each in his own way, reflect these traditions in his work.

Collaboration is a complex concept. Iliazd's printed pages are built from personal, social engagements. He never combined an artist with an author in a production solely for the sake of a business venture. Far from it. *Pirosmanachvili* demonstrates quite clearly Iliazd's approach in its combined dependence on highly personal frames of reference and claims to participation in the trajectory of Modernism. The list of Iliazd's collaborators contains the names of many other distinguished figures, poets and visual artists in the pantheon of twentieth-century art, such as Max Ernst, Joan Miró, Camille Bryen, Raoul Hausmann, and Alberto Giacometti. The list of contributors to the two anthology-like works Iliazd published constitutes a veritable who's who of Modern art. One of these, *Hommage à Roger Lacourière* (1968), was a tribute to the important Parisian printer who editioned etchings and engravings for fine press publishers.[3] The other, arguably among the most important of Iliazd's contributions to twentieth-century arts and letters, is the remarkable *Poésie de mots inconnus (Poetry of Unknown Words)* published in 1949 [Fig. 53].

The tribute to Lacourière was conceived and designed with consummate professional grace and is a tribute to Iliazd's craft as book editor and artist as well as a demonstration of his appreciation of artisanal capability in others. But the *Poetry of Unknown Words* is of another order. The collection marked a critical moment of historical reflection at mid-century, a coming-of-age of self-consciousness

3. A copy of this work, *Hommage à Roger Lacourière,* is held in the Bareiss Collection at the Toledo Museum of Art.

Fig. 53. Henri Laurens from *Poésie de mots inconnus.* Text by Paul Dermée, edited by Iliazd (Paris: Le degré quarante et un (Iliazd), 1949). Etching. Edition: "*compagnon* XXXVI Paul Éluard." Listed in Checklist under Various Artists. The clever wordplay in Paul Dermée's poem, with its variations on individual words, finds a complementary refrain in the suggestive overlay of forms in Henri Laurens's plate, with its combination of identifiable female forms and more vaguely suggestive biomorphic shapes. The Baton typeface used in this book anticipates the use of the Gill sans serif that Iliazd adopted for most of his later publications. This face is heavier, stockier, and better suited to the task of giving these poems a substantive presence on the small pages than the more delicate Gill face.

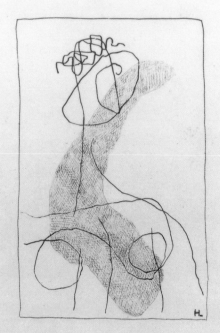

MOTS NOMMÉS TANÉMONES

POUR ILIAZD

I

MON NOM EST ANÉMONE
AMÉTUSE
ANIMOBRE
UN TYMPASE GICOLPHE
EN QUI L'AMOUR ÉDONNE
ET QUE L'ÉNURE ALFONE

MON ROMBLE ÉTAIT MÉSOLE
TAGLÉRÈSE
DÉRÉBROGNE
MOT SIMBRÉ PICLE A TOLDE
AMIGEA RÉLUGÈSE
ET SURDIT PÉTRUVELLE

MORDS NON VEL FARABRÈGE
TARSILLÈNE
ÉPACOLDE
SIFFLERINÉ SUR LES FLARONES
ON M'AUDRIT LOTARD FORS
PALÉGON A TAÈDRE
MOLOMBRE ET TALÉNOME.

II

MON OMBRE ÉTULANT MA LÉMONE
LE POL DE GOMPHE SE TÉVOLE
OFFOGRE LONCHE A MONÉGÈSE
POURGÉ
DARGUVE
ÉLOTIS
GRÈDRE
AUX MANÉTACLES TÉMAROLES

JE TRÉSILLAIS SUR LES POTONES
ÉTAGLÉRÈSES
FARTIBOSOLES
MONÈGRE ALLIMBRE DE LA SOL
UN TRÉMILLAC AU TÉLÉBROGNE
AMÉNIT L'ESPUR DE NÉGÈSE

MONA PONILLE ÉNAMOULONGRE
L'OGISÉRATE A PRIS EMONE
LA TEMPLÉZA
L'ÉTOLA SÈGRE
AUPLIR SOUFFLANT
DES MÉRAS GOMPHES
TURCIDÉLA TON ANÉMONE.

III

MONTS GERDÉS SUR L'ALFUR
DE L'ÉTANG D'ANÉROLE
MONOBRE ELGÉRISAIT
FAGOSSA L'ARDIGELLE
ET MOÈRE OVITANT LA GARFOUILLE
A BRÉLOMME
SORDIPAILLAIT L'OURDE A FAÈZE

MANÉTACLE EST DRUZÉ
DE LA FELLE ILLAROSE
A L'EMBROLE IL AFFILE UN PERGET
DE TANVEURS
SONNE L'ÉTANE ! PORGNE L'ÉPLEURE !
ET PROLINE DANS LES MÉROSES

L'AVÉRÉ DE MÉRONE
A TULLI DE LA JORDE
SINGLINTONS LA GLOTAPHÈRE !
SON NOM EST ALLONÈRE
AMÉTUSE
ANIROLDE

MON NOM EST ANÉMONE...

1925

4. Lettrism was invented by Isidore Isou, a Romanian poet who immigrated to Paris just after the end of World War II. The central precepts of the movement were that letters formed the foundation of all poetics and that their manipulation (including coded glyphs and invented signs) represented the ultimate extreme of imaginative innovation. Gabriel Pommerand and Maurice Lemaître were the two other early members of Isou's Lettrist group and became involved in the production of poetry, visual art, performance, and cinema works in the late 1940s and 1950s. The movement gained considerable visibility in a French context in this period, and adherents to its aesthetics included Iliazd's daughter, Michelle, much to his consternation.

about the earlier achievements of the avantgarde. Produced as a protest to the upstart claims of the Lettrists, Iliazd's anthology collected significant examples of experiments in sound and visual poetry that had been written in the early decades of the twentieth century.[4] In *Poetry of Unknown Words,* poetical works by Velemir Khlebnikov, Alexei Krutchenyhk, Kurt Schwitters, Hugo Ball, Antonin Artaud, Tristan Tzara—nearly two dozen outstanding poets—were printed in conjunction with prints by Léopold Survage, Georges Braque, Jean Metzinger, Sophie Taeuber-Arp, Jacques Villon, and others. A star-studded cast, to be sure, but celebrity showcasing was never, especially not in this instance, Iliazd's intention. Quite the contrary. Iliazd's attitude is embodied in his assessment of the writer Adrien de Montluc, a seventeenth-century wit whose overlooked texts under the name

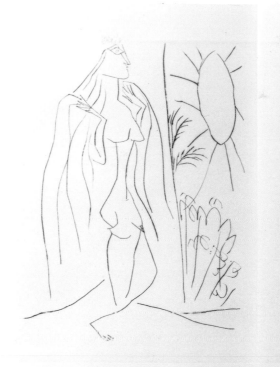

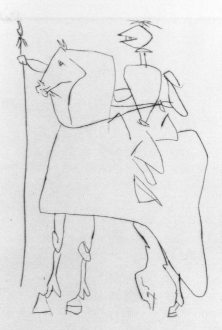

LA QUERELLE D'APELLES & DE PROTOGENES, CELUI QUI VOUS
EUT APPLIQUÉE ENTRE LEURS LIGNES, SANS DOUTE EN EUST EM-
PORTÉ LE PRIX. QUE DONC CES AUARES & SUBTILS LÆSINEURS,
QUI FONT PROFESSION DE PARTIR VN CHEUEU EN DEUX, FACENT
LE SEMBLABLE DE VOSTRE PERSONNE, IE LES EN DÉFIE: QUE

3

S'ILS Y PEUUENT PARUENIR, l'ADUOUERAY QU'ILS MERITENT DE
MESNAGER LES THRESORS, & LES FINANCES DU ROY. SANS DOU-
TE VOUS ESTES CET INDIUIDU VAGUE, SI SOUUENT NOMMÉ PAR
LES LOGICIENS, QUI NE SE DIT DE PERSONNE. LES ENCHAI-
NEURS DE PUCES NE VOUS SÇAUROIENT ATTACHER DE LEURS

4

Guillame de Vaux Iliazd had put into print in *La maigre* [Fig. 54] and *Le courtisan grotesque* [Fig. 55]. "The best fate that can befall an artist," Iliazd proclaimed, "is to fall into obscurity." Publicity for its own sake, star status of any kind — these were anathema to Iliazd. He equated obscurity with the modesty appropriate to artistic vision.

But the poets and artists who figured in *Poetry of Unknown Words* had made major contributions to aesthetic innovation in the context of Russian and Italian Futurism, Dada, and other avantgarde activities. Iliazd's own early work, like that of several of his important Russian counterparts, had explored the possibilities of invented language in the form of *zaum.*[5] Sound poetry, visual poetry, the attentive investigation of the potential of materiality to play a part in meaning — production in artistic expression — these were concerns that had motivated a varied and highly imaginative range of productions. Much of this work had indeed fallen into obscurity or been appropriated to other uses by mid-century. Futurism and Dada were associated with the first great European war and were perceived as dated and outmoded by mid-century. By World War II and its aftermath, the stylistic elements of these early movements become incorporated into the visual language of commerce, decoration, and special effects for window display and film sequences. The once-radical typography of Constructivist or Futurist experiment had been tamed to serve the interests of corporate identity. Dada montage techniques served for propaganda posters and mass-communication campaigns. The once-sharp edge of early radicalism was blunted. The poetic activity of an earlier generation appeared tinged with a sense of quaintness, of a utopianism now out of fashion. The emblematic

5. The term *zaum* means "transmental language" and refers to the efforts of a number of Russian Futurist poets, notably Velemir Khlebnikov and Roman Jakobson, to invent verbal expressions that bypassed normal meaning production and created direct, affective response in a reader or listener. Iliazd's five plays are the most sustained use of *zaum* in works of the 1910s and 1920s.

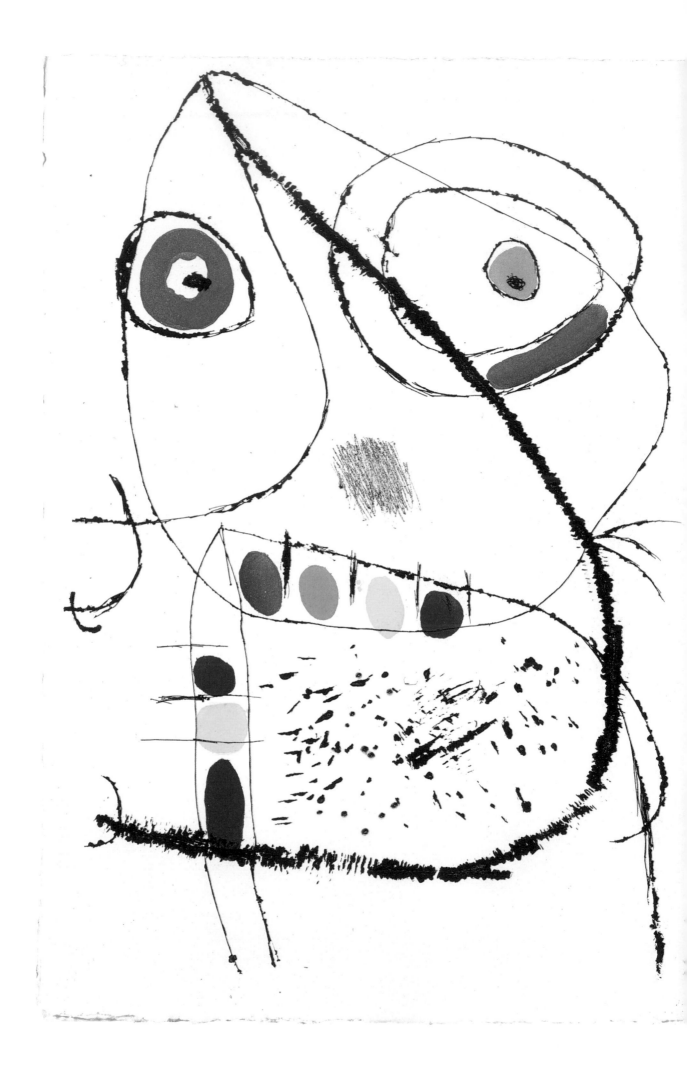

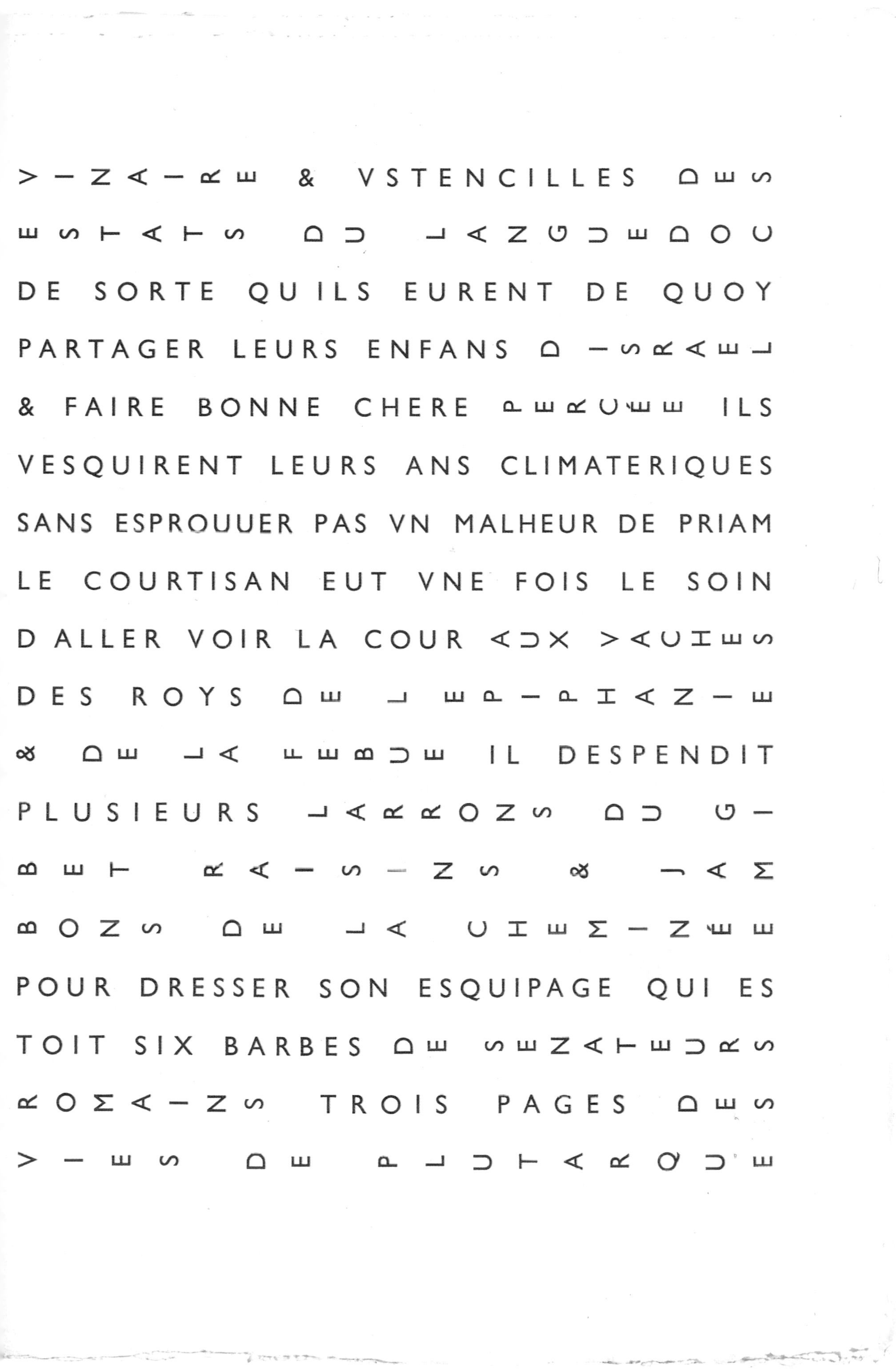

VINAIRE & VSTENCILLES DES

ESTATS DU LANGUEDOU

DE SORTE QUILS EURENT DE QUOY

PARTAGER LEURS ENFANS D ISRAEL

& FAIRE BONNE CHERE PERCUEE ILS

VESQUIRENT LEURS ANS CLIMATERIQUES

SANS ESPROUUER PAS VN MALHEUR DE PRIAM

LE COURTISAN EUT VNE FOIS LE SOIN

D ALLER VOIR LA COUR AUX VACHES

DES ROYS DE L EPIPHAZIE

& DE LA FEBUE IL DESPENDIT

PLUSIEURS LARROZS DU GI

BBET RAISINS & JAM

BOZS DE LA CHEMINEE

POUR DRESSER SON ESQUIPAGE QUI ES

TOIT SIX BARBES DE SENATEURS

ROMAINS TROIS PAGES DES

VIES DE PLUTARQUE

work of the Italian poet Filippo Tommaso Marinetti, whose *Mots en liberté: futuristes,* published in 1919, though a canonical reference for the history of experimental typography and visual poetics, had fallen from favor [Fig. 56]. Artists and intellectuals distanced themselves from Marinetti and his increasingly vocal support of the rising fascist leader Benito Mussolini. Iliazd, who had been an early supporter of the Italian poet and much influenced by his work, clung to his allegiance to the aesthetic sensibility of the older poet, but he was almost alone among his circle in this regard. Such loyalty was characteristic of Iliazd, whose commitments ran deep and clearly had emotional wellsprings that countered intellectual or reasoned judgment. His antipathies were equally profound, and once committed to a campaign on any particular point, he was resolute and indefatigable.[6]

The circumstances that piqued Iliazd's editorial impulse to produce *Poetry of Unknown Words* is typical of this disposition. The arrival of a young Romanian poet, Isidore Isou, into the Paris scene in the years immediately following the close of World War II, brought the concept of Lettrism into the aesthetic milieu. Isou was a careerist, an aesthetic self-promoter and egotist of the first order. His claims for Lettrism were hyperbolic to the extreme. His conviction — that before him all poetry had been produced in expectation of Lettrism's arrival and that after him all poetry would be conceived in its shadow — would have been ludicrous had he not managed to gain support for the 1947 publication of his thick manifesto, *Introduction à une nouvelle poésie et à une nouvelle musique,* through the offices of the prestigious French publisher Gallimard.

Iliazd made contact with Isou in the late 1940s, initially seeing possibilities for a community of fellowship at the nexus of their common interests in the material richness of the letter and of the visual expressiveness of the poem as a form. But Isou's monomaniacal claims permitted no shared vision. The Romanian poet launched an attack on all prior avantgarde experiments, determined to obliterate them from consideration, even going so far as to deny that Dada or Futurism had existed. In a masterwork of perversity, Isou wrote a diatribe against Iliazd without ever mentioning him by name, so determined was he to erase all traces of precedent for his Lettrist works. Iliazd countered the attack by organizing the publication of *Poetry of Unknown Words.*

In this first anthology of visual poetry to gather a representative collection of early-twentieth-century experiments, Iliazd combined visual and verbal works in a compact format. Sheets were printed, folded into quadrants, and collated within stiff folds of the vellum cover. As a statement of editorial intention, the work declares the importance of early-twentieth-century work, protesting its elimination from the history of the era. As a collection that uses typographic variation within a set of fairly constrained parameters — the use of a Gill Baton typeface in, for the most part, a single weight and size — the work gives serious attention to the formal properties of text on a page (but in a radical departure from the virtuoso *zaum* typography of Iliazd's earlier publications). Each poem, by virtue of being set in the same font, achieves its differentiating look through the compositional variants that stress word groups, spacing, repetitive syllables, and morphemes laid out like elements of an orchestral score or transcribed chant. The images printed from wood and metal incise their presence as a striking counterpart to the rich textures of the poetic works. The composition of each page is slightly different. Each collaborative relationship between image and text has its own aesthetic emphasis — the strong

6. Many instances of this aspect of Iliazd's character are exhibited in the notes of correction he sought to publish to any citation that contained misinformation about himself or anyone to whom he felt such loyalty. And the nature of his work, with its repeating themes and continuity across a lifetime of work, exhibits the same determined commitment to Pirosmanasvili, Michel Ledentu, his second wife, the Nigerian princess Ibironké Akinsemoyin (who died of pneumonia in 1945, at the age of twenty-nine, after only a few years of marriage), as well as to Marinetti, Picasso, Max Ernst, Adrien de Montluc, and other figures.

Fig. 56. Filippo Tommaso
Marinetti from *Les mots en
liberté: futuristes.* Text by
Filippo Tommaso Marinetti
(Milano: Edizioni Futuriste
di "Poesia," 1919).
Typographic design. This
most celebrated of typo-
graphically experimental
works serves as the emblem
of an era of radical avant-
garde aesthetics. Iliazd
admired Marinetti's precepts,
and the visual excitement of
Futurist typography served
as crucial inspiration, though
Iliazd's adaptation was more
systematic, extensive, and
measured than that of his
Italian counterparts.

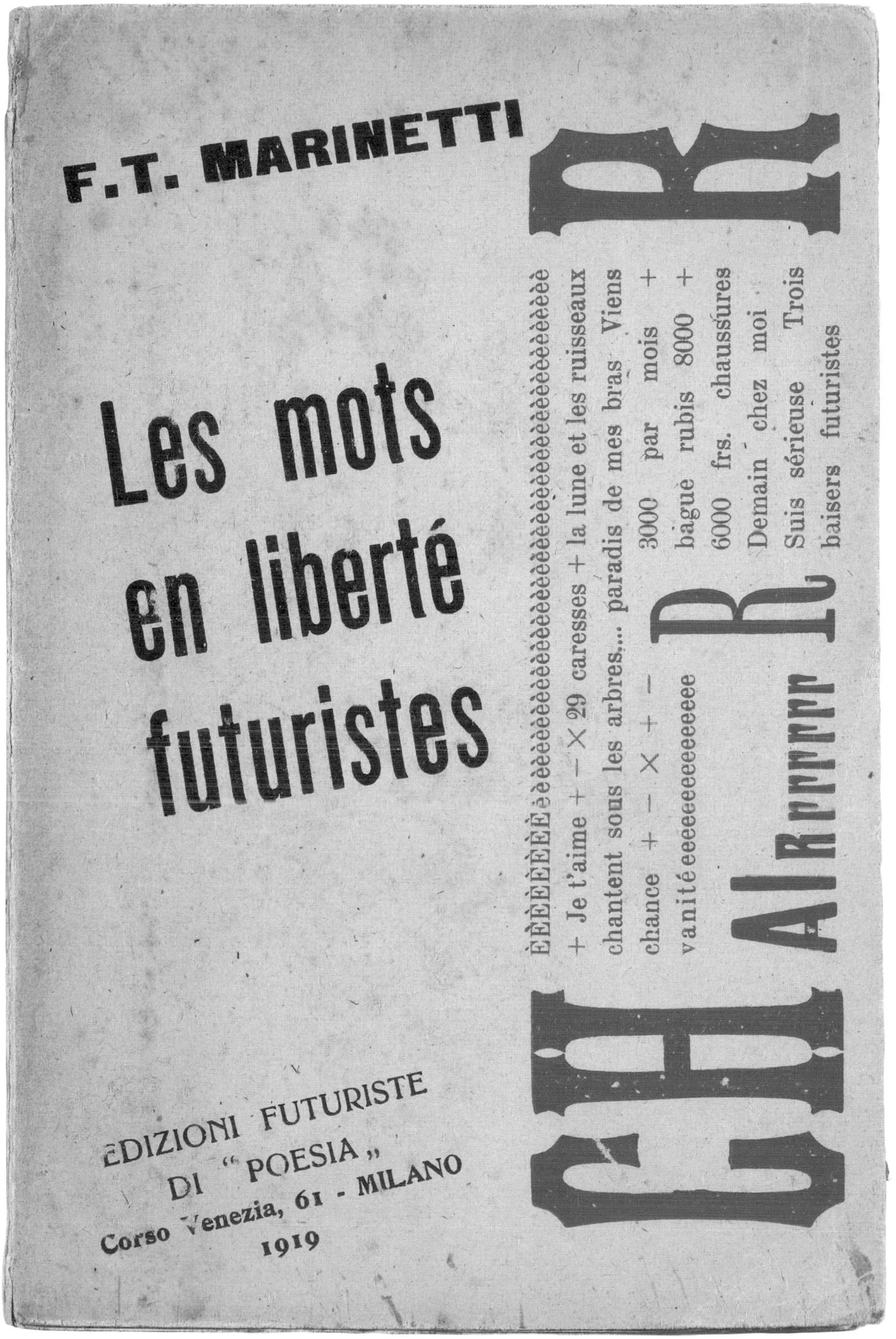

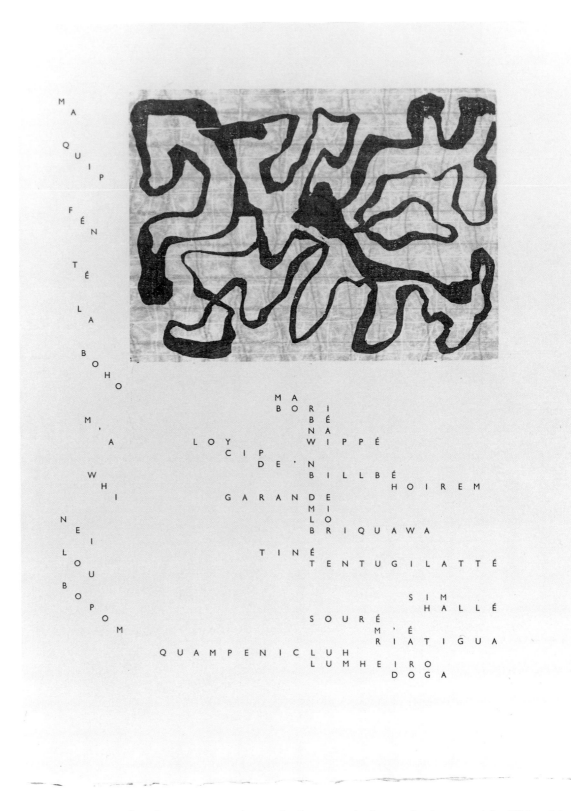

marks of Henri Matisse's simple shapes push the emphatic potential of Ibironké Akinsemoyin's Yoruban text to the fore, just as a softening effect, a slurring together of syllables and phrases, is re-inforced in the way the lines of Matisse's image read against the tone of the Nigerian princess's text. The emphatic repetition and variation that pattern the poetry vibrate against the clean form of the image, enlivening their static shapes with syllabic movement.

Modest in size—approximately five by six inches—but large in intellectual and aesthetic scope, *Poetry* failed in its mission to re-educate Isou. Nor did the book have any immediate or large-scale impact on the literary world. But as a first self-conscious re-assessment of the range of experiments that had been fostered by avantgarde poetics, the work was and remains a crucial landmark. Not until Robert

Motherwell's anthology of Dada poets and painters (published by George Wittenborn in 1951) was another recollective anthology of this scope attempted—and then it was in a more academic and critical framework, produced by an astute member of another generation, not by one of the originators and participants in the early movements.[7]

Poetry marked another turning point within the history of Iliazd's work. His early experiments were over, his engagement with books, their conceptualization, design, and production had begun on a new foundation. From this moment on, he worked on the projects that would establish his identity as one of the premier figures in the tradition of *livres d'artiste*. From the conventions that had been codified in works produced by Ambroise Vollard and others—with their finely produced prints (mainly etchings, drypoints, aquatints, and other intaglio media) and well-designed typography, fine paper, large formats, and luxurious bindings—Iliazd crafted his own specific sensibility. From his highly personal convictions, he made books that realized his individual aesthetic concerns. He made books from the work of obscure authors attentive to the material properties of sound (puns, nonsense, invented language), the work of friends whose writing or imagery had not received as much attention as Iliazd deemed they merited (the poetry of Roch Grey, the etchings of the sculptor Michel Guino, a text by the almost forgotten astronomer Guillaume Tempel, a Spanish travel narrative from a fourteenth-century Franciscan friar, ballets for Renaissance courts by Jehan-François de Boissière), and then a limited number of works of his own composition.

Through sales of the eighteen books he produced after 1949, Iliazd was able to support himself modestly. Printed in quite small numbers, his works verge on the category of artist's books—works made in pursuit of a single artistic vision through the form of a book. His work can be distinguished from other publisher-driven projects, beautiful and elegant though they may be, that are the manifestation of a publishing venture rather than the outcome of irresistible artistic impulses. Specious as it may be to overrate the artistic vision, or to promote a cliché of the romantic artist driven to production, I think it is fair to assess Iliazd's work as the outcome of a drive that was primarily expressive, rather than commercial, in its origins.

A striking instance of such expression is the highly original typography Iliazd designed for setting Raoul Hausmann's works in *Poèmes et bois* (1961) [Fig. 57]. The forms of the woodcuts, made by the German Dada poet/artist, became the driving force for Iliazd's arrangement of the typographic forms on the page. The sensitivity of this mimicry is such that the two elements cross the great traverse usually irremediably inscribed by the presence of two very different media on the same graphic surface. The shapes of the texts are reinforced by the harder outline of the forms on the paper while, vice versa, the images take on a quality of legibility by their proximity to the carefully composed texts. The quality of thoughtfulness in these pages is never forced, and never clever. The pages of *Poetry of Unknown Words* were composed with sufficient constraint to allow their specific aesthetic qualities to stand in striking contrast with those around them. Similarly, in *Poèmes* the use of selective mimicry within fairly limited constraints succeeds in producing a subtly charged dialogue inconceivable without tightly monitored attention to the full sum of graphic effects.

Iliazd's contribution to twentieth-century art remains these singular volumes, each achieved in an exchange that grew from and expanded a relationship. His

7. Robert Motherwell, *Dada Painters and Poets* (New York: Wittenborn Books, 1951).

correspondence is filled with exhortations to colleagues to meet their deadlines, to clarify confusions over details of design or business, or to let him know when they needed plates, or would be able to finish drawings, or any of a million other details essential to production. Another among the works in the Bareiss Collection that attest to his wide-ranging network of friendships is a volume that includes portraits

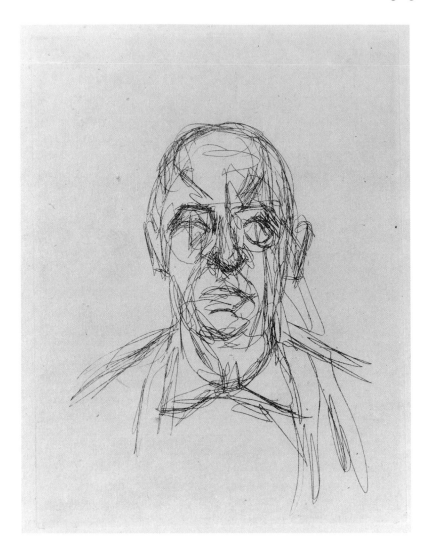

of Iliazd by the Swiss sculptor Alberto Giacometti [Fig. 58]. Titled *Les douze portraits du célèbre Orbandale,* the work is a series of etched images of Iliazd. He had invited Giacometti to provide a frontispiece portrait for the crown of Russian sonnets, *Sentence sans paroles.* Composed in Russian over several years, this work, like *Afat* (1940), *Rahel* (1941), and *Pismo* (1948), found a more limited audience when it appeared in print in 1961 than later works produced with a Francophone audience and readership in mind. Iliazd never conceived of his arrangements with these fellow artists as a business relationship. No contracts except those of informal communications between friends bound the various individuals to Iliazd through his collaborations. Sometimes frustration occurred. Delays caused by distraction or the failure to attend to a deadline, or some confusion over the responsibility for a certain part of the production of an edition, or a misunderstanding about payment—these all happened in the course of Iliazd's career as an editor and publisher. But even in the most difficult circumstances, Iliazd was quick to remind his friends that friendship, above all, must be preserved.

Fig. 58. Alberto Giacometti from *Les douze portraits du célèbre Orbandale* (Paris: Le degré quarante et un (Iliazd), 1962). Soft-ground etching. Edition: 32/40. Giacometti's portraits of Iliazd communicate the focused intensity of his presence. Through their sketchy, open linework they suggest the physically powerful and concentrated energy of a man whose vitality persists.

The books thus have the character of works brought into being through love and communicative exchange. Iliazd had a keen instinct for the rightness of aesthetic choices: of Picasso as artist for the skinny-bones heroine of *La maigre;* of Michel Guino, a sculptor, for production of the solid, simple, almost archetypal images that anchor the exquisitely light phrases of Paul Éluard's poem *Un soupçon* (1965; the title translates as "a hint"); and of Max Ernst for the amazing tour de force *Maximiliana* (1964)—in which Iliazd guided Ernst to produce several very distinct forms of graphic art (aquatints, glyphic-figures, and long etched passages of invented writing). The publication dates on such elaborate works are deceptive, linking them with date-stamped simplicity to their moment of appearance as a finished edition. Some works, like *Maximiliana,* were in the making for almost a decade—Iliazd having conceived the project years earlier and a desire to make a work with Ernst even earlier, in the first years of their acquaintance. Clearly Iliazd understood book production as a merging of sensibilities within the parameters of printing and publishing constraints—and all that such limits offered as a structure for controlled experiment.

But lest Iliazd appear to be outshone in this context by the luminous reputations of the artists with whom he collaborated, his own contribution to the book as a form of creative expression deserves its own recognition. Iliazd was a consummate designer. His understanding of typography had been fostered from early in his life by hands-on experience of the letterpress shop. Trained by a printer in Tiflis, who made the contents of his shop available to Iliazd (though on what basis we are not sure), Iliazd kept a close tie to the print shop alive throughout his decades of publishing. Louis Barnier, the owner of the shop in which Iliazd produced the letterpress portions of his editions, testifies to the engagement Iliazd had with every aspect of production. Photographs show him standing at the typecase, composing stick in hand, almost to the end of his life. Elaborate planning went into each of his editions. He put the designs of his books onto graph paper, marking out the spacing and distribution of type with mathematical precision. The effect is one of exquisite balance and symmetry, equilibrium at the fundamental level of page and book structure. Each book exhibits its own individual expression of these capacities. The architectonic structures of the Hausmann book discussed above contrast dramatically with the delicate scattering of type that steps across the pages of *Récit du nord* (1956), visually matched by the aquatint-spattered textures of Camille Bryen's seemingly frostbitten plates showing the "régions froides" of "Groenland and Frizland" in that work [Fig. 59].

Every volume attests to this care and its effects. Each has its own specific sensibility, unique treatment of the text, and careful articulation of relationships between the pages of language and the images that accompany them. Nowhere is Iliazd's typographic skill more apparent than in the artfully deft handling of typography to indicate puns within the seventeenth-century text of Adrien de Montluc that appears in *Le courtisan grotesque* (1974) [fig. 55]. In that work, Iliazd called attention to the wordplay by setting the phrases containing double entendres sideways within the line. A difficult technical task, one for which Iliazd's early apprenticeship with the elaborate pages of *Ledentu* (1923) had prepared him more than fifty years earlier. The aesthetic judgment with which Iliazd subsumed his youthful exuberant spirit of radical experiment into the almost classical-seeming beauty of the works of his later decades bears tribute to his capacity to preserve the best of his early discoveries within the context of a mature artistic vision.

The capacity to move onward while recapitulating the themes of youth and a life of engagement is perhaps best exemplified in the poetic retrospection embodied in *Boustrophédon* (1971), a useful counterpoint to the iconography of *Pirosmanachvili*, with which this essay opened. In *Boustrophédon* Iliazd touched very briefly, lightly, on the persons whose place in his life had defined his own existence as a man and an artist. Pirosmanasvili is among the figures named in the poems in *Boustrophédon*. Spelled out letter by letter in reverse (thus corresponding to the pattern of reading invoked in the title), these verses form a tribute to the *zaum* experiments that had opened doors of perception for Iliazd in the 1910s. His early work had instilled in him a recognition of the material qualities of language as sound and image, the capacity of words to create suggestive sensation that he believed bypassed reason and the conscious mind. But *Boustrophédon* was a highly calculated work, a memorial tribute not only to the companions of his youth, Michel Ledentu and Pirosmanasvili, but also to his beloved wife Hélène, adoring companion of his final years, and to Adrien de Montluc, a figure whose renegade linguistic tactics had brought him into conflict with Cardinal Richelieu, as well as to others with whose heroic achievements (or failures) Iliazd identified. These figures were the sum of Iliazd's sense of himself as artist, poet, typographer,

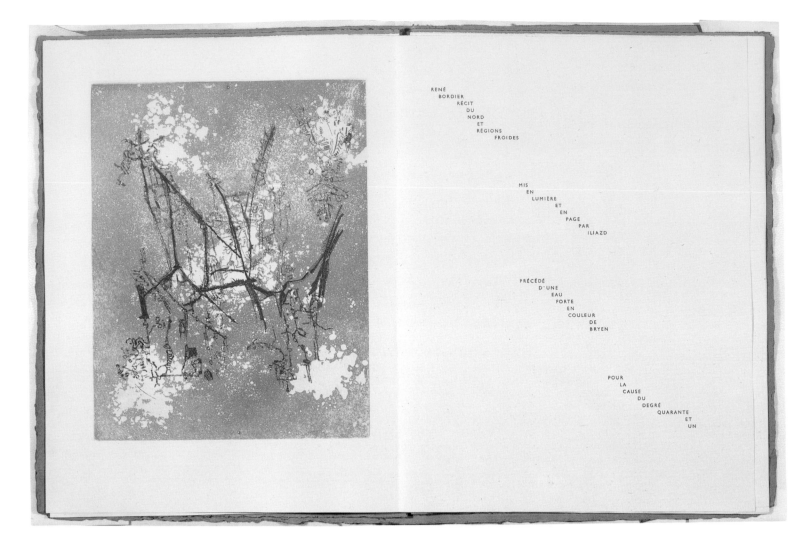

RENÉ
BORDIER
RÉCIT
DU
NORD
ET
RÉGIONS
FROIDES

MIS
EN
LUMIÈRE
ET
EN
PAGE
PAR
ILIAZD

PRÉCÉDÉ
D'UNE
EAU
FORTE
EN
COULEUR
DE
BRYEN

POUR
LA
CAUSE
DU
DEGRÉ
QUARANTE
ET
UN

Fig. 59. Camille Bryen from *Récit du nord et régions froides.* Text by René Bordier (Paris: Le degré quarante et un (Iliazd), 1956). Color etching with aquatint. Edition: 23/45. The typographic design on these pages emphasizes each word, as if it were a solid, physical object encountered in the open landscape of the page. The dramatic use of white space reinforces the sense of each of these words as individually important in its own right as well as within the book as a whole.

publisher—and human being. The text is highly moving, an old man's work, fully cognizant of the finitude of human life and of the preciousness of gathering together, in tribute, those few poetical strands that constitute a self-articulated legacy. As with every work of Iliazd, this book cannot be mistaken for the production of any other editor or publisher. He made use of the Gill sans typeface that had become his signature. The large font size made an unequivocal claim on the pages. The folded sheets were neither sewn nor glued, but held into folded paper and vellum covers in a format large enough to support the importance of the brief poems, but without inflated, hyperbolic claims. Modest, but grand, *Boustrophédon* is a fine testimonial to the self-consciousness of its artist/author—as well as to his understanding of the character of the editioned book as a form of artistic expression.

Throughout the course of his productive life, Iliazd made books. As an artist and writer, editor and publisher, typographer and designer, he found in the book form the fullest potential for expression of his multi-faceted intellect. How many aspects of a man may be made evident in his work? Drawing on his theatrical interests (his first five volumes were works of drama in *zaum,* his own version of transmental language invention also explored by Velemir Khlebnikov and other members of the Russian avantgarde), Iliazd saw the potential for a book space to operate as a series of acts, distinct and interrelated, punctuating time and space with an orchestral sophistication. As a scholar of architecture, particularly the geometric intricacies of Byzantine church forms, he understood the structuring principles of design as a scaffolding by which meaning was made, reading produced, and the book as a whole constructed. As a poet who adored classical forms, obscure works, and avantgarde invention, he was a missionary and pioneer, working to exhume little-known treasures of linguistic invention while asserting the claim of twentieth-century avantgardists to a fuller recognition of their early achievements. He loved to dance, and the lightness of his typographic touch bespeaks an agile sensibility. But he was also renowned for prodigious ability to hike—as a youth in the Caucasus, and as an adult in the Pyrenees and the mountains of the rugged Var region in France. This physical stamina, providing the strength required for the long hours of patient but demanding work in a print shop, is manifest in the unerring balance and tangible structure of his books. Iliazd's work testifies to the many dimensions of his character, just as the content of these works, deeply personal, offers a resolute and uncompromising set of statements culled from the interwoven complexities of an individual life.

I might never have known of these works had I not seen them being studied by a scholar across the tables of the Bibliothèque Jacques Doucet in the winter of 1984. I would surely never have had any insight into the books had I not followed his suggestion to contact Hélène Zdanevich, Iliazd's widow, still living at that time in the tiny apartment with studio on the rue Mazarine that had been Iliazd's since the late 1930s. I will never forget the magical transport I experienced in January 1985 the first afternoon when I visited her. That January was bitter cold. She had a fire in the small grate, and the light from that hearth flickered on walls covered with works by all the individuals with whom Iliazd had collaborated in his life-time—and many others he had known. I felt I had come into an intimate treasure chamber of Modern art and been offered a chance to engage its living legacy directly. Hélène Zdanevich was a grand and generous woman, dedicated to promoting Iliazd's work. I was privileged to collaborate with her for several years following that encounter, and to get to know her as she gave me access to and understanding of Iliazd's life and work. This essay is dedicated to her memory, her wisdom, and her graciousness.

"What I mean is that every time I drive for the point, I go someplace else."

"I know, but those someplace elses are pretty interesting."

Grandpa smiled. "If you're a bullshit artist, Clivey, you are a damned good one."

Banning smiled back, and the darkness of Johnny Brink-mayer's memory seemed to lift from his grandpa. When he spoke again, his voice was more businesslike.

"Anyway! Never mind that swill. Having long time in pain is just a little extry the Lord throws in. You know how a man will save up Raleigh coupons and trade 'em in for something like a brass barometer to hang in his den or a new set of steak knives, Clivey?"

Banning nodded.

"Well, that's what pain-time is like . . . only it's more of a *booby* prize than a real one, I guess you'd have to say. Main thing is, when you get old, regular time—my pretty pony time—changes to *short* time. It's like when you were a kid, only turned around."

"Backwards."

"You got it! I should smile and kiss a pig if you ain't."

The idea that time went *fast* when you got old was beyond the ability of Banning's emotion to understand, but he was a bright enough boy who could already do a little algebra, although

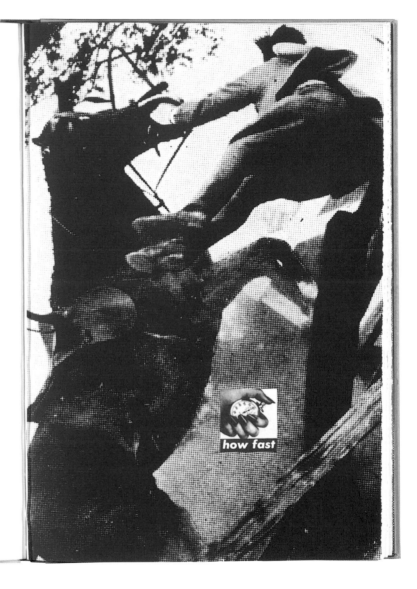

Fig. 60. Barbara Kruger from *My Pretty Pony.*
Text by Stephen King (New York: Library
Fellows of the Whitney Museum of American
Art, 1988). Color lithograph. Edition:
unnumbered/250.

MAY CASTLEBERRY

Publishing's Pleasures and Terrors

For the publisher, artists' books are inherently contradictory. These highly experimental works rarely offer the possibility of reaching the audiences that most publishers depend on for survival, even though they provide access to a rich artistic heritage, both past and present. Although historically these books have often advocated technological change, their future role in the rapidly evolving industry is uncertain. Nonetheless, there will always be artists for whom the book is an essential medium, and there will always be publishers willing to run the risk of bringing artists' books into existence.

On one end of a spectrum there are artists whose books are rooted in private experiment and made with little regard for a larger public forum. These are the artists who, deprived of other means, make books from any available paper and materials in a few copies. Because of the intensely personal nature of these treasures, they and the artists and authors who make them frequently remain anonymous or little known, their secrets locked in the recesses of libraries, book shops, and art collections. Their unconventional formats make few concessions to economies of printing or scale, and they are difficult to reprint or distribute. Some of the best works of this form, as represented in this catalogue, may become known through infrequent exhibitions. Some small, hand-printed editions, by such artists as Cy Twombly or Richard Tuttle, attain recognition in light of the artist's better-known career in another, more public medium.

Then there are artists whose high ambitions for the art of a book are matched by their training and imagination in the worldly arts of design, packaging, or commercial printing. The most adventuresome among those who have reached a broader public include *Andy Warhol's Index (Book)* (1967) [Fig. 61],[1] a fantasy of the Warhol studio, or almost any of Ed Ruscha's self-published early books, such as *Royal Road Test* (1967),[2] an inexpensively produced faux test manual, both a spoof and a genuine product of commercial culture.

Given varied opportunities to publish, these and most other artists who have been committed to the book—including Lázló Moholy-Nagy, El Lissitzky, Dieter Roth, Lawrence Weiner, John Baldessari, Daido Moriyama, and Kiki Smith—never confined themselves to one format or approach. They jumped genres, using and overturning the most distributable forms of their day, from children's books to propagandistic pamphlets to photographic treatises, even while they worked with fine print formats. Some books were rigorously sequential, if not cinematic; other books or aspects of the book reveled in singular images and sculptural bindings.

1. *Andy Warhol's Index (Book)* (New York: Random House, 1967).
2. Mason Williams, Edward Ruscha, and Patrick Blackwell, *Royal Road Test* (Los Angeles: M. Williams and E. Ruscha, 1967).

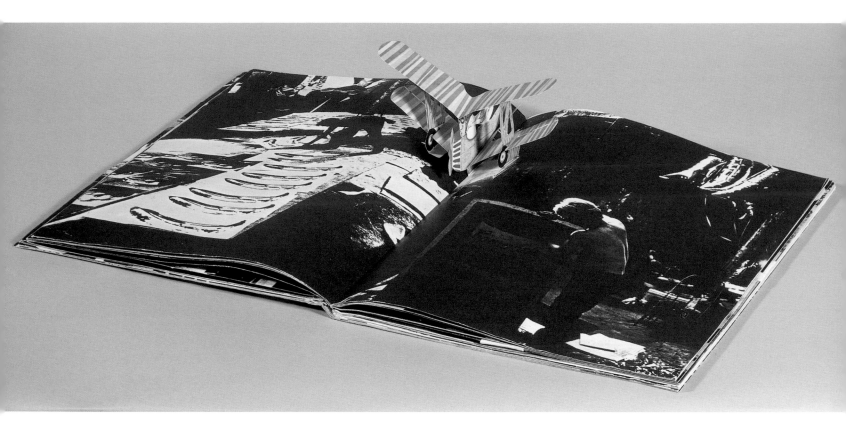

Fig. 61. Andy Warhol from *Andy Warhol's Index
(Book)* (New York: Random House, 1967).
Photomechanical reproductions with pop-up
element.

They adapted whatever materials or technology were available to them to define the artists' book in the broadest sense. They used or re-invented almost every known arrow in the quiver of the modern book form, varying narrative strategies, mixing fine printing and commercial techniques, issuing inexpensive artists' books as well as small, handmade objects. Almost no publisher is fully prepared to meet this range of interests, yet here are the pleasures and perils of publishing books by artists.

As a librarian and a curator, I have found almost every species of book compelling. My interests and experiences as a publisher have been more focused. I have been particularly drawn to books in which artists play a substantial role in the conception and design; in which authors contribute new literary texts; and in which the artist's hand can be seen in small production runs.

I became thoroughly interested in books as artifacts and as artworks just after college, when I studied printmaking at the Columbia University School of Arts at night and worked as a clerk in the general university library by day. I shelved and labeled books designated as possible candidates for "special collections." Once every few weeks several librarians would debate the books' merits and demerits, choose a few gems, and return the rhinestones to the general stacks. The valued items moved on to a more protected life in the Rare Books Library. The unsung treasures re-entered the general stacks to become, once again, available but vulnerable. Compelled to sift through thousands of books and gaze on an array of bindings, papers, stamps, title pages, illustrations, and structures, we clerks came to recognize some of the conventions that identify a book's origins and reputation — and to appreciate the oddities all the more.

In making these choices, the librarians applied some or all of the criteria that have prevailed in the market from the dawn of book collecting: eminence or currency of the author, provenance, condition, rarity, an artistic breakthrough, a provocation, a representation of a cultural moment. These are the foundation — or the shifting sands — on which stand evaluations of some of the most highly valued books, from a first edition of James Joyce's *Ulysses*,[3] to the books discussed in this volume. These discussions helped underscore the enormous gaps between the creation and reception of books conceived as works of art.

Then, as now, New York City offered a vast tutorial in books by artists — but then again, almost anyplace can provide an education in the art of the book, given time, interest, and a good library. Printed Matter, the not-for-profit distributor of artists' books, and still a necessity for the field, the Library and Archives at The Museum of Modern Art (MoMA), and other institutional advocates held extensive collections of recent artists' books: the self-published, inexpensively produced, rigorously sequenced books first made by Ed Ruscha and others in the 1960s. Not since Surrealism's literary and artistic core had adapted the magazine as a vehicle of artistic expression had so many artists been so visibly engaged with book publication as an art form. The artists' book movement of the 1960s presented a crucible for the book as a medium of aesthetic innovation and communication: could experimental books reach large audiences? In retrospect, very few did, in competitive publishing terms, but these books opened new ambitions for artists. And the artists' book movement of the 1960s was my point of entry; it became the subject of my graduate thesis for the Columbia University Library School.

In addition, I visited library collections, storefronts, and bookstores. The Spencer Collection at the New York Public Library and the study collection of the

3. James Joyce, *Ulysses* (Paris: Shakespeare and Company, 1922).

Department of Prints and Illustrated Books of MoMA provided (and still provide) access to wondrous *livres d'artiste* from the twentieth century and earlier to anyone who cared to make an appointment. Other favorites included: The Strand Book Store ("twelve miles of aisles"); Ray Smith's antiquarian American art book shop in New Haven; and Glenn Horowitz, then a private dealer down the street from me in Greenwich Village, now a leading dealer in rare books.

In late 1978 I became Librarian at the Whitney Museum of American Art. This was the one and only staff position in a small but historically rich library, and there were few funds for the reference library, let alone the seemingly luxurious category of books by—not about—artists. Still, I was able to beg slender funds for a variety of books illustrated or created by artists. It was a golden time to buy "vintage" artists' books of the 1960s and early 1970s, undervalued photographic books (a mint first edition of Robert Frank's *The Americans*[4] for a mere $150!), and a variety of books created by artists better known for their painting and sculpture in the Whitney Museum collection. I also became fascinated with a broad range of twentieth-century literary broadsides, books, pamphlets illustrated or created by artists in the Whitney's collection. This catholic pursuit led me to buy beautifully conceived books as diverse and, I thought, necessary to the collection as Max Weber's *Primitives* (1926) and Alexander Calder's *A Bestiary* (1955) [Fig. 62],[5] both designed and printed by the redoubtable Spiral Press. Paul Cummings, the crankily humorous, bookish Curator of Drawings at the Whitney, introduced me to his personal trove of Beat era publications and to a world of small press poetry with work by artists such as Joe Brainard, Wallace Berman, and Bruce Conner. Judith Goldman, the Whitney's Curator of Prints, had recently organized an acute first exhibition of Jasper Johns' and Samuel Beckett's *Foirades / Fizzles* (1976) [Fig. 63],[6] the masterpiece of the *livre d'artiste* of the past few decades.

I was delighted to observe at close hand many *livres d'artiste* and small press books. Many individual books presented a unique mix of commercial and hand-printing, common and uncommon papers, rich inks and letterpress impressions, commercial and hand-bindings. Collectively, they represented some of the most ancient and contemporary technologies. Printed in small editions, they carried texts and images that might never have been published in an offset edition created for large-scale distribution. Unlike most trade publishers' visual books—from photographic books through museum catalogues—these editions did not depend on a high volume of books to pay for the high costs of starting up an offset press,

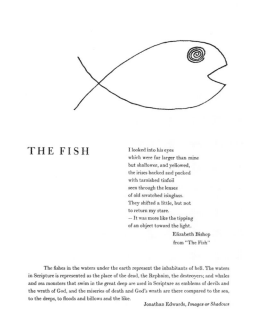

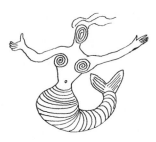

Fig. 62. Alexander Calder from *A Bestiary* (New York: Pantheon Books, 1955). Line block reproductions. Courtesy of the Center for Archival Collections, Bowling Green State University, Bowling Green, Ohio.

4. Robert Frank, *The Americans,* introduction by Jack Kerouac (New York: Grove Press, 1959).
5. Max Weber, *Primitives: Poems and Woodcuts* (New York: Spiral Press, 1926); Richard Wilbur, compiler, *A Bestiary* (New York: Printed at the Spiral Press for Pantheon Books, 1955).
6. Samuel Beckett and Jasper Johns, *Foirades / Fizzles* (London: Petersburg Press, 1976).

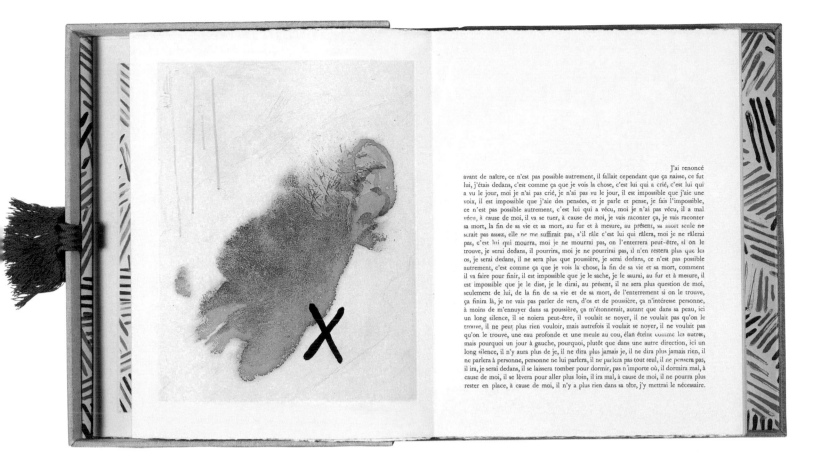

Fig. 63. Jasper Johns from *Foirades / Fizzles*. Text by Samuel Beckett ([London]: Petersburg Press, 1976). Mixed etching. Edition: 167/250. Toledo Museum of Art, Mrs. George W. Stevens Fund. Listed in Checklist under Additional Books.

engage a commercial bindery, and work through national distribution systems. (To break even, a trade art publication must usually reach an audience of well over five thousand. Or else receive support from a philanthropic organization, an art gallery, or another source, commercial or not.) Like many admirers of these books, I had and still have some caveats about small editions. First, they are expensive for the average consumer. But as a printer, I could also see that they were inexpensive for the work involved. In fact, they seemed to be pure labors of love in comparison to more marketable categories of art, whether paintings, prints, or a chair designed by an artist. Second, many of the fine press works appeared obscure or precious, their devotion to craft unsupported by challenging aesthetic goals. Yet, with the culling, or curatorial effort, that is always required to illuminate the best products of any established field of art—be it painting, drawing, graphics, or a flood of inexpensive, second-generation artists' books—one can find remarkable originals that address their time and a larger world of art and ideas. It seemed to me that the very best examples of the *livre d'artiste* and the small press edition present ideal laboratories for art, both for unexpected texts and unconventional visual thinking.

With these examples in mind, I imagined publishing my own volumes. I took courses in printing and design. I wrote about new books and artists' magazines. But my first publishing efforts came about because I was pushed, then encouraged and aided. In 1982, Tom Armstrong, then Director of the Whitney Museum, and Flora Biddle, Chairman of the Board of Trustees, were eager to help me find a way to raise money to expand the library collection and facilities. They appointed Brendan Gill, a Whitney Trustee and a longtime writer for *The New Yorker,* to organize a small Library committee. Together we considered how to proceed. It was clear to me that maintaining the interest and patronage of a far-flung support group for a small library within a museum would be difficult. I had no idea how to ask people for money (I still don't). However, I thought that if we could mix appeals for philanthropy with the promise of a tangible product, we might have a chance. Thus I proposed that we produce a series of books with new work by artists and writers that would explore the arts of the book. Artists, working with designers and printers, would control the design and structure of the book. Members of the Library Fellows would support both the book and the library, and they would receive one copy of each book published in return for their annual donation. Brendan Gill worked tirelessly to assemble a core membership and a program of three meetings a year centered on books and publishing. And so the Library Fellows of the Whitney Museum of American Art was founded in 1982.

From 1982 to 2000 I produced and edited one annual or biannual fine press publication for the Library Fellows. As I was young and inexperienced, the choices of artists and writers for the first books in the series were guided with approvals from members of the Library Fellows. This was necessary at the time, but if I may say now, rule by committee hampers an editor trying to conceive or complete a hands-on project with an artist. In any case, I learned a great deal from our first designer and printer, Gabriel Rummonds. And I often revisit John Hollander's introduction to *Dal Vero*,[7] by John Hollander and Saul Steinberg, which was the first book in the series, published by the Library Fellows in 1983:

> On the facing pages of a book, images and words can confront one another in different ways. A text can interpret, or gloss, or "read" a picture. A picture can "illustrate" a text, by imagining what a fictional person or place or a particular narrative moment looks like; more problematically, it may identify something abstract or implicit in the text and represent that. Pictures can serve as decorations, with at least enough oblique meaning to be appropriate to a particular text. On the other hand, picture and prose can be total strangers, sharing an elevator or taxi at the behest of unknown forces. They may even be secret lovers pretending to be strangers.

With the third book in the series, I chose to work with the artist Vija Celmins, whose exquisite prints of horizon-less seascapes and starry skies seemed an ideal match with the poetry and lapidary printing that only a fine press book can offer. Her work had previously been collected by the Whitney Museum. However, when I began to speak to Vija about publishing a book, in 1984, her full-scale retrospective at the Whitney (and a heightened reputation) was a decade in the future. For this reason, I knew we had to keep the costs relatively low by limiting the number of pages and prints. Luckily it took only a few of her prints to absorb the reader and to carry the book.

Vija and I jointly considered authors, and she proposed the poet Czeslaw Milosz. Working with Milosz's translator and editor, I made a selection of new prose pieces. I also chose an older poem, called "The View," which—in its evocation of landscapes, solitary existences, and the cosmos—seemed to define the artist's and the poet's common ground. In response to these pieces, Vija set to work on the laborious process of creating exquisitely rendered mezzotints (a process by which the artist rubs out every positive surface, leaving the plate to catch inky blacks) of night skies, trees, and globes, printed by the California-based fine printer Doris Simmilink. Eleanor Caponigro designed the book, constantly adjusting the location of the type even as Vija asked to move an image a millimeter to the left or a millimeter to the right, over and over again. (Obsession goes with the territory.) Eleanor

7. John Hollander and Saul Steinberg, *Dal Vero* (New York: Library Fellows of the Whitney Museum of American Art, 1983).

commissioned a black-flecked, handmade paper from Twinrocker, one that very gently suggests the imagery in the book, but in no way competes with the artwork.

It is an introspective and, I think, darkly beautiful book [Fig. 64],[8] published in an edition of 120 copies at $900 each. I doubt we could have sustained the quality of the mezzotints over a larger edition, but at first this seemed almost too many copies. It took over six years to sell the forty copies available for purchase (eighty had been set aside for the fifty Library Fellows and the collaborators). However, this book became scarce when Vija's reputation soared after her retrospective in the early nineties. Even as she was recognized as a key figure in California Pop of the 1960s, she seemed to present a new direction in art making, one in which craft—and obsessive attention to the handmade—could matter anew. When I've offered to present a selection of Library Fellows books to candidates for book projects in the past decade, it has been Vija's book that most artists, from Robert Gober to Fred Tomaselli, have wanted to see.

In 1986 I approached Richard Tuttle to create a book,[9] and he accepted. Together we considered a variety of writers whose poetry or prose might inspire, or connect to, his imagery. A mutual friend, Brad Morrow (writer and editor of the literary magazine *Conjunctions*), suggested we speak with a young poet named Mei-mei Berssenbrugge. We went to dinner, and Richard instantly determined that Mei-mei would become his collaborator. Over the next year Richard and Mei-mei created work in tandem, one responding to the other. They jointly attended to every detail of the book's physical production—handmade papers by the Dieu Donné Papermill, including the colored pulp that Richard

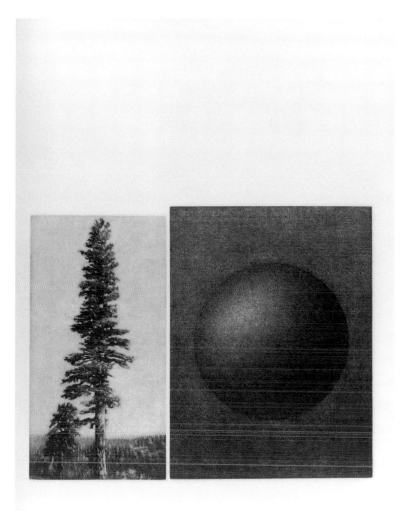

Fig. 64. Vija Celmins from *The View*. Text by Czeslaw Milosz (New York: Library Fellows of the Whitney Museum of American Art, 1985). Mezzotints. Edition: unnumbered/120.

poured over the sheets; and delicate layers of silkscreen and lithography and letterpress-printed type by Judith Solodkin and Peter Kruty at the Solo Press in New York. This, more than any other book in the series, was a true partnership between artist and writer [Fig. 65]. As the binding was close to completion, Richard and Mei-mei were reluctant to part. They married and now live in New York and New Mexico with their daughter, Martha.

The artist Barbara Kruger has much to contribute as an artist and graphic designer, and in 1986 I invited her to lunch to ask her what she might imagine. She almost immediately suggested Stephen King. It made sense: his work is emphatic and of the wider culture that Barbara's work simulated, critiqued, reconsidered, and sometimes just reveled in.

Unlike the Nobel Prize–winning Czeslaw Milosz, or any other writer we attempted to reach, King was surrounded by layers of agents and managers; most letters went unanswered. We asked Brendan Gill to aid us in soliciting a piece from King. Happily, Brendan knew King and had expressed his respect for King's literary (as opposed to popular) skills at a conference some years earlier. This meant a great deal to King. At that time, he had not yet been published in *The New Yorker* or

8. Czeslaw Milosz and Vija Celmins, *The View* (New York: Library Fellows of the Whitney Museum of American Art, 1985).
9. Mei-mei Berssenbrugge and Richard Tuttle, *Hiddenness* (New York: Library Fellows of the Whitney Museum of American Art, 1987)

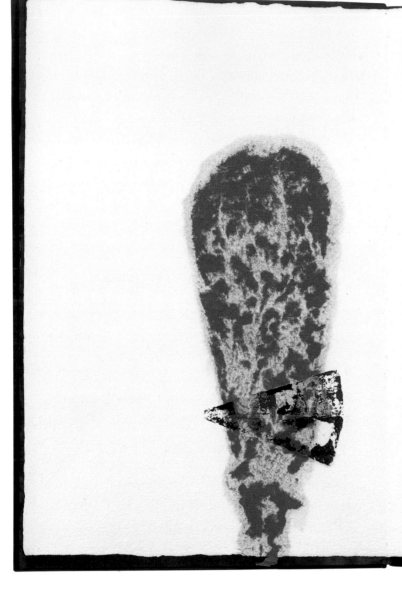

HIDDENNESS

1.

Though relations with oneself and with other people seem negotiated in terms secretly confirmed
by representations, her idea of the person's visibility was not susceptible to representation. No matter
how emphatically a person will control his demeanor, there will be perspectives she cannot foresee or direct,
because there is no assignable end to the depth of us to which representation can reach,
the way part of a circle can be just the memory of a depth. The surface inside its contour,
like the inside of a body, emits more feeling than its surroundings, as if
the volume or capacity of relations would only refer to something inside, that I can't see,
that the other person and I keep getting in the way of, or things in the landscape while they are driving,
instead of the capacity being *of* your person.

2.

If the tree is crimson in the fall in the mercury light by the river, I feel it gather its color *from* the river.
An orange moon is partially hidden in the clouds in the darkness.
Whenever or wherever it is possible to speak of recognition, there was a prior hiddenness or border of the circle,
where private is to mean you would not be able to understand, as if understanding the possibility *of*
were veering slashes of light on a steep track. It is more like driving without headlights on the plain,
the moon's appearance as a lake by a power plant, a dead lake, whose color neither hides nor doesn't hide
a perspective. I would call it color, if the way the texture of the skin on his hand
changes in moonlight were a color, instead of fantasy,
so that the physical idea of his privacy is not made clearer by the idea of his secrecy.
It is the same sentence as trying to explain how her assessment could not wait for her uncertainty.

You could be hiding behind a pane of glass in the atmosphere, or an example inaccessible to what
you are hiding, the way the beauty of a person, perhaps during a daydream, may flash across your mind,
like an animal across the landscape, forcing an exclamation from you, when you might not remember its name.

Fig. 65. Richard Tuttle from *Hiddenness.* Text
by Mei-mei Berssenbrugge (New York: Library
Fellows of the Whitney Museum of American
Art, 1987). Color lithograph with hand stamps.
Edition: unnumbered/120.

recognized in many quarters of the literary world. (Several of the book's critics would conclude at the time that Barbara Kruger's interest in King could only be an act of Post-Modernist irony.)

The previously unpublished piece that King sent, titled "My Pretty Pony," concerned a boy who learns from his grandfather that time speeds up as you get older; the grandfather reveals an uncanny secret of recalling the long summers of childhood and arresting time: chant "My Pretty Pony" [Fig. 60]. It was an old-fashioned story, with a literally driving narrative about the control of time. Barbara loved the story, as literature and as a slightly off-kilter but fundamentally archetypal American tale, with a wonderfully logical progression of the marvelous. As a story based in mid-century America, it was perfect for an old-fashioned, Century Schoolbook type that Barbara loved. Its propulsive narrative, concerned with the fact and illusion of time and progression, inspired her to create a parallel, time-based visual structure that followed the story. Each of a series of twelve oversize lithographs (printed beautifully by Maurice Sanchez at Derrière L'Étoile Studios, New York) carried a word or two of the story's motto: "Time ain't got nothing to do with how fast you can count." The words MY PRETTY PONY were printed in an exaggerated format on screen-printed pages, and placed to appear at regular intervals throughout the book; these pages were meant to work as a kind of graphic incantation for the reader who wished to stop time. Each copy of the special edition of *My Pretty Pony*[10] was bound in stainless steel embedded with a working clock. On the one hand, the book looked like an oversize children's picture book; on the other hand, a tabloid paper. It seemed to mix comfort and menace as it combined seemingly opposed genres in American publishing.

This was one of the few books I have published that had immediate commercial appeal, thanks to Stephen King's reputation. There was no difficulty in locating a trade publisher: working in association with Knopf, we published a smaller-size, offset printed trade edition of the book in 15,000 copies in 1989.

Thus far the most challenging book I have produced was *The Magic Magic Book*,[11] by Ricky Jay, with contributions from Vija Celmins, Jane Hammond [Fig. 67], Justen Ladda, Glenn Ligon, Philip Taaffe, and William Wegman (1994) [Fig. 66]. For some years before its publication I had admired the visual traditions of the magic book and had wondered about its rich trove of illusion, deception, and iconography as a likely source for contemporary artists. In the late 1980s one of the members of the Library Fellows kindly put me in touch with Ricky, a scholar of magic, an illusionist, and a great collector of magic books.

One of the most surprising groups of books in Ricky's collection was an almost forgotten genre of magic book that flourished from the seventeenth to the nineteenth centuries. These were called "blow books," because with a flick of the hand or a blow of the breath, a performing magician could manipulate tabs on the pages to create several different sequences of images within one volume. In centuries past, an itinerant magician could pull out one volume and astound innocent audiences with what seemed to be several books within one book. A single volume might contain a set of figures from the commedia dell'arte; a story-telling sequence about the unrequited loves of a monk; fire-eating devils; and eye-popping abstractions. Ricky and I decided to re-create a blow book, reproducing historical imagery and adding original contributions by contemporary artists. He began writing a substantial volume for our publication on the history and use of this virtually unknown category of book.

10. Stephen King and Barbara Kruger, *My Pretty Pony* (New York: Library Fellows of the Whitney Museum of American Art, 1988).
11. Ricky Jay, *The Magic Magic Book* (New York: Library Fellows of the Whitney Museum of American Art, 1994).

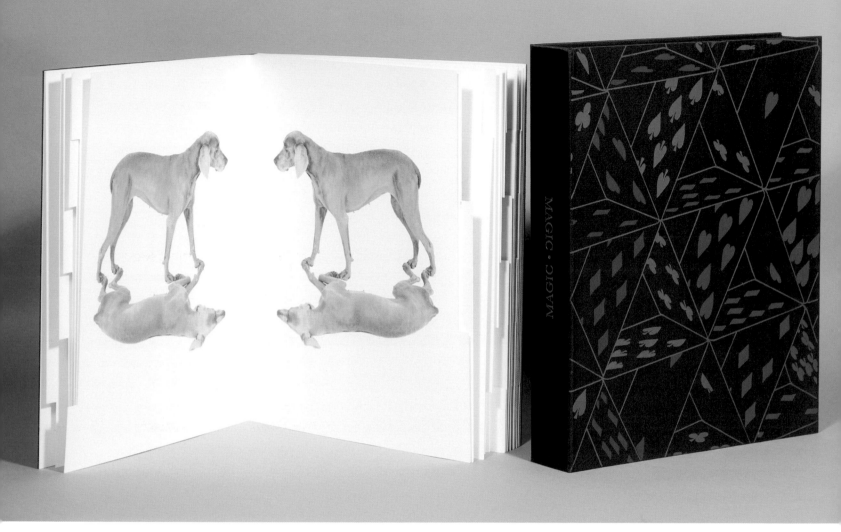

Fig. 66. William Wegman from *The Magic Magic Book*. Text by Ricky Jay, cover design for box by Justen Ladda (New York: Library Fellows of the Whitney Museum of American Art, 1994). Photomechanical reproduction. Toledo Museum of Art, Gift of Reba and Dave Williams.

The process of selecting contemporary artists for the project was unlike any other for the books I had put together. I made proposals, and together we "interviewed" artists. One of the first artists we visited was Vija Celmins, whom of course I already knew from the previous book. Her hypnotically illusionistic woodcuts seemed to recall some of the historic work Ricky and I had seen, and was therefore ideal for one of the sections in *The Magic Magic Book*. As an artist making works involving an almost fanatical degree of observation and skill, no one is more concerned with connections between the hand and the eye than Vija. Nor do I know anyone more skeptical. For an illusionist, this describes the person you want to trick. Ricky, who is considered by many to be the greatest sleight-of-hand artist in the world, pulled out the pack of cards he carries with him at all times. Though he almost never performs privately, he treated Vija to a small, dazzling performance. She was hooked and created a hypnotically detailed woodcut of an ocean surface; it was repeated four times in the book, though each time it seemed to be different, seen in a different context and light.

William Wegman, who shared stories with Ricky about nineteenth-century dog acts, created photographs of real dogs in real but seemingly impossible positions. Philip Taaffe, who learned that he had grown up near the same pool hall in Elizabeth, New Jersey, that was frequented by Ricky, contributed a set of optically charged abstractions. Responding to sequences of pictures of runaway slaves in an early American blow book, Glenn Ligon gave us a series of vanishing figures, overlaid with the first paragraph of Ralph Ellison's *Invisible Man*. Jane Hammond's work, which is often filled with mystical images culled from the troves of history, seemed ideal to capture the iconography of magic from centuries past. Ricky asked if she would respond to a rich tradition of silhouetted images found in historical blow books. She was duly inspired and created silhouettes drawn from some of the enduring symbols of conjuring—cards, keys, hats, and ancient soothsayers. The artist Justen Ladda created a puzzle-like image of a house of cards for the cover. He proposed that we bring in termites to do the laborious work of cutting wood. For a book on chance, it was not inappropriate, but by the time we were ready to produce the cover we had had our fill of chance operations, and instead he worked with the binder Craig Jensen to emboss the book with interlocking metal plates, a challenge in itself.

The printing and binding for *The Magic Magic Book* were tours de force. The relief prints were proofed by Leslie Miller of the Grenfell Press and finally printed by Leslie and Patrick Reagh. Pat also designed and printed the text-based volume of the two-volume set, which featured Ricky's extensive history of the blow book. For a time, we thought we had encountered a lost secret of bookmaking: no binder could determine how the printed and tabbed pages should fall, or how such a book could be bound. Finally, the hand-bookbinder Claudia Cohen, working with Leslie, laid out a plan.

The entire project took over three years, and I worried throughout about recouping our costs. Ricky was not well known. Here was a book that was fraught with delays and high expenses, additionally problematic as we struggled to maintain the Library Fellows membership in a recession. But timing counted for a lot: Ricky's off-Broadway show opened with enormous success and to media attention just after we published the book in 1994. Most copies of the edition of 250 sold easily at $1,200; its success ultimately depended on a bibliophilic niche audience of

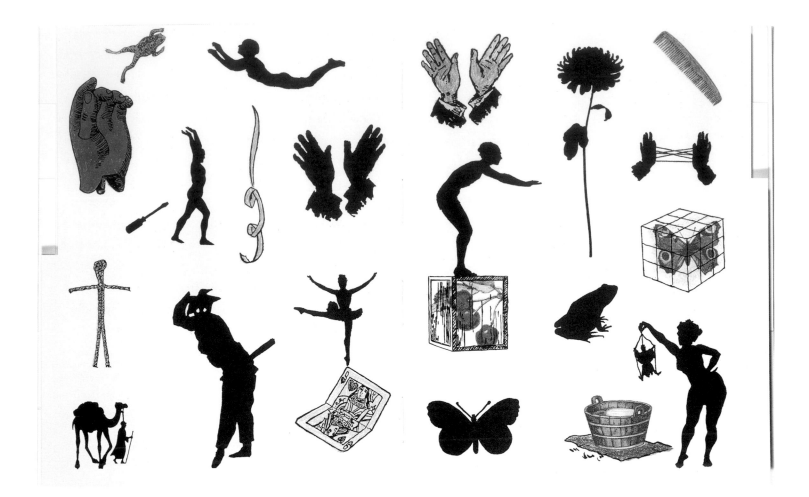

Fig. 67. Jane Hammond from *The Magic Magic Book*. Text by Ricky Jay (New York: Library Fellows of the Whitney Museum of American Art, 1994). Mixed media with offset additions. Toledo Museum of Art, Gift of Reba and Dave Williams.

the magic and theater worlds in which Ricky was becoming an increasingly revered figure, as opposed to the art market.

For a time, we hoped to produce *The Magic Magic Book* as a trade edition as well, but the publisher's production staff quickly recognized a book whose complex structure could not easily be replicated at a commercial bindery and declared that the book could not be brought in at a viable price for trade distribution. This was one of many experiences that convinced me that there was no reason to feel guilty about creating a small edition of a handmade book, as long as such a book found a core constituency and some copies made their way to public collections.

Some say that the art of printing will always survive, since an art form only needs the love of children and lunatics to keep going. In this scheme, artists' books have a lot going for them. Our very first experiences with picture books, as children, establish our deepest connections with words and images. And the tactile pleasures of ink and paper on a hand-held object will always be important to some of us, no matter what our psychological condition or the technological marvels of electronic publishing.

Still, even the most passionate publishers can maintain a lack of concern for audience and finances only temporarily. Writing retrospectively, as I do here, about books and publishing situations that worked out in the end, it is easy to forget the potential disasters that loom with every new publication. Overestimating the audience for a particular book, unnecessary production expenses, a preoccupied artist or author, or a downturn in the economy can take a book that is at best narrowly profitable into a deep hole. And even within a seemingly well-funded institution, like the Whitney Museum, the Artists and Writers Series depended on a fragile ecosystem. In addition to the fundamental generosity and enthusiasm of artists, we needed the philanthropy of patrons who believed in the larger program and an ongoing institutional belief in the book as an art form.

I am all the more conscious of the possibilities and problems as I begin work in a new institution. I am now editing a new series of books sponsored by The Museum of Modern Art's new Library Council and working with MoMA's Chief of the Library and Archives, Milan Hughston, in support of MoMA's magnificent collections. The Library Council's publishing program is dedicated to artistic and literary collaboration and the art of the book, and MoMA's international focus gives us the opportunity to combine the work of artists, artisans, and book traditions from around the globe. As we begin the program, I am ever aware of the enormous privilege of working with artists, for an institution that is dedicated to both the past and the future of the artists' book. As I begin to speak with the artists about the first two books in the series, I am inspired by their interest in the most optically challenging printing and unconventional materials that the handmade book provides. I am worrying about finances and preaching the creativity of constraint and repetition. Then I am reminded that artists will always keep re-inventing the book, and that publishers must always keep re-inventing audiences.

Endocrinology Story and Notes

In the beginning of the 1990s I was asked to organize an exhibition of my work at the Institute of Contemporary Art (ICA) in Amsterdam. This was to be the second show at what was then a new institution. The first exhibition was the work of Richard Tuttle. Richard had, for a short time, assisted my father and lived with us when I was a teenager, which was enormously influential to me. However, I had very little contact with him since that time. This exhibition was my first in Europe and occasioned the publication of the first book about my work. Richard gave his wife, poet Mei-mei Berssenbrugge, a copy of my catalogue. She became interested in a collaboration and contacted me. **I**

One night I had a dream that I should go to Santa Fe. I had absolutely no knowledge of the city whatsoever and hadn't a clue why I should go there. Shortly thereafter I went to an astrologer and she said I should go to Santa Fe. So when Mei-mei called from New Mexico to say she was interested in a collaboration, but it was difficult for her to travel, I took it as a sign and agreed to go shortly thereafter.

Before this I had been involved in only one other collaborative work, with my close friend Lynn Tillman, in which I illustrated her words. I think that from the beginning Mei-mei made it clear that she wanted our project to be a true collaboration. **2**

Coming from the East Coast, I was totally physically overwhelmed by New Mexico. I immediately had an anxiety attack getting off the plane. The enormity of the landscape was too much to bear. All I could think was that there was no place

I This book contained photographs of work that was powerfully visceral, emotional, and at the same time seemed to tell a story connected to history and society from the point of view of a spiritual witness and a mourner. I was ill and had been trying to learn how to live with suffering, through humility and a kind of transmutation of bodily suffering into spirit. I was excited by the polarities between us. I'm an abstract, ethereal writer. With Kiki, I hoped to learn about the concrete power of emotion in the real and to learn this with narrative. She suggested a book in which black organs become white or lit, which struck me as a marvelous armature for narrative. She introduced me to the word "fem," which she expresses among other ways in handwork. During our meetings, she set a book of anatomy in front of her and drew on stiff paper, cutting out shapes that would become the blue monoprints of endocrine organs for our book. She proposed for our subject the endocrine system, the source of emotions and of form of the body, and I wanted to include the fantastic, subvisible components of the immune system.

2 I had an idea of self as a core, a center, or "emitter" of work. Now I wonder if perhaps an "essential" core self is an illusion we have, a cultural concept. I wonder if there is another way to look at the self of sensibility as a

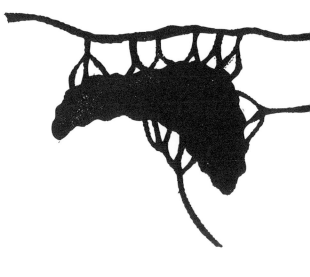

to hide. I got a ride with some acquaintances who dropped me at the Wild Oats Market, where Mei-mei and Richard with their new baby, Martha, came to greet me. Mei-mei was incredibly beautiful to me. She had rented a guest house for me in Galisteo. Richard and Mei-mei told me to walk up the long road, the car road, and then up the drive to their house, which was perhaps a mile. I saw that there was a shortcut to town next to the graveyard and past some houses and asked Mei-mei why she didn't take it. She replied that she didn't like to be seen walking out on the land. Being from New York, I found this one of the most eccentric things I had ever heard.

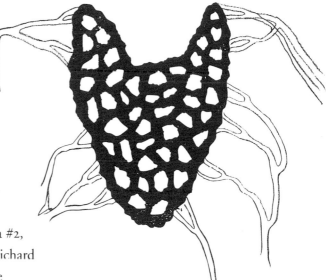

One of the first things Mei-mei did in New Mexico was read her work to me out loud. This was absolutely mesmerizing. She had the most beautiful, fluid, soft-spoken, tender voice I had ever heard. While it is sometimes difficult for me to read poetry, hearing it made it all come together for me. What was amazing to me about her work was that it was at once both extremely concrete and abstract. It was like witnessing thought. These thoughts seemed to have a three-dimensional quality to them.

The next day we drove, taking turns, from Galisteo over to Hopi Mesa #2, which was about a three- or four-hour drive. We stopped in Gallup, and Richard bought me a small jeweler's file. We went to watch the corn dance with the Kachinas, these enormous, life-size creatures who gave presents and then submerged into the ground. To me, the dance was the closest I had come to seeing Santa Claus. Mei-mei remarked that there was very little land on the mesa, that it was mostly sky. We drove back and they dropped me at the airport in Albuquerque. The next morning, I went to Washington State, where I was submerged in green and somehow felt a hundred percent safer. Thus began our collaboration.

Shortly after this first trip I was invited by Dwight Hackett to work at bronze casting in his art foundry. With that I began more frequent travels to New Mexico, over a period of five to seven years. Sometimes I went every six weeks, staying two weeks at a time. It was during this time that Mei-mei and I made our book. I stayed in various guest houses and she would come by. When we first began working, Mei-mei would ask me questions about my life. I had just split up with someone and, while it wasn't a particularly significant relationship, I was totally overwhelmed and would start crying every other sentence. One thing I remember telling her was that I had to get more light inside my organs. She had recently been diagnosed with environmental illness, and its concerns attracted her to the body issues of my work. Someplace shortly into it we chose to make it a book about the endocrine system and the lymph system [Fig. 68]. I was, at the time, trying to go through the different systems of the body and make representations of them and she was reading medical books about the different systems. I quickly made the images for the book. They were copied from a coloring book of human anatomy.

shifting and layered "neighborhood" of responses: memories, you as others see you, what society expects from you, emission and transmission at the same time, how you perceive how others see you, genetic makeup and its mutations, the dynamics of metabolism, etc.

And I like collaboration because it transfers the focus of art activity from the individual core out to an area between people. A plaza, a dance floor.

When I work with Kiki it is as if I become a circumference, the space of half an arena for her vision for her, and I think what of my self to bring to this space for a "good show." That double space becomes the self of the collaboration. For me, it marvelously dissolves the intransigent limits of working by "my self," vaporization, expansion. It's feminine in relation to context and empathy.

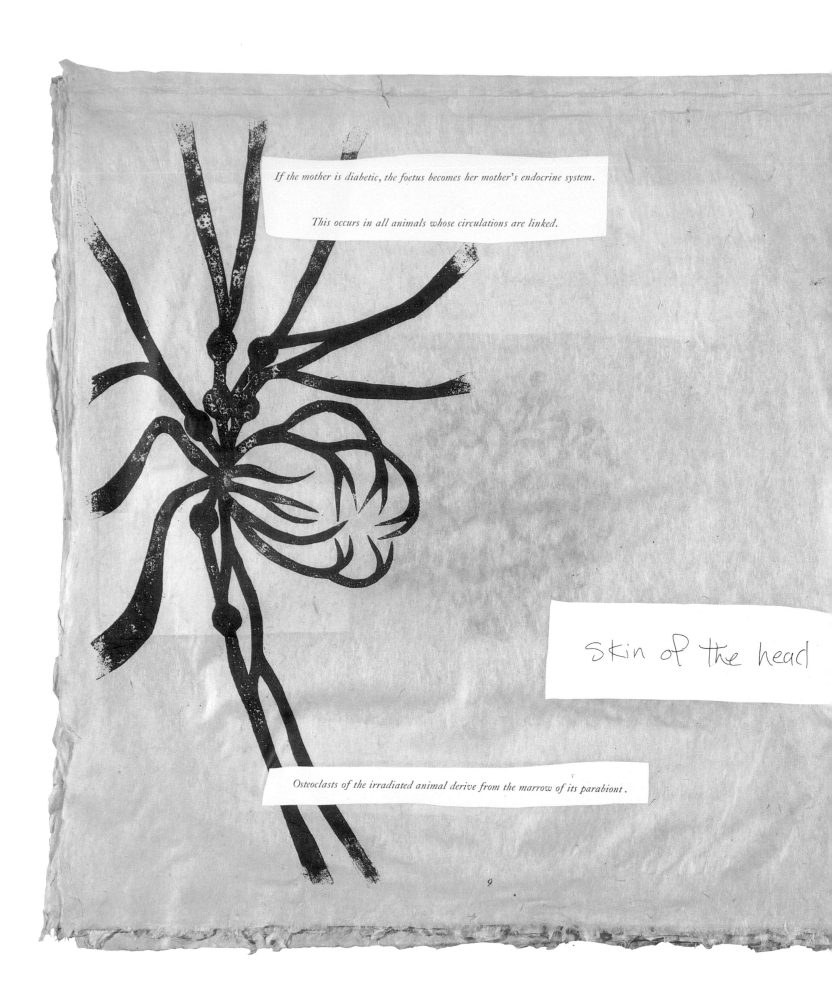

If the mother is diabetic, the foetus becomes her mother's endocrine system.

This occurs in all animals whose circulations are linked.

skin of the head

Osteoclasts of the irradiated animal derive from the marrow of its parabiont.

9

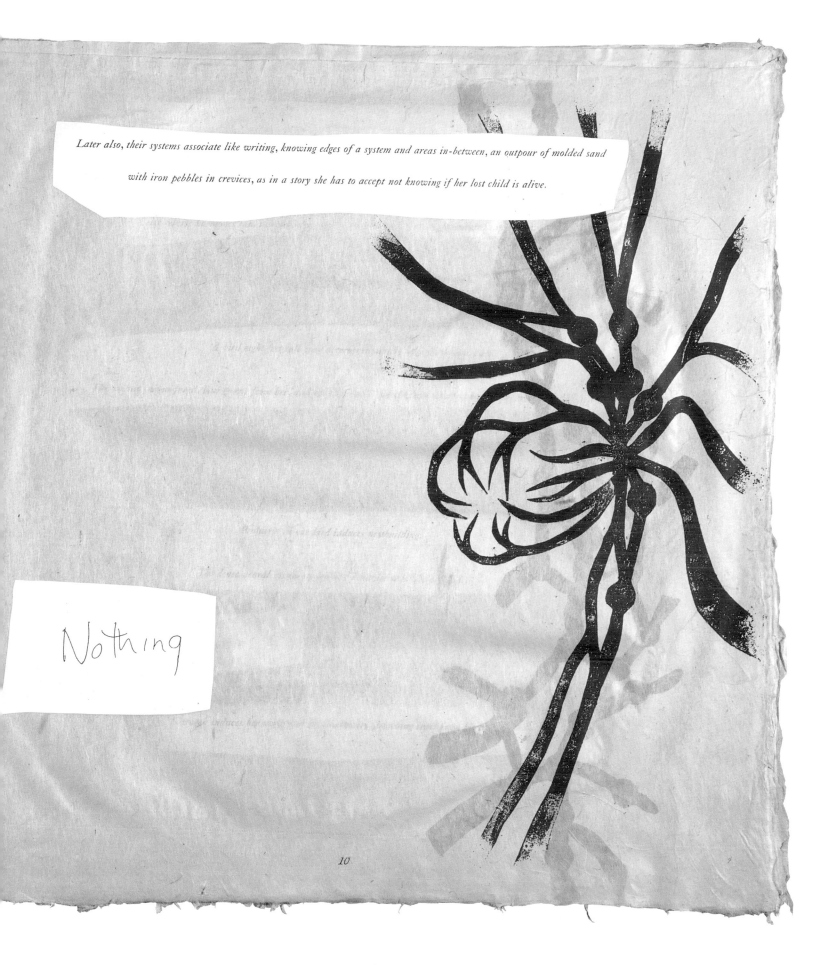

Later also, their systems associate like writing, knowing edges of a system and areas in-between, an outpour of molded sand with iron pebbles in crevices, as in a story she has to accept not knowing if her lost child is alive.

Nothing

10

Fig. 68. Kiki Smith from *Endocrinology.* Text by
Mei-mei Berssenbrugge ([West Islip, New York]:
Universal Limited Art Editions, 1997). Color mono-
prints. Edition: 8/40.

My interest was to use rudimentary printmaking techniques of inking a piece of cut paper and directly transferring that onto another piece of paper, monoprinting, and thus circumventing a press. We would work, Mei-mei would ask questions, I would cry, and later I would go to her house to eat because she is a very wonderful cook.

Originally, Rena Rosenwasser asked Mei-mei to make a book for Kelsey Street Press and asked whom she wanted to do it with. Rena and her friend Penny had been some of the first to collect my work. She has a small press based in Berkeley, California, that specializes in women poets. I worked with ULAE (Universal Limited Art Editions), one of the great print publishers in the United States, which originally started out printing artist-writer collaborations, and I thought it might be interesting to make both a fine arts edition and a trade edition. So, I asked Bill Goldston at ULAE if he was willing.

3 Richard Tuttle, besides being a super fabulous person and one of the really great living American artists, has probably made more books and more rigorously artistic books than any other living artist.

Not to be competitive, but it considerably upped the ante in trying to make a book. I finished my prints that were indigo on Nepal paper, the originals being cut-out stencils on Saunders paper.

At some point, Mei-mei came up with a list of words and asked me to respond with words. My words ended up being a kind of singular entry on the page that functioned similarly to the images. We enlisted Richard to advise us on typography because of his deep interest in it. At some point Mei-mei finished the poem. **4**

I had by then lost all the original images from New Mexico and then remade them. Mei-mei gave ULAE the text. We decided to use offset lithography as opposed to a traditional letterpress book. It seemed too fussy in relation to the simplicity of the images and also because of the wide range of typefaces.

Someone typed in the text in our size of choice and we laid out the images. Since eighteen is the day of my birth, we decided on an eighteen-inch square book that would open to thirty-six inches. We decided the trade edition would be a nine-inch square. Once we started into production there were many questions of typeface scale, cover material, images for the cover, boxing, etc. Mei-mei and I went on one of her visits to the East Coast to discuss issues at ULAE. It was important that we share monetarily in the proceeds from the book, even though traditionally art books lose money for presses and have to be subsidized by other printmaking activities. Later, on Bill Goldston's birthday, Mei-mei and I boarded the train with flowers and images to make the layout, and in my enthusiasm I

3 Our project continues an exploration I began with Richard Tuttle on *Hiddenness* [Fig. 65] (Library Fellows of the Whitney Museum of American Art, 1987) to try and align the visual and verbal mental planes. So often in a book or in life, one focuses on the visual image and then shifts to words, as if switching to another mental level. Some books in which the words and pictures occupy the same world are illuminated manuscripts, Chinese scrolls, Toulouse-Lautrec. Kiki and I treated the visual and verbal as a continuum of material, and the valence was the energy of our interaction. Because strips are pasted onto a page, and because one can see through to pages underneath, our book seems to be 3-D, using a sculptural space to embrace or unify words and images.

4 We meet in New York, in New Mexico. I'm trying to absorb her whole work and also the person not in the work. One week I tape the monoprints around my kitchen, spread out my notes, and write the poem, while my family is away. There are five stanzas, not enough text for twenty images. On the floor with scissors, I cut the stanzas apart into sentences and fit them with the images. My poem changes from five stanzas into a field or surface tension of words that float across the whole. During our next meeting, Kiki lays out the book, with marvelous directness and speed. She scotch-tapes strips of my typewriter sentences onto translucent rice paper printed with blue anatomical images, like flowers. Layers of transparency appear. Opening the book, you can look through pages, as through human tissue. The book is like a body, layered with blue organs and ligaments of text. A plain expanse of cover, like skin. A spine. The handwritten words create an extra layer of floating linguistic and visual meaning like meaning outside the story.

once again left all the flowers and all of my drawings for the book on the train. Mei-mei at that point wondered if I had issues with making the book. I liked to think of it as a test of perseverance. So I had to make all of the images again. Bill pressured me to come up with a cover, and I said I wanted a picture of Mei-mei. That day we took pictures of her. Then Craig Zammiello took pictures of me for the back cover.

I laid out the cut-out sentences, for which Mei-mei had carefully made the decisions on line breaks, as well as my whimsical handwritten words and images. Since nothing at ULAE ends up as what it appears to be, Bill pushed that we make a real facsimile or copy of the layout. So each page was then printed with the blue image of the endocrine or lymph system and then dry-mounted with the cut-outs, painstakingly mimicking my loose cuts of paper. The book was then bound with a cardboard cover with our photos on the front and back. Then it came to making the second version nine by nine inches square for the Kelsey Press. Mei-mei had as a last thought to dedicate the book to her husband and to my friend Barry Le Va. Rena Rosenwasser's brother, Robert, designed the layout. Somehow it wasn't possible for him to make a direct copy because some places the text had to be lowered on the page and in some places it wasn't. Rena asked if we would make a special edition copy with a small print to help pay for the publication. Bill Goldston reduced one of the images from the original book and printed it, I think.

Sometime during the making of the images for the first book early in New Mexico, Mei-mei was giving me a ride home in her Cadillac. In general I felt that I wasn't a person compelled to collaborate and wasn't sure I knew where any of the book was going. I said to Mei-mei that meeting her had changed my life. During the last eight to ten years what began as a collaboration has become a significant and deep friendship and we have chosen to continue to collaborate.

Maybe her many years spent in the New Mexican landscape, and the fact that she is a mother, have helped to shape her as one of the most loving people I've ever met. Her deep intellect, compassion, and silence have created a rare, open heart.

5 By coincidence, each of us bought our first statues of Kuan Yin, the Chinese goddess of compassion, on the same day. Kiki made a black sculpture of Kuan Yin speaking words I wrote on the subject of hearing, because she is "the hearer of all the cries in the world." This collaboration, using photographs and a CD, will become our second book at ULAE.

6 Of all my work, I've found that students ask me most about collaboration. It's exciting and freeing to them. You can move beyond your personal intransigence and your own limits. Perhaps they intuit that a new world needs a sensibility and creativity beyond the individual achiever, a world which, in some ways, they already practice in life on the internet. I was born in Beijing, and I've always felt a shadow of loneliness growing up in the United States. I've read about this shadow and its many forms in philosophy, particularly as the idea of "the other." I love the idea of opening to the questioning of "the other," of incorporating the sensibility of another so intimately in one's own writing. It seems to me Kiki has lived her life as an artist with that incorporating energy: as a founding member of Collab in the Lower East Side, as an emergency medical technician, with printmaking, in collaborations, in moral dialogue with her city.

ENDOCRINOLOGY

1

The bird watches the man and woman dance. He touches her stomach. There's circulation around her
in intercapillary space, empty or hollow, in relation to organs. A virus transfers firefly genes
to a tobacco plant. The plant glows in the dark. How much evolution derives from "something in the air",
not a square of light above a niche in a white wall. Light, your intestines. Fluid, lines of light. As if,
when you think about something, it already has a frame that's a priori. Think before that moment, freedom is inside there.
Think before the man and woman, their freedom of the animal among silver trees. Which trunks the light hits is an endocrine
permutation, a state of being or a physical state. Hormones are molecules, material, invisible. Their flow is random,
mesh through which a body is sensed, not an image. The form of her body is important,
as how she is here, though there's no physical evidence of her physical suffering.

2

Hormones provide a mechanism by which the body relays chemical signals through cells perfused by blood.
There's a structural need to make tectonic episodes which might otherwise become pliant.
Conceiving of the body as a space of culture tends not to refer to it as nature, unless it's been taken away by disease,
hairy ears, genital ambiguities, like a shamanistic object, not generic. Because she's in a body, it makes decisions.
Black rock in a dry river, weeds tangled at its base, something heavy enmeshes with something light.
The material, of non-negotiable contingency, the feeling, a different structure on different physical levels.
A pool in the forest gleams with organic matter, its depth of the possibility of an imbalance in the body,
when luminosity detaches itself from feeling as emanation, transparency, a structural need to become
disorganized. What is physical light inside the body? A white cloth in a gold and marble tomb, to focus the expression of the tomb.
Shortly after phagocytosing material, leucocytes increase their oxygen consumption and chemically produce light.
During pregnancy, the foetoplacental unit under the curve acts as a gland.
If the mother is diabetic, the foetus becomes her mother's endocrine system. This occurs in all animals
whose circulations are linked. Osteoclasts of an irradiated animal derive from the marrow of its parabiont.
Later, also, their systems associate like writing, knowing edges of a system and areas in-between,
an outpour of molded sand with iron rocks in crevices, as in a story she accepts not knowing if her lost child is alive.

3

The bird sings on a strawberry the size of a melon. Cells release hormones into intracellular space, where they enter local,
fenestrated capillaries.
A bird eight feet tall with disproportionately huge claws and beak.
The woman, moon-faced, hair grows from her, and she feels desire for the man touching her abdomen,
that feels like love. Prolactin in our bird induces nestbuilding.
Estrogen induces her concept of his luminosity, detaching itself from his color. Her hands enlarge.
She can't see where her sadness ends and someone else's is.
The line between chemical and emotion is the horizon inside a niche in her body, transferring non-being to utility
She lives on moisture from dew condensed on soil surfaces from night air.
The strawberry sprouts a fantail of petals. Air flames on her skin.
She believes the body, though densely saturated, is generic, dreaming the same nightmare as the child.
His presence triggers latent feeling beyond feeling for her, with enormous affection for her body.
Blood drips under a white feather of the wounded bird. A vein puts the organ in the background.
She concentrates on manipulating her organs to pull the white square of light precisely into the niche.

4

A woman leans her arms on the table, forearms abnormally long.

Her milk flows and flows. She cries and cries.

These are unaccountable imperfections in the numerical fabric, not mysteries.

A wire crosses in front of a line on a wall, while its shadow seems to cross behind it.

The place where a word originates in her body is the physical source of her sense of beauty, so you can

change the word for "happiness" that was formerly, "innocence". The respiratory system, when stimulated produces

a characteristic sighing. The thymus expends itself during stress and collapses, so an autopsy finds only a membrane.

Touching a wall produces the sound of touch on the other wall. Feedback between health and fate unfolds

so fast, there's no way one step in the chain can be based on the previous one.

An associative smear or aura requires her to be in a body, in order to make decisions.

Lack of cloud cover causes thermal energy on the desert to return rapidly to the sky at night.

Oxygenating molecules makes light. Lighting the organs, they turn white.

He loved her body as much as he loved her as an individual.

5

There is a space. You see something at the far edge, and your eye going over this space

makes a whole, like watery mass in a gourd, the feeling of old organs no longer crucial to or inside themselves,

while remembering people you loved, which flowed from the physical, about which you made decisions.

To make this whole, any object, brings into being something not in nature, an interior measurement,

yourself, not yourself, bursts of growth when you sleep. Her back bleeds. A spray

of blood on the snow. She sits on her hands physically preventing herself from scratching.

The child, her sense of the world being crucial to or inside itself, of memory and specificity, like script.

B cells grow for years in a petri dish. The sick, immortalized cells don't know to stop growing.

Where your eye goes over space to the horizon makes a whole, but where the sky meets the earth, the fragment

is not the same as a whole. Desert ferns covered with reflecting hair may insulate the fronds.

Radiations of a state barely embodied, then dissolving in counter-reflections of light.

There's an engine. He cannot separate from the loved person, to shed the loved body.

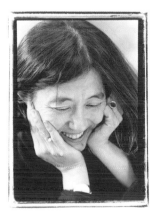
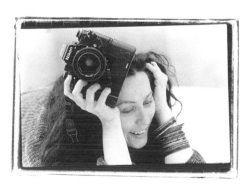

Figs. 69. Kiki Smith and Craig Zammiello,
Untitled: Mei-mei Berssenbrugge and Kiki Smith,
1997. Photographs. Courtesy of Kiki Smith and
Craig Zammiello.

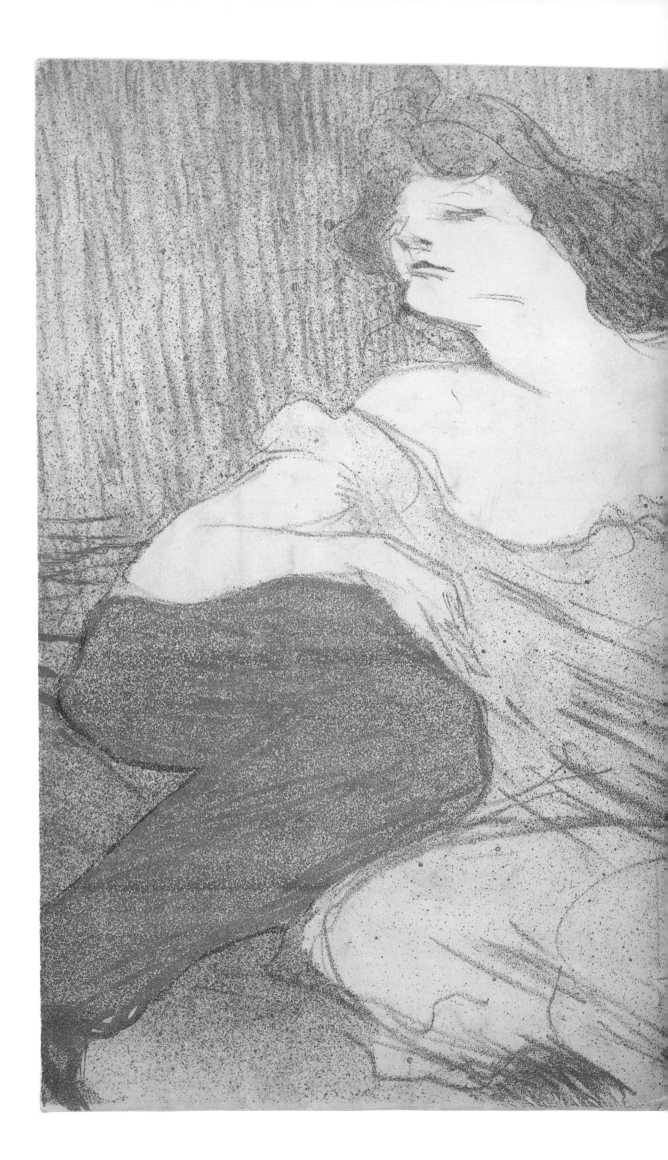

Plates

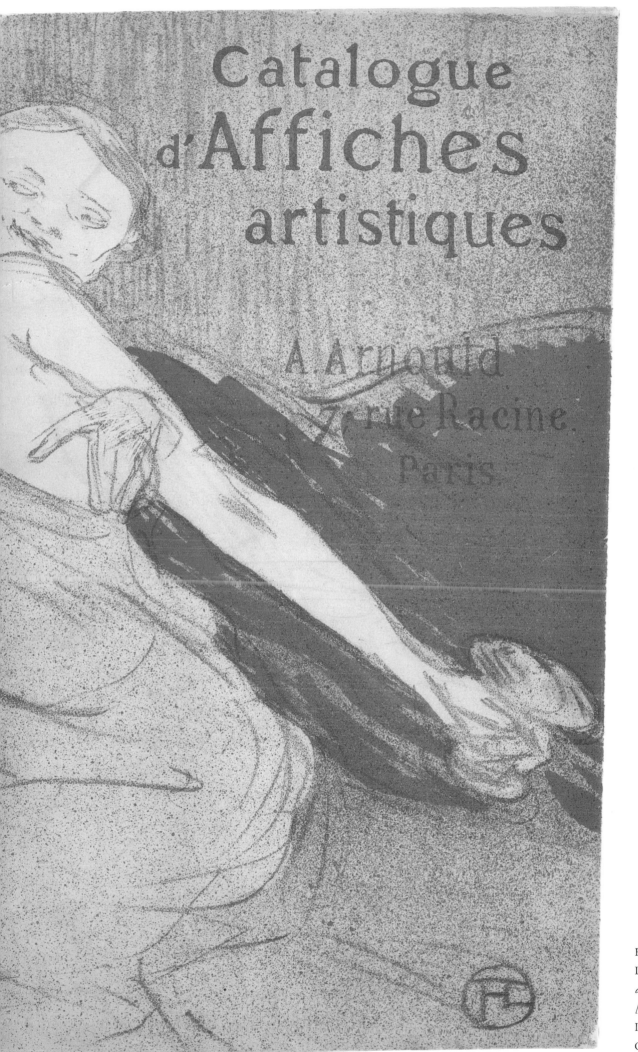

Fig. 70. Henri de Toulouse-
Lautrec from *Catalogue
d'affiches artistiques, français
[et] étrangère, estampes* (Paris:
Imprimerie Henon, 1896).
Color lithograph.

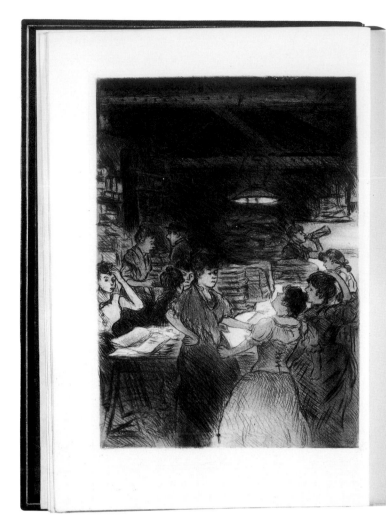

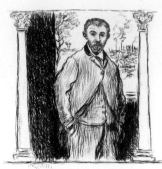

Fig. 71. J.-F. Raffaëlli from
Les soeurs Vatard. Text by
Joris-Karl Huysmans (Paris:
Librairie des amateurs,
1909). Color etching with
drypoint. Edition: 224/250.

Fig. 72. Jules Pascin from
*Aus den Memoiren des Herrn
von Schnabelewopski*. Text by
Heinrich Heine (Berlin:
Paul Cassirer, 1910). Transfer
lithograph with added
pochoir color. Edition:
84/250.

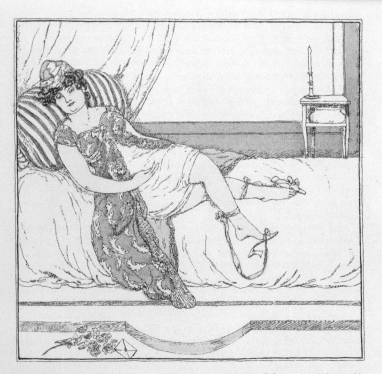

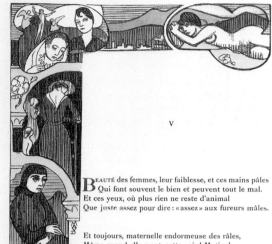

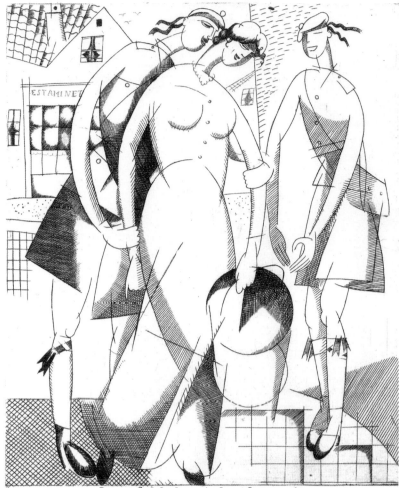

V

ʙᴇᴀᴜᴛᴇ́ des femmes, leur faiblesse, et ces mains pâles
Qui font souvent le bien et peuvent tout le mal.
Et ces yeux, où plus rien ne reste d'animal
Que juste assez pour dire : «assez» aux fureurs mâles.

Et toujours, maternelle endormeuse des râles,
Même quand elle ment, cette voix! Matinal
Appel, ou chant bien doux à vêpre, ou frais signal,
Ou beau sanglot qui va mourir au pli des châles!...

Hommes durs! Vie atroce et laide d'ici-bas!
Ah! que du moins, loin des baisers et des combats,
Quelque chose demeure un peu sur la montagne,

Quelque chose du cœur enfantin et subtil,
Bonté, respect! Car qu'est-ce qui nous accompagne,
Et vraiment, quand la mort viendra, que reste-t-il?

SAGESSE   15

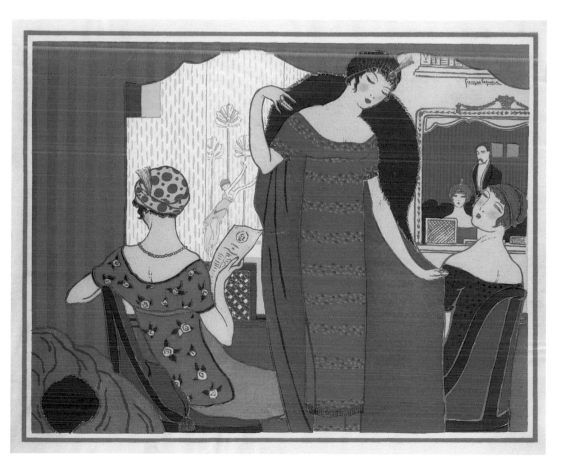

Fig. 73. Maurice Denis from *Sagesse* Text by Paul Verlaine (Paris: Ambroise Vollard, 1911). Color wood-engraving. Edition: 122/250.

Fig. 74. Jean-Émile Laboureur from *Petites images de la guerre sur le front britannique.* Text by Roger Allard (Paris: L'imprimerie d'A. Vernant, 1917). Engraving. Edition: 88/120.

Fig. 75. Georges Lepape from *Les choses de Paul Poiret, vues par Georges Lepape* (Paris: Paul Poiret, 1911). Color lithograph with added pochoir color. Edition: "exemplaire d'état."

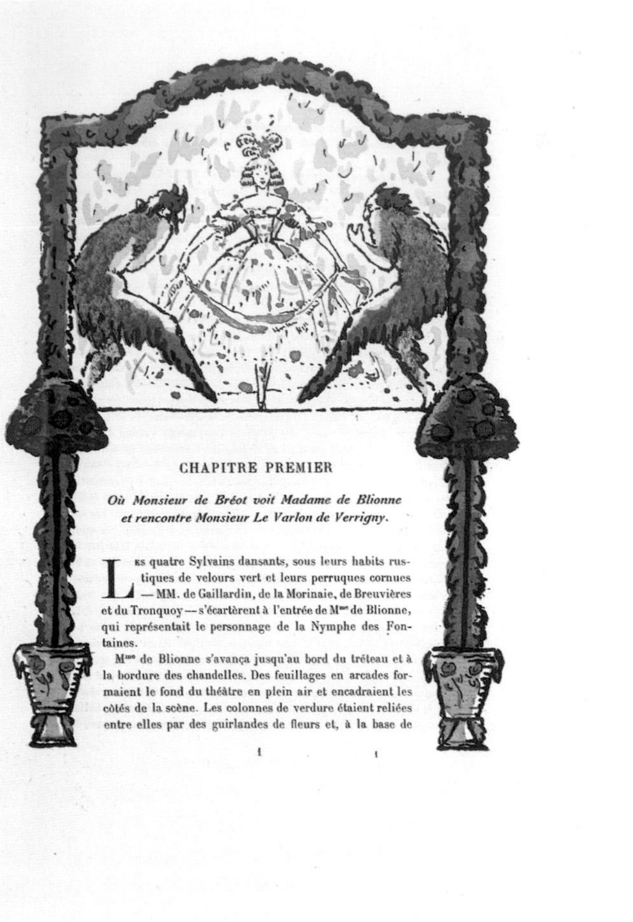

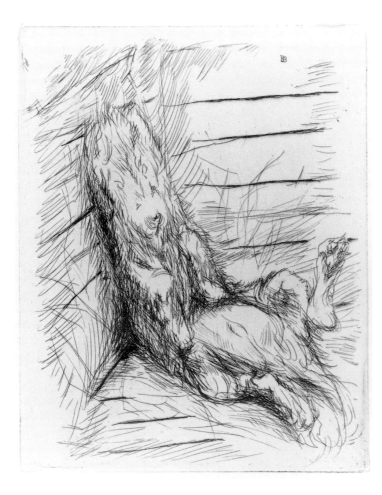

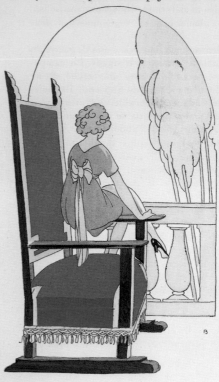

Fig. 76. Robert Bonfils from *Les rencontres de M. de Bréot.* Text by Henri de Régnier (Paris: René Kieffe, 1919). Line block reproduction with added watercolor. Edition: 158/500.

Fig. 78. Pierre Bonnard from *Dingo.* Text by Octave Mirbeau (Paris: Ambroise Vollard, 1924). Etching with drypoint. Edition: 199/350.

Fig. 77. Umberto Brunelleschi from *Phili: ou, par-delà le bien et le mal: Conte moral.* Text by Abel Hermant ([Paris?]: Éditions de la Guirlande, 1921). Line block reproduction with added pochoir color. Edition: 11/275.

Fig. 79. George Grosz from *Ecce Homo* (Berlin: Der Malik-Verlag, [1923]). Photomechanical reproduction.

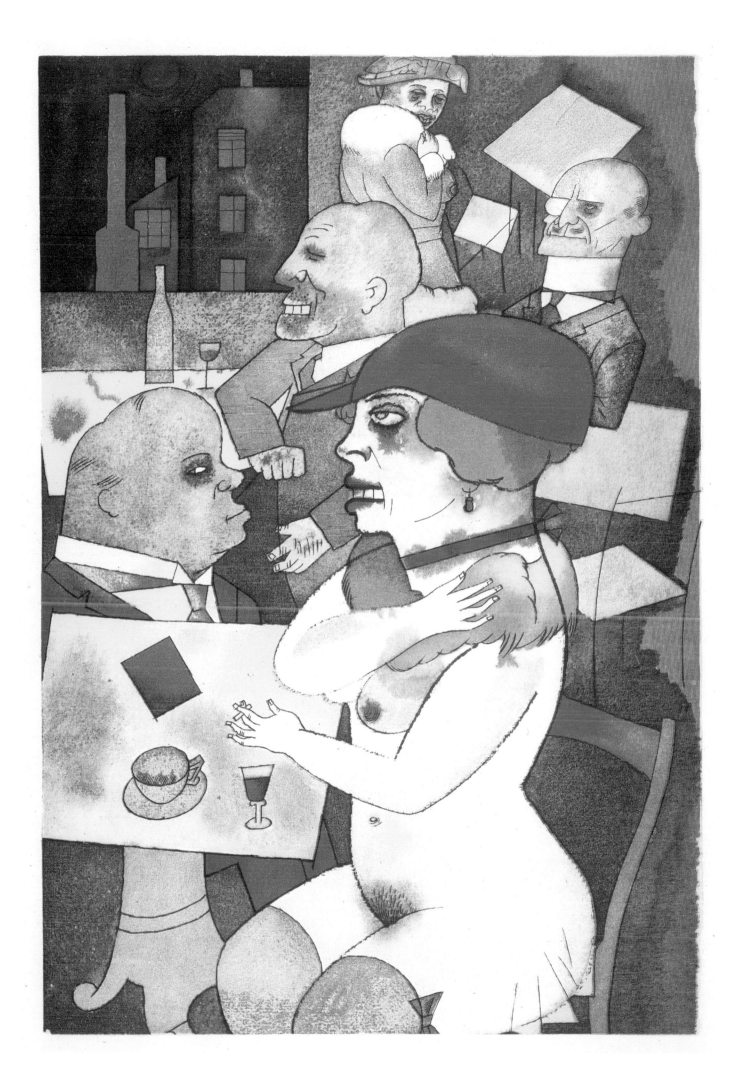

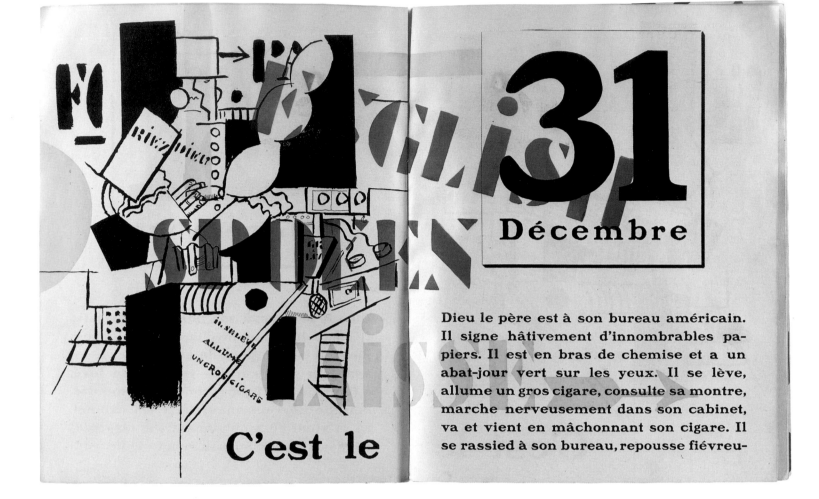

Dieu le père est à son bureau américain. Il signe hâtivement d'innombrables papiers. Il est en bras de chemise et a un abat-jour vert sur les yeux. Il se lève, allume un gros cigare, consulte sa montre, marche nerveusement dans son cabinet, va et vient en mâchonnant son cigare. Il se rassied à son bureau, repousse fiévreu-

Fig. 80. Fernand Léger from *La fin du monde filmée par l'ange N.-D.* Text by Blaise Cendrars (Paris: Éditions de la sirène, 1919). Color pochoir print with line block elements. Edition: 1,115/1,225.

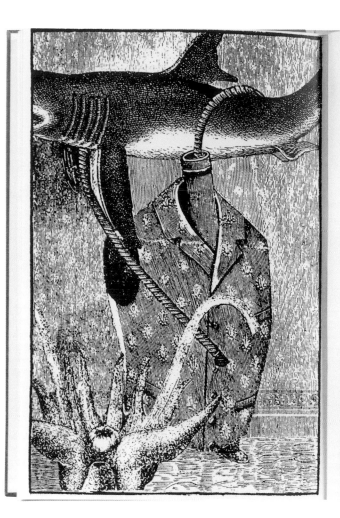

Fig. 81. Max Ernst from *Les
malheurs des immortels*.
Texts by Max Ernst and
Paul Éluard (Köln: Galerie
der Spiegel, [1965? 1st ed.
1922]). Line block reproduction. Edition: 85/335.

Fig. 82. Heinrich Hoffmann
from *Das Struwwelpeter-
Manuscript* [facsimile]. Text
by Heinrich Hoffmann and
G. A. E. Bogeng (Frankfurt
am Main: Literarische
Anstalt Rütten & Loening,
1925). Collotype. Edition:
104/550.

following pages:
Fig. 83. Ernst Ludwig
Kirchner from *Umbra vitae:
nachgelassene Gedichte*. Text
by Georg Heym (München:
Kurt Wolff, 1924). Color
woodcut. Edition: 201/510.

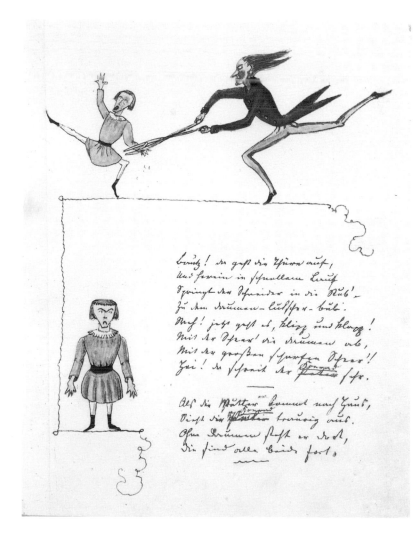

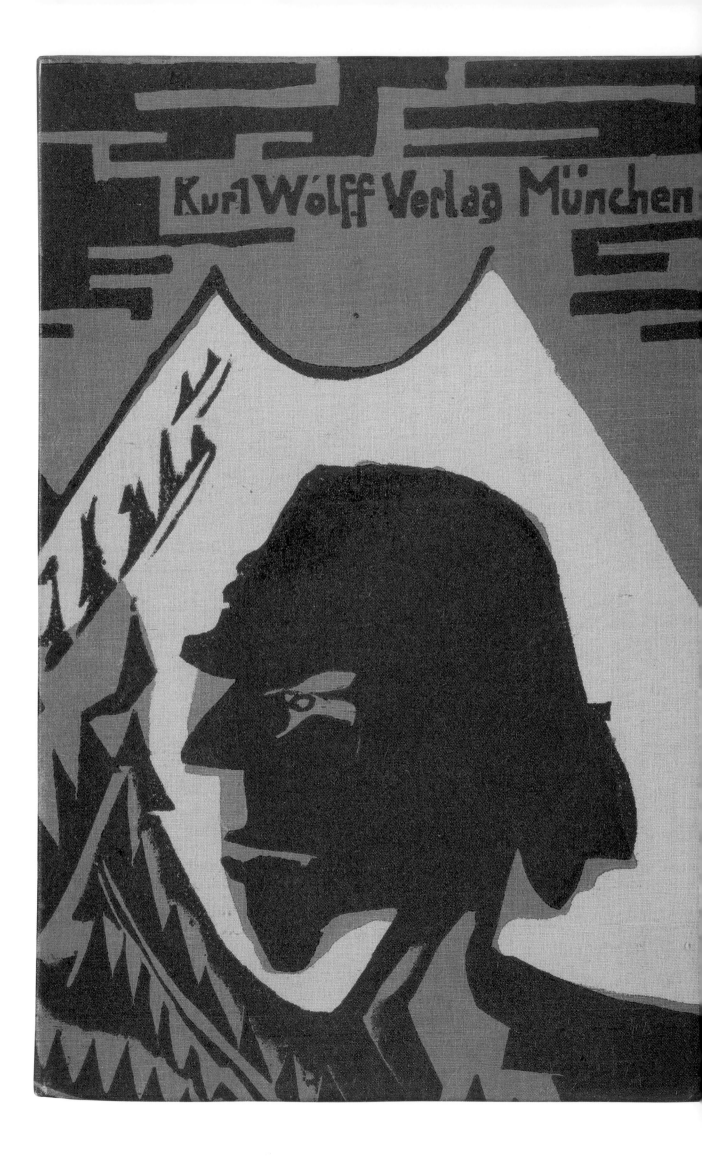

Kurt Wolff Verlag München

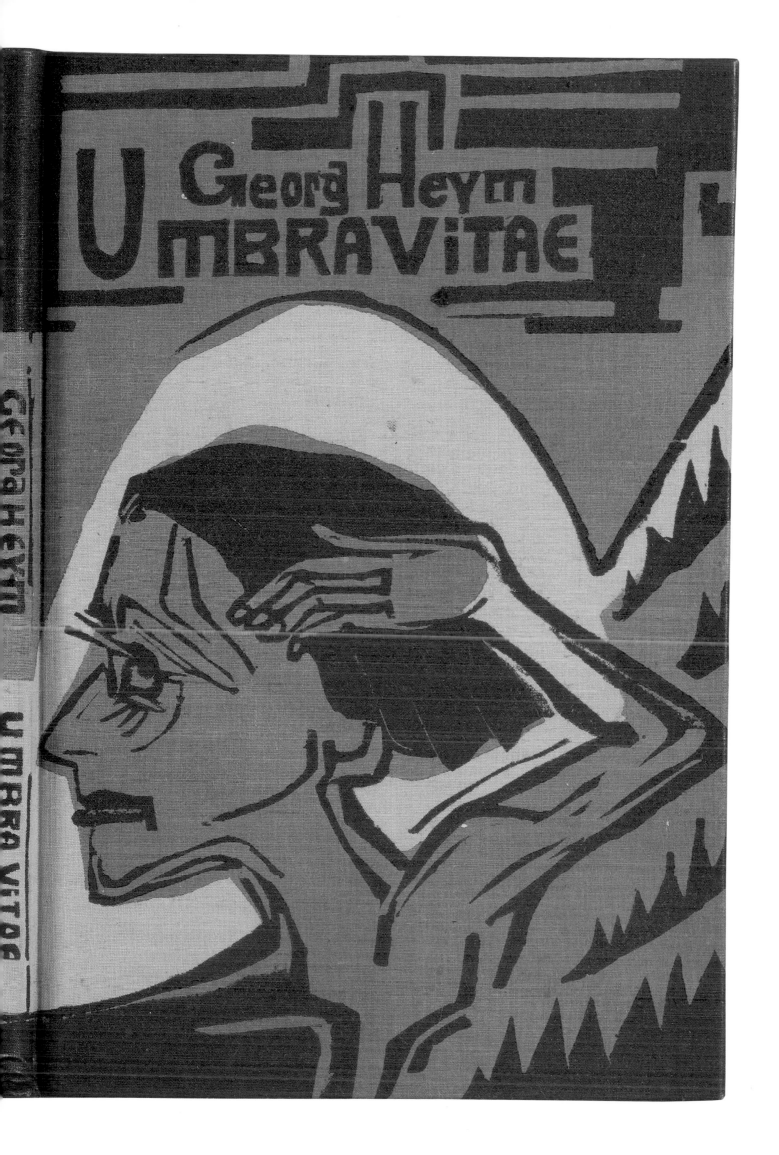

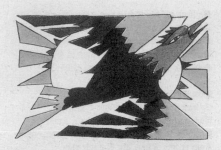

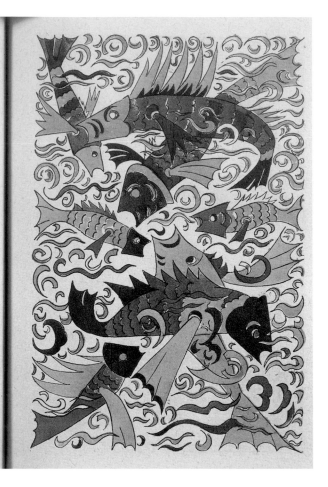

An der Donau singen und saufen die Speere.
Klagend ertönt von den Zinnen Putiwls
Jaroslawnas Stimme in der Morgenstunde,
Wie des Kuckucksweibchens wehmüt'ger Schrei:
„Als Kuckuck flieg ich zum Donauflusse,
Den mit Biberpelz verbrämten Ärmel
Meines Gewandes will ich ins Wasser
Der Kajala tauchen, am tapfern Leibe
Des Fürsten zu waschen die blutigen Wunden."

Klagend tönt von den Zinnen Putiwls
Jaroslawnas Stimme in der Morgenstunde:
„O Herre Wind! Was wehst du so heftig?
Was treibst du schwirrend auf leichten Schwingen
Die Geschosse des Chans gegen die Scharen
Meines Geliebten? Laß dir's genug sein,
Die weißen Wolken am Himmel zu wiegen,
Die Schiffe im blauen Meere zu schaukeln!

42

Fig. 84. Natalia Gontcharova from *Die Mär von der Heerfahrt Igors*. Text by Arthur Luther (München: Orchis, 1924; title page, 1923). Line block reproductions with added pochoir color. Edition: unnumbered/700.

Fig. 85. Raoul Dufy from *Raoul Dufy*. Text by Marcelle Berr de Turique (Paris: Librairie Floury, 1930). Collotype with added pochoir color. Edition: 744/unknown.

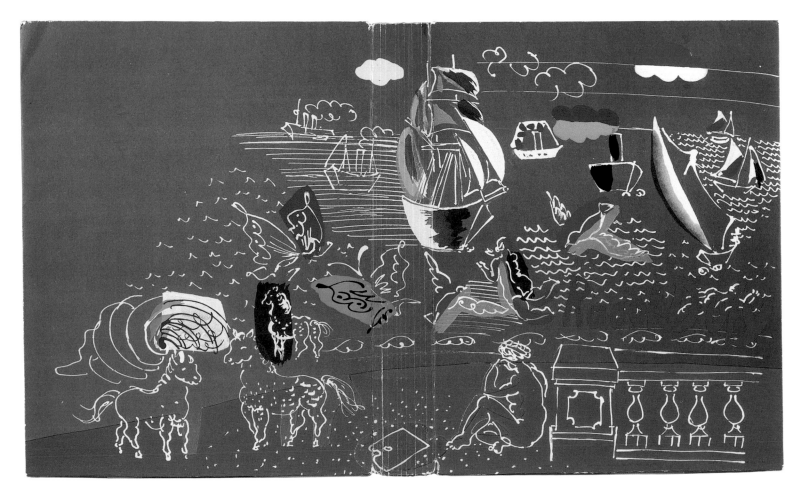

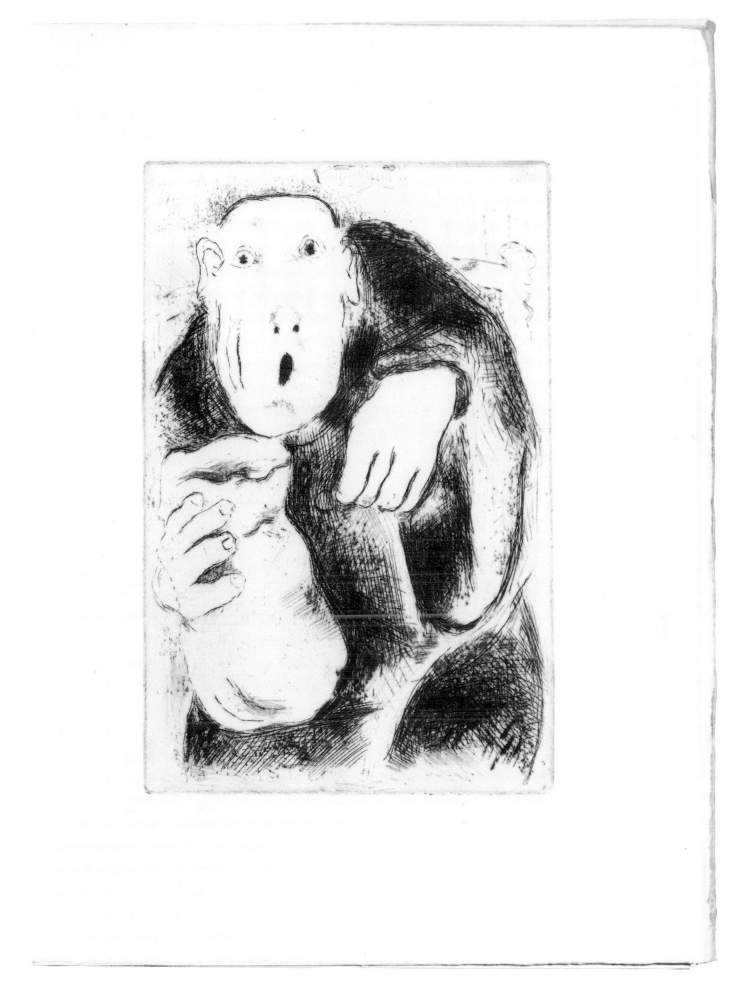

Fig. 86. Marc Chagall from *Les sept péchés*
capitaux (Paris: Simon Kra, [1926]).
Etching. Edition: 23/300.

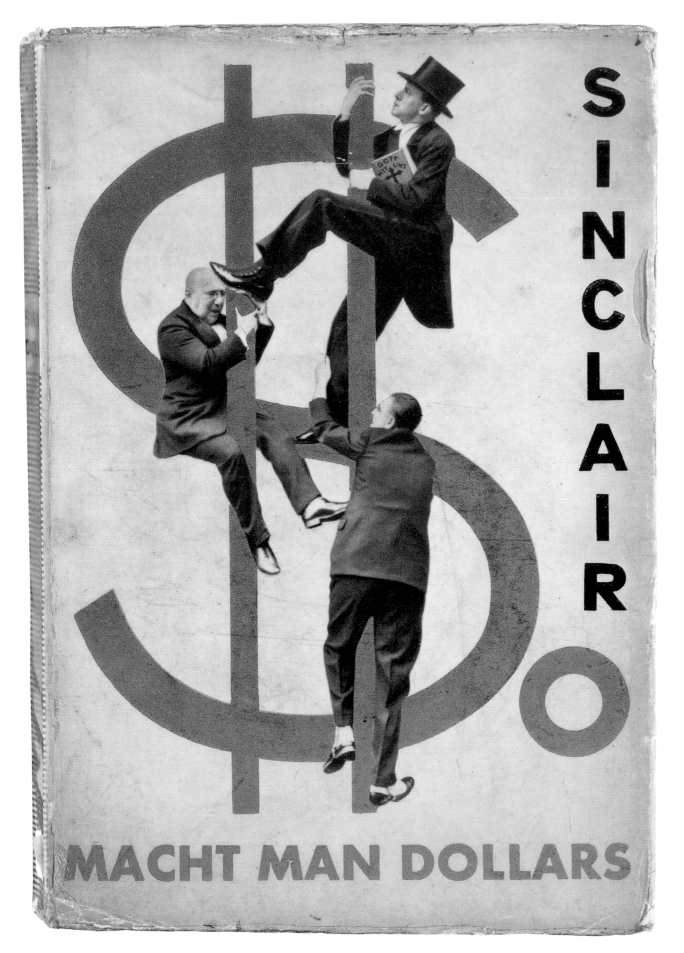

Fig. 87. John Heartfield from *So macht Man Dollars*. Text by Upton Sinclair (Berlin: Malik-Verlag, 1931). Photomechanical reproduction with line block element. Edition: unnumbered/35,000.

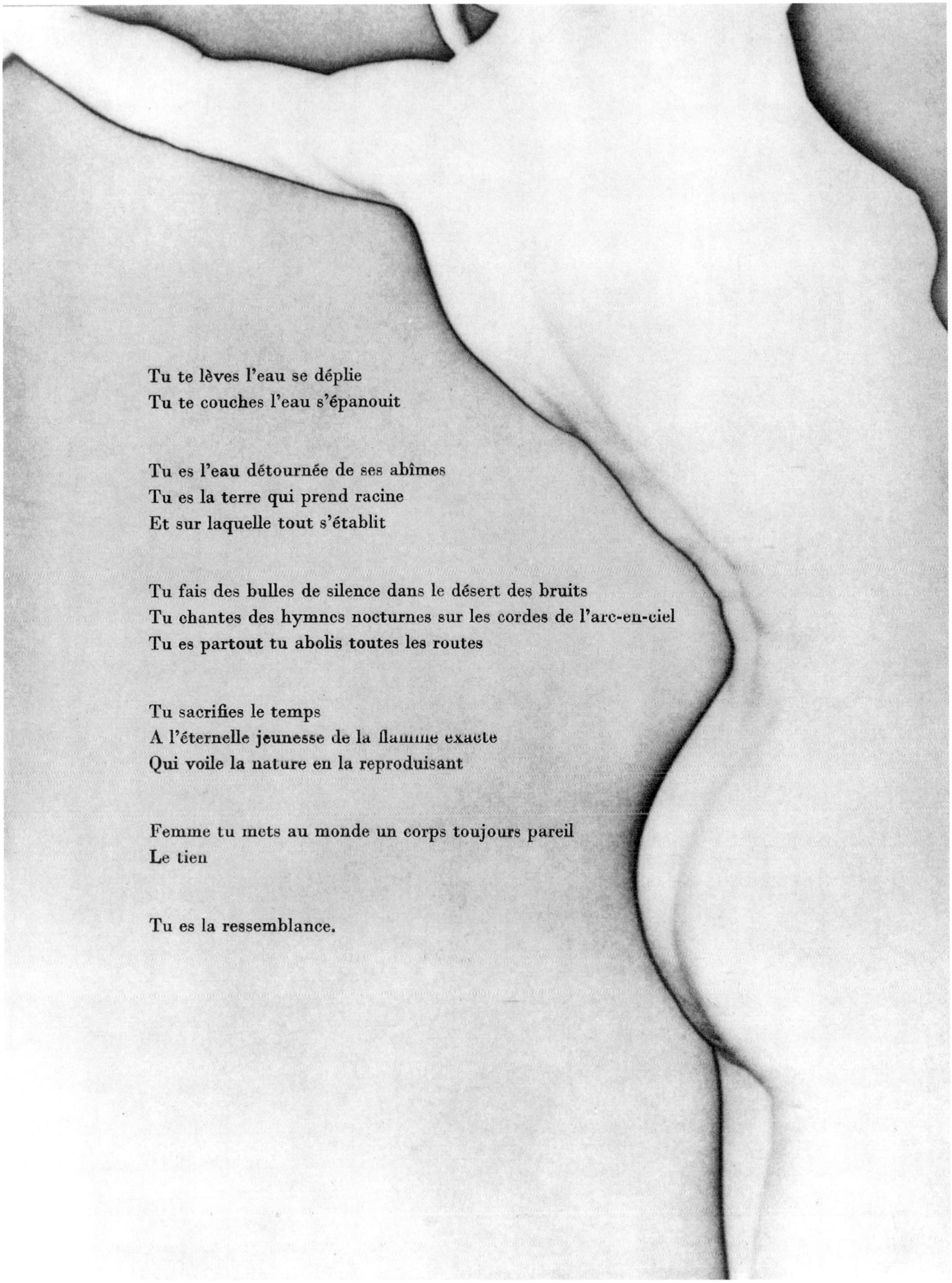

Tu te lèves l'eau se déplie
Tu te couches l'eau s'épanouit

Tu es l'eau détournée de ses abîmes
Tu es la terre qui prend racine
Et sur laquelle tout s'établit

Tu fais des bulles de silence dans le désert des bruits
Tu chantes des hymnes nocturnes sur les cordes de l'arc-en-ciel
Tu es partout tu abolis toutes les routes

Tu sacrifies le temps
A l'éternelle jeunesse de la flamme exacte
Qui voile la nature en la reproduisant

Femme tu mets au monde un corps toujours pareil
Le tien

Tu es la ressemblance.

Fig. 88. Man Ray from *Facile*. Text by Paul
Éluard (Paris: Éditions G.L.M., 1935).
Photomechanical reproduction. Edition:
841/1,020. .

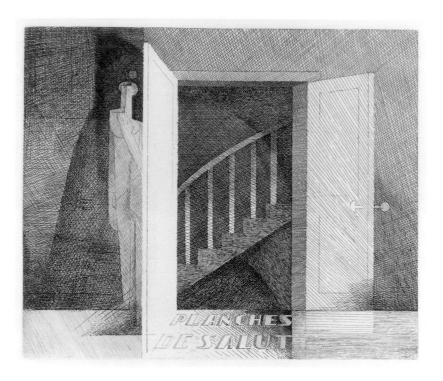

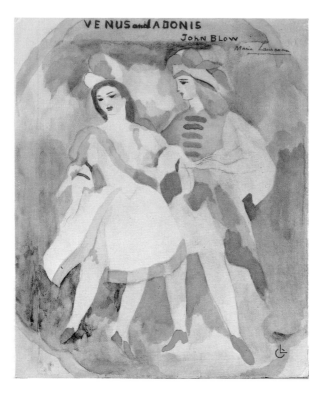

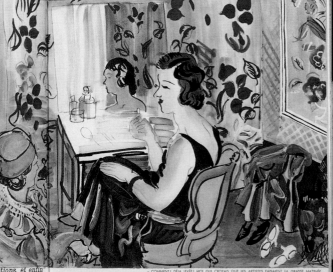

Fig. 89. Louis Marcoussis from *Planches de salut*. Text by Tristan Tzara (Paris: Éditions Jeanne Bucher, 1931). Mixed etching. Edition: 65/71.

Fig. 90. Marie Laurencin from *Venus and Adonis*. Music by John Blow (Paris: Éditions de l'oiseau lyre, 1939). Collotype with added pochoir color. Edition: XIV/L.

Fig. 91. Raoul Dufy from *Mon docteur le vin*. Text by Gaston Derys (Paris: Draeger frères, 1936). Photomechanical reproduction.

Fig. 92. Karl Schrag from *The Suicide Club*. Text by Robert Louis Stevenson (New York: Pierre Bères, 1941). Etching with aquatint and drypoint. Edition: 70/100.

Fig. 93. Jean Dubuffet from *L'homme du commun, ou Jean Dubuffet*. Text by Pierre Seghers ([Paris]: Éditions poésie, 1944). Color lithograph. Edition: 140/150.

following pages:
Fig. 94. André Derain from *Pantagruel*. Text by François Rabelais (Paris: Albert Skira, 1943). Woodcuts from hand-painted blocks. Edition: 146/250.

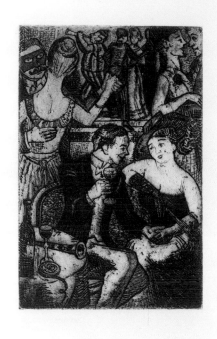

ROBERT LOUIS STEVENSON

The Suicide Club

WITH 18 ORIGINAL AQUATINT ETCHINGS BY
KARL SCHRAG

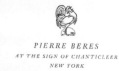

PIERRE BERES
AT THE SIGN OF CHANTICLEER
NEW YORK

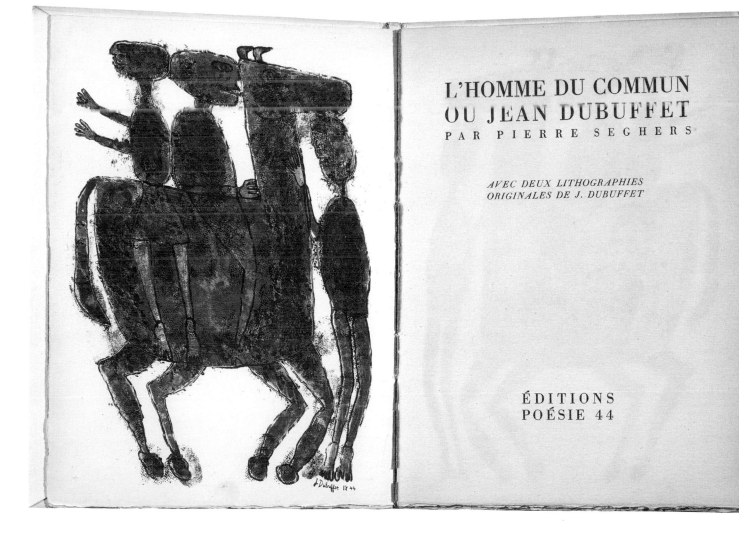

L'HOMME DU COMMUN
OU JEAN DUBUFFET
PAR PIERRE SEGHERS

*AVEC DEUX LITHOGRAPHIES
ORIGINALES DE J. DUBUFFET*

ÉDITIONS
POÉSIE 44

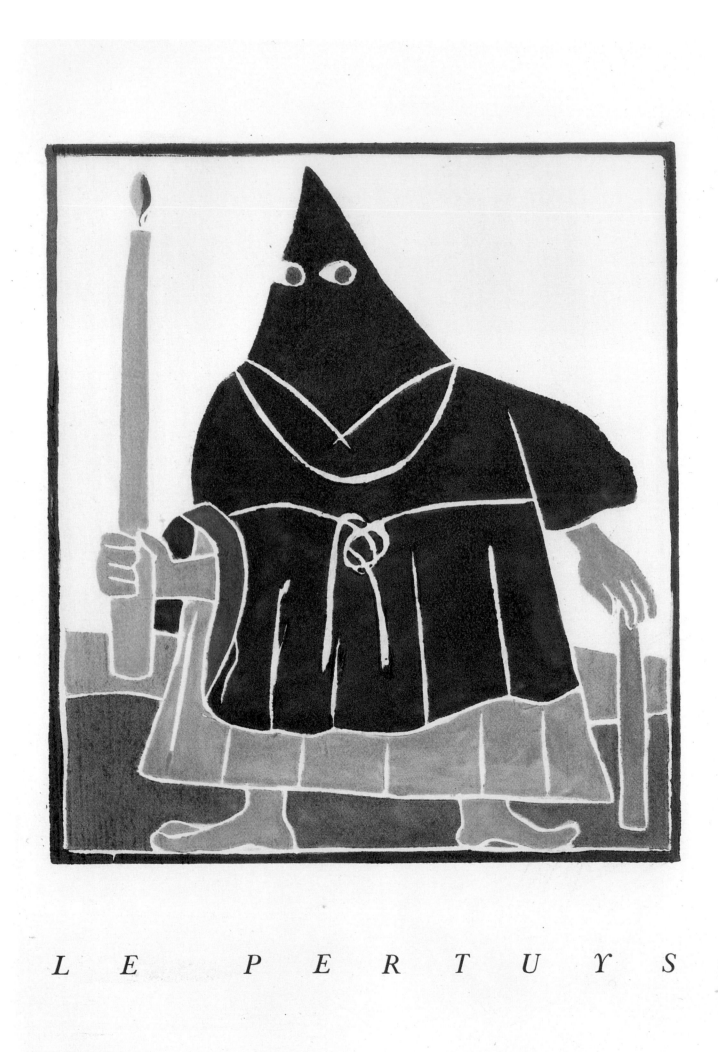

LE PERTUYS

La conclusion du present livre et l'excuse de l'auteur

CHAPITRE XXXIV

R, Messieurs, vous avez ouy un commencement de l'Histoire horrificque de mon maistre et seigneur Pantagruel. Icy je feray fin à ce premier livre; la teste me faict un peu de mal, et sens bien que les registres de mon cerveau sont quelque peu brouillez de ceste purée de septembre.

Vous aurez la reste de l'histoire à ces foires de Francfort prochainement venantes, et là vous verrez : comment Panurge fut marié, et cocqu dès le premier moys de ses nopces ; et comment Pantagruel trouva la pierre philosophale, et la maniere de la trouver et d'en user ; et comment il passa les Mons Caspies ; comment il naviga par la mer Athlanticque, et deffit les caniballes, et conquesta les isles de Perlas ; comment il espousa la fille du roy de Inde, nommée Presthan ; comment il combatit contre les diables et fist brusler cinq chambres d'enfer, et mist à sac la grande chambre noire, et getta Proserpine au feu, et rompit quatre dentz à Lucifer et une corne au cul; et comment il visita les regions de la lune pour sçavoir si, à la verité, la lune n'estoit entiere, mais que les femmes en avoient troys quartiers

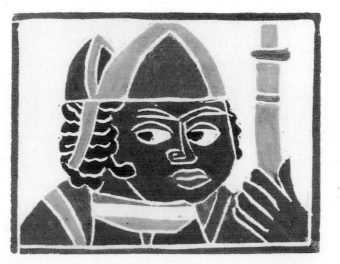

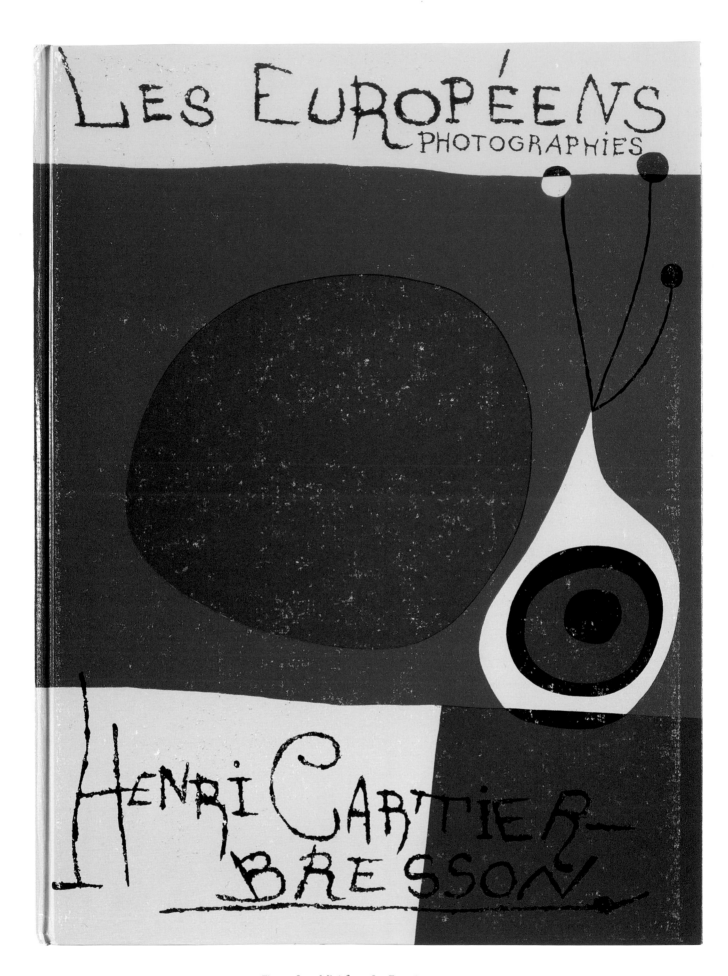

Fig. 95. Joan Miró from *Les Européens:*
Photographies par Henri Cartier-Bresson. Text by
Henri Cartier-Bresson (Paris: Éditions de la revue
Verve, 1955). Photomechanical reproduction.
Listed in Checklist under Cartier-Bresson.

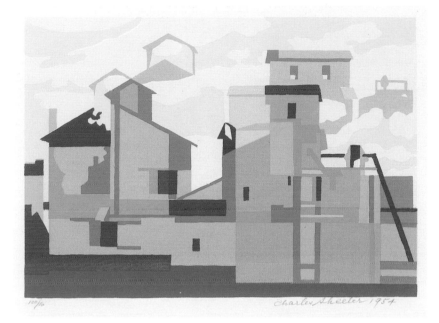

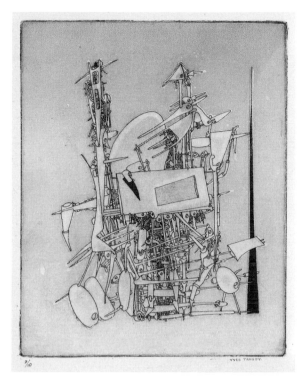

Fig. 96. Charles Sheeler from
*Charles Sheeler: A Retrospective
Exhibition.* Texts by Bartlett
H. Hayes, Jr., and Frederick
S. Wight (Los Angeles: The
Art Galleries, University of
California, 1954). Color screen
print. Edition: 10/100.

Fig. 97. Yves Tanguy from
Le grand passage. Text by Jean
Laude (Paris: Les presses
littéraires de France, 1954).
Etching with monotype color.
Edition: G/J.

Fig. 98. Juan Gris from *Au
soleil du plafond.* Text by Pierre
Reverdy (Paris: Éditions de la
revue Verve, 1955). Color
lithograph. Edition: 20/205.

following pages:
Fig. 99. Le Corbusier from
Poème de l'angle droit. Text by
Le Corbusier (Paris: Tériade,
1955). Color lithograph.
Edition: 68/250.

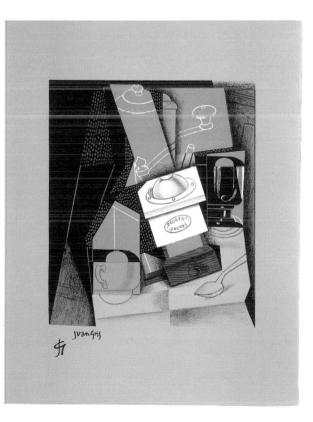

pupilles ouvertes que les regards
croisés ont pu conduire à
l'acte foudroyant de communion:
" L'épanouissement les grands
silences " ....

La mer est redescendue
au bas de la marée pour
pouvoir remonter à l'heure.
Un temps neuf s'est ouvert
une étape un delai un relai

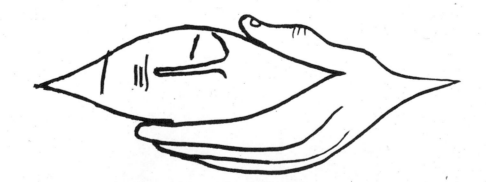

Alors ne serons-nous pas
demeurés assis à coté de nos vies.

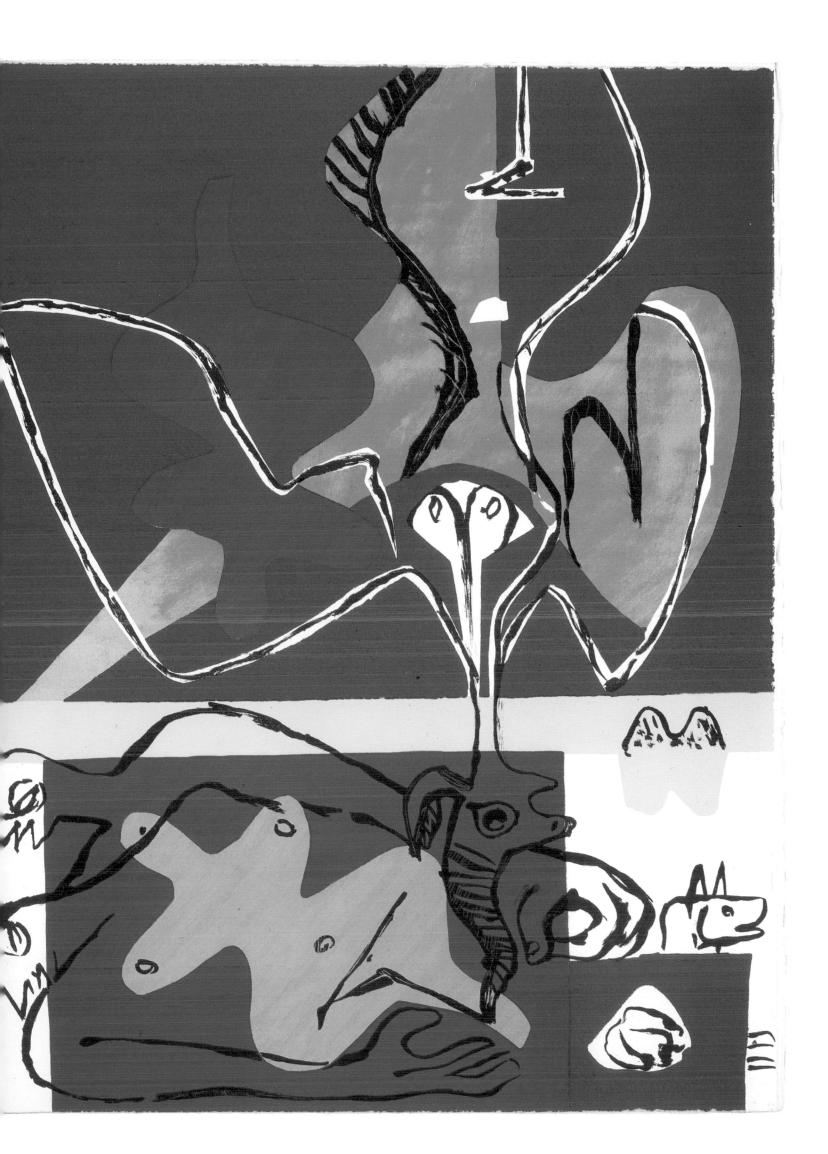

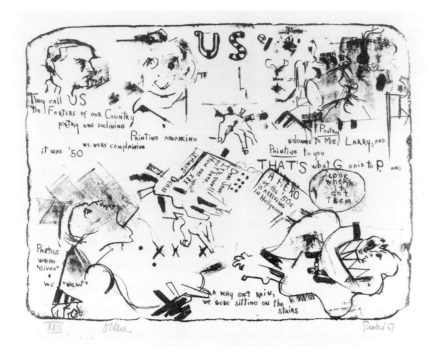

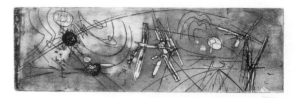

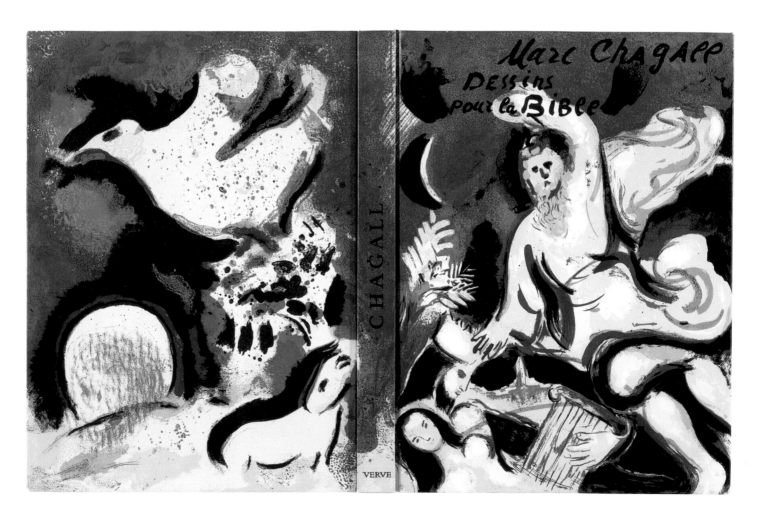

Fig. 100. Larry Rivers from *Stones*. Text by Frank O'Hara (West Islip, New York: Universal Limited Art Editions, 1959). Lithograph. Edition: XXII/XXV.

Fig. 101. Matta (Roberto Matta Echaurren) from *Come detta Dentro vo Significando*. Text by Matta (Lausanne: Éditions Meyer, 1962). Color mixed etching. Edition: 54/100.

Fig. 102. Marc Chagall from *Verve: Dessins pour la Bible*. Text by Gaston Bachelard (Paris, Édition de la revue Verve, 1960). Color lithograph. Listed in Checklist under Various Artists.

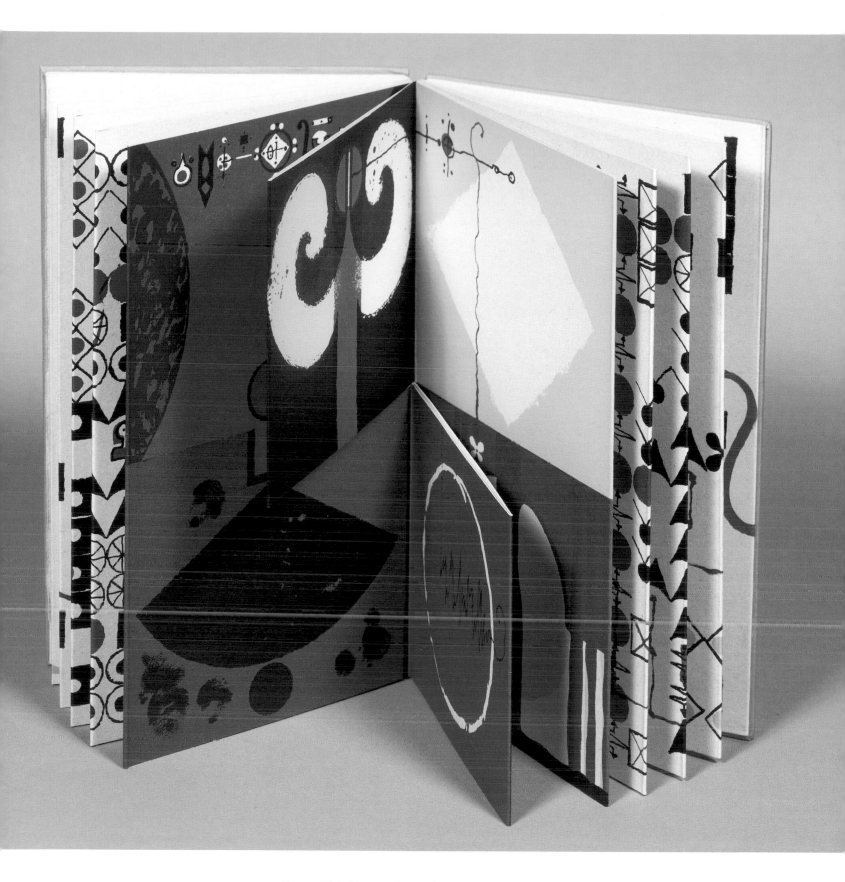

Fig. 103. Warja Honegger-Lavater from *Homo sapiens?* (Basel: Basilius Presse, 1965). Color lithographs.

following pages:
Fig. 104. James Rosenquist from *1¢ Life*. Text by Walasse Ting, edited by Sam Francis (Bern: E. W. Kornfeld, 1964). Color lithograph. Listed in Checklist under Various Artists. Edition: 1,417/2,000.

HAPPILY AND LONG INTO THE NIGHT WE DRINK
TILL ALL ARE DRUNK
THERE IS NO RETIRING
HOW CAN A MAN BITE HIS NAVEL?

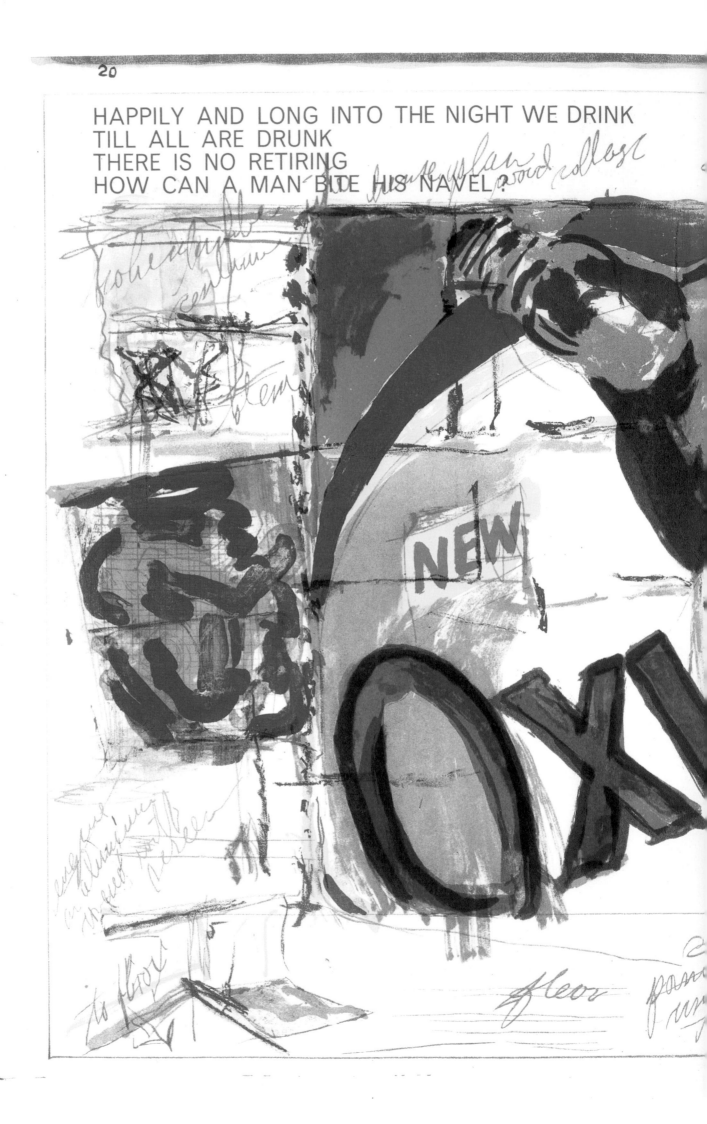

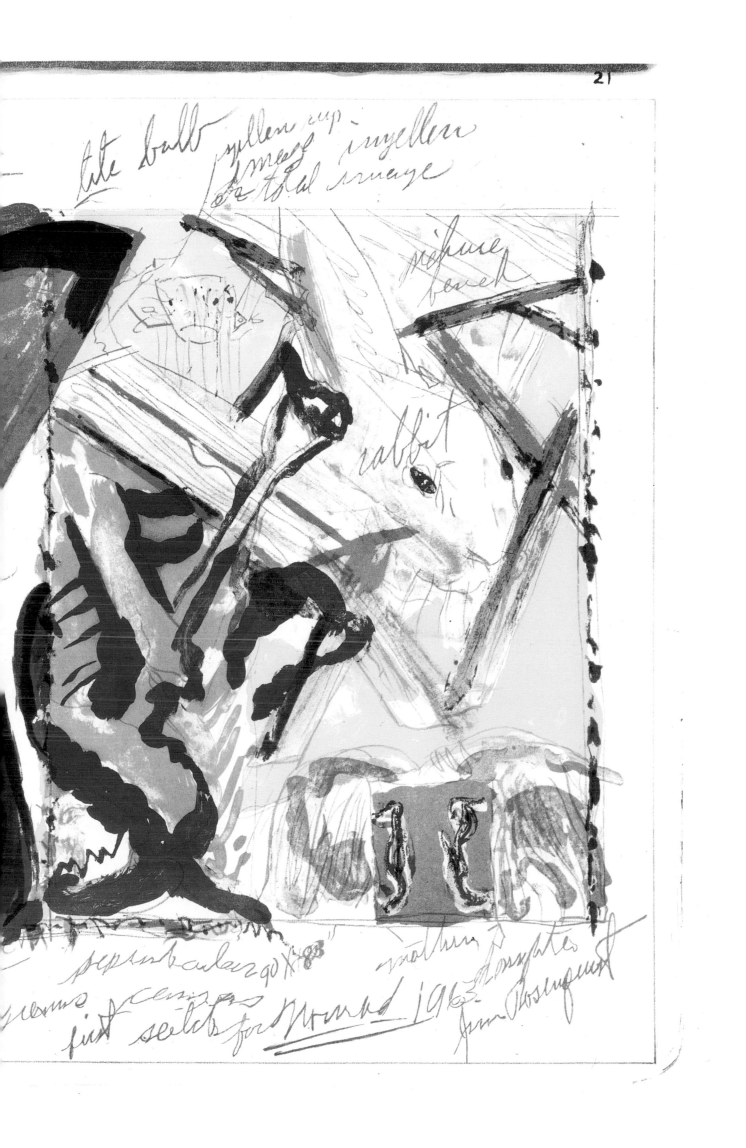

21

Ce n'était pas un jeu

Et d'en sortir jamais à mon honneur
Et sans aucun dommage
Ce n'était peut-être pas
    D'ailleurs
Un simple tremblement
Ou à peine un frisson

    Un fragment

Mais tout avait craqué

18

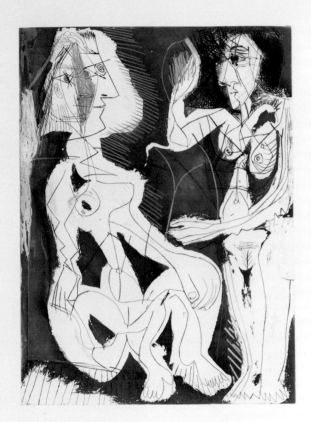

Fig. 105. Pablo Picasso from *Sable mouvant.*
Text by Pierre Reverdy (Paris: Louis Broder,
1966). Aquatint. Edition: 51/220.

Fig. 106. Joan Miró from *Miró: Oiseau
solaire, oiseau lunaire, étincelles* (New York:
Pierre Matisse Gallery, 1967). Collotype with
die cut. Edition: 106/1,200.

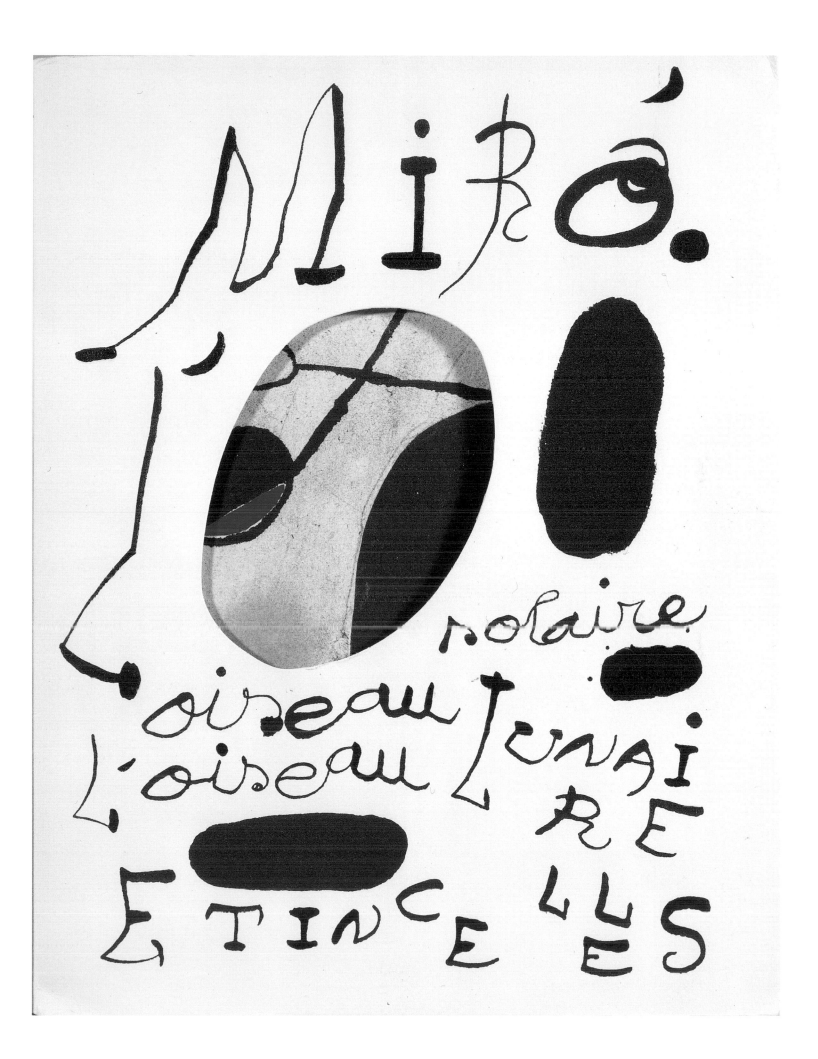

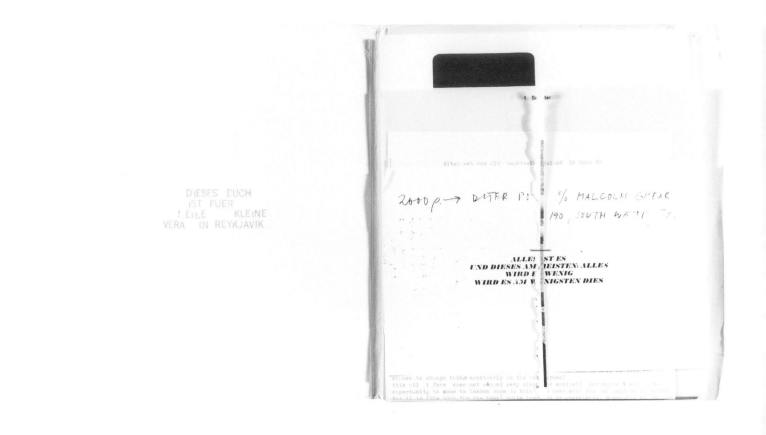

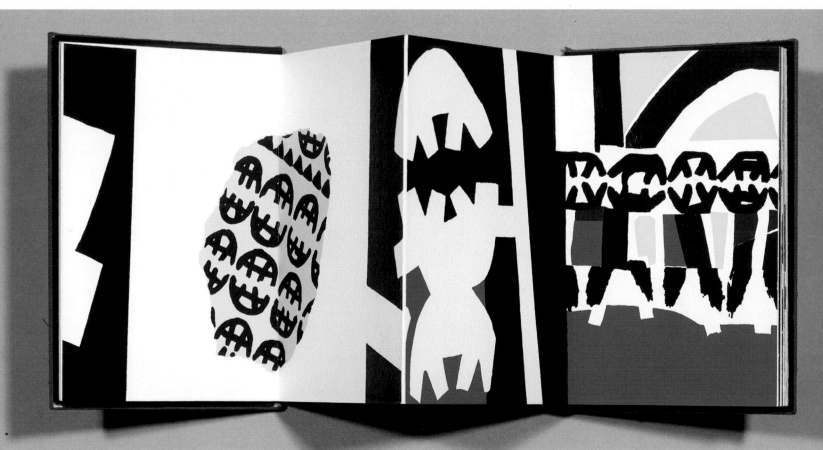

Fig. 107. Dieter Roth (Diter Rot) from *Diter Rot* (Chicago: William and Noma Copley Foundation, 1965). Photomechanical reproductions on various size pages stapled closed.

Fig. 108. Giuseppe Capogrossi from *Capogrossi* (Venezia: Cavallino, 1966). Color screen print. Edition: 50/200.

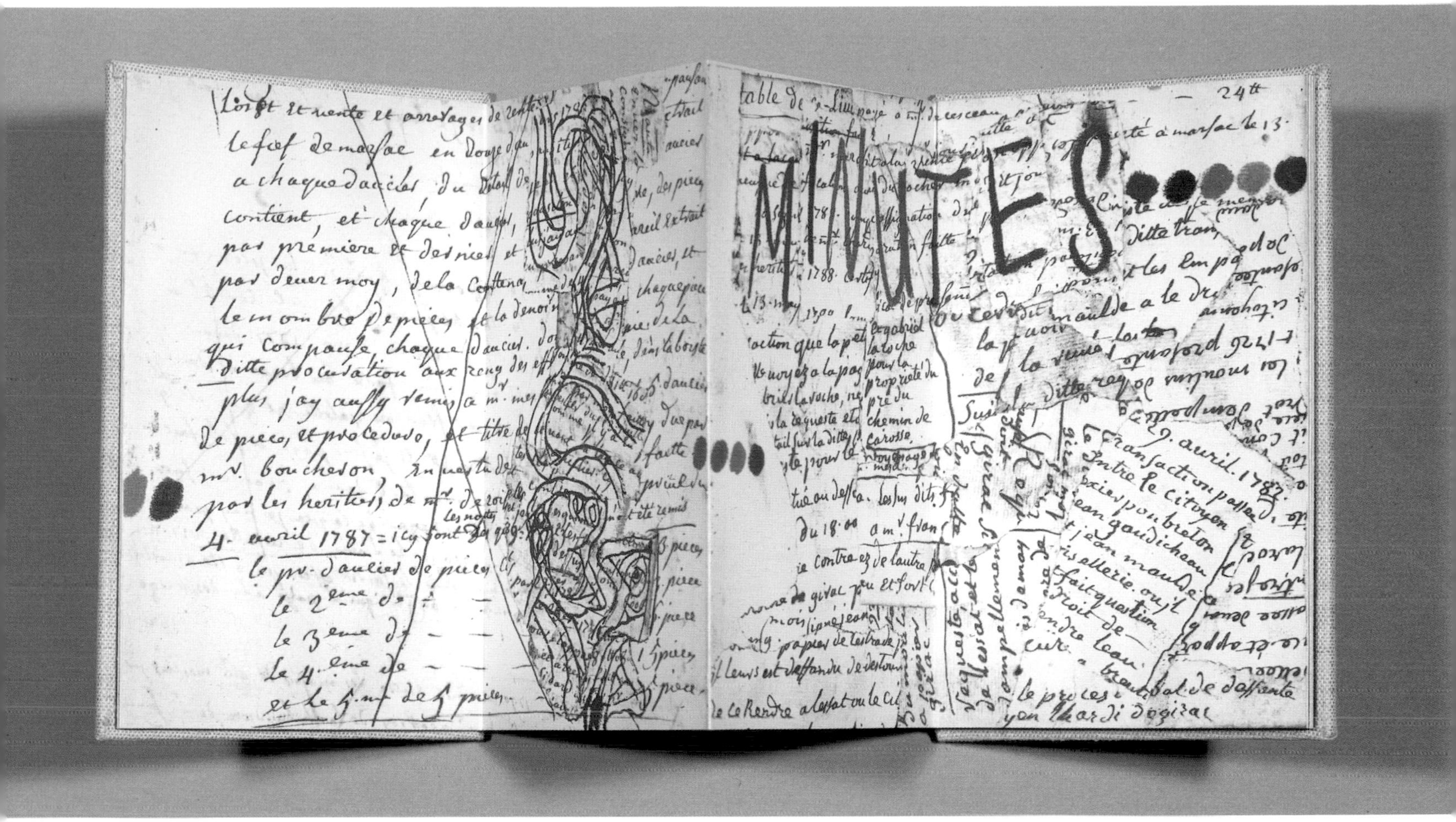

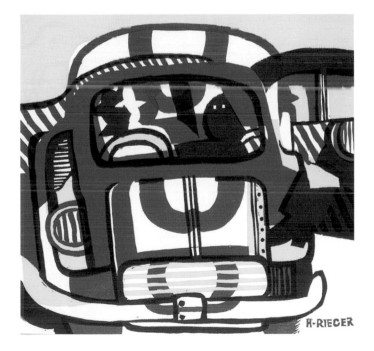

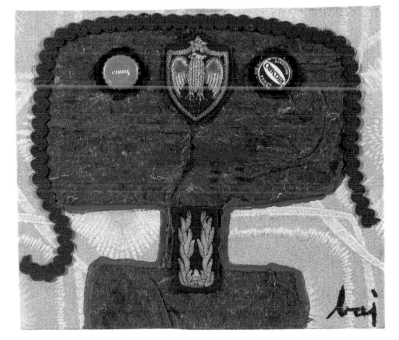

Fig. 109. Pierre Alechinsky from *Minutes* (Venezia: Cavallino, 1967). Photomechanical reproduction. Edition: 24/200.

Fig. 110. Helmut Rieger from *SPUR WIR* ([München?]: SPUR WIR, 1965). Color linoleum cut. Edition: unnumbered/1,500. Listed in Checklist under Various Artists.

Fig. 111. Enrico Baj from *Les incongruités monumentales.* Text by André Pieyre de Mandiargues (Paris: Michel Cassé, 1967). Collage with fabric, bottle caps, and paint. Edition: 5/100.

following pages: Fig. 112. Werner Pfeiffer from *Liber Mobile. An Experimental Book* (Brooklyn, New York: Pratt Adlib Press, 1967). Typographic designs with die cuts. Edition: 101/130.

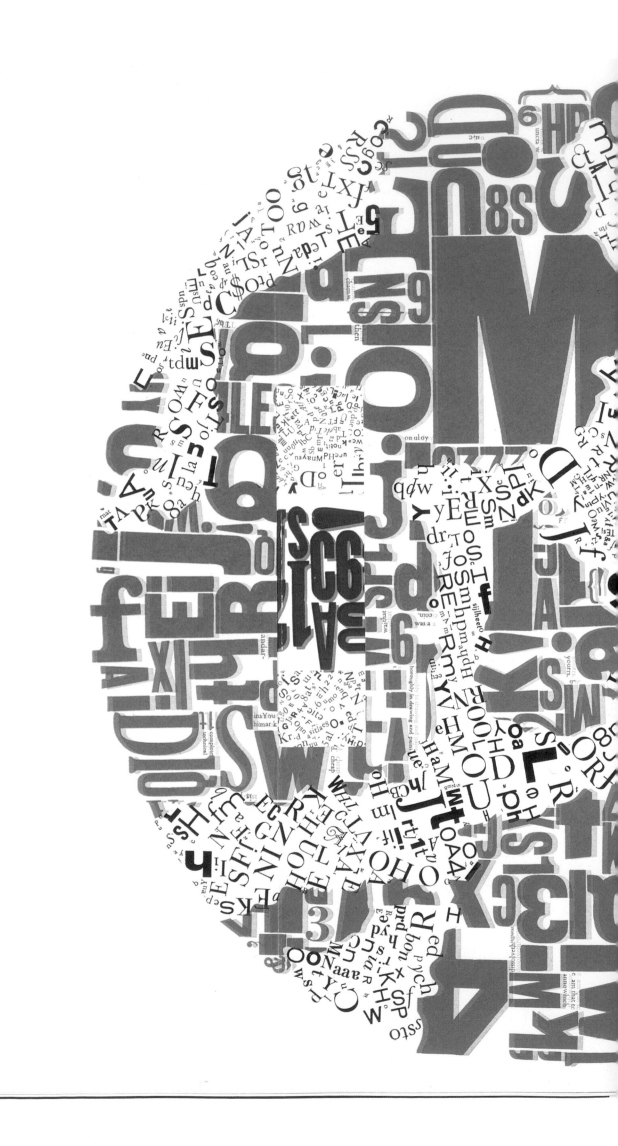

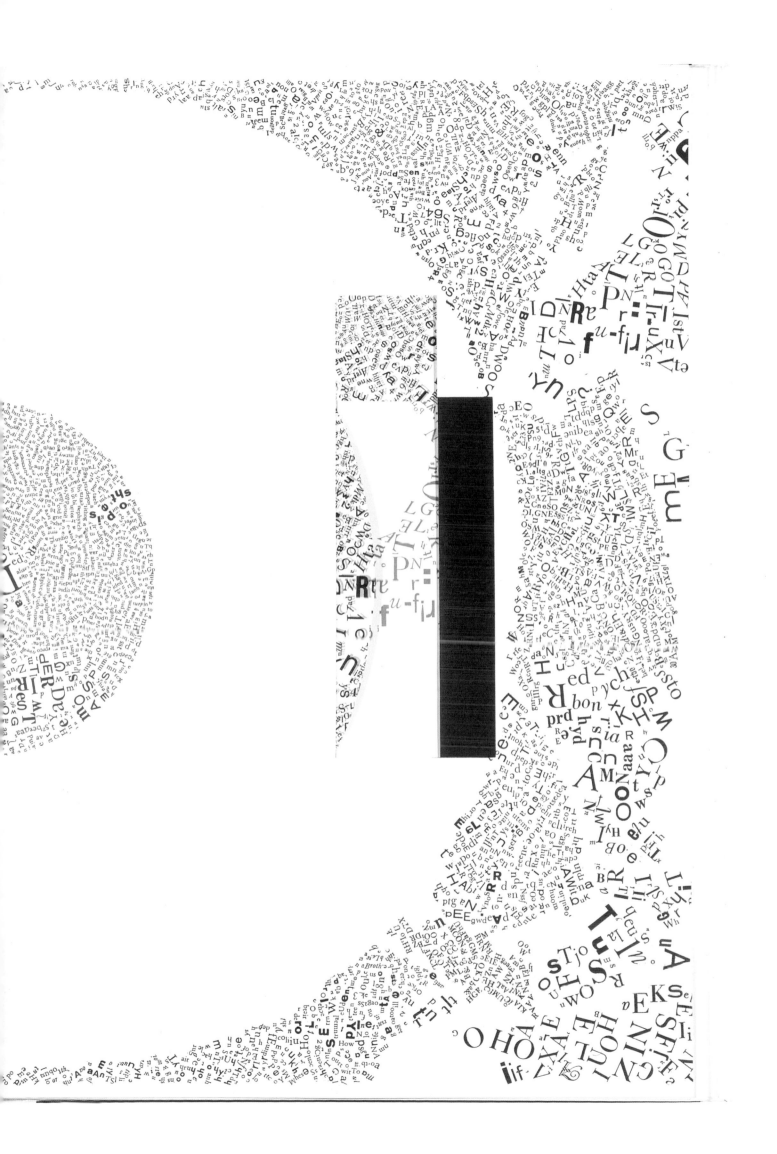

Fig. 113. Bruno Munari from *Libro Illeggibile N.Y. 1* (New York: The Museum of Modern Art, 1967). Book object: die-cut pages with pochoir color, stamping, and thread. Edition: 1,291/unknown.

Fig. 114. Joseph Beuys from *Beuys.* Texts by Johannes Cladders and Hans Strelow (Mönchengladbach, Deutschland: Städtisches Museum Abteiberg, 1967). Relief-printed felt and box. Edition 273/330.

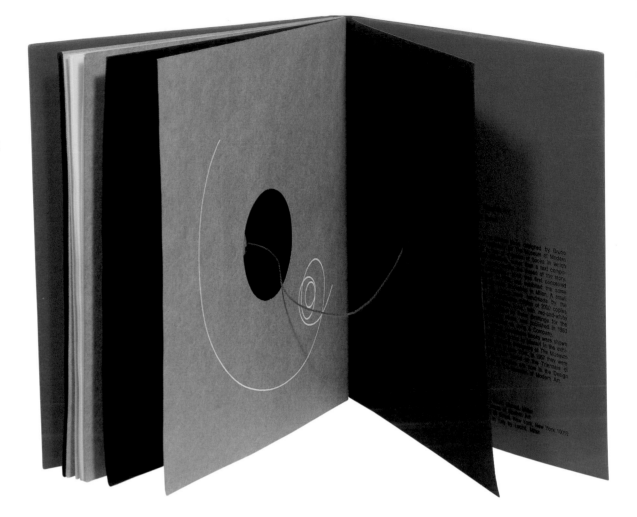

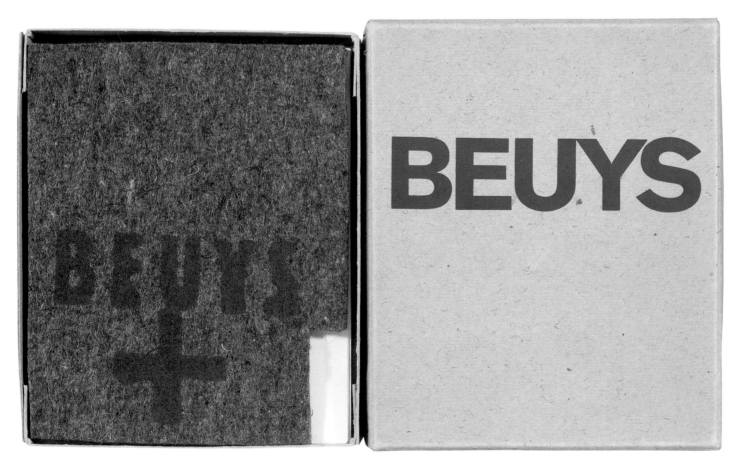

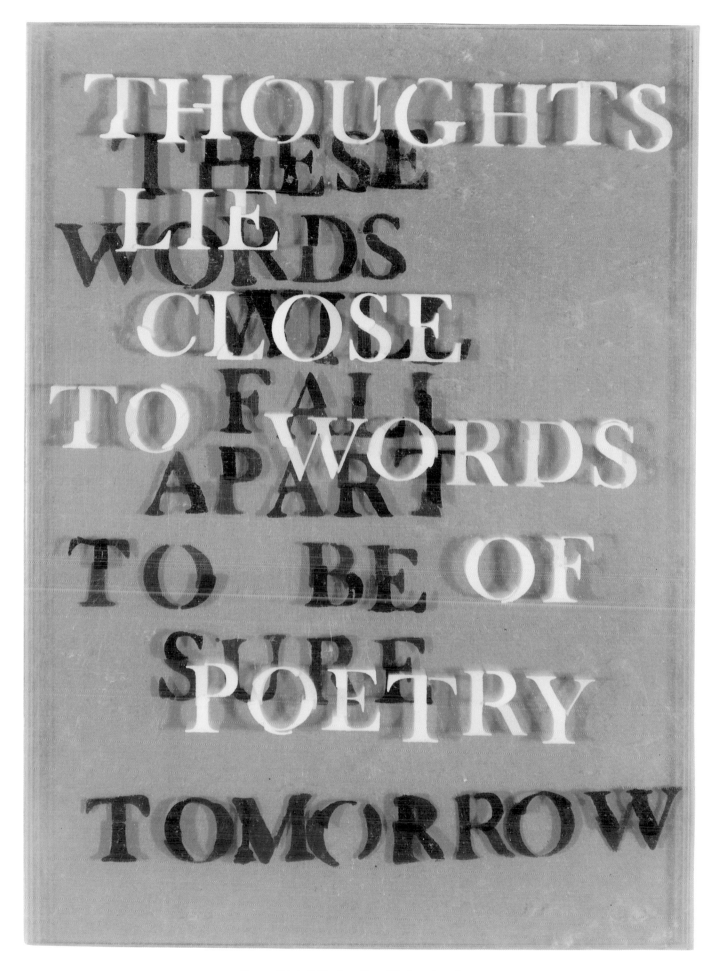

Fig. 115. Edwin Schlossberg from *Wordswordswords*.
Text by Edwin Schlossberg (West Islip, New York:
Universal Limited Art Editions, 1968). Lithographs
on Plexiglas. Edition: 25/25

Fig. 116. Various artists
including Su Braden,
Christo, Richard Hamilton,
Julien Levy, and Nancy
Reitkopf from *S.M.S.*
(No. 1, February 1968).
Photomechanical reproduc-
tions, some with die cuts.
Listed in Checklist under
Various Artists.

Fig. 117. Karin Székessy from
Porträt Nr. 7 (Hannover:
Dieter Brusberg, 1969).
Color screen print. Edition:
45/60. Listed in Checklist
under Voss.

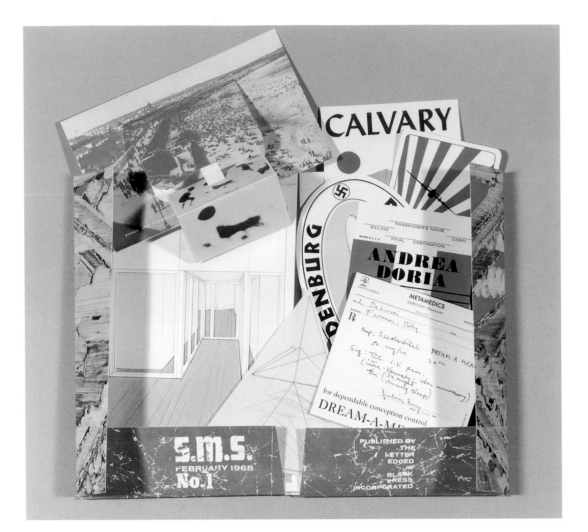

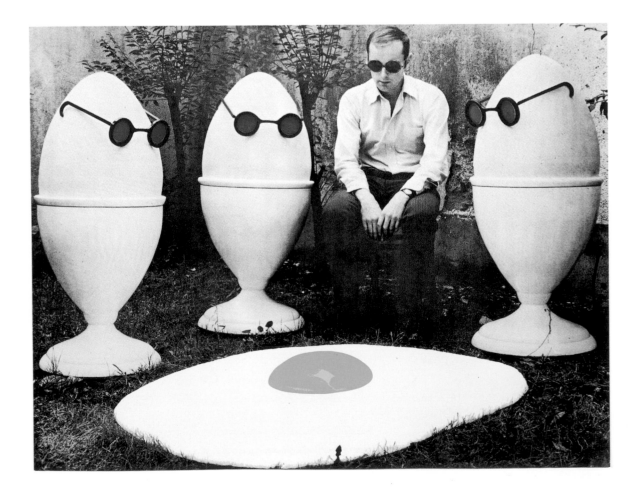

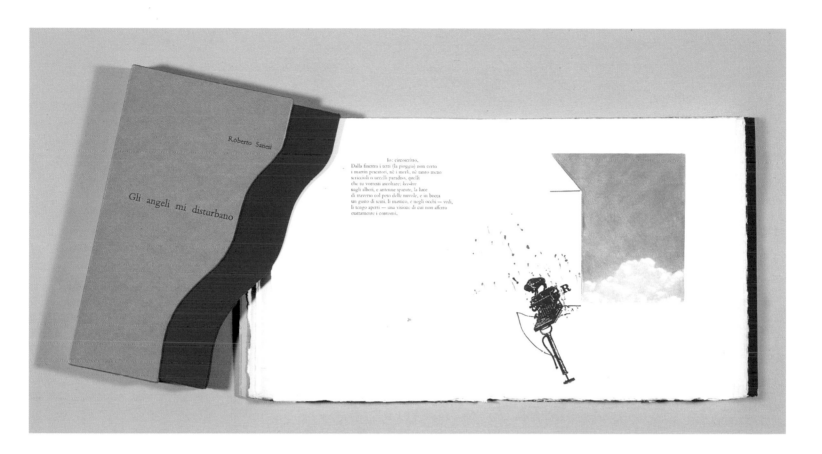

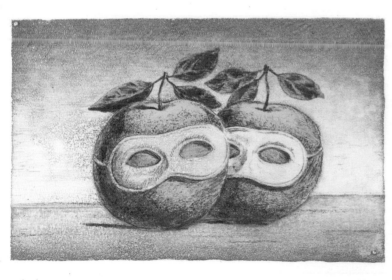

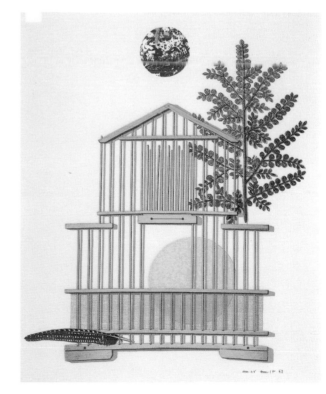

Fig. 118. Masuo Ikeda from *Gli angeli mi disturbano*. Text by Roberto Sanesi (Milano: Edizioni d'Arte Grafica Uno, 1969). Color mixed etching. Edition: 54/99.

Fig. 119. René Magritte from *Signes de survie aux temps d'amour*. Text by Gui Rosey (Paris: Éditions Georges Visat, 1968). Color etching. Edition: 8/150.

Fig. 120. Max Ernst from *Dent prompte*. Text by René Char (Paris: Galerie Lucie Weill, 1969). Color lithograph. Edition: 31/240.

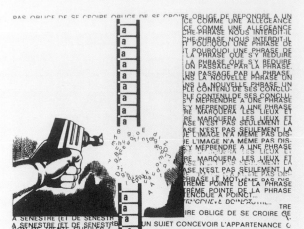

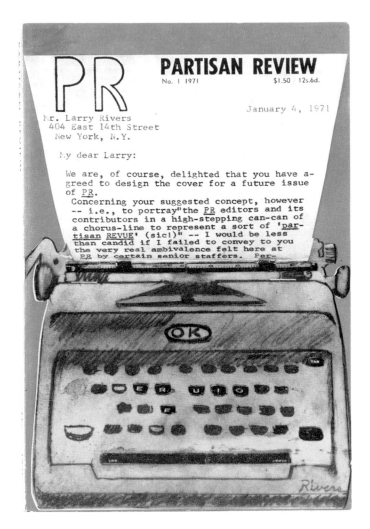

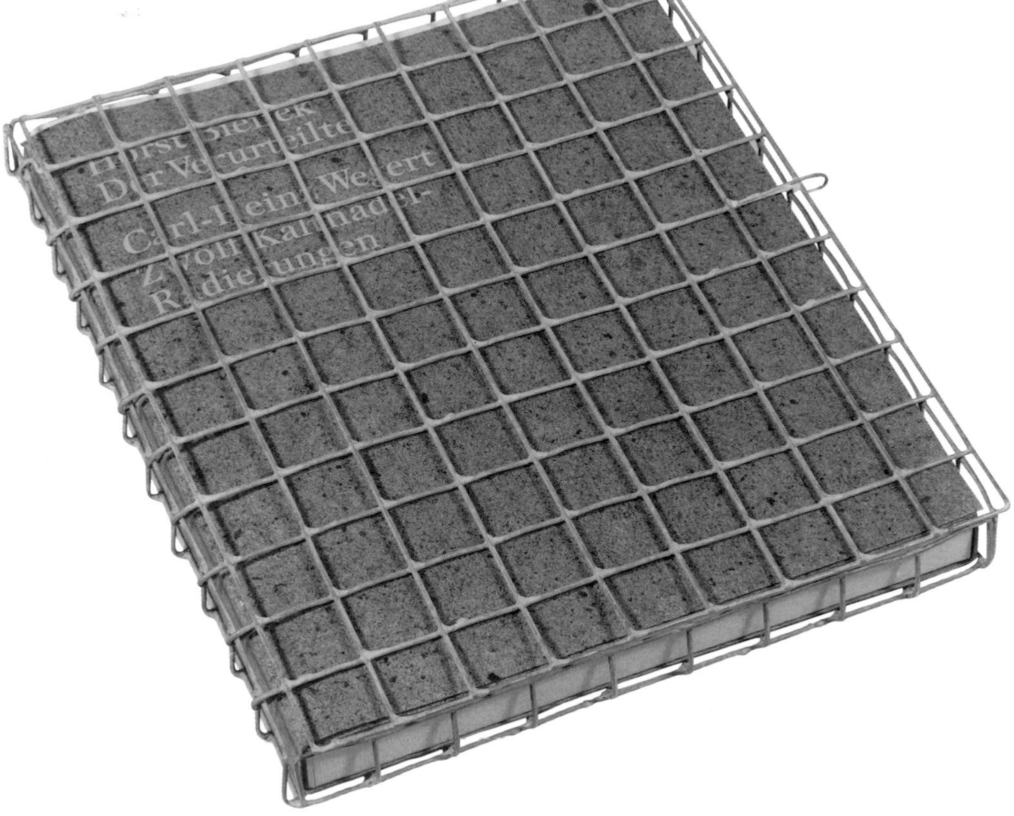

Fig. 121. Jean-François Bory from *Post-scriptum.* Text by Jean-François Bory ([S.l.]: Eric Losfeld, 1970). Line block reproduction.

Fig. 122. Larry Rivers from *Partisan Review.* Text by Terry Southern (New Brunswick, New Jersey, Rutgers University, 1971). Photomechanical reproduction.

Fig. 123. Carl-Heinz Wegert from *Der Verurteilte.* Text by Horst Bienek (München: Edition Günter Stöberlein, 1972). Wire box with hinged lid and clasp. Edition: 7/27 (Edition A).

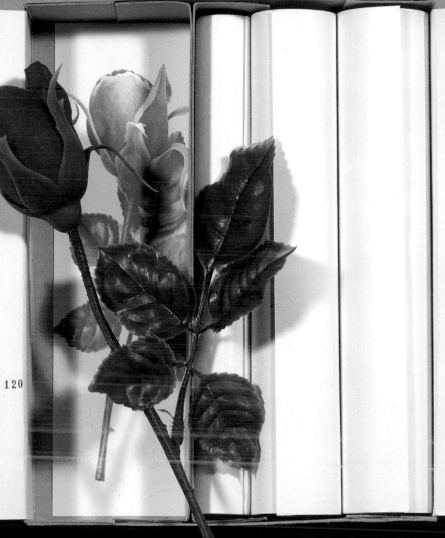

Der Text „A Rose is a Rose..." ist einem Gedicht von Gertru[...] Stein aus 1922 entnomm[...] Emblem-Form verwandt[...] auf ihren Briefbogen.

Dieser Katalog begleitet [...] zeichnis und Abbildungen und [...] als verbale und intermediale Interpretation seines Werks die Ausstellung:

STÄDTISCHES MUSEUM
MÖNCHENGLADBACH

JASPER JOHNS
DAS GRAPHISCHE WERK
1960 - 1970

22. JUNI BIS 1. AUGUST 1971

Auflage des Katalogs:
550 Exemplare

Dies ist Exemplar   № 120

Gesamtherstellung des Katalogs
Heinrich Schlechtriem Mönchengladbach

Ein Ding, das sich in einer Richtung auswirkt.
Ein anderes Ding, das sich in einer anderen Richtung
Ein Ding das zu *verschiedenen Zeiten* verschieden

Einen Gegenstand nehmen.
Etwas an ihm tun.
Etwas anderes an ihm tun.

. . . . .

Eine Leinwand nehmen.
Ein Zeichen darauf setzen.
Ein anderes Zeichen darauf setzen.

. . . . . .

Etwas machen.
Eine Verwendung dafür finden.
UND / ODER
Eine Funktion erfinden.
Einen Gegenstand dazu suchen.

Jasper Johns

(aus „Art and Literature", 4, 1965 übersetzt von Carlo Huber.)

Fig. 124. Jasper Johns from *Jasper Johns: Das graphische Werk, 1960–1970.* Texts by Jasper Johns, Johannes Cladders, and Carlo Huber (Mönchengladbach, Deutschland: Städtisches Museum Abteiberg, [1971]). Molded plastic rose, photomechanical reproduction. Edition: 120/550.

following pages:
Fig. 125. Jean Dubuffet from *La botte à nique.* Text by Jean Dubuffet ([Lausanne]: Albert Skira, 1973). Photomechanical reproduction. Edition: 3/200.

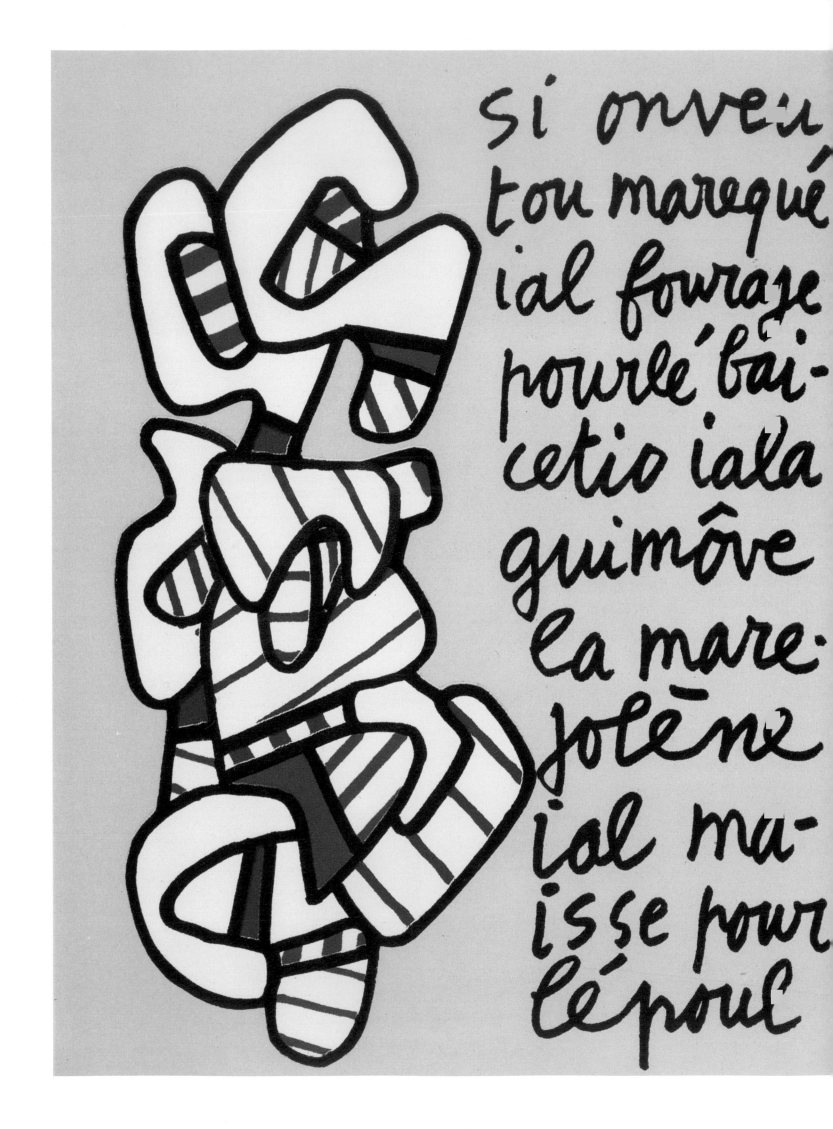

si on veu,
tou marequé
ial fouraze
pourlé bai-
cetio iala
guimôve
la mare-
jolène
ial ma-
isse pour
lé poul

iala paye.
pour lai
matla dai
sauleda
oprintan
alaure
selmoman
dla monté
dla saive
ia dla
pouciaire

Fig. 126. Jean Tinguely from *"Méta,"* text by Karl Gunnar Pontus Hultén (Paris: Pierre Horay, 1973; 1st ed. 1972). Photomechanical reproductions.

Fig. 127. Marcel Broodthaers from *Marcel Broodthaers: Sixteen Photographic Portraits, 1957–1967, and One Self-Portrait, 1974.* Text by Wieland Schmied (New York: Marian Goodman Gallery and Multiples, Inc., in collaboration with Sander Gallery, 1983). Gelatin silver print. Edition: 2/50.

Fig. 128. Wifredo Lam from *Contre une maison sèche.* Text by René Char ([Paris]: Jean Hugues, 1975). Etching with aquatint. Edition: 52/135.

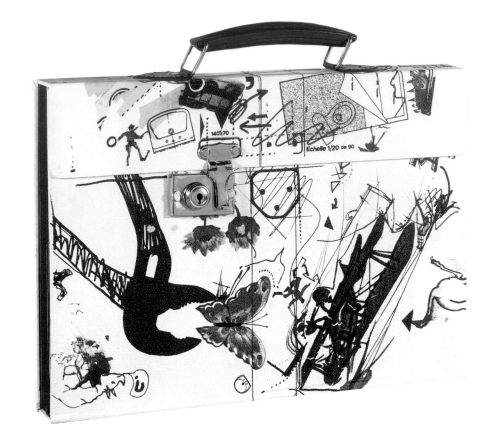

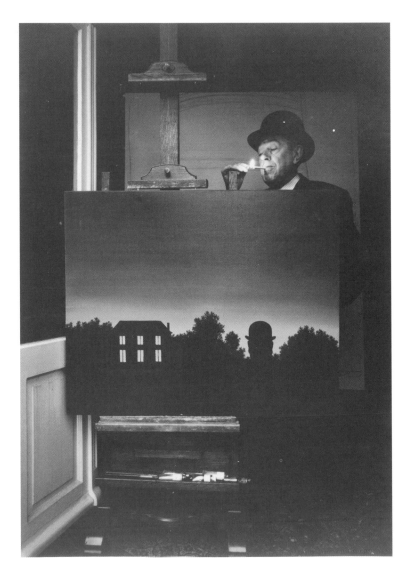

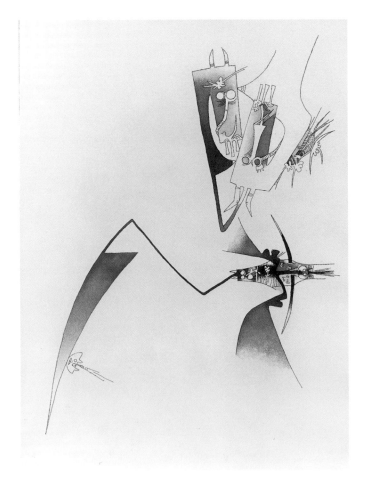

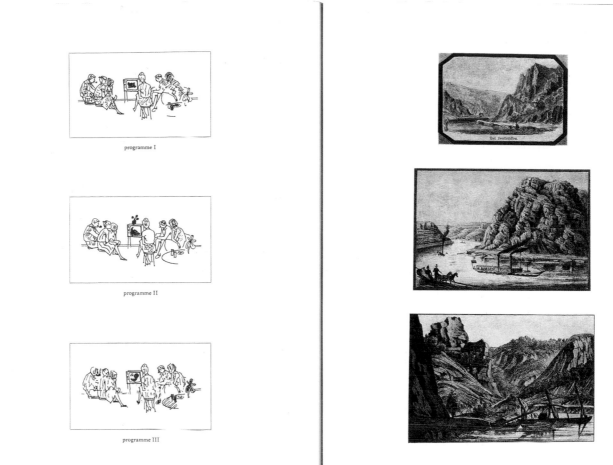

programme I

programme II

programme III

Fig. 129. Marcel Broodthaers from *En lisant la Lorelei. Wie ich die Lorelei gelesen habe.* Text by Marcel Broodthaers (München: Edition der Galerie Heiner Friedrich; Paris: Yvon Lambert, 1975). Photomechanical reproductions. Edition: 39/100.

Fig. 130. David Hockney from *The Blue Guitar; Etchings by David Hockney Who Was Inspired by Wallace Stevens Who Was Inspired by Pablo Picasso.* Text by Wallace Stevens (London: Petersburg Press, 1977). Photomechanical reproduction.

following pages:
Fig. 131. Anselm Kiefer from *Brünhilde schläft* (unique book) ([S.l.: Anselm Kiefer, 1980]). Photographs with added acrylic emulsion, paint, graphite, and chalk.

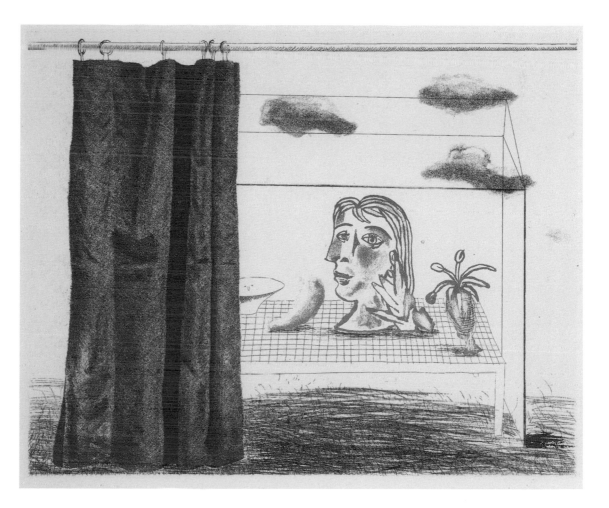

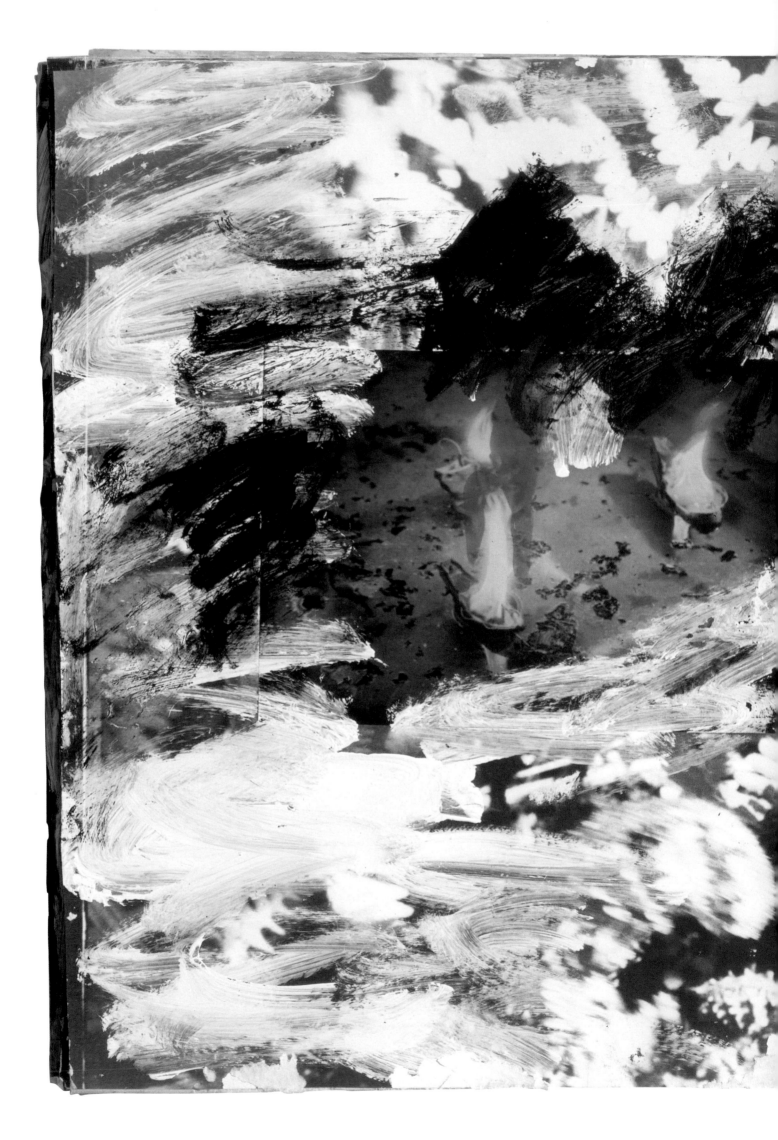

Fig. 132. Robert Rauschenberg from *Traces suspectes en surface*. Text by Alain Robbe-Grillet (West Islip, New York: Universal Limited Art Editions, [1978]). Color lithograph. Edition: 20/36.

Fig. 133. *Self Portrait in a Convex Mirror*. Text by John Ashbery (San Francisco: Arion Press, 1984). Stainless steel film canister with convex mirror. Edition: 75/150. Listed in Checklist under Various Artists.

Fig. 134. Arnulf Rainer from *Körpersprache* (München: Van de Loo und Prelinger, 1980). Photogravure overworked with drypoint, photomechanical reproduction (cover). Edition: 110/1,000.

Fig. 135. Emmett Williams from *Faustzeichnungen* (Berlin: Rainer, 1983). Photomechanical reproduction. Edition: 99/130.

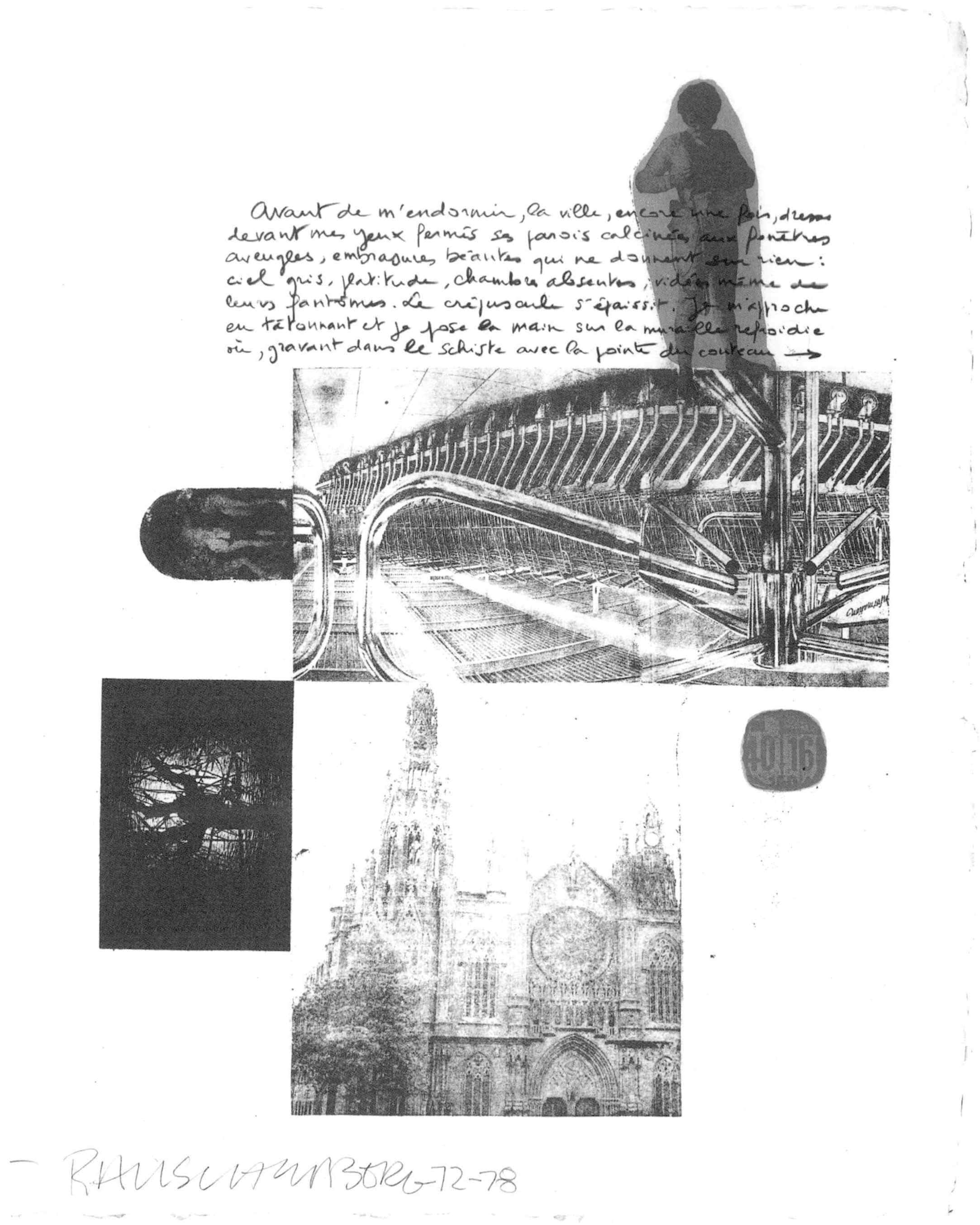

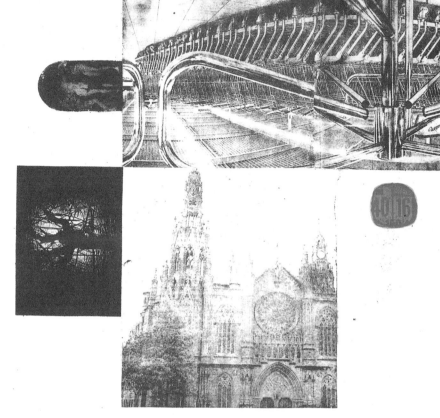

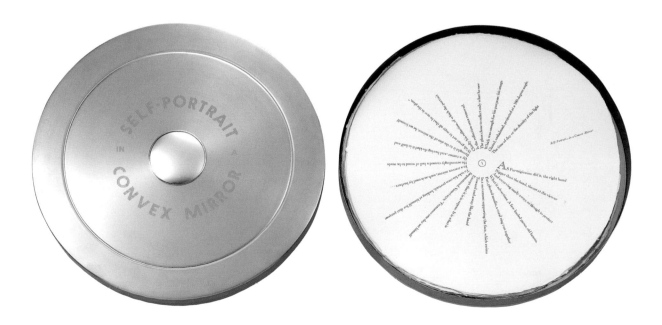

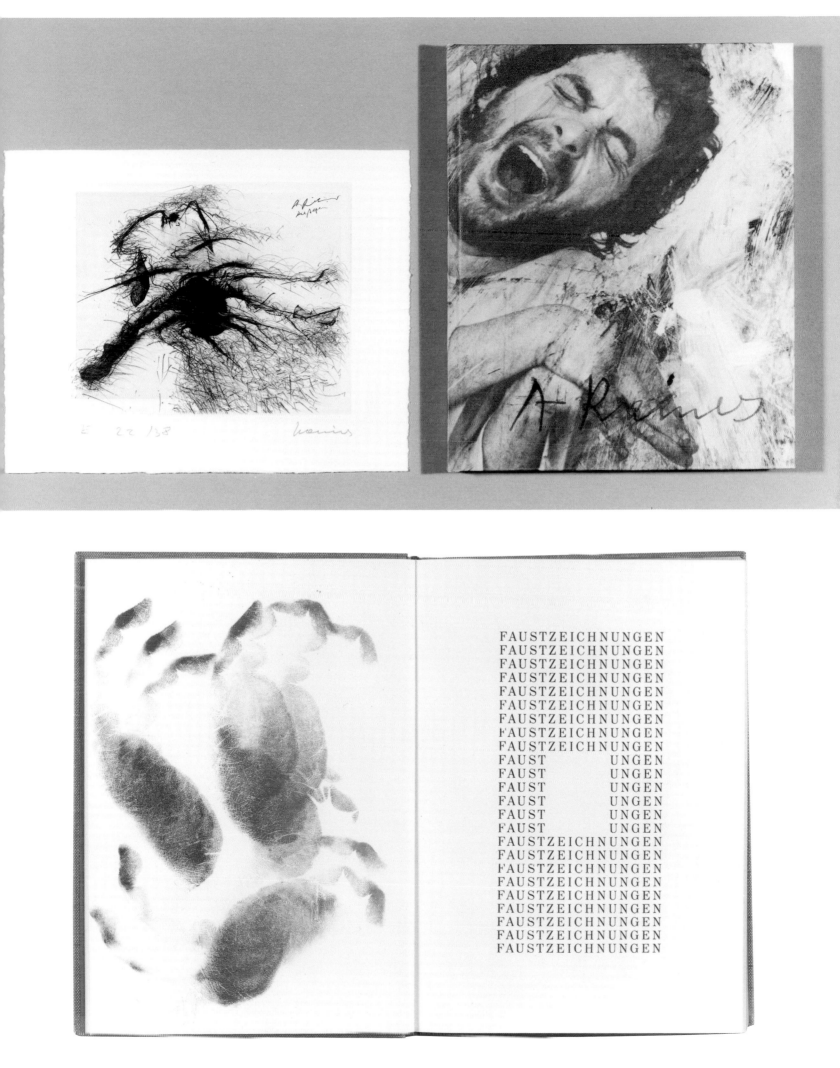

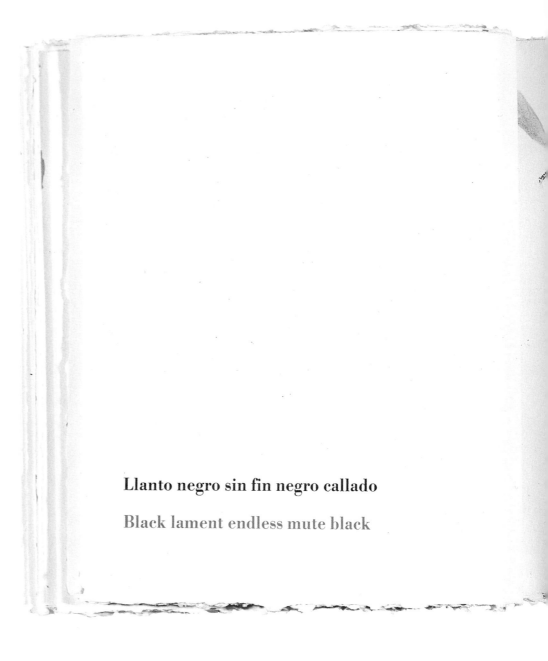

Llanto negro sin fin negro callado

Black lament endless mute black

Fig. 136. Robert Motherwell from *El Negro*. Text
by Rafael Alberti (Bedford Village, New York: Tyler
Graphics, 1983). Color lithograph. Edition: 39/51.

Fig. 137. Roz Chast from *Three Small Books: Mondo Boxo. The Small Pamphlet of Things. Somebody Goes to the White House, by Vera Lee Marlone, in Diary Form.* Text by Roz Chast ([New York]: Kathryn Markel, 1982). Line block reproductions.

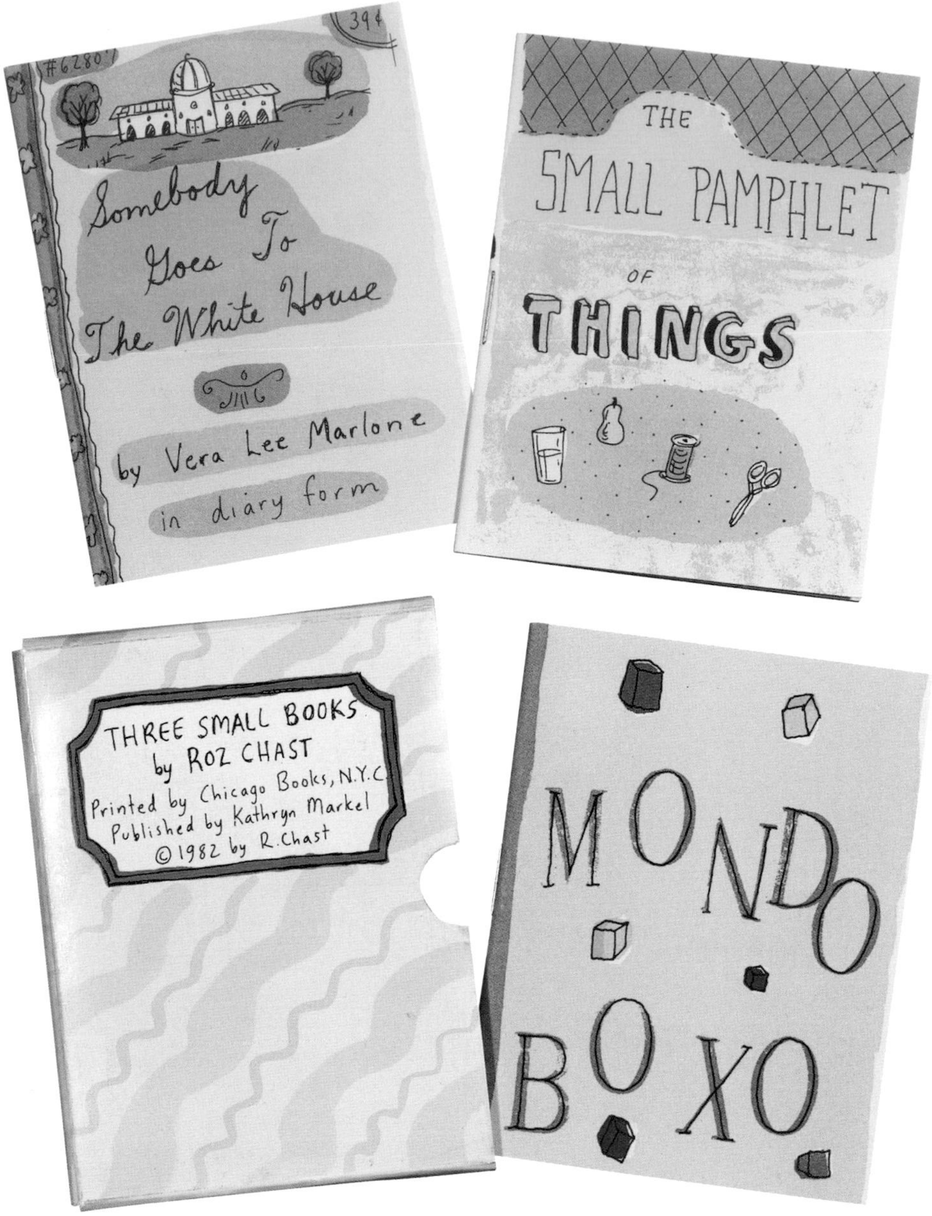

Fig. 138. Jörg Immendorff from *Grüsse von der Nordfront.* Text by A. R. Penck (München: Fred Jahn, 1982). Color linoleum cut. Edition: 2/30.

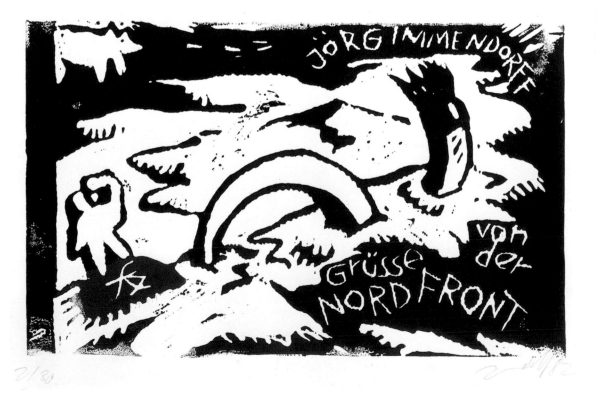

Fig. 139. A. R. Penck from
4 mm: Westkeller / Endstation
([S.l.]: Weltmelodie, 1983).
Photo-mechanical reproduction.

Fig. 140. Jasper Johns from
Poems. Text by Wallace Stevens
(San Francisco: Arion Press,
1985). Etching. Edition: 159/300.

following pages:
Fig. 141. Francesco Clemente
from *The Departure of the
Argonaut.* Text by Alberto
Savinio ([London]: Petersburg
Press, 1986). Color lithograph.
Edition: 64/200.

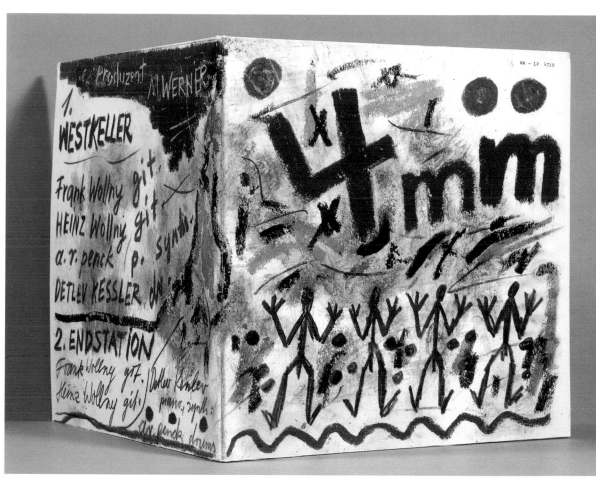

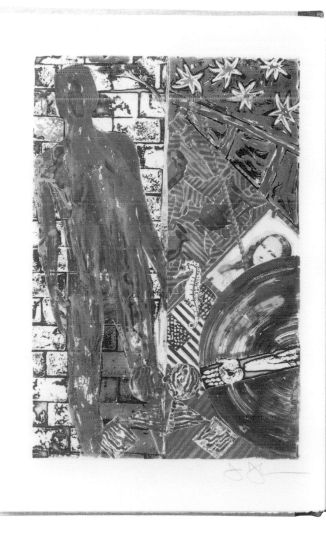

WALLACE STEVENS

POEMS

SELECTED AND WITH AN INTRODUCTION BY
HELEN VENDLER

THE ARION PRESS
SAN FRANCISCO
1985

phantoms glide by in a drama that is ripping the continents apart, its treacherous back is bent under the heavy stride of a hostile humanity ... in that smoke on the horizon ... in that fat steamer lethargically pulling out of the harbor which I can sight between the prongs of the masts on that battleship down there ...

Facts accumulate, signs become denser, reality is accentuated and, in the end, I have the feeling that I'm moving into a shadow; the shadow of a roof, the roof of a station, the station at Taranto!

I pack up my things and vacate the room where I've spent three days and two nights and it gives out a shriek at the loss. I step out of the coach — that is, I leave home for the last time — and, as if compelled by some desperate warning, I turn around to look at the train which has taken me this far ... Had I ever really gotten to know her properly during my stay within her flanks? ... It's as if I were seeing her for the first time: small, pathetic, lost among the enormous freight cars and powerful locomotives jamming the tracks, as if she had insinuated herself amidst all this grandness like some insulting intrusion, nearly crushed beneath the thundering arch of the trestle ... I don't have the kind of eyes that can cry for a train, *tout-de-même*! With my heart breaking, I walk down the ramp and enter the modern sector of the city. Everything is totally new to me, as if I'd thrown myself into an abyss. Held back by useless guardrails, I look about for a reference point of a more abstract nature, something of note on which to fix my mind, something dominant, characteristic, that municipal place in every city whose fame preceeds it and which attracts the arriving traveler like a magnet (St. Peter's in Rome, the Eiffel Tower in Paris, the Statue of Liberty in New York, *el palacio del gobernador* in Mexico City), which in this enormous armed buoy of a town is the *Bridge of Two Seas.*

So I head out, keep on walking and in fact come across a bridge. But what a disappointment! It can't be this steel bridge, lace-like and full of energy, which when it opens its embrace gives free flight to the naval fleet, and when it closes gathers all into its watery bowels. No: it's this stone bridge here, built like that other bridge, between two seas, but which is altogether stiff and bedraggled.

The magic of the new begins to spread and I easily slip into a sort of familiarity with my surroundings as my olfactory sense thrills to the strong odor of fried food mixed with the dull scent of algae, one of the most enjoyable qualities of port cities. This tangy mixture has always disturbed me, like the smell of a sawdust circus which used to trouble my childhood, or the trail of springtime that the armpits of certain woman leave behind in a fragrant wake, which so troubled my seething adolescence.

I cross the bridge and find myself facing a square whose name is taken from its fountains. Each new square invites one to take a look, so I make the rounds with my eyes, halting my gaze just opposite a white canvas booth on which large black letters are printed. This isn't the first time I've uncovered a link binding me in brotherhood to that unlucky Pinocchio – I really enjoy juggling acts and will go to any lengths to witness a puppet show. I get the impression that this canvas booth is advertising a magic show, and so I skip past the fountains, raise my nose to the letters and read the program: "Command Post for the Troops assigned to Albania and Macedonia." My nose plunges to my navel, lickity split! It takes its time rising again, since this show is continuous, and before my nose has the chance to buy a ticket to the "Troops of Macedonia" theater, my overwhelming instinct of self-preservation tells me to push off and find lodgings.

I knock on hotel doors – I go from the "Abyssinia" to the "Two Worlds," I go up to the "Sun" and down to the "Moon," then I run from the "Stag" to the "Horse," but to no avail. I feel like I'm being enveloped by a dark conspiracy, the *famuli* greet me with obvious hostility, even the chambermaids deny me bed and commode with a

Fig. 142. Timothy C. Ely from *Approach to the Site* (New York: Water Street Press, 1986). Color lithograph. Edition: 16/49.

Fig. 143. Mark Beard from *Utah Reader*. Text by Mark Beard (New York: Vincent FitzGerald & Company, 1986). Linoleum cut with hand color and collage. Edition: 18/40.

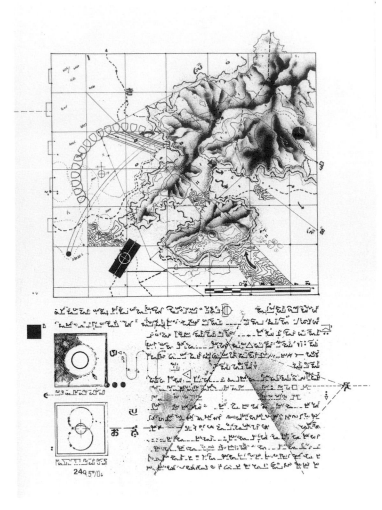

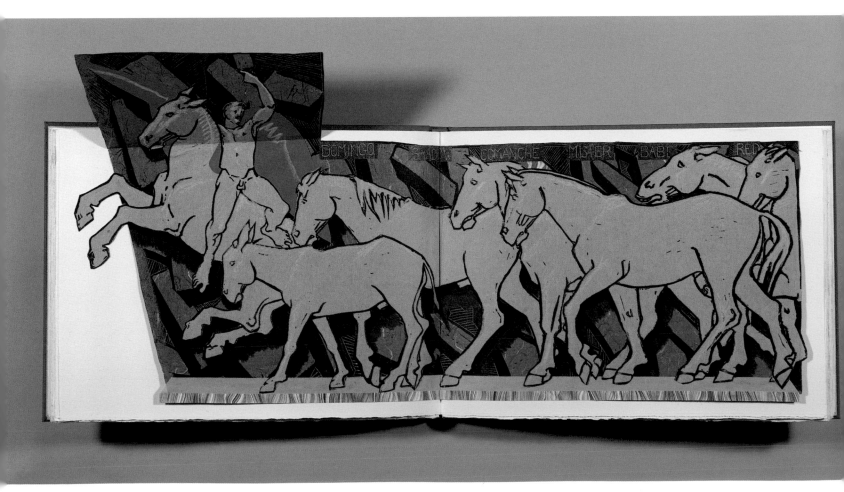

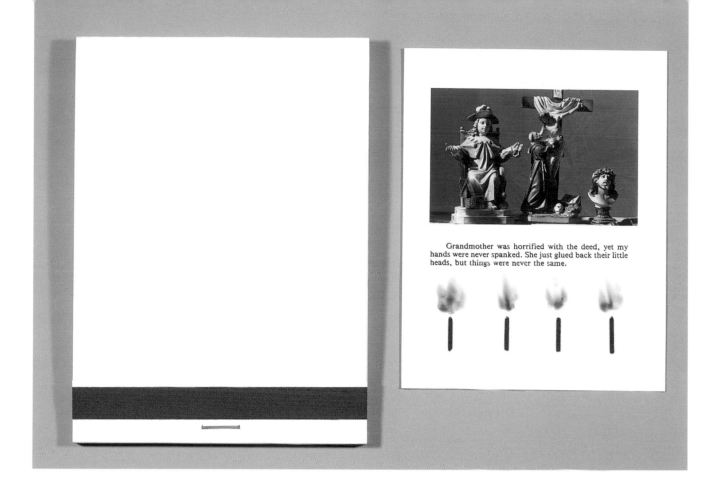

Grandmother was horrified with the deed, yet my hands were never spanked. She just glued back their little heads, but things were never the same.

Fig. 144. Celia Alvarez Muñoz from *Enlightenment #1* (Arlington, Texas: Enlightenment Press, 1982–87). Gelatin silver print with book matches and scorching. Edition 3/10

Fig. 145. Hermann Nitsch from *Die Arkitektur des Orgien Mysterien Theaters: Mappe I* (München: Fred Jahn, 1987). Etching reworked with tusche, tint, and stamping. Edition: 23/35.

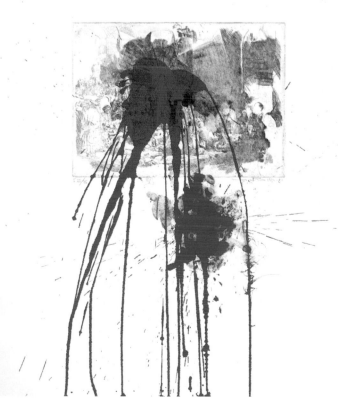

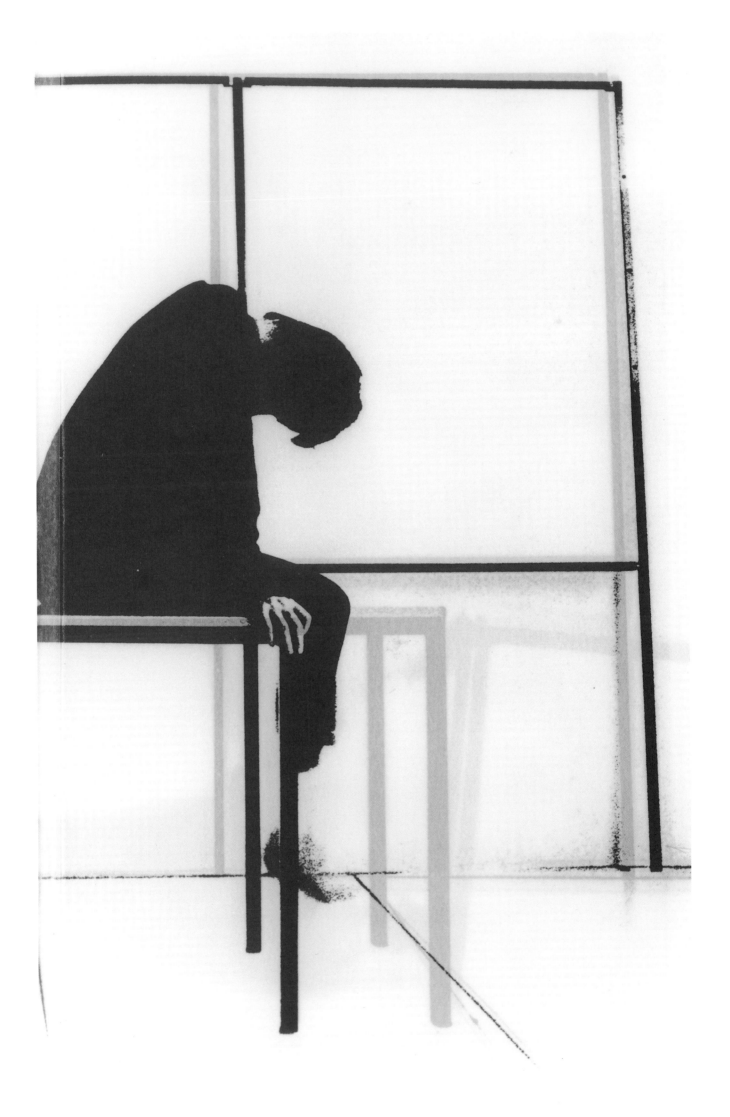

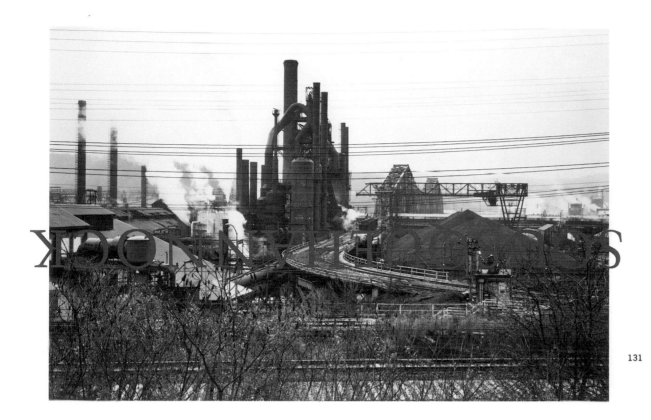

131

Fig. 146. Ines von Ketelhodt from *Konzept II* (Offenbach am Main, Deutschland: Unica T, 1989). Photocopies on Plexiglas and transparent paper. Edition: 8/30.

Fig. 147. Lothar Baumgarten from *Carbon*. Texts by Lothar Baumgarten and Michael Oppitz ([S.l.]: Pentti Kouri in conjunction with the Museum of Contemporary Art, Los Angeles, 1991). Photomechanical reproduction. Edition: unnumbered/1,750.

Fig. 148. Carla Rippey from *Five Afternoons in the Garden* ([S.l.: Carla Rippey, 1995]). Photomechanical reproduction. Edition: 3/10.

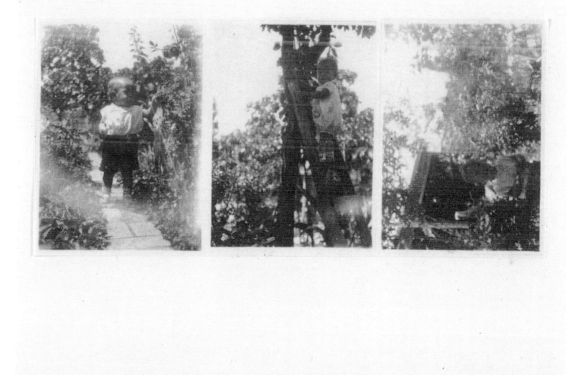

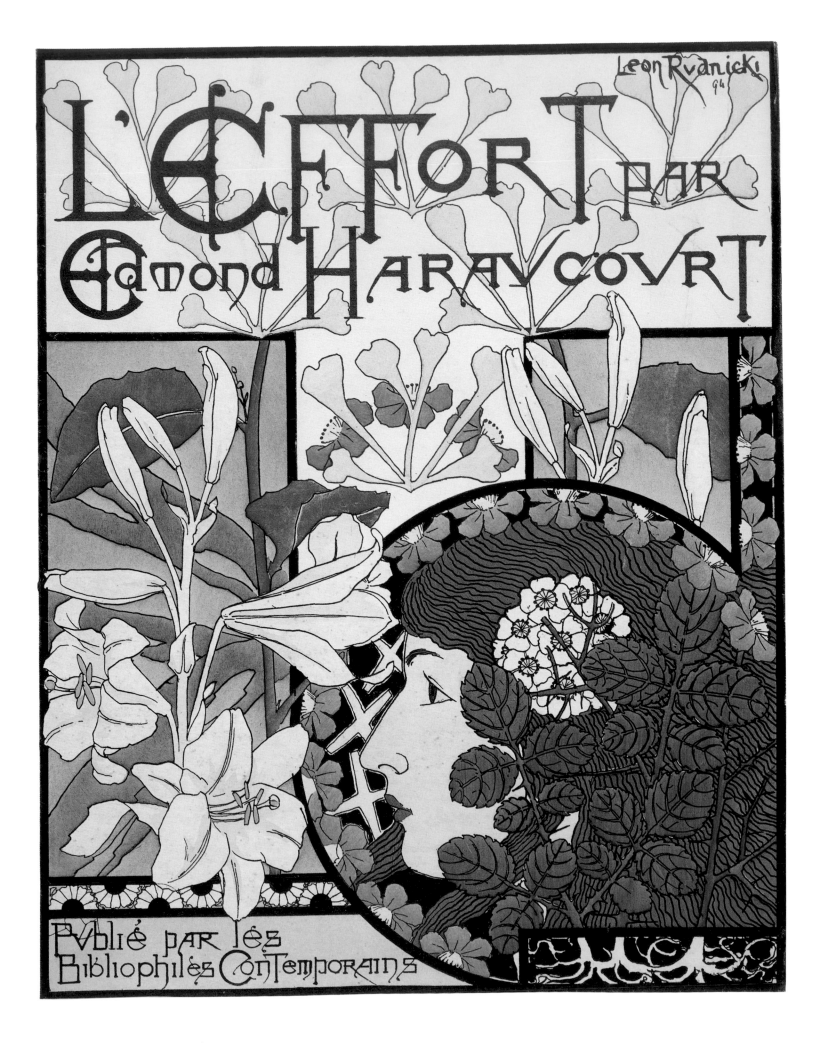

A Note about the Checklist

Fig. 149. Léon Rudnicki from *L'effort: La madone. L'antéchrist. L'immortalité. La fin du monde.* Texts by Edmond Haraucourt (Paris: Les sociétaires de l'Académie des beaux livres, Bibliophiles contemporains, 1894). Line block reproduction with added pochoir color. Edition: 97/180. Listed in Checklist under Various Artists.

This checklist offers concise citations for the more than 1,400 titles in the Bareiss Collection at the Toledo Museum of Art. Extensive cataloguing records for each book are available on a database that will be linked to the Museum's website in the future.

This checklist is arranged in three sections. The first includes books listed alphabetically by the artist's last name. Books including the work of up to three artists are listed under the first artist's name, with other artists' names cross-referenced. Books including the work of more than three artists are listed alphabetically by title under the heading "Various Artists." Both artists and authors who publish under a pseudonym are listed under that pseudonym, such as "Cply" rather than William Nelson Copley. Alternative name forms of artists are cross-referenced in the checklist.

Entry description:
Artist, Nationality, Dates
Title
Author, Nationality, Dates; Translator, Nationality, Dates
Place of publication: Publisher (Person responsible for publication), Date of publication
Number and medium(s) of works of art. Edition number/size of edition
Donor, Accession number
Bibliographic reference(s)
Illustration figure number

The title is transcribed from the title page, whenever possible. Square brackets are used only when we supply information not found in the book. The name of the city of publication is given in the language of the book, and the country name is sometimes added to further identify the location. If the place of publication is not known, "s.l." is used (*sine loco* or without a place). If the publisher is not known "s.n." is used (*sine nome* or without a name). The edition is noted in its simplest form; a complete edition statement will be available on our database.

The second section lists books without artwork or an artist's contribution and so is arranged alphabetically by title.

The third section is a list of sixteen additional books that were already in the collection of the Toledo Museum of Art when the Bareiss Collection was donated. The duplicate books were returned to the Bareiss family, but we wish to recognize them as part of the original gift.

Periodicals are listed under "Various Artists" unless we hold only one issue or if the original art in each issue features one artist, such as the periodical *Derrière le miroir.* In this case, the issue is listed under the individual artist. In addition, if a particular artist is responsible for the majority of issues, the complete set is listed under that artist, with added names cross-referenced, such as A. R. Penck's *Krater und Wolke.* Monographic series titles have not been listed unless the entire run is catalogued under that title; in such a case, titles are individually described with information on artists and mediums.

An index to authors and publishers follows the checklist.

Only nine bibliographic references are included in this checklist. Additional references will be available on the collection database.

Castleman
Riva Castleman, *A Century of Artists Books* (New York: The Museum of Modern Art, 1994).

Drucker
Johanna Drucker, *The Century of Artists' Books* (New York: Granary Books, 1995).

Garvey
Eleanor M. Garvey, *The Artist & the Book, 1860–1960* (Boston: Museum of Fine Arts, 1961).

Hogben
Carol Hogben and Rowan Watson, editors, *From Manet to Hockney: Modern Artists' Illustrated Books* (London: Victoria & Albert Museum, 1985).

Johnson
Robert Flynn Johnson, *Artists' Books in a Modern Era 1870–2000* (San Francisco: Fine Arts Museums of San Francisco, 2001).

Phillips
Elizabeth Phillips and Tony Zwicker, *The American Livre de Peintre* (New York: Grolier Club, 1993).

Strachan
W. J. Strachan, *The Artist and the Book in France, The 20th Century Livre d'Artiste* (New York: George Wittenborn, 1969).

Symmes
Marilyn F. Symmes, *The Bareiss Collection of Modern Illustrated Books from Toulouse-Lautrec to Kiefer* (Toledo: The Toledo Museum of Art, 1985).

Wheeler
Monroe Wheeler, *Painters and Sculptors as Illustrators* (New York: The Museum of Modern Art, 1946).

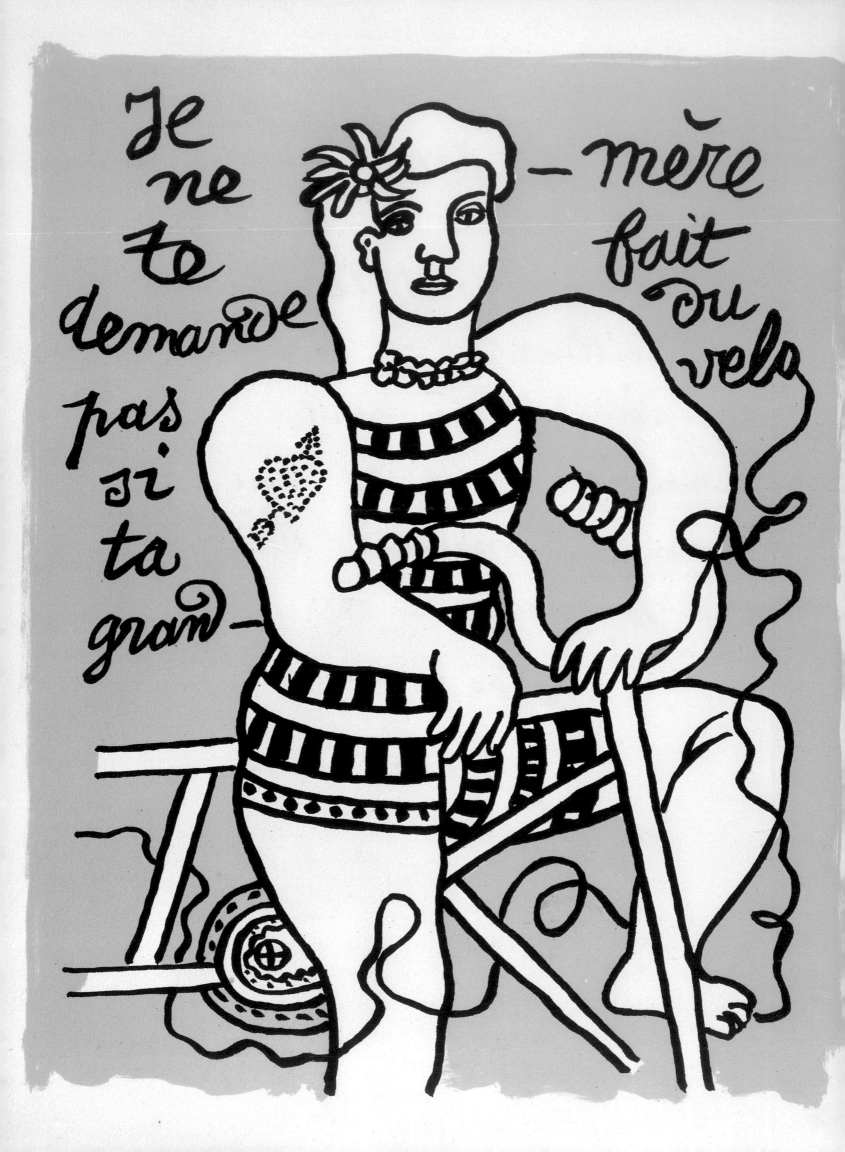

Checklist

Ivor Abrahams, British, born 1935
Oxford Gardens: A Sketchbook
London: Bernard Jacobson, 1977
One color screen print, photomechanical reproductions.
Edition: 1,000/1,000
Gift of Molly and Walter Bareiss, 1984.181

Josef Albers, American (born Germany), 1888–1976
Poems and Drawings
Text by Josef Albers
New Haven, CT: Readymade Press, 1958
Line block reproductions
Gift of Molly and Walter Bareiss, 1984.182

L. Alcopley (Alfred Lewin Copley), American (born Germany), 1910–1992
Listening to Heidegger and Hisamatsu
Text by L. Alcopley; Martin Heidegger, German, 1889–1976; Shin'ichi Hisamatsu, Japanese, 1889–1980
Kyoto: Bokubi Press (Shiryu Morita), 1963
Photomechanical reproductions. Edition: 344/800
Gift of Molly and Walter Bareiss, 1985.74

Pierre Alechinsky, Belgian, active France, born 1927
Moi qui j'avais
Text by Christian Dotremont, Belgian, 1922–1979
Paris: G. Girard, 1961
One ink drawing with coffee wash, one color lithograph, line block reproductions. Edition: 103/300
Gift of Molly and Walter Bareiss, 1984.183

Les tireurs de langue
Text by Amos Kenan, born 1927
Torino: Edizione d'Arte Fratelli Pozzo; Paris: Guy Le Prat, [1962?]
Photomechanical reproductions
Gift of Molly and Walter Bareiss, 1984.184

À la gare
Text by Amos Kenan, born 1927
Milano: Edizioni d'Arte Grafica Uno (Giorgio Upiglio), 1964
10 color etchings, plus suite of 10 color etchings.
Edition: 35/110
Gift of Molly and Walter Bareiss, 1984.185

Carré blanc
Text by Joyce Mansour, active France, born 1928
Paris: Éditions du soleil, Le soleil noir, 1965
5 color etchings. Edition: 67/2,705
Gift of Molly and Walter Bareiss, 1984.186

Le tout venant
Text by Pierre Alechinsky
Paris: Galerie de France, [1966]
Photomechanical reproductions. Edition: unnumbered/3,000
Gift of Molly and Walter Bareiss, 1984.187

Pierre Alechinsky: 20 Jahre Impressionen
Text by Yvon Taillandier, French, born 1926
München: Galerie van de Loo, 1967
One lithograph (jacket), photomechanical reproductions.
Edition: unnumbered/2,000
Gift of Molly and Walter Bareiss, 1984.188

Minutes
Venezia: Cavallino, 1967
Photomechanical reproductions. Edition: 24/200
Gift of Molly and Walter Bareiss, 1984.189
Fig. 109

Le rêve de l'ammonite
Text by Michel Butor, French, born 1926
[Montpellier, France]: Fata Morgana, [1975]
10 color lift-ground aquatints, 29 lithographs.
Edition: 66/155
Gift of Molly and Walter Bareiss, 1984.190
Ref.: Castleman p. 195

Marc Allégret, French, 1900–1973
Voyage au Congo suivi du Retour du Tchad
Text by André Gide, French, 1869–1951
Paris: Librairie Gallimard, 1929

Photomechanical reproductions. Edition: 34/1,500
Gift of Molly and Walter Bareiss, 1984.518

Vivian Alper, American; **Lynda Kalman,** American
Pratt Graphic Talent 1965
Text by Jacob Landau, American, born 1917
Brooklyn, NY: Pratt Adlib Press, 1965
One color letterpress print, one linoleum cut (?), photomechanical reproductions
Gift of Molly and Walter Bareiss, 1984.1219

Otmar Alt, German, born 1940
Pic-nic
Text by Herbert Asmodi, German, born 1923
München: Gernot von Pape, Edition X (Fred Jahn), 1968
9 color screen prints. Edition: 53/100
Gift of Molly and Walter Bareiss, 1984.191

Gerhard Altenbourg, German, 1926–1989
Ein Lauschender auf blauer Au
Text by Theodor Däubler, Swiss, 1876–1934
München: "Graphikum" (Heinrich Mock), 1963
One lithograph, photomechanical reproductions.
Edition: 12/300
Gift of Molly and Walter Bareiss, 1984.192

Carl Andre, American, born 1935
Carl Andre
Text by Carl Andre; Johannes Cladders, German, born 1924
Mönchengladbach, Deutschland: Städtisches Museum Abteiberg (Johannes Cladders), 1968
Cloth table runner with screen-printed or photolithographed text. Edition: 389/660
Gift of Molly and Walter Bareiss, 1984.193

Carl Andre; Ana Mendieta, American (born Cuba), 1948–1985
Pietre / Foglie
Roma: Edizioni R. R. Bulla (Romolo and Rosalba Bulla), 1984
20 transfer lithographs (10 by Andre, 10 by Mendieta).
Edition: 24/40
Molly and Walter Bareiss Art Fund, 1988.35

Horst Antes, German, born 1936
Horst Antes, Bilder aus Florenz und Rom
Köln: Galerie der Spiegel, 1963
7 lithographs, most in colors, photomechanical reproductions. Edition: unnumbered/250
Gift of Molly and Walter Bareiss, 1984.194

Buch der Feste
Text by Walter Euler, 1896–1975
[Köln]: Galerie der Spiegel, 1964
One ink drawing, mimeographs (one with added ink).
Edition: 24/48
Gift of Molly and Walter Bareiss, 1984.195

Stierstädter Gartenbuch
Text by Dieter Hoffmann, born 1934
Stierstadt im Taunus, Deutschland: Eremiten-Presse, 1964
30 relief prints. Edition: 153/300
Gift of Molly and Walter Bareiss, 1984.196

Horst Antes: Radierungen zu siebzehn Gedichten von Cesare Pavese
Text by Cesare Pavese, Italian, 1908–1950
München: Galerie Stangl, [1966]
21 etchings, plus one canceled zinc plate. Edition: 12/70
Gift of Molly and Walter Bareiss, 1984.202

Original-Prägung von Horst Antes: (Figur)
Basel: Ernst Beyeler, 1969
Etching in blind with added embossing. Edition: 250/380
Gift of Molly and Walter Bareiss, 1984.197

Ratschläge für einen jungen Dichter
Text by Max Jacob, French, 1876–1944
München: Kösel-Verlag (Friedhelm Kemp), 1969
Photomechanical reproductions. Edition: unnumbered/40
Gift of Molly and Walter Bareiss, 1984.198

Fig. 150. Fernand Léger from *Cirque*. Text by Fernand Léger (Paris: Tériade, 1950). Color lithograph. Edition: 28/280.

Horst Antes: Ausstellung Bilder, Zeichnungen, Keramik und Plastik
München: Galerie Stangl, 1972
Photomechanical reproductions. Edition: 434/800
Gift of Molly and Walter Bareiss, 1984.199

Für Billy und Alan Davie
Venezia: Cavallino, 1973
Photomechanical reproductions, with collaged fabric and paper elements. Edition: 119/200
Gift of Molly and Walter Bareiss, 1984.200

Horst Antes '75
München: Galerie Stangl, 1975
One lithograph, photomechanical reproductions
Gift of Molly and Walter Bareiss, 1984.201

Horst Antes (see also listing under HAP Grieshaber)

Garo Z. Antreasian, American, born 1922
Fragments: 12 Lithographs by Garo Z. Antreasian
Los Angeles: Tamarind Lithography Workshop, 1961
14 lithographs, including title page and colophon, some in colors (one with added gold leaf and collage). Edition: 10/12
Gift of Molly and Walter Bareiss, 1984.203a–n

Ikuma Arishima, Japanese, 1882–1973
Cent phrases pour eventails
Text by Paul Claudel, French, 1868–1955
Tokyo: La maison Koshiba, 1927
Lithographs. Edition: 64/200
Gift of Molly and Walter Bareiss, 1984.352a–c

Arman (Armand Fernandez), American (born France), born 1928
Cardiogramme
Text by Jacques Lepage, French
Paris: Aux dépens d'un amateur, 1966
2 monoprints (one printed on x-ray film), photomechanical reproductions. Edition: 44/60
Gift of Molly and Walter Bareiss, 1984.204

Jean (Hans) Arp, French (born Alsace), 1887–1966
Phantastische Gebete
Text by Richard Huelsenbeck, German, 1892–1974
Zürich: Collection Dada, 1916
7 woodcuts
Gift of Molly and Walter Bareiss, 1984.205

Die Wolkenpumpe
Text by Jean (Hans) Arp
Hannover: Paul Steegemann, 1920
One woodcut (wrappers)
Gift of Molly and Walter Bareiss, 1984.207

Cinéma calendrier du coeur abstrait: maisons
Text by Tristan Tzara, French (born Romania), 1896–1963
Paris: Au sans pareil, 1920
19 woodcuts. Edition: 78/150
Gift of Molly and Walter Bareiss, 1984.208
Ref.: Garvey cat. 3, Hogben cat. 56, Symmes cat. 1
Fig. 39

La sphère du sable
Text by Georges Hugnet, French, 1906–1974
Paris: Robert-J. Godet, 1943
Line block reproductions. Edition: 161/176
Gift of Molly and Walter Bareiss, 1984.210
Fig. 38

Temps troué
Text by Camille Bryen, French, 1907–1977
Paris: Le soleil noir, 1951
6 woodcuts, photomechanical reproduction, line block reproductions. Edition: unnumbered/320
Gift of Molly and Walter Bareiss, 1984.212

Multiple femme: poèmes
Text by Yvan Goll, French, 1891–1950
Paris: Caractères (Bruno Durocher), 1956
8 woodcuts, line block reproduction (wrappers). Edition: unnumbered/50
Gift of Molly and Walter Bareiss, 1984.213

Le voilier dans la forêt
Texts by Jean (Hans) Arp; Paul Éluard, French, 1895–1952
Paris: Louis Broder, 1957
6 color woodcuts. Edition: 99/115
Gift of Molly and Walter Bareiss, 1984.214
Ref.: Garvey cat. 5, Strachan p. 325

Mondsand
Text by Jean (Hans) Arp
Pfullingen, Deutschland: Günther Neske, 1959
7 etchings. Edition: 89/300
Gift of Molly and Walter Bareiss, 1984.215

Vers le blanc infini
Text by Jean (Hans) Arp
Lausanne and Paris: Rose des vents, 1960
8 soft-ground etchings. Edition: 41/499
Gift of Molly and Walter Bareiss, 1984.216
Ref.: Johnson cat. 138

Arp
Text by Gaston Puel, French, born 1924
Veilhes, Tarn, France: G. P. (Gaston Puel), 1966
4 color linoleum cuts. Edition: XIX/XL
Gift of Molly and Walter Bareiss, 1984.217

Jean (Hans) Arp; Marcel Duchamp, American (born France), 1887–1968; **Francis Picabia,** French, 1878–1953
691
Texts by various authors; edited by Pierre André Benoit, French, 1924–1993
Alès, France: PAB (Pierre André Benoit), 1961
One paper collage (Arp), photomechanical reproductions, line block reproduction. Edition: 47/90
Gift of Molly and Walter Bareiss, 1984.1290

Jean (Hans) Arp; Raoul Hausmann, Austrian, active Germany, France, 1886–1971
Ultimistischer Almanach
Texts by various authors; edited by Klaus M. Rarisch
Köln: Wolfgang Hake, 1965
2 woodcuts, line block reproduction (cover). Edition: 484/1,000
Gift of Molly and Walter Bareiss, 1984.1319a–c

Jean (Hans) Arp; Walter Helbig, German, active Switzerland, 1878–1965
Moderner Bund: Zweite Ausstellung
Zürich: Kunsthaus, 1912
3 woodcuts, photomechanical reproductions, line block reproductions. Edition: "Gratis Exemplar"
Gift of Molly and Walter Bareiss, 1984.1293

Jean (Hans) Arp; Walter Helbig; Arthur Segal, Romanian, 1875–1944
Ausstellung: H. Arp, H. Berger, E. Egger, W. Helbig, A. Segal
[Zürich]: Kunstsalon Wolfsberg, [1919?]
Photomechanical reproductions
Gift of Molly and Walter Bareiss, 1984.206b

Jean (Hans) Arp; Marcel Janco, Israeli (born Romania), 1895–1984; **Hans Richter,** German, active United States, Switzerland, 1888–1976
Ausstellung die neue Kunst
Text by W. Jollos, 1886–19??
Zürich: Kunstsalon Wolfsberg, 1918
4 woodcuts (2 by Arp, one each by Janco and Richter)
Gift of Molly and Walter Bareiss, 1984.206a

Jean (Hans) Arp; Wassily Kandinsky, French (born Russia), 1866–1944; **Leo Leuppi,** Swiss, 1893–1972
Onze peintres vus par Arp
Text by Jean (Hans) Arp
Zürich: Editions Girsberger, 1949
3 color woodcuts (one each by Arp, Kandinsky, Leuppi), 13 collotypes, line block reproductions. Edition: 11/200
Gift of Molly and Walter Bareiss, 1984.211

Jean (Hans) Arp; Sophie Taeuber-Arp, Swiss, 1889–1943
De nos oiseaux: poèmes
Text by Tristan Tzara, French (born Romania), 1896–1963
Paris: Éditions Kra, [1929] (1st ed. 1923)

10 woodcuts (2 by or after Taeuber-Arp)
Gift of Molly and Walter Bareiss, 1984.209

Jean (Hans) Arp (see also listings under Various Artists, *XXe siècle; Additional Books*)

Christian Ludwig Attersee, Austrian, born 1941
Komm mit nach Österreich: ein Führer durch Österreich für ausserirdische Wesen, Wien 1965
Text by Gerhard Rühm, Austrian, born 1930
Grenchen, Schweiz: Edition Konus-Presse, 1976
9 color screen prints, photomechanical reproductions, line block reproduction. Edition: 99/390
Gift of Molly and Walter Bareiss, 1984.218

Ay-O, Japanese, active United States, born 1931
Ouzel
Text by Ay-O
Tokyo: Chikumasyobo Publishing, 1972
Drawings, collotypes, photomechanical reproductions, line block reproductions, hand-coloring, rubber-stamping, embossing, collage. Edition: 140/unknown
Gift of Molly and Walter Bareiss, 1984.219

Giorgio Azzaroni, Italian, born 1939
I Lembi Scoloriti ma Sempre Sfarzosi delle Terre ad Oriente. Suoni della Pioggia dell'Est
Text by Giorgio Azzaroni
Venezia: Cavallino, 1968
One color lithograph. Edition: 142/200
Gift of Molly and Walter Bareiss, 1984.220

Enrico Baj, Italian, active France, born 1924
Dames et généraux
Text by Benjamin Péret, French, 1899–1959
Paris: Berggruen; Milano: Schwarz, 1964
10 soft-ground etchings with aquatint and added collage. Edition: 21/100
Gift of Molly and Walter Bareiss, 1984.221

Pochette militaire
Text by André Pieyre de Mandiargues, French, 1909–1991
Paris: Berggruen, 1965
One collotype, photomechanical reproductions
Gift of Molly and Walter Bareiss, 1984.222

L'intérieur
Text by Edoardo Sanguineti, Italian, born 1930
Milano: Edizioni d'Arte Grafica Uno (Giorgio Upiglio), 1966
6 color aquatints, 4 color etchings. Edition: 81/125
Gift of Molly and Walter Bareiss, 1984.223

Les incongruités monumentales
Text by André Pieyre de Mandiargues, French, 1909–1991
Paris: Michel Cassé, 1967
One collage with fabric, bottle caps, added paint; 33 hand-colored lithographs. Edition: 5/100
Gift of Molly and Walter Bareiss, 1984.224
Fig. 111

Julius Baltazar, French, born 1949
Colloque des mouches
Text by Michel Butor, French, born 1926
Nice: J. Matarasso, 1980
5 drypoint engravings with embossing. Edition: 37/63
Gift of Molly and Walter Bareiss, 1984.225

Ballade à toute vitesse
Text by Michel Butor, French, born 1926
Ivry and Nice: [Julius] Baltazar, 1981
One drypoint with added color pencil. Edition: 3/10
Gift of Molly and Walter Bareiss, 1984.326

Heinz Balthes, German, born 1937
Freizeitkatalog
Text by Hubert Gersch, German
Stierstadt im Taunus, Deutschland: Eremiten-Presse, 1965
30 color woodcuts. Edition: 100/250
Gift of Molly and Walter Bareiss, 1984.226

Eduard Bargheer, German, 1901–1979
Ischia: 10 Farblithographien

Stuttgart: Galerie Valentien, 1965
10 color lithographs. Edition: 40/120
Gift of Molly and Walter Bareiss, 1984.227a–j

Ernst Barlach, German, 1870–1938
Der Tote Tag: Drama in fünf Akten
Text by Ernst Barlach
Berlin: Paul Cassirer, 1918 (1st ed. 1912)
Line block reproductions
Gift of Molly and Walter Bareiss, 1984.228
Ref.: Garvey cat. 7

Der Kopf
Text by Reinhold von Walter, German, 1882–1956
Berlin: Paul Cassirer, 1919
11 woodcuts
Gift of Molly and Walter Bareiss, 1984.229
Ref.: Symmes cat. 2

Die echten Sedemunds
Text by Ernst Barlach
Berlin: Paul Cassirer, 1920
Photomechanical reproductions
Gift of Molly and Walter Bareiss, 1984.230

Walpurgisnacht
Text by Johann Wolfgang von Goethe, German, 1749–1832
Berlin: Paul Cassirer, 1923
20 woodcuts "printed by galvanotype" from the original woodblocks
Gift of Molly and Walter Bareiss, 1985.75
Ref.: Wheeler p. 97

Die Sündflut: Drama in 5 Teilen
Text by Ernst Barlach
Berlin: Paul Cassirer, 1925 (1st ed. 1924?)
Photomechanical reproductions
Gift of Molly and Walter Bareiss, 1984.231

Der arme Vetter: Drama in fünf Akten
Text by Ernst Barlach
Berlin: Paul Cassirer, 1926 (1st ed. 1918)
Photomechanical reproduction, line block reproduction (cover)
Gift of Molly and Walter Bareiss, 1984.232
Ref.: Garvey cat. 8, Wheeler p. 97

Zeichnungen zum "Michael Kohlhaas"
Berlin: Friends of Ernst Barlach (Ulrich Riemerschmidt), 1940
52 collotypes, plus suite of 12 collotypes. Edition: 510/1,000
Gift of Molly and Walter Bareiss, 1984.233

Maurice Barraud, Swiss, 1889–1954 or 1955
La bohème et mon cœur
Text by Francis Carco, French, 1886–1958
Genève: Éditions du milieu du monde, 1943
11 mixed etchings. Edition: 184/299
Gift of Molly and Walter Bareiss, 1984.234

Georg Baselitz, German, born 1938
Walter Bareiss Ex Libris
Unpublished, 1974
Etching. Edition: unnumbered/2,000
Gift of Molly and Walter Bareiss, 1990.96
Fig. 1

Die Gesänge des Maldoror
Text by comte de Lautréamont (Isidore Ducasse), French, 1847–1870; translation by Ré Soupault, French, 1901–1996
München: Rogner & Bernhard, 1976
Photomechanical reproductions
Gift of Molly and Walter Bareiss, 1984.235
Ref.: Symmes cat. 4
Fig. 26

Georg Baselitz
Texts by Carla Schulz-Hoffmann; Gunther Gercken; Johannes Gachnang, German, born 1939
München: Galerieverein München e.V., Staatsgalerie moderner Kunst, 1976
Photomechanical reproductions
Gift of Molly and Walter Bareiss, 1984.236

Georg Baselitz: Zeichnungen zum Strassenbild
Text by Heribert Heere
Köln: Galerie Michael Werner, 1982
One linoleum cut, photomechanical reproductions.
Edition: 47/50
Gift of Molly and Walter Bareiss, 1984.237

"Sächsische Motive"
Berlin: Rainer in association with Berliner Künstlerprogramm des Deutschen Akademischen Austauschdienstes (Rainer Pretzell), 1985
Photomechanical reproductions. Edition: unnumbered/1,300
Gift of Molly and Walter Bareiss, 1987.60

Georg Baselitz (see also listing under A. R. Penck)

Leonard Baskin, American, 1922–2000
A Poem Called The Tunning of Elynour Rummynge, the Famous Ale-Wife of England
Text by John Skelton, British, 1463–1529
Worcester, [MA]: Gehenna Press (Leonard Baskin), 1953
15 color wood-engravings. Edition: 78/118
Gift of Molly and Walter Bareiss, 1984.238

Blake and the Youthful Ancients
Text by Bennett Schiff
Northampton, MA: Gehenna Press (Leonard Baskin), 1956
19 wood-engravings. Edition: 21/50
Gift of Molly and Walter Bareiss, 1984.239

Voyages: Six Poems from White Buildings
Text by Hart Crane, American, 1899–1932
New York: The Museum of Modern Art (Monroe Wheeler), 1957
7 wood-engravings, some in color, one woodcut.
Edition: 428/975
Gift of Molly and Walter Bareiss, 1984.240
Ref.: Castleman p. 204, Garvey cat. 13, Phillips cat. 4

A Passover Haggadah
Text by W. Gunther Plaut, born 1912
[New York]: Grossman Publishers, Viking Press, 1974
Photomechanical reproductions
Gift of Molly and Walter Bareiss, 1984.242

Leonard Baskin; Thomas Bewick, British, 1753–1828
An ABC with Best Wishes for 1958
[Northampton, MA: Gehenna Press (Leonard Baskin), 1957]
10 wood-engravings (5 by Bewick, 3 by Baskin, 2 by anonymous engravers). Edition: unnumbered/500
Gift of Molly and Walter Bareiss, 1984.241

Leonard Baskin (see also listing under Additional Books)

Willi Baumeister, German, 1889–1955
The Tempest
Text by William Shakespeare, British, 1564–1616
Stuttgart: Gerd Hatje, [1946]
One lithograph, 33 collotypes, line block reproduction.
Edition: 85/500
Gift of Molly and Walter Bareiss, 1984.243

Willi Baumeister: 8 Original-Lithos
[S.l.]: Alfred Eichorn, [1947?]
8 color lithographs, photomechanical reproduction (cover)
Gift of Molly and Walter Bareiss, 1984.244a–h

Lothar Baumgarten, German, born 1944
Die Namen der Bäume: Hylaea
Texts by various authors
Eindhoven, Nederland: Stedelijk van Abbemuseum, 1982
One photograph, photomechanical reproductions. Edition: 111/240
Gift of Molly and Walter Bareiss, 1987.277a–b

Makunaíma
Text by Alejo Carpentier, 1904–1980
New York: Marian Goodman Gallery, 1987
Photomechanical reproductions. Edition: unnumbered/950
Gift of Molly and Walter Bareiss, 1988.106

Carbon
Texts by Lothar Baumgarten; Michael Oppitz, active Germany, Switzerland, born 1942
[S.l.]: Pentti Kouri in conjunction with the Museum of Contemporary Art, Los Angeles, 1991
Photomechanical reproductions. Edition: unnumbered/1,750
Molly and Walter Bareiss Art Fund, 1993.15
Fig. 147

Thomas Bayrle, German, born 1937; **Bernhard Jäger,** German, born 1935
Gesichter
Stierstadt im Taunus, Deutschland: Eremiten-Presse, 1962
12 color lithographs. Edition: 51/100
Gift of Molly and Walter Bareiss, 1984.245

1–10
Text by Dietrich Mahlow, born 1920
Hannover: Galerie Dieter Brusberg, 1964
17 color lithographs. Edition: 5/30
Gift of Molly and Walter Bareiss, 1984.247a–l

Bayrle & Jäger: Gulliver-Presse
Text by Franz Mon, born 1926
München: Galerie Buchholz, [1965?]
Photomechanical reproductions
Gift of Molly and Walter Bareiss, 1984.248

Jean (René) Bazaine, French, 1904–2001
Ancienne mémoire
Text by André Frénaud, French, 1907–1993
[Paris?]: Le Divan, 1960
One etching. Edition: 33/120
Gift of Molly and Walter Bareiss, 1984.249

Derrière le miroir (n° 170, mars 1968)
Texts by René Char, French, 1907–1988; Jean Tardieu, French, 1903–1995; André Frénaud, French, 1907–1993
Paris: Maeght éditeur (Aimé Maeght), 1968
6 color lithographs, photomechanical reproductions
Gift of Molly and Walter Bareiss, 1984.1228

Derrière le miroir (n° 197, avril 1972)
Text by Marcel Jouhandeau, French, 1888–1979
Paris: Maeght éditeur (Aimé Maeght), 1972
14 color lithographs, photomechanical reproductions
Gift of Molly and Walter Bareiss, 1984.1226

Mark Beard, American, born 1956
Manhattan Third Year Reader
Text by Mark Beard
New York: Vincent FitzGerald & Company, 1984
35 linoleum cuts with hand color and collage, photomechanical reproductions. Edition: 30/30
Gift of Molly and Walter Bareiss, 1984.250

Neo-Classik Comix: Adventures on 27th Street
Text by Mark Beard
New York: Vincent FitzGerald & Company, 1985
71 drypoints with hand color and collage. Edition: 2/11
Gift of Molly and Walter Bareiss, 1985.64

The Côte d'Azur Triangle
Text by Harry Kondoleon, American, 1955–1994
New York: Vincent FitzGerald & Company, 1985
One aquatint, 15 lithographs with etching, aquatint, cut-out, collage. Edition: 34/119
Gift of Molly and Walter Bareiss, 1985.76

Utah Reader
Text by Mark Beard
New York: Vincent FitzGerald & Company, 1986
Linoleum cuts with hand color and collage. Edition: 18/40
Gift of Molly and Walter Bareiss, 1986.109
Ref.: Phillips cat. 5
Fig. 143

Moses and the Shepherd
Text by Jalaluddin Mohammad Rumi (Jalal al-Din Rumi), Persian, 1207–1273; translation by Zahra Partovi and David Rattray
New York: Vincent FitzGerald & Company, 1987

20 etchings with aquatint. Edition: 4/100
Gift of Molly and Walter Bareiss, 1987.41

Aubrey Beardsley, British, 1872–1898
Salome: A Tragedy in One Act
Text by Oscar Wilde, Irish, 1854–1900; translation
by Lord Alfred Douglas, British, 1870–1945
London: John Lane, The Bodley Head; New York:
John Lane Company, 1907 (1st ed. 1894)
Line block reproductions, photomechanical reproduction
Gift of Molly and Walter Bareiss, 1984.251
Ref.: Castleman p. 104, Garvey cat. 17

Salomé: Drame en un acte
Text by Oscar Wilde, Irish, 1854–1900
Söcking, Deutschland: Heinrich F. S. Bachmair, 1949
(1st ed. 1894)
Line block reproductions. Edition: 1,793/2,100
Gift of Molly and Walter Bareiss, 1984.252
Ref.: Castleman p. 104, Garvey cat. 17

Salome: Tragödie in einem Akt
Text by Oscar Wilde, Irish, 1854–1900; translation
by Hedwig Lachmann, German, 1865–1918
Wiesbaden: Insel-Verlag, 1959 (1st ed. 1894)
Line block reproductions
Gift of Molly and Walter Bareiss, 1984.253
Ref.: Castleman p. 104, Garvey cat. 17

Unter dem Hügel: Eine romantische Erzählung
Text by Aubrey Beardsley; translation by Rudolf Alexander
Schröder, German, 1878–1962
Frankfurt am Main: Insel-Verlag, 1965 (1st ed. 1904)
Line block reproductions
Gift of Molly and Walter Bareiss, 1984.254

Cecil Beaton, British, 1904–1980
A Young Man Comes to London
Text by Michael Arlen, British, 1895–1956
London: [s.n.] in conjunction with Dorchester
Hotel, [1932]
Photomechanical reproductions, line block reproductions
Gift of Molly and Walter Bareiss, 1984.255

Henning H. Beck, German
In den Wind
Text by Christine Koller, German, born 1925
Stierstadt im Taunus, Deutschland: Eremiten-Presse
(V. O. Stomps, Dieter Hülsmanns, Friedolin Reske), 1967
6 color lithographs. Edition: 67/170
Gift of Molly and Walter Bareiss, 1984.256

Max Beckmann, German, 1884–1950
Die Hölle
Berlin: Graphisches Kabinett J. B. Neumann, 1919
Photomechanical reproductions. Edition: unnumbered/
1,000
Gift of Molly and Walter Bareiss, 1984.257

Faust: Der Tragödie zweiter Teil
Text by Johann Wolfgang von Goethe, German, 1749–1832
München: Prestel-Verlag, 1970
Photomechanical reproductions
Gift of Molly and Walter Bareiss, 1984.258

Hans Sebald Beham (see listing under Albrecht Dürer)

Hans Bellmer, German, active France, 1902–1975
*Mon arrestation du 26 août. Lettre inédite suivie des Étrennes
philosophiques*
Text by D. A. F. de Sade (le marquis de Sade), French,
1740–1814
Paris: Jean Hugues, 1959
One engraving. Edition: 15/184
Gift of Molly and Walter Bareiss, 1984.259

Mode d'emploi
Text by Hans Bellmer
Paris: Éditions Georges Visat, 1967
7 engravings, plus a suite of 7 engravings. Edition: 58/150
Gift of Molly and Walter Bareiss, 1984.260

Les marionnettes
Text by Heinrich von Kleist, German, 1777–1811

Paris: Éditions Georges Visat, 1969
11 engravings with added pochoir color, plus a suite
of 11 engravings. Edition: 43/150
Gift of Molly and Walter Bareiss, 1984.261

Georges Beltrand (see listing under A.-E. Marty)

Richard Bennett, American, 1899–1971
Humility, Concentration, & Gusto
Text by Winthrop Sargeant, American, 1903–1986
Brooklyn, NY: Pratt Adlib Press, 1960
9 woodcuts, including one in color (wrappers).
Edition: 172/300
Gift of Molly and Walter Bareiss, 1984.262

Charlotte Berend, German, 1880–1967
Valeska Gert
Text by Oscar Bie, German, 1864–1938
München: Verlagsanstalt D. & R. Bischoff, 1920
8 hand-colored lithographs. Edition: XIII/XXV
Gift of Molly and Walter Bareiss, 1984.263a–h

Charlotte Berend-Corinth (see Charlotte Berend)

Paul Berger, American, born 1948
Seattle Subtext
Rochester, NY: Visual Studies Workshop Press; Seattle:
Real Comet Press, 1984
Photomechanical reproductions
Molly and Walter Bareiss Art Fund and Printed Matter
Matching Gift Fund for Libraries, 1987.62

Miguel Berrocal, Spanish, born 1933
La Mini-Maria
Text by Michel Tapié, 1909–1987
[S.l.]: Multicetera, 1970
Photomechanical reproductions. Edition: 2,107/10,000
Gift of Molly and Walter Bareiss, 1984.264

René Bèrtholo, Portuguese, active France, born 1935
Il faut ce qu'il faut
Text by André Balthazar, born 1934
[S.l.: s.n., 1964]
32 color screenprints. Edition: 10/30
Gift of Molly and Walter Bareiss, 1984.265

Gianni Bertini, Italian, active France, born 1922
Stèle pour Adam de La Halle
Text by Jean-Jacques Lévêque, French, born 1931
Anduze, France: Édition du Castel Rose, 1962
21 screen prints, some in color. Edition: 28/200
Gift of Molly and Walter Bareiss, 1984.266

Werner Beulecke, born 1935
Mosis Magische Geisterkunst
Text attributed to Moses
München: Chris-Verlag, 1968
Line block reproductions
Gift of Molly and Walter Bareiss, 1984.267

Joseph Beuys, German, 1921–1986
Beuys
Texts by Johannes Cladders, German, born 1924;
Hans Strelow
Mönchengladbach, Deutschland: Städtisches Museum
Abteiberg (Johannes Cladders), 1967
Gray felt with relief-printed text, photomechanical
reproductions. Edition: 273/330
Gift of Molly and Walter Bareiss, 1984.268
Fig. 114

Joseph Beuys: Zeichnungen 1947–59, I
Text by Joseph Beuys; Hagen Lieberknecht
Köln: Schirmer, 1972
40 collotypes, photomechanical reproductions. Edition:
unnumbered/2,000
Gift of Molly and Walter Bareiss, 1984.269

Joseph Beuys: Zeichnungen von 1946–1971, II
Text by Joseph Beuys
[Düsseldorf]: Galerie Schmela, [1972?]
Photomechanical reproductions. Edition: 341/500
Gift of Molly and Walter Bareiss, 1984.270

Tod im Leben, Gedicht für Joseph Beuys
Text by Heiner Bastian, German, born 1942
München: Carl Hanser, 1972
Photomechanical reproductions
Molly and Walter Bareiss Art Fund, 1988.147

[Die Empfehlung (Fettbriefe)]
Heidelberg: Edition Staeck, [1973]
5 sheets of fat-treated stationery. Edition: 33/125
Molly and Walter Bareiss Art Fund, 1988.142a–e

Fotoreport: Prof. Beuys im Einbaum über den Rhein
Frankfurt: Deutsche Presse Agentur, 1973
One photograph
Molly and Walter Bareiss Art Fund, 1988.143

*Stiftung zur Foerderung der Kuenste: Zertifikat bezüglich
Opus Nr. IV/2.2-033/125*
Heidelberg: Edition Staeck, 1973
One lithographed certificate. Edition: 33/125
Molly and Walter Bareiss Art Fund, 1988.141

[Postkarten 1968–1974]
Text by Joseph Beuys
Heidelberg: Edition Staeck, [1974]
Photomechanical reproductions. Edition: 101/120
Molly and Walter Bareiss Art Fund, 1988.154a–n

Postkarten: Holzpostkarte
Heidelberg: Edition Staeck, [1974]
Block of wood with screen-printed text. Edition: 101/120
Molly and Walter Bareiss Art Fund, 1988.151

Postkarten: Honey Is Flowing
Text by Joseph Beuys
Heidelberg: Edition Staeck, [1974]
PVC plastic with screen-printed text. Edition: 101/120
Molly and Walter Bareiss Art Fund, 1988.152

Postkarten: Joseph Beuys auf dem Flug nach Amerika
Heidelberg: Edition Staeck, [1974]
Photomechanical reproductions. Edition: 101/120
Molly and Walter Bareiss Art Fund, 1988.153a–p

Abendunterhaltung
Achberg, Deutschland: Achberger Verlangsanstalt;
Hamburg: Geisteswissenschaftliche Dokumentation, 1977
Photomechanical reproductions. Edition: 743/unknown
Molly and Walter Bareiss Art Fund, 1988.150

Honigpumpe am Arbeitsplatz
Heidelberg: Edition Staeck (Free International University
Editions), [1977]
Photomechanical reproductions
Molly and Walter Bareiss Art Fund, 1988.113a–k

Die beste Stadt für Blinde, und andere Berichte
Text by Jürg Federspiel, Swiss, born 1931
Zürich: Suhrkamp, 1980
Photomechanical reproduction with added ink drawing
and holograph script; collage elements. Edition: 12/20
Molly and Walter Bareiss Art Fund, 1988.149

Art-Rite: "I love you by 8 mutton kidneys more"
[Bonn: Galerie Klein, 1981]
Ink drawing on newspaper. Edition: 26/66
Molly and Walter Bareiss Art Fund, 1988.145

Sciora: mythisch Beleven
Text by Dirk Rochtus, Belgian, born 1961; translation by
Annette De Wachter
Lier, België: Uitgeverij J. van In, 1981
Photomechanical reproductions. Edition: 29/40
Molly and Walter Bareiss Art Fund, 1988.148

F.I.U.: Difesa della Natura
Bonn: Galerie Klein, 1982
Photomechanical reproductions
Molly and Walter Bareiss Art Fund, 1988.144a

*Freie Internationale Hochschule für Kreativität und
Interdisziplinäre Forschung E.V.: Joseph Beuys, 7000 Eichen*
Düsseldorf: FIU-Geschäftsstelle Kunstakademie Atelier
Beuys, 1982
Photomechanical reproduction
Molly and Walter Bareiss Art Fund, 1988.144d

Postkarte: "Ich denke sowieso mit dem Knie"
[S.l: s.n., 1982?]
Photomechanical reproduction
Molly and Walter Bareiss Art Fund, 1988.144c

Postkarte: Nr. 2, Joseph Beuys vor der Rheinüberfahrt
Achberg, Deutschland: Achberger Verlag, [1982?]
Photomechanical reproduction
Molly and Walter Bareiss Art Fund, 1988.144b

Cornelis van Beverloo (see Corneille)

Thomas Bewick (see listing under Leonard Baskin)

Gustave Blanchot (see Gus Bofa)

Marc Blocker, American
The Printing House in Hell
Text by William Blake, British, 1757–1827
Portland, OR: Charles Seluzicki, 1985
Hand-colored relief prints. Edition: 33/50
Molly and Walter Bareiss Art Fund, 1987.188

Mel Bochner, American, born 1940
Mel Bochner: Zeichnungen
München: Fred Jahn, 1990
One aquatint, photomechanical reproductions.
Edition: 16/20
Gift of Molly and Walter Bareiss, 1990.84

Arnold Bode, German, 1900–1976
Aus dem Reiseskizzenbuch 1965
[S.l.: Arnold Bode, 1965?]
Photomechanical reproductions, line block reproductions
Gift of Molly and Walter Bareiss, 1984.271

Gus Bofa, French, 1888–1968
Voyages de Gulliver
Text by Jonathan Swift, British, 1667–1745
Bruxelles. Éditions du nord (Albert Parmentier), 1929
30 etchings, 36 color wood-engravings. Edition: 284/360
Gift of Molly and Walter Bareiss, 1984.272a–b

Karl Bohrmann, German, 1928–1998
Fall: 5 Radierungen 1965
[S.l.]: Karl Bohrmann, 1965
5 etchings with drypoint. Edition: 3/20
Gift of Molly and Walter Bareiss, 1984.391a–e

Die Weltmaschine
Text by Paolo Volponi, 1924–1994
[S.l.: Karl Bohrmann, 1966 or after]
One ink drawing (cover), 15 hand-colored etchings,
some mixed. Edition: 2/20
Gift of Molly and Walter Bareiss, 1984.273

Robert Bonfils, French, 1886–1972
Les rencontres de M. de Bréot
Text by Henri de Régnier, French, 1864–1936
Paris: René Kieffe, 1919
Line block reproductions with added watercolor.
Edition: 158/500
Gift of Molly and Walter Bareiss, 1984.274
Fig. 76

Pierre Bonnard, French, 1867–1947
Petit solfège illustré
Music by Claude Terrasse, French, 1867–1923
Paris: Ancienne maison Quantin, Librairies-imprimeries
réunies, [1893]
Relief etchings. Edition: unnumbered/2,000
Gift of Molly and Walter Bareiss, 1984.275
Ref.: Symmes cat. 5
Fig. 21

Petites scènes familières pour piano
Text by Franc-Nohain, French, 1873–1934; music
by Claude Terrasse, French, 1867–1923
Paris: E. Fromont, [1893]
20 lithographs
Gift of Molly and Walter Bareiss, 1984.276
Ref.: Garvey cat. 25, Hogben cat. 8, Symmes cat. 6

La lithographie originale en couleurs
Text by André Mellerio, French, 1862–1943

Paris: L'estampe et l'affiche, 1898
2 color lithographs. Edition: unnumbered/1,000
Gift of Molly and Walter Bareiss, 1984.279
Ref.: Garvey cat. 26

Parallèlement
Text by Paul Verlaine, French, 1844–1896
Paris: Ambroise Vollard, 1900
109 lithographs, wood-engraved vignettes, plus a suite
of 109 lithographs. Edition: 5/200
Gift of Molly and Walter Bareiss, 1984.280
Ref.: Castleman pp. 86–87, Garvey cat. 27, Hogben
cat. 17, Johnson cat. 11, Strachan p. 326, Symmes cat. 8,
Wheeler p. 98
Fig. 17

Parallèlement [title page]
One lithograph
Gift of Molly and Walter Bareiss, 1984.180

Almanach illustré du Père Ubu (XXe siècle)
Texts by Alfred Jarry, French, 1873–1907; Ambroise Vollard,
French, 1867–1939
[Paris: Ambroise Vollard, 1901]
Relief etchings. Edition: unnumbered/1,000
Gift of Molly and Walter Bareiss, 1984.281

Les pastorales de Longus; ou Daphnis et Chloé
Text by Longus, Greek, active 2nd–3rd centuries C.E.;
translation by Jacques Amyot, French, 1513–1593;
completed by Paul-Louis Courier, French, 1772–1825
Paris: Ambroise Vollard, 1902
151 lithographs, one wood-engraving after Bonnard.
Edition: 211/250
Gift of Molly and Walter Bareiss, 1984.282
Ref.: Garvey cat. 28, Hogben cat. 18, Strachan p. 326,
Symmes cat. 9, Wheeler p. 98

[Les pastorales de Longus; ou Daphnis et Chloé] [single
gathering]
4 lithographs
Gift of Molly and Walter Bareiss, 1984.282bis

La 628-E8
Text by Octave Mirbeau, French, 1848–1917
Paris: Librairie Charpentier et Fasquelle (Eugène
Fasquelle), 1908
Line block reproductions. Edition: 28/225
Gift of Molly and Walter Bareiss, 1984.283

Histoire du poisson scie et du poisson marteau
Text by Léopold Chauveau, French, 1870–1940
Paris: Payot & cie., 1923 (© 1922)
Line block reproductions
Gift of Molly and Walter Bareiss, 1984.284

Dingo
Text by Octave Mirbeau, French, 1848–1917
Paris: Ambroise Vollard, 1924
55 etchings, some with drypoint, including suite of 14
etchings, line block reproduction. Edition: 199/350
Gift of Molly and Walter Bareiss, 1984.285
Ref.: Garvey cat. 30, Symmes cat. 10, Wheeler p. 98
Fig. 78

Bonnard
Text by Charles Terrasse, French, 1893–1982
Paris: Henry Floury, 1927
One etching, collotypes, photomechanical reproductions,
line block reproductions. Edition: 1,125/unknown
Gift of Molly and Walter Bareiss, 1984.286

Sainte Monique
Text by Ambroise Vollard, French, 1867–1939
Paris: Ambroise Vollard, 1930
29 transfer lithographs, 17 etchings, 178 wood-engravings
from drawings on the blocks by Bonnard. Edition: 293/340
Gift of Molly and Walter Bareiss, 1984.287
Ref.: Wheeler p. 98

Éloge de Pierre Bonnard
Text by Léon Werth, 1878–1955
[Paris]: Manuel Bruker, 1946
10 lithographs after drawings. Edition: 143/200
Gift of Molly and Walter Bareiss, 1984.288

Pierre Bonnard; Georges Braque, French, 1882–1963;
Henri Matisse, French, 1869–1954
Le vent des épines
Text by Jacques Kober, French
Paris: Éditions pierre à feu, Maeght éditeur
(Adrien Maeght), 1947
Photomechanical reproduction, line block reproductions.
Edition: 223/270
Gift of Molly and Walter Bareiss, 1984.1328

Pierre Bonnard; Alfred Jarry, French, 1873–1907
Répertoire des pantins
Texts by Alfred Jarry; Franc-Nohain, French, 1873–1934,
music by Claude Terrasse, French, 1867–1923
Paris: Mercure de France, 1898
No. 1: *Du pays tourangeau*, transfer lithograph by Bonnard
No. 2: *Malheureuse Adèle!*, transfer lithograph by Bonnard
No. 3: *Velas, ou l'officier de fortune*, transfer lithograph by
Bonnard
No. 4: *La complainte de Monsieur Benoît*, transfer litho-
graph by Bonnard
No. 5: *Paysage de neige*, transfer lithograph by Bonnard
No. 6: *Berceuse obscène*, transfer lithograph by Bonnard
No. 7: *La chanson du décervelage*, transfer lithograph by
Jarry
No. 8: *Ouverture d'Ubu Roi*, transfer lithograph by Jarry
No. 9: *Marche des polonais*, transfer lithograph by Jarry
Gift of Molly and Walter Bareiss, 1984.277a–i; 1984.278a–i
Ref.: Symmes cat. 7

George G. Booth, American, 1884–1949
The Dictes and Sayings of the Philosophers
Texts by various authors
Detroit, MI: Cranbrook Press (George G. Booth), 1901
Wood-engravings. Edition: 141/244
Gift of Molly and Walter Bareiss, 1993.58
Fig. 5

Jean-François Bory, French, born 1938
Post-scriptum
Text by Jean-François Bory
[S.l.]: Eric Losfeld, 1970
Photomechanical reproductions, line block reproductions
Gift of Molly and Walter Bareiss, 1984.289
Fig. 121

Richard Bosman, American, born 1944
Captivity Narrative of Hannah Dustin
Texts by various authors
San Francisco: Arion Press (Andrew Hoyem), 1987
35 woodcuts. Edition: unnumbered/425
Molly and Walter Bareiss Art Fund, 1988.21

Sandro Botticelli, Italian, 1444/45–1510
*La divina commedia: or, The Divine Vision of Dante
Alighieri*
Text by Dante Alighieri, Italian, 1265–1321
[London]: Nonesuch Press (Francis Meynell), 1928
42 collotypes. Edition: 749/1,475
Gift of Molly and Walter Bareiss, 1984.290

George Bottini, French, 1874–1907
La maison Philibert
Text by Jean Lorrain (Paul Duval), French, 1855–1906
Paris: Librairie Universelle, 1904
Photomechanical reproductions, line block reproductions
Gift of Molly and Walter Bareiss, 1984.291

Bourdonnaye, Alain de La (see La Bourdonnaye,
Alain de)

Jean-Louis Boussingault, French, 1883–1943
D'après Paris
Text by Léon-Paul Fargue, French, 1876–1947
Paris: Librairie de France, for Les amis de l'amour de
l'art, 1931
16 lithographs. Edition: 74/120
Gift of Molly and Walter Bareiss, 1984.294

Georges Braque, French, 1882–1963
Le piège de Méduse
Text by Érik Satie, French, 1866–1925

Paris: Éditions de la Galerie Simon, André Simon et cie. (under the direction of Daniel-Henry Kahnweiler), 1921
3 color woodcuts. Edition: 22/100
Gift of Molly and Walter Bareiss, 1984.295
Ref.: Castleman p. 172, Garvey cat. 33, Johnson cat. 29, Symmes cat. 11, Wheeler p. 99
Fig. 24

Cinq sapates
Text by Francis Ponge, French, 1899–1988
Paris: [Maeght éditeur], 1950
5 etchings with lift-ground aquatint. Edition: 65/95
Gift of Molly and Walter Bareiss, 1984.297
Ref.: Garvey cat. 37

La bonne heure
Text by Tristan Tzara, French (born Romania), 1896–1963
Paris: Raymond Jacquet, 1955
One etching with aquatint. Edition: 26/42
Gift of Molly and Walter Bareiss, 1984.298
Ref.: Symmes cat. 12

Georges Braque: grands livres illustrés
Texts by Roger Vieillard, French, 1907–1989; Antoine Tudal, born 1931
Paris: Maeght éditeur (Adrien Maeght), 1958
One color lithograph (cover), photomechanical reproductions. Edition: unnumbered/900
Gift of Molly and Walter Bareiss, 1984.299

Georges Braque: oeuvre graphique original
Text by René Char, French, 1907–1988
Genève: [s.n.], 1958
Photomechanical reproductions, line block reproduction (cover). Edition: 669/1,500
Gift of Molly and Walter Bareiss, 1984.300

Passionné
Text by Édith Boissonnas, French, 1904–1989
Alès, France: PAB (Pierre André Benoit), 1958
One lithograph. Edition: 50/60
Gift of Molly and Walter Bareiss, 1984.301

Août
Text by Antoine Saint-Pol-Roux, French, 1861–1948
[Paris]: Louis Broder, [1958]
4 mixed etchings, including one in color. Edition: 101/120
Gift of Molly and Walter Bareiss, 1984.302
Ref.: Garvey cat. 41, Symmes cat. 13

Georges Braque; Alberto Giacometti, Swiss, active France, 1901–1966
Sentence sans paroles
Text by Iliazd, Russian, active France, 1894–1975
Paris: Le degré quarante et un (Iliazd), 1961
2 etchings. Edition: 57/62
Gift of Molly and Walter Bareiss, 1984.303

Georges Braque; Man Ray, American, active France, 1890–1977; **Jean Cocteau,** French, 1889–1963
Les fâcheux
Texts by Louis Laloy, French, 1874–1944; Jean Cocteau
Paris: Quatre chemins, 1924
47 collotypes, most with added pochoir color, line block reproduction. Edition: LV/LXXV
Gift of Molly and Walter Bareiss, 1984.296a–b

Georges Braque (see also listing under Pierre Bonnard)

Brassaï (see listing under Henri Matisse)

Victor Brauner, Romanian, active France, 1903–1966
Main forte
Text by Benjamin Péret, French, 1899–1959
[Paris]: Éditions de la revue fontaine, 1946
Line block reproductions. Edition: 226/925
Gift of Molly and Walter Bareiss, 1984.304

Ce château pressenti
Text by Ghérasim Luca, Romanian, active France, 1913–1994
[S.l.]: Méconnaissance, 1958
One hand-colored etching, line block reproduction.

Edition: 6/388
Gift of Molly and Walter Bareiss, 1984.305

Uwe Bremer, German, born 1940
Nachrichten über den Leviathan
Text by Volker von Törne, German, born 1934
Stierstadt im Taunus, Deutschland: Eremiten-Presse, 1964
One woodcut (cover), 14 lithographs (8 with second color added by relief printing). Edition: 123/250
Gift of Molly and Walter Bareiss, 1984.306

Marcel Breuer, American (born Hungary), 1902–1981
Marcel Breuer: Sun and Shadow, The Philosophy of an Architect
Texts by Marcel Breuer; Rufus Stillman
New York: Dodd, Mead & Company, 1955
Photomechanical reproductions
Gift of Molly and Walter Bareiss, 1984.307

Marcel Broodthaers, Belgian, active Great Britain, 1924–1976
A Voyage on the North Sea
Text by Marcel Broodthaers
London: Petersburg Press, 1974
Photomechanical reproductions, line block reproduction (wrappers). Edition: unnumbered/1,100
Gift of Molly and Walter Bareiss, 1984.308
Ref.: Drucker pp. 224–25

Un jardin d'hiver
London: Petersburg Press; Bruxelles: Société des expositions, 1974
Line block reproductions with added pochoir color, typographic designs. Edition: 100/100
Molly and Walter Bareiss Art Fund, 1988.36

En lisant la Lorelei. Wie ich die Lorelei gelesen habe
Text by Marcel Broodthaers
München: Edition der Galerie Heiner Friedrich; Paris: Yvon Lambert, 1975
Photomechanical reproductions. Edition: 39/100
Gift of Molly and Walter Bareiss, 1984.310
Ref.: Drucker pp. 316–17
Fig. 129

Marcel Broodthaers: Editionen (1964–1975)
München: Edition der Galerie Heiner Friedrich, 1978
Photomechanical reproductions. Edition: unnumbered/ 1,500
Gift of Molly and Walter Bareiss, 1984.309

Catalogue des livres 1957–1975
Köln: Galerie Michael Werner, 1982
Photomechanical reproductions
Gift of Molly and Walter Bareiss, 1984.312

Je m'en lave les mains
Text by Marcel Broodthaers
Zürich: Seedorn, 1982
Letterpress (text only). Edition: unnumbered/500
Gift of Molly and Walter Bareiss, 1984.311

Marcel Broodthaers: Sixteen Photographic Portraits, 1957–1967, and One Self-Portrait, 1974
Text by Wieland Schmied, German, born 1929
New York: Marian Goodman Gallery and Multiples, Inc., in collaboration with Sander Gallery, 1983
17 photographs. Edition: 2/50
Gift of Molly and Walter Bareiss, 1984.313a–q
Fig. 127

Umberto Brunelleschi, Italian, active France, 1879–1949
Phili: ou, par-delà le bien et le mal: Conte moral
Text by Abel Hermant, French, 1862–1950
[Paris?]: Éditions de la Guirlande, 1921
12 engravings with added pochoir color, 12 engravings without color, line block reproductions, some with added pochoir color. Edition: 11/275
Gift of Molly and Walter Bareiss, 1984.314
Fig. 77

Günter Brus, Austrian, born 1938
Zerreissprobe
Text by Günter Brus

München: Edition Hundertmark, 1970One color pencil and gouache drawing, 2 color screen prints, 5 photographs.
Edition: 1/unknown
Gift of Molly and Walter Bareiss, 1984.315

Die Schastrommel: Organ der Österr. Exilregierung
Texts by various authors; edited by Günter Brus
Bolzano, Italia: [s.n.]
Nr. 2, Mai 1970: One pencil drawing, one photograph, 10 color screen prints, 9 lithographs (by various artists). Edition: unnumbered/100
Nr. 6, März 1972: 8 color screen prints (Brus), including cover, photomechanical reproductions
Gift of Molly and Walter Bareiss, 1984.1339, 1984.1338

Der blaue Wald
Text by Günter Brus
Berlin: Edition Hundertmark, 1974
17 color pencil drawings, 2 screen prints. Edition: 17/30
Gift of Molly and Walter Bareiss, 1984.316

Hohes Gebrechen
Text by Günter Brus
Altona [Hamburg], Hohengebraching: Arnulf Meifert, 1976
Photomechanical reproductions (cover). Edition: 206/350
Gift of Molly and Walter Bareiss, 1984.317

Die Gärten in der Exosphäre
Text by Günter Brus
Altona [Hamburg]: Das Hohe Gebrechen, 1979
Photomechanical reproductions. Edition: unnumbered/600
Gift of Molly and Walter Bareiss, 1984.318

Behauptungen und Beschreibungen zum Projekt des Origien Mysterien Theaters (Ordensregeln)
Text by Hermann Nitsch, Austrian, born 1938
Altona [Hamburg], Hohengebraching: Das Hohe Gebrechen, 1981
Photomechanical reproductions. Edition: unnumbered/660
Gift of Molly and Walter Bareiss, 1985.86

Ana: 1. Aktion, 1964
[Wien]: Galerie Heike Curtze, Galerie Krinzinger, [1984?]
7 photographs. Edition: 17/35
Gift of Molly and Walter Bareiss, 1988.103a–g
Fig. 6

Selbstbemalung I, 1964
[Vienna]: Galerie Heike Curtze, Galerie Krinzinger, [1985?]
15 photographs. Edition: 32/35
Gift of Molly and Walter Bareiss, 1988.104a–o

Camille Bryen, French, 1907–1977
Récit du nord et régions froides
Text by René Bordier, active 1614–1658
Paris: Le degré quarante et un (Iliazd), 1956
One color etching with aquatint. Edition: 23/45
Gift of Molly and Walter Bareiss, 1984.319
Fig. 59

Jeu de glace de Camille Bryen
Text by Roger Bordier, French, born 1923
[Alès, France]: PAB (Pierre André Benoit), 1958
One color etching with aquatint. Edition: 47/50
Gift of Molly and Walter Bareiss, 1984.320

Gernot Bubenik, German, born 1942
Das Komplexe Gedicht
Text by Gernot Bubenik
[S.l.]: Gernot Bubenik, 1965
8 color screen prints, line block reproductions. Edition: 67/230
Gift of Molly and Walter Bareiss, 1984.321

Marguerite Burnat-Provins, French, 1872–1950
Petits tableaux Valaisans
Text by Marguerite Burnat-Provins
Vevey, Suisse: Imprimerie Säuberlin & Pfeiffer, 1903
122 color wood-engravings. Edition: 214/562
Gift of Molly and Walter Bareiss, 1984.322

Pol Bury, Belgian, active France, born 1922
À bras le corps
Text by André Balthazar, born 1934

La Louvière, België: Daily-Bul, [1966]
8 lithographs, some in colors. Edition: 63/100
Gift of Molly and Walter Bareiss, 1984.323

Milano: Cinetizzazioni
Venezia: Cavallino, 1967
Photomechanical reproductions. Edition: 242/400
Gift of Molly and Walter Bareiss, 1984.324

Wilhelm Busch, German, 1832–1908
Busch Bilderbogen (Band II)
Text by Wilhelm Busch
München: Braun & Schneider, [1875 or after?]
Photomechanical reproductions
Gift of Molly and Walter Bareiss, 1984.325

James Lee Byars, American, 1932–1997
James Lee Byars im Westfälischen Kunstverein
Texts by James Lee Byars; Thomas Deecke, born 1940
Münster: Westfälischer Kunstverein, 1982
Photomechanical reproductions
Gift of Molly and Walter Bareiss, 1984.327

James Lee Byars (see also listing under A. R. Penck)

Michel Cadoret, French, 1912–1985
La passoire à connerie
Texts by Michel Cadoret; Edgar Varèse, American
(born France), 1883–1965
[New York: Galerie Norval, 1960]
Photomechanical reproductions, line block reproduction
(of signature and musical notes by Marcel Duchamp)
Gift of Molly and Walter Bareiss, 1984.328

Michael C. Caine
The Blue Dream
Text by Louis Aragon, French, 1897–1982
[S.l.: s.n., 1981?]
9 color woodcuts (one with monoprint color), including
one after photograph by Baron Adolf de Meyer. Edition:
10/15
Gift of Molly and Walter Bareiss, 1984.329

Alexander Calder, American, 1898–1976
Selected Fables
Text by Jean de La Fontaine, French, 1621–1695;
translation by Eunice Clark, born 1911
New York: George Braziller, 1957 (1st ed. 1948)
Line block reproductions
Gift of Molly and Walter Bareiss, 1984.330

Cycle
Text by Michel Butor, French, born 1926
Paris: La Hune, 1962
Photomechanical reproductions (one with line block
element). Edition: 381/500
Gift of Molly and Walter Bareiss, 1984.331

Derrière le miroir (n° 141, novembre 1963)
Texts by James Jones, American, 1921–1977; Michel
Ragon, born 1924
Paris: Maeght éditeur (Aimé Maeght), 1963
8 color lithographs, photomechanical reproductions
Gift of Molly and Walter Bareiss, 1984.1237

Alexandre Calder
Text by Giovanni Carandente, Italian
Genève: Galerie Krugier & cie., 1966
Photomechanical reproductions. Edition:
unnumbered/2,500
Gift of Molly and Walter Bareiss, 1984.332

Alexander Calder (see also listing under Additional Books)

Giuseppe Capogrossi, Italian, 1900–1972
Capogrossi
Venezia: Cavallino, 1966
Color screen prints. Edition: 50/200
Gift of Molly and Walter Bareiss, 1984.333
Fig. 108

Giuseppe Capogrossi; Mino Guerrini, Italian, born 1927
*Forma 2, Quaderni Tecnico-Informativi di Arte
Contemporanea: Omaggio a W. Kandinsky* (n. 1, maggio 1950)

Texts by various authors
Roma: Edizioni Age d'or, 1950
2 lithographs, photomechanical reproductions, line
block reproduction (folder). Edition: 160/200
Gift of Molly and Walter Bareiss, 1984.1320a–c

Ernst Caramelle, Austrian, born 1952
Forty Found Fakes 1976–1978
New York: Thomas Way & Company, 1979
Photomechanical reproductions. Edition: 787/1,000
Molly and Walter Bareiss Art Fund and Printed Matter
Matching Gift Fund for Libraries, 1987.52
Ref.: Drucker pp. 328–29

Henri Cartier-Bresson, French, born 1908; **Joan Miró,**
Spanish, active France, 1893–1983
Les européens: photographies par Henri Cartier-Bresson
Text by Henri Cartier-Bresson
Paris: Éditions Verve (Tériade), 1955
Photomechanical reproductions (including cover by Miró)
Gift of Molly and Walter Bareiss, 1984.334
Fig. 95

Henri Cartier-Bresson (see also listing under Henri
Matisse)

A. M. Cassandre, French (born Russia), 1901–1968
Le spectacle est dans la rue
Montrouge, Seine, France: Draeger frères, [1936?]
Photomechanical reproductions
Gift of Molly and Walter Bareiss, 1984.335

Lourdes Castro, Portuguese, active France, born 1930
Lourdes Castro
Text by Pierre Restany, French, born 1930
Munchen: Galerie Buchholz, 1965
One color screen print, photomechanical reproductions.
Edition: 14/60
Gift of Molly and Walter Bareiss, 1984.336

Vija Celmins, American (born Latvia), born 1939
The View
Text by Czeslaw Milosz, American (born Lithuania),
born 1911
New York: Library Fellows of the Whitney Museum
of American Art (May Castleberry), 1985
6 mezzotints, line block reproduction. Edition:
unnumbered/120
Molly and Walter Bareiss Art Fund, 1987.65
Fig. 64

Paul Cézanne, French, 1839–1906
*Paul Cézanne: Sketch Book Owned by the Art Institute
of Chicago* [facsimile]
Text by Carl O. Schniewind, American, 1900–1957
New York: Curt Valentin, 1951
Collotypes. Edition: unnumbered/1,500
Gift of Molly and Walter Bareiss, 1984.338a–b

Album de Paul Cézanne [facsimile]
Text by Adrien Chappuis, French
Paris: Berggruen & cie., 1966
Collotypes, some in colors, photomechanical
reproductions. Edition: "pour Walter Bareiss"
Gift of Molly and Walter Bareiss, 1984.339a–b

Paul Cézanne: Sketchbook 1875–1885 [facsimile]
Text by John Rewald, American (born Germany),
1912–1994
[New York]: Johnson Reprint Corporation; Harcourt
Brace Jovanovich, 1982
Photomechanical reproductions. Edition: 277/500
Gift of Molly and Walter Bareiss, 1984.340a–b

Marc Chagall, Russian, active France, 1887–1985
Les sept péchés capitaux
Texts by various authors
Paris: Simon Kra, [1926]
15 etchings with drypoint, some with aquatint,
plus a suite of 16 etchings. Edition: 23/300
Gift of Molly and Walter Bareiss, 1984.341

Ref.: Johnson cat. 42, Symmes cat. 14
Fig. 86
Fables
Text by Jean de La Fontaine, French, 1621–1695
Paris: Tériade, 1952
One watercolor drawing, 102 etchings, some with
engraving and drypoint. Edition: 126/185
Gift of Molly and Walter Bareiss, 1984.342a–b
Ref.: Garvey cat. 52, Hogben cat. 79, Strachan p. 327,
Symmes cat. 15, Wheeler p. 99
Fig. 10

Derrière le miroir (n° 147, juin 1964)
Text by Marcel Arland, 1899–1986
Paris: Maeght éditeur (Aimé Maeght), 1964
3 lithographs (2 in color), photomechanical reproductions,
line block reproduction
Gift of Molly and Walter Bareiss, 1984.1232

Le cirque d'Izis
Text by Jacques Prévert, French, 1900–1977
Monte Carlo: André Sauret, 1965
Photomechanical reproductions
Gift of Molly and Walter Bareiss, 1984.343

Derrière le miroir (n° 198, mai 1972)
Text by Louis Aragon, French, 1897–1982
Paris: Maeght éditeur (Aimé Maeght), 1972
3 color lithographs, photomechanical reproductions
Gift of Molly and Walter Bareiss, 1984.1227

Marc Chagall (see also listing under Various artists,
XXe siècle; Verve)

John Chamberlain, American, born 1927
Conversations with Myself
Text by John Chamberlain
[New York]: Pace Editions, 1992
One drypoint, line block reproductions. Edition: 14/108
Molly and Walter Bareiss Art Fund, 1993.23a–b

Roz Chast, American, born 1954
*Three Small Books: Mondo Boxo. The Small Pamphlet
of Things. Somebody Goes to the White House, by Vera
Lee Marlone, in Diary Form*
Text by Roz Chast
[New York]: Kathryn Markel, 1982
Line block reproductions
Gift of Molly and Walter Bareiss, 1984.344a–c
Fig. 137

Eduardo Chillida, Spanish, 1924–2002
Derrière le miroir (n° 143, avril 1964)
Text by Carola Giedion-Welcker
Paris: Maeght éditeur (Aimé Maeght), 1964
5 lithographs, photomechanical reproductions, line
block reproductions
Gift of Molly and Walter Bareiss, 1984.1231

Le chemin des devins, suivi de Ménerbes
Text by André Frénaud, French, 1907–1993
Paris: Maeght éditeur (Adrien Maeght), 1966
One ink drawing, 12 etchings, including one in blind
(wrappers). Edition: 8/175
Gift of Molly and Walter Bareiss, 1984.345
Ref.: Strachan p. 328
Fig. 41

Meditation in Kastilien
Text by Max Hölzer, Austrian, 1915–1984
St. Gallen, Schweiz: Erker-Presse (Franz Larese, Jürg
Janett), 1968
7 lithographs. Edition: 41/145
Gift of Molly and Walter Bareiss, 1984.346

Die Kunst und der Raum
Text by Martin Heidegger, German, 1889–1976
St. Gallen, Schweiz: Erker-Presse (Franz Larese, Jürg
Janett), 1969
8 collaged lithographs, plus a suite of 7 lithographs.
Edition: 6/150
Gift of Molly and Walter Bareiss, 1984.347a–b,

1984.349a–g
Ref.: Castleman p. 194
Fig. 23

Martin Heidegger / Eduardo Chillida: Die Kunst und der Raum [sound recording]
Texts by Martin Heidegger, German, 1889–1976; Erhart Kästner, German, 1904–1974
St. Gallen, Schweiz: Erker-Presse (Franz Larese, Jürg Janett), 1970
One woodcut, photomechanical reproduction (album cover). Edition: 49/100
Gift of Molly and Walter Bareiss, 1984.348a–b

Pantheon: Edition Eduardo Chillida
Text by Reinhold Hohl, born 1929
München: Studio Bruckmann (Erhardt D. Stiebner), 1975
One woodcut, photomechanical reproductions. Edition: 21/100
Gift of Molly and Walter Bareiss, 1984.1341

Giorgio de Chirico, Italian (born Greece), 1888–1978
Siepe a Nordovest: Rappresentazione
Text by Massimo Bontempelli, Italian, 1878–1960
Roma: Edizioni di "Valori Plastici," [1922]
Photomechanical reproductions
Gift of Molly and Walter Bareiss, 1984.350

Charles Clément, Swiss, 1889–1972
Une nuit dans la forêt: premier fragment d'une autobiographie
Text by Blaise Cendrars, French (born Switzerland), 1887–1961
Lausanne: Au Verseau, 1929
3 etchings. Edition: 292/450
Gift of Molly and Walter Bareiss, 1984.353

Francesco Clemente, Italian, born 1952
The Departure of the Argonaut
Text by Alberto Savinio, Italian (born Greece), 1891–1952
[London]: Petersburg Press, 1986
49 lithographs, some in colors. Edition: 64/200
Gift of Molly and Walter Bareiss and Mrs. George W. Stevens Fund, 1986.45
Ref. Castleman p. 217, Johnson cat. 169, Phillips cat. 11
Fig. 141

Jean Cocteau, French, 1889–1963
Dessins
Paris: Librairie Stock, Delamain, Boutelleau & cie., 1924 (1st ed. 1923)
Line block reproductions
Gift of Molly and Walter Bareiss, 1984.354
Fig. 151

Dessins en marge du texte des Chevaliers de la Table Ronde
Text by Jean Cocteau
Paris: Gallimard, 1941
Photomechanical reproductions. Edition: 70/1,880
Gift of Molly and Walter Bareiss, 1984.356

Jean Cocteau (see also listing under Georges Braque)

Peter Collien, German, born 1938
Pierrot lunaire
Text by Albert Giraud, Belgian, 1860–1929
Berlin: Rembrandt Verlag, 1968
6 engravings. Edition: H/J
Gift of Molly and Walter Bareiss, 1984.357

Lawrence Compton (Kolawole), American, born 1931
Verstümmelte Sprünge
Text by Gisela (Maria von) Frankenberg, 1925–1985
[S.l.: s.n.], 1967
10 etchings. Edition: 3/50
Gift of Molly and Walter Bareiss, 1984.358a–j

William Nelson Copley (see Cply)

Lovis Corinth, German, 1858–1925
Antike Legenden
Text by Julius Meier-Graefe, German (born Hungary), 1867–1935
München: Verlag der Marées-Gesellschaft, R. Piper & Co., 1920

12 etchings with drypoint. Edition: 61/150
Gift of Molly and Walter Bareiss, 1984.359a–l

Bei den Corinthern
Text by Lovis Corinth; Wilhelm Hausenstein, German, 1882–1957
Leipzig: E. A. Seemann, 1920
One etching, photomechanical reproductions. Edition: 11/100
Gift of Molly and Walter Bareiss, 1984.360

Corneille, Dutch (born Belgium), active France, born 1922
Les portes de l'été
Text by Jean-Jacques Lévêque, French, born 1931
Alès, France: PAB (Pierre André Benoit), 1961
2 lithographs. Edition: 11/40
Gift of Molly and Walter Bareiss, 1984.361

Thomas Browne Cornell, American, born 1937
The Monkey
Text by Thomas Henry Huxley, British, 1825–1895
[Northampton, MA]: Apiary Press (Smith College Student Printing Office), 1959
13 etchings (one in color). Edition: 3/60
Gift of Molly and Walter Bareiss, 1984.362

Eugène Courboin (see listing under Various Artists, *L'effort*)

François Courboin, French, 1865–1926
A Street of Paris and Its Inhabitant
Text by Honoré de Balzac, French, 1799–1850; translation by Henri Pène du Bois, French, 1858–1906
New York: Meyer Brothers and Company, 1900
Photomechanical reproductions, plus a suite of reproductions. Edition: 227/400
Gift of Molly and Walter Bareiss, 1984.363

Cply, American, 1919–1996
Ballads
New York: Alexandre Iolas, [1967?]
One color lithograph (wrappers), photomechanical reproductions
Gift of Molly and Walter Bareiss, 1984.364

Cply (see also listing under Various artists, *S.M.S.*)

Roberto Crippa, Italian, 1921–1972
I Contemporanei / Les contemporains / The Contemporaries, v. II: Roberto Crippa
Text by Tristan Sauvage, Italian (born Egypt), born 1924
Milano: Galleria Schwarz, 1962
10 etchings, some in colors. Edition: 31/75
Gift of Molly and Walter Bareiss, 1984.1323

Michaël Croissant (see listing under Ursula Rusche-Wolters)

Henri-Edmond Cross, French, 1856–1910
Carnet de dessins [facsimile]
Text by John Rewald, American (born Germany), 1912–1994
Paris: Berggruen & cie., 1959
Collotypes, some with added color. Edition: "for Mr. and Mrs. Walter Bareiss"
Gift of Molly and Walter Bareiss, 1984.365a–b

K. F. Dahmen, German, 1917–1981
Chronik des Galilei
Text by Walter Aue, Czech, born 1930
Köln: Wolfgang Hake, 1965
4 etchings with embossing. Edition: 1/400
Gift of Molly and Walter Bareiss, 1984.366

Salvador Dalí, Spanish, active France, 1904–1989
Les chants de Maldoror
Text by comte de Lautréamont (Isidore Ducasse), French, 1847–1870
Paris: Albert Skira, 1934
42 etchings, some with drypoint and engraving, plus a suite of 44 etchings. Edition: 18/200
Gift of Molly and Walter Bareiss, 1984.367a–b
Ref.: Castleman p. 94, Garvey cat. 67, Hogben cat. 99,

Johnson cat. 106, Strachan p. 329, Symmes cat. 16, Wheeler p. 99
Fig. 32

The Maze
Text by Maurice Yves Sandoz, Swiss?, 1892–1958
Garden City, NY: Doubleday, Doran and Co., 1945
Photomechanical reproductions
Gift of Molly and Walter Bareiss, 1984.368

50 Secrets of Magic Craftsmanship
Text by Salvador Dalí
New York: Dial Press, 1948
One ink drawing, photomechanical reproductions
Gift of Molly and Walter Bareiss, 1984.369
Ref.: Phillips cat. 12

Hermine David, French, 1886–1970
Cressida
Text by André Suarès, French, 1868–1948
Paris: Éditions Émile-Paul frères, 1926
32 drypoints. Edition: 194/225
Gift of Molly and Walter Bareiss, 1984.370

Luciano De Vita, Italian, born 1929
Cantata di Bomarzo
Text by Manuel Mujica Láinez, Argentinian, 1910–1984
Verona: Plain Wrapper Press, 1981
7 color etchings. Edition: "for Walter Bareiss" 38/83
Gift of Molly and Walter Bareiss, 1984.385a–b

François Deck, French, born 1945
Et je m'épuise d'être là …
Text by Roger Giroux, French, 1925–1974
Provence: Éditions Unes, 1982
One etching with aquatint. Edition: XV/XXI
Gift of Molly and Walter Bareiss, 1984.371

Miles DeCoster, American
Television
Text by Miles DeCoster
[S.l.: Miles DeCoster?], 1985
Photomechanical reproductions. Edition: unnumbered/2,500
Molly and Walter Bareiss Art Fund and Printed Matter Matching Gift Fund for Libraries, 1987.50
Ref.: Drucker pp. 298–99

Eugène Delacroix, French, 1798–1863
Faust: Ein Tragödie
Text by Johann Wolfgang von Goethe, German, 1749–1832
Leipzig: Insel-Verlag, 1912 (1st ed. 1828, in French)
Collotypes. Edition: 168/615
Gift of Molly and Walter Bareiss, 1984.372
Ref.: Wheeler p. 100

Le voyage de Eugène Delacroix au Maroc: fac-similé de l'album du Château de Chantilly [facsimile]
Text by Jean Guiffrey, French, 1870–19??
Paris: J. Terquem & cie. (P. Lemare), 1913
Collotypes. Edition: 157/200
Gift of Molly and Walter Bareiss, 1984.373a–b

Album de croquis [facsimile]
Text by Maurice Sérullaz, French, 1914–1997
Paris: Quatre chemins-éditart, 1961
Collotypes. Edition: 11/500
Gift of Molly and Walter Bareiss, 1984.374a–b

Robert Delaunay, French, 1885–1941
Allô! Paris!
Text by Joseph Delteil, French, 1894–1978
Paris: Éditions des Quatre chemins, 1926
20 lithographs. Edition: 151/325
Gift of Molly and Walter Bareiss, 1984.375
Ref.: Garvey cat. 72, Johnson cat. 53

Sonia Delaunay (see listing under Various Artists, *XXe siècle*)

Maurice Denis, French, 1870–1943
Le voyage d'Urien
Text by André Gide, French, 1869–1951

Paris: Librairie de l'art indépendant, 1893
30 color lithographs, one wood-engraving (cover).
Edition: 202/300
Gift of Molly and Walter Bareiss, 1984.376
Ref.: Garvey cat. 76, Hogben cat. 5, Symmes cat. 17

Sagesse
Text by Paul Verlaine, French, 1844–1896
Paris: Ambroise Vollard, 1911
89 color wood-engravings. Edition: 122/250
Gift of Molly and Walter Bareiss, 1984.377
Ref.: Garvey cat. 77, Hogben cat. 4, Symmes cat. 18,
Wheeler p. 100
Fig. 73

André Derain, French, 1880–1954
Le calumet
Text by André Salmon, French, 1881–1969
Paris: Éditions de la Nouvelle revue française, Librairie
Gallimard, 1920
61 woodcuts, including one in color. Edition: 593/750
Gift of Molly and Walter Bareiss, 1984.378
Ref.: Wheeler p. 101

La cassette de plomb
Text by Georges Gabory, French, 1899–1978
Paris: Imprimerie François Bernouard, [1920]
2 etchings. Edition: 49/130
Gift of Molly and Walter Bareiss, 1984.379

Les travaux et les jeux
Text by Vincent Muselli, French, 1879–1956
Paris: J. E. Pouterman, 1929
41 color lithographs, plus a suite of 40 lithographs.
Edition: "pour Jacques Schiffrin"
Gift of Molly and Walter Bareiss, 1984.380
Ref.: Wheeler p. 101

Pantagruel
Text by François Rabelais, French, ca. 1494–1553
Paris: Albert Skira, 1943
180 color woodcuts. Edition: 146/250
Gift of Molly and Walter Bareiss, 1984.381
Ref.: Garvey cat. 81, Hogben cat. 111, Johnson cat. 118,
Strachan p. 330, Symmes cat. 19, Wheeler p. 101
Figs. 94, jacket back

A Tribute to Precious Stones
Text by René Héron de Villefosse, French, born 1903
Paris: Cartier (Jean Vigneau), 1947
One color lithograph. Edition: 513/1,472
Gift of Molly and Walter Bareiss, 1984.382

Contes et nouvelles en vers
Text by Jean de La Fontaine, French, 1621–1695
Paris: "Aux dépens d'un amateur," 1950
67 lithographs, plus a suite of 67 lithographs. Edition:
39/200
Gift of Molly and Walter Bareiss, 1984.383a–c
Ref.: Strachan p. 330

Charles Despiau, French, 1874–1946
Poèmes de Baudelaire
Text by Charles Baudelaire, French, 1821–1867
Paris: Éditions Gonin frères, 1933
44 lithographs, 7 wood-engravings, some in colors.
Edition: "pour Charles Despiau"
Gift of Molly and Walter Bareiss, 1984.384
Ref.: Garvey cat. 83, Strachan p. 330, Wheeler p. 101

Martin Dessecker, German, born 1958
Zungen Gurken und Einzeller
München: Galerie Biedermann, 1992
Photomechanical reproductions, including 3 with
overpainting. Edition: 7/20
Molly and Walter Bareiss Art Fund, 1992.87

Jan Dibbets, Dutch, born 1941
Roodborst Territorium / Sculptuur 1969
Text by Jan Dibbets
Köln: Gebr. König (Seth Siegelaub), 1970
Photomechanical reproductions, line block reproductions

Gift of Molly and Walter Bareiss, 1984.386
Ref: Drucker pp. 315–16

Jim Dine, American, born 1935
*The Picture of Dorian Gray: A Working Script for the Stage
from the Novel by Oscar Wilde with Original Images & Notes
on the Text by Jim Dine*
Text by Oscar Wilde, Irish, 1854–1900
London: Petersburg Press, 1968
12 color lithographs, plus a suite of 6 color lithographs,
photomechanical reproductions. Edition: 167/200
Gift of Molly and Walter Bareiss, 1984.387a–g
Ref.: Hogben cat. 142, Symmes cat. 20

*The Apocalypse: The Revelation of St. John the Divine
(The Last Book of the New Testament from the King James
Version of the Bible, 1611)*
San Francisco: Arion Press (Andrew Hoyem), 1982
29 woodcuts. Edition: 57/150
Gift of Molly and Walter Bareiss, 1984.388
Ref.: Castleman p. 133, Hogben cat. 165, Johnson cat. 168,
Phillips cat. 13, Symmes cat. 21

The Temple of Flora
Texts by various authors
San Francisco: Arion Press (Andrew Hoyem), 1984
One bas-relief cast in bonded bronze (cover), 29 drypoints
and engravings. Edition: 40/175
Gift of Molly and Walter Bareiss, 1984.389
Ref.: Symmes cat. 22

Ding Xiong Quan (see Walasse Ting)

César Doméla, Dutch, active France, 1900–1992
Diana Trivia
Text by Jean Laude, French, born 1922
[Paris]: Brunidor, 1973
10 color lithographs. Edition: XXVII/XXX
Gift of Molly and Walter Bareiss, 1984.392

Oscar Dominguez, Spanish, active France, 1906–1958
Les deux qui se croisent
Text by Oscar Dominguez
[Paris]: Revue fontaine (Henri Parisot), 1947
One ink drawing, line block reproduction. Edition:
388/400
Gift of Molly and Walter Bareiss, 1984.393

Poésie et vérité 1942
Text by Paul Éluard, French, 1895–1952
Paris: Librairie "Les nourritures terrestres," 1947
One ink drawing, 32 etchings, one color lift ground
aquatint
Gift of Molly and Walter Bareiss, 1984.394

Auguste Donnay, Belgian, 1862–1911
L'almanach des poètes
Texts by various authors
Paris: Mercure de France, 1895
Photomechanical reproductions
Gift of Molly and Walter Bareiss, 1984.395

Piero Dorazio, Italian, born 1927
Unbewohnbar die Trauer
Text by Peter Huchel, German, 1903–1981
St. Gallen, Schweiz: Erker-Presse (Franz Larese, Jürg
Janett), 1976
8 color lithographs, plus a double suite of 16 lithographs,
one sound recording. Edition: 14/40
Gift of Molly and Walter Bareiss, 1984.397a–b

Piero Dorazio
Text by Giuseppe Ungaretti, Italian, 1888–1970
St. Gallen, Schweiz: Erker-Presse (Franz Larese, Jurg
Janett), 1971
One color lithograph, photomechanical reproductions.
Edition: 9/100
Gift of Molly and Walter Bareiss, 1984.398

La Luce: Poesie 1914–1961 [reduced facsimile]
Text by Giuseppe Ungaretti, Italian, 1888–1970
St. Gallen, Schweiz: Erker-Presse (Franz Larese, Jürg
Janett), 1978 (1st ed. 1971)

Photomechanical reproductions
Gift of Molly and Walter Bareiss, 1984.396

Piero Dorazio
Text by Eugène Ionesco, French (born Romania),
1912–1994
St. Gallen, Schweiz: Erker-Presse (Franz Larese, Jürg
Janett), 1981
4 color lithographs. Edition: 81/200
Gift of Molly and Walter Bareiss, 1984.399

Hans Dörflinger, German, born 1941
Tarot
Texts by Hans Dörflinger; David Sylvester, American,
born 1924
London: Fischer Fine Art in association with Propyläen,
Berlin and Galerie Valentien, Stuttgart, 1975
22 color "granolithographs." Edition: "a.p."
Gift of Molly and Walter Bareiss, 1984.390

Helen Douglas (see listing under Telfer Stokes)

Jean Dubuffet, French, 1901–1985
L'homme du commun, ou Jean Dubuffet
Text by Pierre Seghers, French, 1906–1987
[Paris]: Éditions poésie, 1944
2 lithographs (one in color). Edition: 140/150
Gift of Molly and Walter Bareiss, 1984.400
Fig. 93

Matière et mémoire, ou les lithographes à l'école
Text by Francis Ponge, French, 1899–1988
Paris: Fernand Mourlot, 1945
34 lithographs, some in colors. Edition: 21/50
Gift of Molly and Walter Bareiss, 1984.401
Ref.: Johnson cat. 117, Strachan p. 330

Élégies
Text by Eugène Guillevic, French, born 1907
Paris: Éditions le Point du jour, 1946
One color lithograph. Edition: IV/X
Gift of Molly and Walter Bareiss, 1984.402
Ref.: Garvey cat. 87

Ler dla canpane
Text by Jean Dubuffet
[Paris: Jean Dubuffet, 1948]
3 linoleum cuts, 3 woodcuts
Gift of Molly and Walter Bareiss, 1984.403

La métromanie, ou les dessous de la capitale
Text by Jean Paulhan, French, 1884–1968
Paris: [s.n.], 1949
Lithographs. Edition: hors commerce
Gift of Molly and Walter Bareiss, 1984.404
Ref.: Strachan p. 330

Les murs
Text by Eugène Guillevic, French, born 1907
[Paris]: Éditions du livre, 1950
15 lithographs. Edition: 67/160
Gift of Molly and Walter Bareiss, 1984.405
Ref.: Garvey cat. 88, Hogben cat.122, Johnson cat. 128,
Strachan p. 330, Symmes cat. 24
Fig. 25

*La djingine du Théophélès, avec les "Corps de dames" de
Jean Dubuffet*
Text by André Martel, French, born 1930
Saint-Maurice d'Etalan, France: L'air du temps, 1954
Line block reproductions with blind embossing.
Edition: 9/75
Gift of Molly and Walter Bareiss, 1984.406

Demain Monsieur Silber
Text by Kay Sage, American (born France), 1898–1963
Paris: Pierre Seghers, 1957
2 collotypes, photomechanical reproduction (wrappers).
Edition: 70/500
Gift of Molly and Walter Bareiss, 1984.407

Les assemblages de Jean Dubuffet
Text by Pierre Volboudt
Paris: XXe siècle (F. Hazan), 1958

One color lithograph, 18 collotypes, some in color.
Edition: 34/750
Gift of Molly and Walter Bareiss, 1984.408

Oukiva trene sebot par Jandu Bufe G. O. O G G
Text by Jean Dubuffet; Pierre Bettencourt, French,
born 1917
[Paris?]: Collège de Pataphysique [(Jean Dubuffet), 1958]
Line block reproductions. Edition: 427/557
Gift of Molly and Walter Bareiss, 1984.430

Phénomènes, nᵒˢ 7, 9, 11–13
[Paris]: Jean Dubuffet, 1959–60
18 lithographs each. Edition: various/XXII
Gift of Molly and Walter Bareiss, 1984.409, 1984.410,
1984.411, 1984.414, 1984.415

Phénomènes (color series), nᵒˢ 4–9
[Paris]: Jean Dubuffet, 1960–62
10 color lithographs each. Edition: various/XX
Gift of Molly and Walter Bareiss, 1984.412, 1984.413,
1984.416, 1984.417, 1984.418, 1984.419

La fleur de barbe
Text by Jean Dubuffet
[Paris]: L'imprimerie Duval, 1960
5 collotypes. Edition: 231/500
Gift of Molly and Walter Bareiss, 1981.135

Oreilles gardées
Text by Pierre André Benoit, French, 1924–1993
Paris and Alès, France: PAB (Pierre André Benoit), 1962
Line block reproductions. Edition: 105/300
Gift of Molly and Walter Bareiss, 1984.420

*Algèbre de l'hourloupe: 52 figures extrapolatoires de
Jean Dubuffet*
Paris: Éditions Jeanne Bucher; Basel: [Galerie] Beyeler,
[1963 or after]
Photomechanical reproductions
Gift of Molly and Walter Bareiss, 1984.427

L'hourloupe
Text by Jean Dubuffet
Paris: Noël Arnaud, 1963
Photomechanical reproductions. Edition: unnumbered/850
Gift of Molly and Walter Bareiss, 1984.424

La lunette farcie
Text by Jean Dubuffet
Paris, Alès, France: PAB (Pierre André Benoit), 1963
11 lithographs (10 in colors). Edition: 34/50
Gift of Molly and Walter Bareiss, 1984.423
Ref.: Castleman p. 153, Symmes cat. 25

Le mirivis des naturgies
Text by André Martel, French, born 1930
Paris: Alexandre Loewy, 1963
16 lithographs, some in color. Edition: 71/110
Gift of Molly and Walter Bareiss, 1984.421
Ref.: Johnson cat. 147, Strachan p. 331

Trémolo sur l'oeil
Text by Jean Dubuffet
Veilhes, Lavaur, France: Gaston Puel, 1963
Photomechanical reproductions. Edition: unnumbered/300
Gift of Molly and Walter Bareiss, 1984.422

Vignettes lorgnettes (Ler dla canpane)
Text by Jean Dubuffet
Basel: Galerie Beyeler, 1963
11 woodcuts, 13 linoleum cuts, one woodblock.
Edition: 12/20
Gift of Molly and Walter Bareiss, 1984.425

Parade funèbre pour Charles Estienne
Text by Jean Dubuffet
Paris: Éditions Jeanne Bucher, 1967
Zinc block reproductions. Edition: 371/400
Gift of Molly and Walter Bareiss, 1984.426

La botte à nique
Text by Jean Dubuffet
[Lausanne]: Albert Skira, 1973
One color screen print, photomechanical reproductions.

Edition: 37/200
Gift of Molly and Walter Bareiss, 1984.428
Fig. 125

Il y a
Text by Jacques Berne, French, born 1947
[Montpellier, France]: Fata Morgana, 1979
15 collotypes. Edition: 32/80
Gift of Molly and Walter Bareiss, 1984.429

Jean Dubuffet (see also listing under Various Artists,
XXe siècle)

Marcel Duchamp, American (born France), 1887–1968
*First Papers of Surrealism: Hanging by André Breton,
His Twine Marcel Duchamp*
Text by R. A. Parker, 1889?–1970
New York: Coordinating Council of French Relief
Societies, 1942
Photomechanical reproduction with die-cut holes
by Duchamp (cover), photomechanical reproductions
of work by various artists
Gift of Molly and Walter Bareiss, 1984.1215

From the Green Box
Text by Marcel Duchamp
New Haven, CT: Readymade Press [Graphic Arts
Department, Yale University], 1957
Photomechanical reproduction (cover). Edition:
unnumbered/400
Gift of Molly and Walter Bareiss, 1984.432, 2000.1

L'équilibre
Text by Francis Picabia, French, 1879–1953
Alès, France: PAB (Pierre André Benoit), 1958
One etching. Edition: 26/40
Gift of Molly and Walter Bareiss, 1984.433

Première lumière
Text by Pierre André Benoit, French, 1924–1993
Alès, France: PAB (Pierre André Benoit), 1959
One etching. Edition: 31/40
Gift of Molly and Walter Bareiss, 1984.434

Tiré à 4 épingles
Text by Pierre de Massot, French, 1900–1969
Alès, France: PAB (Pierre André Benoit), 1959
One drypoint. Edition: 23/30
Gift of Molly and Walter Bareiss, 1984.435

Marcel Duchamp; Richard Hamilton, British, born 1922
*The Bride Stripped Bare by Her Bachelors, Even: A
Typographic Version by Richard Hamilton of Marcel
Duchamp's Green Box*
Text by Marcel Duchamp; translation by George Heard
Hamilton, American, born 1910
New York: George Wittenborn, [1960]
Photomechanical reproductions
Gift of Molly and Walter Bareiss, 1984.436

Marcel Duchamp (see also listings under Jean (Hans) Arp,
Michel Cadoret, Alberto Giacometti, Georges Hugnet)

Raoul Dufy, French, 1877–1953
Le poète assassiné
Text by Guillaume Apollinaire, French, 1880–1918
Paris: Au sans pareil, 1926
36 lithographs, one color woodcut (cover). Edition:
427/450
Gift of Molly and Walter Bareiss, 1984.437
Ref.: Garvey cat. 92, Symmes cat. 27, Wheeler p. 101

Raoul Dufy
Text by Marcelle Berr de Turique, French, 1894–19??
Paris: Librairie Floury, 1930
One etching, one collotype with added pochoir color
(wrappers), 175 collotypes. Edition: 744/unknown
Gift of Molly and Walter Bareiss, 1984.439
Fig. 85

*Le bestiaire, ou cortège d'Orphée, supplement: Les deux
poèmes refusés (no 4)*
Text by Guillaume Apollinaire, French, 1880–1918
Paris: "Aux dépens d'un amateur," 1931

2 woodcuts. Edition: 4/29
Gift of Molly and Walter Bareiss, 1984.440
Ref.: Garvey cat. 91, Wheeler p. 101

Mon docteur le vin
Text by Gaston Derys, French, 1875–19??
Paris: Draeger frères, 1936
Photomechanical reproductions
Gift of Molly and Walter Bareiss, 1984.441
Fig. 91

*Dessins et croquis: extraits des cartons et carnets
de Raoul Dufy*
Text by Louis Carré, French, 1897–1977
Paris: Louis Carré, 1944
Collotypes. Edition: 63/703
Gift of Molly and Walter Bareiss, 1984.442

La source des jours
Text by Gaston Massat, French
Paris: Bordas, 1948 (© 1947)
One lithograph, photomechanical reproductions.
Edition: 244/300
Gift of Molly and Walter Bareiss, 1984.443

Raoul Dufy; Pierre-Auguste Renoir, French, 1841–1919
Catalogue complet des éditions Ambroise Vollard
Text by Ambroise Vollard, French, 1867–1939
Paris: Le Portique, 1930
One etching (Dufy), line block reproduction (Renoir).
Edition: 58/625
Gift of Molly and Walter Bareiss, 1984.438

André Dunoyer de Segonzac, French, 1884–1974
Dunoyer de Segonzac
Text by Paul Jamot, French, 1863–1939
Paris: Librairie Floury, 1929
One etching, collotypes, some in colors. Edition:
391/unknown
Gift of Molly and Walter Bareiss, 1984.1078

L'appel du clown: comédie en un acte
Text by Régis Gignoux, French, 1878–1931
[Paris]: [s.n.], 1930
25 etchings with drypoint. Edition: 71/120
Gift of Molly and Walter Bareiss, 1984.1079
Ref.: Wheeler p. 110

La treille muscate
Text by Colette, French, 1873–1954
[Paris?: s.n.], 1932
35 etchings. Edition: 146/150
Gift of Molly and Walter Bareiss, 1984.1080
Ref.: Garvey cat. 280, Strachan p. 341, Wheeler p. 110

Albrecht Dürer, German, 1471–1528
Albrecht Dürer: Niederländisches Reiseskizzenbuch, 1520–1521
[facsimile]
Text by Heinrich Wölfflin, Swiss, 1864–1945
Frankfurt am Main: Prestel-Verlag, 1928
Collotypes. Edition: 740/1,200
Gift of Molly and Walter Bareiss, 1984.445

Albrecht Dürer; Hans Leonhard Schäuffelein, German,
ca. 1480–1537/40; **Hans Sebald Beham,** German,
1500–1550
*Originalholzschnitte aus dem 16. Jahrhundert: Dürer,
Schäuffelein, u.a.*
München: Gesellschaft für Zeichnende Künste
(Walter Biehl), 1923
Line block reproductions. Edition: 431/440
Gift of Molly and Walter Bareiss, 1984.444

Anthony van Dyck, Flemish, 1599–1641
*A Description of the Sketch-book by Sir Anthony Van Dyck,
Used by Him in Italy, 1621–1627, and Preserved in the
Collection of the Duke of Devonshire, K.G. at Chatsworth*
[facsimile]
Text by Lionel Cust, British, 1859–1929
London: George Bell and Sons, 1902
Collotypes
Gift of Molly and Walter Bareiss, 1984.446

Yan Bernard Dyl, French
Les oraisons amoureuses de Jeanne-Aurélie Grivolin, Lyonnaise
Texts by Jeanne-Aurélie Grivolin, French, 1784–1869;
Roger Pillet, born 1917
Paris: "La Connaissance," Galerie de la Madeleine, 1926
15 drypoints with added pochoir and hand color, line block
reproductions, including 2 with added pochoir color (wrappers). Edition: 272/500
Gift of Molly and Walter Bareiss, 1984.447

Roberto Matta Echaurren (see Matta)

Fritz Eichenberg, American (born Germany), 1901–1990
Eleonora
Texts by Edgar Allan Poe, American, 1809–1849; Richard
Wilbur, American, born 1921
Cleveland: Print Club of Cleveland, 1979
2 wood-engravings (from same block). Edition: 220/264
Gift of Molly and Walter Bareiss, 1984.448a–b

Timothy C. Ely, American, born 1949
Approach to the Site
New York: Water Street Press, 1986
Painted boards with collage (binding), color lithographs.
Edition: 16/49
Gift of Molly and Walter Bareiss, 1987.285
Fig. 142

Jean Epstein, French (born Poland), 1897–1953
Bonjour cinéma
Text by Jean Epstein
Paris: Éditions de la sirène, 1921
Photomechanical reproductions, line block reproductions
Gift of Molly and Walter Bareiss, 1985.77

Wolfram Erber, German, born 1939
*65 Aufnahmen aus meiner Atelier: Projektionen und
Lichtobjekte aus den Jahren 1977–78*
Berlin: Wolfram Erber, 1979
65 photographs. Edition: 2/12
Gift of Molly and Walter Bareiss, 1984.449

*Wolfram Erber: Pastelle und Zeichnungen zu ein Würfelwurf
von Stephane Mallarmé*
Text by Stéphane Mallarmé, French, 1842–1898
München: D. P. Druck und Publikations, 1980
Photomechanical reproductions. Edition: 1/300
Gift of Molly and Walter Bareiss, 1984.450

24 Kombinationen nach dem J Ging für Altflöte Solo
[Berlin: Wolfram Erber, 1982]
Photomechanical reproductions. Edition: 4/100
Gift of Molly and Walter Bareiss, 1987.286

Hans Erni, Swiss, active France, born 1909
Hans Erni: Weg und Zielsetzung des Künstlers
Text by Konrad Farner, German, 1903–1974
Zürich: Amstutz, Herdeg & Co., 1943
One ink drawing, 2 etchings, photomechanical reproductions, line block reproductions. Edition: III/XII
Gift of Molly and Walter Bareiss, 1984.451

Max Ernst, French (born Germany), 1891–1976
Le cœur à gaz
Text by Tristan Tzara, French (born Romania), 1896–1963
Paris: G.L.M. (Guy Lévis Mano), 1946
One color drypoint with etching and aquatint. Edition:
20/380
Gift of Molly and Walter Bareiss, 1984.453

Almanach surréaliste du demi-siècle
Texts by various authors; edited by André Breton, French,
1896–1966
[Paris]: Éditions du sagittaire, 1950
2 color lithographs, photomechanical reproductions,
line block reproductions of work by various artists.
Edition: 12/65
Gift of Molly and Walter Bareiss, 1984.1317

Das Schnabelpaar
Text by Max Ernst
Basel: Galerie Ernst Beyeler, 1953

8 color etchings with aquatint, one blind embossing.
Edition: 17/30
Gift of Molly and Walter Bareiss, 1984.454a–i

Le poème de la femme 100 têtes
Text by Max Ernst
Paris: Jean Hugues, 1959
One etching. Edition: 3/350
Gift of Molly and Walter Bareiss, 1984.455
Ref.: Garvey cat. 102

Histoire naturelle
Texts by Max Ernst; Paul Éluard, French, 1895–1952;
Jean (Hans) Arp, French (born Alsace), 1887–1966
Köln: Galerie der Spiegel, 1965
One color lithograph (wrappers), photomechanical reproductions, line block reproductions. Edition: 192/700
Gift of Molly and Walter Bareiss, 1984.456

Les malheurs des immortels
Texts by Max Ernst; Paul Éluard, French, 1895–1952;
translation by Ulrich Serbser
Köln: Galerie der Spiegel, [1965?] (1st ed. 1922)
One color etching with aquatint, line block reproductions.
Edition: 85/335
Gift of Molly and Walter Bareiss, 1984.452
Ref.: Hogben cat. 66, Wheeler p. 101
Fig. 81

*The Hunting of the Snark: An Agony in Eight Fits. Die Jagd
nach dem Schnark: Agonie in acht Krämpfen*
Text by Lewis Carroll, British, 1832–1898
Stuttgart: Manus Presse, 1968
22 lithographs, some in colors. Edition: 64/130
Gift of Molly and Walter Bareiss, 1984.457

Dent prompte
Text by René Char, French, 1907–1988
Paris: Galerie Lucie Weill, 1969
11 color lithographs. Edition: 31/240
Gift of Molly and Walter Bareiss, 1984.458
Fig. 120

*Caspar David Friedrich: Seelandschaft mit Kapuziner;
Paysage marin avec un Capucin*
Texts by Heinrich von Kleist, German, 1777–1811; Achim
von Arnim, German, 1781–1831; Clemens Brentano,
German, 1778–1842; translation by Max Ernst
Zürich: Edition Hans Bolliger, 1972
One lithograph, photomechanical reproductions. Edition:
134/577
Gift of Molly and Walter Bareiss, 1984.459

La ballade du soldat
Text by Georges Ribemont-Dessaignes, French, 1884–1974
Vence, France: Pierre Chave, 1972
36 color lithographs. Edition: 47/199
Gift of Molly and Walter Bareiss, 1984.460
Fig. 153

Max Ernst; Joan Miró, Spanish, active France, 1893–1983;
Yves Tanguy, American (born France), 1900–1955
*L'antitête: Monsieur Aa l'antiphilosophe. Minuits pour géants.
Le désespéranto*
Texts by Tristan Tzara, French (born Romania), 1896–1963
[Paris]: Bordas, 1949
8 color etchings with aquatint, plus a suite of 8 hand-colored etchings (Ernst, *Monsieur Aa*), 8 etchings with
added pochoir color, plus a suite of 8 etchings with added
watercolor (Miró, *Le désespéranto*), 7 color etchings with
aquatint, plus a suite of 7 hand-colored etchings (Tanguy,
Minuits pour géants). Editions: 187/200 and 20/200
Gift of Molly and Walter Bareiss, 1984.948a–c (without
suites), 1984.949a–c
Ref.: Garvey cat. 298, Johnson cat. 57, 125
Fig. 18

Max Ernst (see also listing under Additional Books)

Erró, Icelandic, active France, born 1932
Tableaux chinois
Text by Jean-Christophe Ammann, German, born 1939

München: Edition Godula Buchholz, [1975?]
Photomechanical reproductions
Gift of Molly and Walter Bareiss, 1984.461

Erté, French (born Russia), 1892–1990
Ermyntrude and Esmeralda: An Entertainment
Text by Lytton Strachey, British, 1880–1932
London: Anthony Blond, 1969
Photomechanical reproductions
Gift of Molly and Walter Bareiss, 1984.462

José Escada (see listing under Various Artists, *KWY*)

Georges d'Espagnat, French, 1870–1950
Simone: poème champêtre
Text by Remy de Gourmont, French, 1858–1915
Paris: Librairie du Mercure de France (Édition du Mercure
musical), 1907
Line block reproductions
Gift of Molly and Walter Bareiss, 1984.463

Maurice Estève, French, born 1904
Tombeau de mon père
Text by André Frénaud, French, 1907–1993
Paris: Éditions Galanis, 1961
7 mezzotints with etching, some in color. Edition: 64/100
Gift of Molly and Walter Bareiss, 1984.464
Ref.: Strachan p. 331

Hans Falk, Swiss, born 1918
Der Besuch der alten Dame: Eine tragische Komödie
Text by Friedrich Dürrenmatt, Swiss, 1921–1990
Lausanne: André and Pierre Gonin, 1964
21 lithographs, most with added color, graphite, and sand.
Edition: 107/174
Gift of Molly and Walter Bareiss, 1984.465

…zart wie dein Bild
Texts by Guillaume Apollinaire, French, 1880–1918;
Madeleine Pagès, French; Elisabeth Brock-Sulzer, Swiss,
1903–1981
Zürich: Alpha-Presse, 1965
13 lithographs, some in color, 8 machine-printed lithographs, photomechanical reproduction (wrappers). Edition:
74/130
Gift of Molly and Walter Bareiss, 1984.466

Henri Fantin-Latour, French, 1836–1904; **G. Simoes da
Fonseca,** 1874–19??; **Denys Puech,** French, 1854–1942
Les bucoliques
Text by André-Marie de Chénier, French (born Turkey),
1762–1794
Paris: "Maison du livre" (Charles Meunier), 1905
12 lithographs by Fantin-Latour (each repeated twice), 22
lithographed decorations by Simoes da Fonseca (each
repeated twice), one bronze relief plaque by Puech (cover).
Edition: 32/177
Gift of Molly and Walter Bareiss, 1984.467

Lyonel Feininger, American, active Germany, 1871–1956
Lyonel Feininger: Drawings
Text by Lyonel Feininger
New York: Curt Valentin, 1951
16 collotypes, photomechanical reproduction (portfolio
cover). Edition: unnumbered/1,000
Gift of Molly and Walter Bareiss, 1984.468

Lore Feininger aus der Werkstatt Vater Lyonels
Text by Lore Feininger, American, born 1909
Berlin: Archivarion, Deutscher Archiv-Verlag, 1957
Photomechanical reproductions. Edition: 8/500
Gift of Molly and Walter Bareiss, 1984.469

Leonor Fini, Italian (born Argentina), active France,
1908–1996
Jardins
Text by Jean-Paul Guibbert, French, born 1942
Montpellier, France: L.E.O., 1965
4 etchings, plus 2 suites of 4 etchings. Edition: 3/60
Gift of Molly and Walter Bareiss, 1984.470

Leonor Fini (see also listing under Henri Matisse)

Ian Hamilton Finlay, British (born Bahamas), born 1925
Sea-Poppy 2 (Fishing Boat Names)
[Dunsyre, Scotland]: Wild Hawthorn Press, 1968
Letterpress (text only)
Molly and Walter Bareiss Art Fund, 1997.278

Blue Water's Bark
[Little Sparta, Scotland: Wild Hawthorn Press, 1992]
One color lithograph
Molly and Walter Bareiss Art Fund, 1997.279

Diamond Studded Fish Net
[Little Sparta, Scotland: Wild Hawthorn Press, 1992]
One color lithograph
Molly and Walter Bareiss Art Fund, 1997.280

'Im dunkeln Laub die Gold-Orangen glühn'
Little Sparta, [Scotland]: Wild Hawthorn Press, [1994]
Photomechanical reproduction
Molly and Walter Bareiss Art Fund, 1997.277

2 Notices
[Little Sparta, Scotland]: Wild Hawthorn Press, [1995]
Letterpress (text only)
Molly and Walter Bareiss Art Fund, 1997.270

3 Constructions
[Little Sparta, Scotland]: Wild Hawthorn Press, [1995]
Photolithographed text
Molly and Walter Bareiss Art Fund, 1997.259

Elegy
[Little Sparta, Scotland]: Wild Hawthorn Press, [1995]
Line block reproduction
Molly and Walter Bareiss Art Fund, 1997.267

The Mastless Barges (2)
[Little Sparta, Scotland]: Wild Hawthorn Press, [1995]
Photolithographed text
Molly and Walter Bareiss Art Fund, 1997.275

Sound Shanty
[Little Sparta, Scotland]: Wild Hawthorn Press, [1995]
Letterpress (text only)
Molly and Walter Bareiss Art Fund, 1997.262

Untitled (Wall Text Series)
[Little Sparta, Scotland]: Wild Hawthorn Press, [1995]
Photolithographed text
Molly and Walter Bareiss Art Fund, 1997.272

Boreas: Plank Bender
[Little Sparta, Scotland]: Wild Hawthorn Press, [1996]
Photomechanical reproduction
Molly and Walter Bareiss Art Fund, 1997.264

Hesiod: An Epigram on the Common Fisheries Policy
Little Sparta, [Scotland]: Wild Hawthorn Press, [1996]
Photolithographed text
Molly and Walter Bareiss Art Fund, 1997.276

Homage to Post-Impressionism
[Little Sparta, Scotland]: Wild Hawthorn Press, [1996]
Photomechanical reproduction
Molly and Walter Bareiss Art Fund, 1997.269

Reef Points
[Little Sparta, Scotland: Wild Hawthorn Press, 1996]
7 color lithographs
Molly and Walter Bareiss Art Fund, 1997.282a–g

A Seychelles Stradivarius
[Little Sparta, Scotland]: Wild Hawthorn Press, [1996]
Photomechanical reproduction
Molly and Walter Bareiss Art Fund, 1997.274

Ian Hamilton Finlay; Laura Gerahty
Calypso
Little Sparta, [Scotland]: Wild Hawthorn Press, [1996]
Text by Andrew Lang, Scottish, 1844–1912
Photomechanical reproductions
Molly and Walter Bareiss Art Fund, 1997.273

Ian Hamilton Finlay; Richard Grasby, British;
Nicholas Sloan, British
Talismans and Signifiers with Sphere into Cube

Edinburgh: Graeme Murray Gallery, 1984
Photomechanical reproductions. Edition: unnumbered/1,000
Molly and Walter Bareiss Art Fund and Printed Matter
Matching Gift Fund for Libraries, 1987.58

Ian Hamilton Finlay; Michael Harvey, British, born 1946
'For the Temples of the Greeks Our Homesickness Lasts Forever'
[Little Sparta, Scotland]: Wild Hawthorn Press, [1995]
Photomechanical reproduction
Molly and Walter Bareiss Art Fund, 1997.260

Purse Seine
[Little Sparta, Scotland: Wild Hawthorn Press, 1995]
Photomechanical reproduction
Molly and Walter Bareiss Art Fund, 1997.263

Ian Hamilton Finlay; Gary Hincks, British, born 1949
Citron Bleu
[Little Sparta, Scotland]: Wild Hawthorn Press, [1994]
One color lithograph
Molly and Walter Bareiss Art Fund, 1997.281

Found Poem: The Mastless Barges
[Little Sparta, Scotland: Wild Hawthorn Press, 1995]
Photomechanical reproduction
Molly and Walter Bareiss Art Fund, 1997.265

Building the Hull
[Little Sparta, Scotland]: Wild Hawthorn Press, [1996]
Line block reproduction
Molly and Walter Bareiss Art Fund, 1997.268

Expectation
[Little Sparta, Scotland]: Wild Hawthorn Press, [1996]
Photomechanical reproduction
Molly and Walter Bareiss Art Fund, 1997.261

Ian Hamilton Finlay; Kathleen Lindsley
After Theocritus
[Little Sparta, Scotland]: Wild Hawthorn Press, [1996]
Photomechanical reproduction
Molly and Walter Bareiss Art Fund, 1997.266

Ian Hamilton Finlay; Annet Stirling
Olsen's Fisherman's Nautical Alphabet
Little Sparta, [Scotland]: Wild Hawthorn Press, [1992]
Photomechanical reproductions
Molly and Walter Bareiss Art Fund, 1997.271

Hans Fischer, Swiss, 1909–1958
La coquinaille
Text by the Brothers Grimm: Jakob Grimm, German,
1785–1863, Wilhelm Grimm, German, 1786–1859; transla-
tion by Gustave Roud, born 1907
Zürich: Edition Wolfsberg; [Paris]: Collection dix sur dix,
Delpire, 1945
Photomechanical reproductions
Gift of Molly and Walter Bareiss, 1984.471

Le chat botté
Text by Charles Perrault, French, 1628–1703
Lausanne: André et Pierre Gonin, 1960 (1st ed. 1957)
Color lithographs. Edition: 42/270
Gift of Molly and Walter Bareiss, 1984.472
Ref.: Garvey cat. 107

Kaspar Fischer, Swiss, 1938–2000
Metamorphosen I
Bern: Zytglogge, 1977 (1st ed. 1971)
Photomechanical reproductions
Gift of Molly and Walter Bareiss, 1984.473

Eric Fischl, American, born 1948
Sketchbook with Voices
Text by Eric Fischl; Jerry Saltz, American, born 1951
New York: Alfred van der Marck Editions, 1986
Line block reproduction
Molly and Walter Bareiss Art Fund and Printed Matter
Matching Gift Funds for Libraries, 1987.59

Annie, Gwen, Lilly, Pam and Tulip
Text by Jamaica Kincaid, American (born Antigua),
born 1949

New York: Library Fellows of the Whitney Museum of
American Art (May Castleberry), 1986
9 lithographs, most in color. Edition: "for Eugene V. Thaw"
Gift of Molly and Walter Bareiss, 1987.276
Ref.: Phillips cat. 16

Georg Flegel, German, 1563–1638
Georg Flegel: Sechs Aquarelle
Text by Friedrich Winkler, 1888–1965
Berlin: Deutscher Verein für Kunstwissenschaft, 1954
6 collotypes, photomechanical reproductions
Gift of Molly and Walter Bareiss, 1984.474

Dean Flemming (see listing under Peter Forakis)

Jean-Michel Folon, Belgian, born 1934
Le portmanteau
Paris: Éditions des Jumeaux, 1969
Line block reproductions
Gift of Molly and Walter Bareiss, 1984.476

La vie sentimentale de Folon
Text by Giorgio Soavi, Italian, born 1923
Milano: Milano Libri, 1970
Line block reproductions. Edition: unnumbered/1,000
Gift of Molly and Walter Bareiss, 1984.477

Le message
Paris: Hermann, éditeurs des sciences et des arts, 1974
(1st ed. 1967)
Photomechanical reproductions
Gift of Molly and Walter Bareiss, 1984.475

Lucio Fontana, Italian (born Argentina), 1899–1968
*Dix eaux-fortes: illustrées par Alain Jouffroy; L'épée dans l'eau:
en hommage à Lucio Fontana*
Text by Alain Jouffroy, French, born 1928
Milano: Galleria Schwarz, 1962
10 etchings, some in color. Edition: 32/75
Gift of Molly and Walter Bareiss, 1984.478

Jean Louis Forain, French, 1852–1931; **J.-F. Raffaëlli,**
French, 1850–1924
Croquis parisiens
Text by Joris-Karl Huysmans, French, 1848–1907
Paris: Henri Vaton, 1880
10 etchings (6 by Forain, 4 by Raffaëlli)
Gift of Molly and Walter Bareiss, 1984.982
Ref.: Garvey cat. 108

Peter Forakis, American, born 1957; **Phyllis Yampolsky;
Dean Flemming**
Grope (vol. 1, no. 1, January 1964)
Edited by Peter Forakis
New York: Tibor-de-Nagy Editions, 1964
Photomechanical reproductions. Edition: unnumbered/500
Gift of Molly and Walter Bareiss, 1984.1202

Ruth Francken, Czech, active France, born 1924
Köpfe
Berlin: Steinpresse Jochen Luft, 1964
8 lithographs. Edition: 6/60
Gift of Molly and Walter Bareiss, 1984.479

Antonio Frasconi, American (born Uruguay), born 1919
The Work of Antonio Frasconi
Cleveland: Print Club of Cleveland; The Cleveland
Museum of Art, 1952
One color woodcut (wrappers), photomechanical reproduc-
tions, line block reproductions
Gift of Molly and Walter Bareiss, 1984.480

12 Fables of Aesop
Text by Aesop, Greek, 620?–?560 B.C.E.
New York: The Museum of Modern Art, 1954
20 linoleum cuts, including one in color. Edition: 271/975
Gift of Molly and Walter Bareiss, 1984.491
Ref.: Castleman p. 121, Garvey cat. 111

*See and Say—Guarda e Parla—Regarde et parle—Mira y
Habla: A Picture Book in Four Languages*
Text by Antonio Frasconi
New York: Harcourt, Brace and Company, 1955

Line block reproductions
Gift of Molly and Walter Bareiss, 1984.481

Birds from My Homeland; with Notes from W. H. Hudson's
"Birds of La Plata"
Text by W. H. Hudson, British, 1841–1922
[South Norwalk, CT]: Antonio Frasconi, 1958
14 woodcuts, including 11 with added color. Edition:
114/200
Gift of Molly and Walter Bareiss, 1984.482

The Face of Edgar Allan Poe
South Norwalk, CT: Antonio Frasconi, 1959
13 color woodcuts (including publisher's device). Edition:
116/250
Gift of Molly and Walter Bareiss, 1984.483

A Whitman Portrait
Text by Walt Whitman, American, 1819–1892
South Norwalk, CT: Antonio Frasconi, [1960]
19 color woodcuts (including publisher's device).
Edition: 204/525
Gift of Molly and Walter Bareiss, 1984.484
Ref.: Garvey cat. 112

Known Fables Illustrated by Frasconi
Text by Aesop, Greek, 620?–?560 B.C.E.
South Norwalk, CT: Antonio Frasconi, 1964
12 woodcuts, some in color. Edition: 254/500
Gift of Molly and Walter Bareiss, 1984.486

A Sunday in Monterey
New York: Harcourt, Brace & World, 1964
Photomechanical reproductions
Gift of Molly and Walter Bareiss, 1984.485

Bestiary / Bestiario
Text by Pablo Neruda, Chilean, 1904–1973; translation by
Elsa Neuberger, American, 1907–2000
New York: Harcourt, Brace & World, 1965
One woodcut in colors, line block reproductions. Edition:
287/300
Gift of Molly and Walter Bareiss, 1984.487

Love Lyrics
Texts by various authors
New York: Odyssey Press, 1965
Photomechanical reproductions
Gift of Molly and Walter Bareiss, 1984.488

A Vision of Thoreau, with His 1849 Essay: Civil Disobedience
Text by Henry David Thoreau, American, 1817–1862
South Norwalk, CT: Antonio Frasconi, 1965
15 woodcuts (including publisher's device). Edition: 18/530
Gift of Molly and Walter Bareiss, 1984.489

Kaleidoscope in Woodcuts
New York: Harcourt, Brace & World, 1968
Photomechanical reproductions
Gift of Molly and Walter Bareiss, 1984.490

Andrea Fraser, American, born 1965
Woman 1 / Madonna and Child 1506–1967
New York: Andrea Fraser, 1984
Photomechanical reproductions
Molly and Walter Bareiss Art Fund and Printed Matter
Matching Gift Fund for Libraries, 1987.66

Caspar David Friedrich, German, 1774–1840
Caspar David Friedrich: Skizzenbuch 1806–1818 [facsimile]
Text by Ludwig Grote, German, 1893–1974
Berlin: Gebr. Mann, 1942
48 collotypes, some in colors
Gift of Molly and Walter Bareiss, 1984.493a–b

Robert Frontier, American (book designer)
The Alphabet Book in Venezia
Text by A. M. K., American
Venezia: Legatoria Piazzesi, 1975
Typographic design. Edition: 1/300
Gift of Molly and Walter Bareiss, 1984.494

Il libro del gallo
Text by A. M. K., American

Venezia: Legatoria Piazzesi, 1976
Relief prints. Edition: 8/25
Gift of Molly and Walter Bareiss, 1984.495

Hamish Fulton, British, born 1946
Camp Fire
Texts by David Reason; Michael Auping, American, born
1949
Eindhoven, Nederland: Stedelijk van Abbemuseum, 1985
Photomechanical reproductions. Edition: unnumbered/
2,000
Molly and Walter Bareiss Art Fund and Printed Matter
Matching Gift Fund for Libraries, 1987.51

Paul Gauguin, French, 1848–1903
L'oeuvre gravé de Gauguin
Text by Marcel Guérin, French, 1873–1948
Paris: H. Floury, 1927
103 collotypes. Edition: 73/550
Gift of Molly and Walter Bareiss, 1984.496a–b

Paul Gauguin: carnet de croquis [facsimile]
Text by Raymond Cogniat, French, 1896–19??
New York: Hammer Galleries, 1962
Collotypes. Edition: 826/900
Gift of Molly and Walter Bareiss, 1984.497a–c

Paul Gauguin (see also listing under Additional Books)

after **Paul Gavarni,** French, 1804–1866
Oeuvres nouvelles: Les bohèmes
Paris: Librairie Nouvelle (Calmann Lévy), 1853
20 lithographs, 2 wood-engravings after Gavarni (covers)
Gift of Molly and Walter Bareiss, 1984.498a–b
Fig. 7

Rupprecht Geiger, German, born 1908
Rupprecht Geiger
München: Galerie Stangl, 1961
One color screen print, photomechanical reproductions.
Edition: 30/50
Gift of Molly and Walter Bareiss, 1984.499

Pyr
München: Galerie Stangl, 1962
7 color screen prints (including cover). Edition: 10/25
Gift of Molly and Walter Bareiss, 1984.500a–f

K. (Karl) Domenig Geissbühler, Swiss, born 1932
Oscar Wilde: Aphorismen
Text by Oscar Wilde, Irish, 1854–1900
[Zürich]: Origo-Verlag, 1965
Photomechanical reproductions. Edition: unnumbered/600
Gift of Molly and Walter Bareiss, 1984.501

Ernst Geitlinger, German, 1895–1972
Ernst Geitlinger
München: Galerie Christoph Dürr, [1970]
One color screen print, line block reproductions.
Edition: 11/50
Gift of Molly and Walter Bareiss, 1984.502a–b

Fritz Genkinger, German, born 1934
Der Schwätzer
Text by Louis-René des Forêts, French, born 1918
München: Kösel-Verlag (Friedhelm Kemp), 1968
Photomechanical reproduction (wrappers)
Gift of Molly and Walter Bareiss, 1984.503

Unter der Lampe: Gedichte und Prosa
Text by Léon-Paul Fargue, French, 1876–1947
München: Kösel-Verlag (Friedhelm Kemp), 1970
Photomechanical reproduction (wrappers)
Gift of Molly and Walter Bareiss, 1984.504

Franco Gentilini, Italian, 1909–1981
Oggetti figure animali per una storia
Venezia: Cavallino, 1965
Photomechanical reproductions. Edition: 73/200
Gift of Molly and Walter Bareiss, 1984.505

Laura Gerahty (see listing under Ian Hamilton Finlay)

Alberto Giacometti, Swiss, 1901–1966
La folie Tristan
Text by unknown author; translation by Gilbert Lély,
French, 1904–1985
Paris: Jean Hugues, 1959
One etching. Edition: 15/50
Gift of Molly and Walter Bareiss, 1984.507

L'épervier
Text by Jacques Dupin, French, born 1927
Paris: G.L.M. (Guy Lévis Mano), 1960
One etching. Edition: 21/495
Gift of Molly and Walter Bareiss, 1984.508

Dans la chaleur vacante
Text by André du Bouchet, French, born 1924
Paris: Mercure de France, 1961
One etching. Edition: 25/520
Gift of Molly and Walter Bareiss, 1984.511

Pomme endormie
Text by Léna Leclercq, French
Décines, France: L'arbalète (Marc Barbezat), 1961
24 lithographs, plus 2 suites of 8 lithographs each.
Edition: XVIII/XX
Gift of Molly and Walter Bareiss, 1984.509
Ref.: Strachan pp. 190, 333

Vivantes cendres, innommées
Text by Michel Leiris, French, 1901–1990
Paris: Jean Hugues, 1961
19 etchings, plus a suite of 6 etchings. Edition: 18/90
Gift of Molly and Walter Bareiss, 1984.510
Ref.: Johnson cat. 141, Strachan pp. 190, 333

Les douze portraits du célèbre Orbandale: Pris sur le vif et
gravés a l'eau forte par Alberto Giacometti
Paris: Le degré quarante et un (Iliazd), 1962
12 soft-ground etchings. Edition: 32/40
Gift of Molly and Walter Bareiss, 1984.512
Fig. 58

L'inhabité
Text by André du Bouchet, French, born 1924
Paris: Jean Hugues, 1967
6 etchings. Edition: 25/125
Gift of Molly and Walter Bareiss, 1984.514

Paris sans fin
Text by Alberto Giacometti
Paris: Tériade, 1969
150 lithographs. Edition: 158/250
Gift of Molly and Walter Bareiss, 1984.515
Ref.: Hogben cat. 145, Johnson cat. 150

Alberto Giacometti; Marcel Duchamp, American (born
France), 1887–1968
La double vue, suivi de l'inventeur du temps gratuit
Paris: [Éditions du soleil], Le soleil noir, 1964
One etching (Giacometti), one die-cut paper construction
(Duchamp). Edition: 25/111
Gift of Molly and Walter Bareiss, 1984.513

Alberto Giacometti (see also listing under Georges Braque)

Giovanni Giacometti, Swiss, 1868–1933
Engadiner Märchen
Text by Gian Bundi, 1872–1936
Samedan, Schweiz: Engadin Press AG, 1971 (1st ed. 1902)
Photomechanical reproductions
Gift of Molly and Walter Bareiss, 1984.516

Robert Gibbings, British, 1889–1958
A Circle of the Seasons: A Translation of the Ritu-Samhara
of Kalidasa Made from Various European Sources by E.
Powys Mathers
Text by Kalidasa, Indian, active late 4th–early 5th century;
translation by E. Powys Mathers, British, 1892–1939
Waltham St. Lawrence, Berkshire, Britain: Golden Cockerel
Press (Robert Gibbings), 1929
4 engravings. Edition: 44/500
Gift of Molly and Walter Bareiss, 1984.517

Gilbert and George: Gilbert, British (born Italy), born 1943; and **George,** British, born 1942
The Red Sculpture Album
Text by Gilbert and George
[London: Art for All, 1975?]
12 color photographs. Edition: 32/100
Gift of Molly and Walter Bareiss, 1984.519

Dark Shadow
Text by Gilbert and George
London: Art for All, Nigel Greenwood Inc., 1976
Photomechanical reproductions. Edition: 730/2,000
Gift of Molly and Walter Bareiss, 1984.520
Ref.: Drucker pp. 263–64

Adolphe Giraldon, French, 1855–1933
Les eglogues de Virgile
Text by Virgil, Roman, 70–19 B.C.E.; translation by Henri Goelzer, 1853–1929
Paris: Plon-Nourrit et cie., 1906
40 color wood-engravings from designs by Giraldon.
Edition: unnumbered/300
Gift of Molly and Walter Bareiss, 1984.522

Barbara Girod, German, born 1942
Und doch: Gedichte und Bilder
Text by Barbara Girod
Stierstadt im Taunus, Deutschland: Eremiten-Presse (V. O. Stomps, Dieter Hülsmanns, Friedolin Reske), 1967
Photomechanical reproductions. Edition: 50/170
Gift of Molly and Walter Bareiss, 1984.523

Vincent van Gogh, Dutch, active France, 1853–1890
Vincent Van Gogh, a Biographical Study
Text by Julius Meier-Graefe, German (born Hungary), 1867–1935
London: Medici Society Limited, 1922 (1st ed. 1921)
Collotypes. Edition: 14/100
Gift of Molly and Walter Bareiss, 1984.524a–b

Michael Goldberg, American, born 1924
Odes
Text by Frank O'Hara, American, 1926–1966
New York: Tiber Press (Tibor de Nagy), 1960
5 color screen prints. Edition: 16/200
Gift of Molly and Walter Bareiss, 1984.1218a
Ref.: Johnson cat. 142

Leon Golub, American, born 1922; **David Reynolds,** American
Facings
[New York]: Chicago Books, 1986
Photomechanical reproductions
Molly and Walter Bareiss Art Fund and Printed Matter Matching Gift Fund for Libraries, 1987.46

Natalia Gontcharova (Goncharova), Russian, 1881–1962
Die Mär von der Heerfahrt Igors
Text by Arthur Luther, German, 1876–1955
München: Orchis, 1924 (title page, 1923)
Line block reproductions with added pochoir color.
Edition: unnumbered/700
Gift of Molly and Walter Bareiss, 1984.525
Fig. 84

Hanns Gött, German, 1883–1974
Ovid: Drei Bücher über die Liebeskunst; Heilmittel gegen die Liebe
Text by Ovid, Roman, 43 B.C.E.–17 C.E.; translation by Otto M. Mittler, 1888–19??
München: Georg Müller, 1920
10 lithographs. Edition: 85/300
Gift of Molly and Walter Bareiss, 1984.526

Toni Grand, French, born 1935
Dragon's Blood
Text by John Yau, American, born 1950
Colombes, France: Collectif génération, 1988
Book object: paintings with acrylic, resin, and découpage, die cuts. Edition: 19/30
Molly and Walter Bareiss Art Fund, 1991.43

Richard Grasby (see listing under Ian Hamilton Finlay)

Derrick Greaves, British, born 1927
Studio International (vol. 174, no. 895, December 1967)
Texts by various authors
London: Cory, Adams & Mackay, 1967
Color screen print, photomechanical reproductions of work by various artists
Gift of Molly and Walter Bareiss, 1984.1250

HAP Grieshaber, German, 1909–1987
Poesia typographica
Text by HAP Grieshaber
Köln: Galerie der Spiegel, 1962 (1st ed. 1957)
Line block reproductions. Edition: unnumbered/1,000
Gift of Molly and Walter Bareiss, 1984.529

HAP Grieshaber
Köln: Galerie der Spiegel, 1964
5 color woodcuts, photomechanical reproductions.
Edition: unnumbered/350
Gift of Molly and Walter Bareiss, 1984.532

HAP Grieshaber: Der Holzschneider
Text by Margot Fuerst, German
Stuttgart: Gerd Hatje, 1964
16 woodcuts, some in colors, photomechanical reproductions
Gift of Molly and Walter Bareiss, 1984.531a–b

Scherben
Text by Albrecht Fabri, German, 1911–1998
Köln: Galerie der Spiegel, 1964
6 color woodcuts. Edition: 21/240
Gift of Molly and Walter Bareiss, 1985.78

Carmina Burana
Music, lyrics by Carl Orff, German, 1895–1982; text by Jacques Prévert, French, 1900–1977
Stuttgart: Manus Presse, 1965
16 color woodcuts, including one repeated twice in different colors. Edition: 27/200
Gift of Molly and Walter Bareiss, 1984.534

Der Rhein
Texts by Albrecht Fabri, German, 1911–1998; Heinrich Böll, German, 1917–1985
Köln: Galerie der Spiegel, 1965
11 woodcuts, some in colors, photomechanical reproductions. Edition: unnumbered/1,000
Gift of Molly and Walter Bareiss, 1984.535

Der grosse Garten
Text by Friedrich Rasche, German, 1900–1965
Hannover: Fackelträger-Verlag Schmidt-Küster, 1965
16 color woodcuts, photomechanical reproductions.
Edition: 580/900
Gift of Molly and Walter Bareiss, 1984.533

Totentanz von Basel mit den Dialogen des Mittelalterlichen Wandbildes
Text by unknown author
Dresden: VEB Verlag der Kunst, 1966
40 color woodcuts
Gift of Molly and Walter Bareiss, 1984.536

Kreuzweg: Meditationen von Stefan Kardinal Wyszynski
Texts by Stefan Wyszynski, Polish, 1901–1981; Fridolin Stier, German, born 1902
Berlin: Rembrandt Verlag, 1967
14 color woodcuts, photomechanical reproductions (wrappers, endpapers). Edition: 322/3,000
Gift of Molly and Walter Bareiss, 1984.537

HAP Grieshaber; various artists
Der Engel der Geschichte, Nr. 1–5, 7, 8
Texts by various authors
Stuttgart: Manus Presse, 1964–67
Nr. 1: color woodcut with screen printing? (Grieshaber), photomechanical reproductions. Edition: unnumbered/500
Nr. 2: color woodcuts (Grieshaber), color lithographs (Horst Antes), photomechanical reproductions. Edition: unnumbered/500
Nr. 3: color woodcuts (Grieshaber, Ivar Radowitz), color lithograph (Rudolf Hoflehner), photomechanical reproductions, line block reproductions. Edition: unnumbered/500
Nr. 4: woodcuts, some in colors (Grieshaber, Gerhard Köhler), photomechanical reproductions. Edition: unnumbered/500
Nr. 5: color woodcut (Grieshaber), color lithographs (Horst Antes, Georg Meistermann). Edition: unnumbered/500
Nr. 7: color woodcuts (Grieshaber), photomechanical reproductions. Edition: unnumbered/1,000
Nr. 8: color woodcuts (Grieshaber), zinc relief print (Hoflehner). Edition: unnumbered/1,000
Gift of Molly and Walter Bareiss, 1984.530a

Juan Gris, Spanish, active France, 1887–1927
Beautés de 1918
Text by Paul Dermée, French, 1886–1951
[Paris]: Éditions de "l'esprit nouveau," 1919
Line block reproductions. Edition: 52/200
Gift of Molly and Walter Bareiss, 1984.538

La guitare endormie
Text by Pierre Reverdy, French, 1889–1960
[Paris]: Contes et poèmes, 1919
Line block reproductions. Edition: 55/110
Gift of Molly and Walter Bareiss, 1984.539

Le casseur d'assiettes: pièce en un acte
Text by Armand Salacrou, French, 1899–1989
Paris: Éditions de la Galerie Simon, André Simon et cie. (under the direction of Daniel-Henry Kahnweiler), 1924
5 lithographs. Edition: 90/100
Gift of Molly and Walter Bareiss, 1984.540
Ref.: Garvey cat. 125, Strachan p. 333, Symmes cat. 29, Wheeler p. 102

Au soleil du plafond
Text by Pierre Reverdy, French, 1889–1960
Paris: Éditions Verve (Tériade), 1955
11 color lithographs. Edition: 20/205
Gift of Molly and Walter Bareiss, 1985.79
Ref.: Symmes cat. 30
Fig. 98

Rudolf Grossmann, German, 1882–1941
Ganymed: Blätter der Marées Gesellschaft (Erster Band)
Texts by various authors
München: R. Piper & Co., 1919
5 lithographs, 28 collotypes
Gift of Molly and Walter Bareiss, 1984.541

George Grosz, American (born Germany), 1893–1959
Ecce Homo
Berlin: Der Malik-Verlag, [1923]
Photomechanical reproductions, line block reproductions
Gift of Molly and Walter Bareiss, 1984.542
Ref.: Castleman p. 160
Fig. 79

Mino Guerrini (see listing under Giuseppe Capogrossi)

Michel Guino, French, born 1926
Un soupçon
Text by Paul Éluard, French, 1895–1952
Paris: Le degré quarante et un (Iliazd), 1965
16 drypoint etchings, some in colors. Edition: 49/70
Gift of Molly and Walter Bareiss, 1984.543

Olaf Gulbransson, Norwegian, 1873–1958
Es war einmal
Text by Olaf Gulbransson
München: R. Piper & Co., 1934
One etching, line block reproductions. Edition: 59/150
Gift of Molly and Walter Bareiss, 1984.544

Sprüche und Wahrheiten
Text by Olaf Gulbransson
Leipzig: Philipp Reclam, 1939
Line block reproductions
Gift of Molly and Walter Bareiss, 1984.545

Idyllen und Katastrophen: Heitere Bildergeschichten mit versen von Dr. Owlglass
Text by Olaf Gulbransson
München: R. Piper & Co., 1962 (1st ed. 1951)

Line block reproductions
Gift of Molly and Walter Bareiss, 1984.546

Gudmundur Gudmundsson (see Erró)

Richard Hamilton (see listing under Marcel Duchamp)

Jane Hammond, American, born 1950
Paysan Comme (Quatre fois)
Text by James Sacré, French, born 1939
Colombes, France: Collectif génération, 1989
Gouache paintings. Edition: 15/20
Molly and Walter Bareiss Art Fund, 1991.44

Fritz Harnest, German, born 1905
Fritz Harnest: Acht farbige Holzschnitte
Text by Eugen Gomringer, Swiss, born 1925
München: Galerie Stangl, 1959
8 color woodcuts. Edition: 6/25
Gift of Molly and Walter Bareiss, 1984.547

Grace Hartigan, American, born 1922
Salute
Text by James Schuyler, American, 1923–1991
New York: Tiber Press (Tibor de Nagy), 1960
5 color screen prints. Edition: 16/200
Gift of Molly and Walter Bareiss, 1984.1218c
Ref.: Castleman p. 207, Johnson cat. 142, Phillips cat. 21

Hans Hartung, French (born Germany), 1904–1989
Un monde ignoré vu par Hans Hartung
Text by Jean Tardieu, French, 1903–1995
[Paris]: Éditions d'art Albert Skira, 1974
Photomechanical reproductions. Edition: 475/999
Gift of Molly and Walter Bareiss, 1984.548

Michael Harvey (see listing under Ian Hamilton Finlay)

Raoul Hausmann, Austrian, active Germany, France,
1886–1971
Poèmes et bois
Text by Raoul Hausmann
Paris: Le degré quarante et un (Iliazd), 1961
5 color woodcuts. Edition: 26/50
Gift of Molly and Walter Bareiss, 1984.549
Fig. 57

Raoul Hausmann (see also listing under Jean (Hans) Arp)

John Heartfield, German, 1891–1968
So macht Man Dollars
Text by Upton Sinclair, American, 1878–1968; translation
by Paul Baudisch (1899–19??)
Berlin: Malik-Verlag, 1931
Photomechanical reproduction with line block element
(cover). Edition: unnumbered/35,000
Gift of Molly and Walter Bareiss, 1984.550
Fig. 87

Erich Heckel, German, 1883–1970
The Ballad of Reading Gaol
Text by Oscar Wilde, Irish, 1854–1900
New York: Ernst Rathenau, 1963
Line block reproductions. Edition: 79/600
Gift of Molly and Walter Bareiss, 1984.551

Walter Helbig (see listing under Jean (Hans) Arp)

Al Held, American, born 1928
Der Philosoph
Text by Helmut Heissenbüttel, German, 1921–1996
Zürich: Verlag 3 (Sybil Albers, Hans Bolliger, Dölf
Hürlimann), 1983
6 etchings, plus a suite of 6 etchings. Edition: 9/140
Gift of Molly and Walter Bareiss, 1984.552

Margaret Henn, German
Taos Sketch Book
Arroyo Seco, NM: Margaret Henn, 1978
Photomechanical reproductions. Edition: 130/500
Gift of Molly and Walter Bareiss, 1984.553

Marshall Henrichs, American
Time and the Machine

Text by Sebastian de Grazia, American, born 1917
Brooklyn, NY: Pratt Adlib Press, 1963
16 woodcuts. Edition: unnumbered/500
Gift of Molly and Walter Bareiss, 1984.527

Jacques Hérold, Romanian, active France, 1910–1987
*La vanille et la manille: Lettre inédite à Madame de Sade
écrite au donjon de Vincennes en 1783*
Text by D. A. F. de Sade (le marquis de Sade), French,
1740–1814
[Paris?]: Collection Drosera, 1950
5 etchings. Edition: 68/96
Gift of Molly and Walter Bareiss, 1984.554

Anton Heyboer, Dutch (born Indonesia), born 1924
Anton Heyboer 1963
Text by Anton Heyboer; J. H. Piers
Köln: Galerie der Spiegel, 1963
6 etchings, including 2 with added red chalk, photo-
mechanical reproductions, line block reproduction.
Edition: unnumbered/250
Gift of Molly and Walter Bareiss, 1984.555

Gary Hincks (see listing under Ian Hamilton Finlay)

Franz Hitzler, German, born 1946
Franz Hitzler
Düsseldorf: Galerie Heike Curtze, 1978
Photomechanical reproductions with overpainting
Gift of Molly and Walter Bareiss, 1984.556

Die stille Angst der Hoffnung
Text by Franz Hitzler
München: D. P. Druck und Publikations, 1980
One photomechanical reproduction with overpainting,
photomechanical reproductions. Edition: 1/30
Gift of Molly and Walter Bareiss, 1984.557, 1984.558
(without overpainting)

Franz Hitzler: Skulpturen und Keramiken, 1968 bis 1982
München: Galerie Biedermann (Fred Jahn, Margret
Biedermann), 1982
One ink and color pencil drawing, photomechanical repro-
ductions. Edition: unnumbered/280
Gift of Molly and Walter Bareiss, 1984.559

Fliessen heisst
Text by Katharina Ponnier
München: D. P. Druck und Publikations, 1986
13 drypoints. Edition: 13/20
Gift of Molly and Walter Bareiss, 1987.283

Antonius Hockelmann, German, 1937–2000
Turf
Köln: Wolfgang Hake, 1980
One graphite drawing, photomechanical reproductions.
Edition: 254/300
Gift of Molly and Walter Bareiss, 1984.560

David Hockney, British, active United States, born 1937
Fourteen Poems
Text by C. P. (Constantine) Cavafy, Greek, 1863–1933;
translation by Nikos Stangos, born 1936, and Stephen
Spender, British, 1909–1995
London: Editions Alecto Limited, 1967 (© 1966)
12 etchings, some with aquatint. Edition: 83/500
(Edition A)
Gift of Molly and Walter Bareiss, 1984.561
Ref.: Castleman p. 212, Hogben cat. 137, Symmes cat. 31

Six Fairy Tales [reduced facsimile]
Text by the Brothers Grimm: Jakob Grimm, German,
1785–1863, Wilhelm Grimm, German, 1786–1859; transla-
tion by Heiner Bastian, German, born 1942
London: Petersburg Press in association with Kasmin
Gallery, 1970
Line block reproductions
Gift of Molly and Walter Bareiss, 1984.562
Ref.: Hogben cat. 146

*The Blue Guitar; Etchings by David Hockney Who Was
Inspired by Wallace Stevens Who Was Inspired by Pablo Picasso*
Text by Wallace Stevens, American, 1879–1955

London: Petersburg Press, 1977
Photomechanical reproductions
Gift of Molly and Walter Bareiss, 1984.563
Ref: Hogben cat. 157
Fig. 130

David Hockney (see also listing under Additional Books)

Heinrich Hoffmann, German, 1809–1894
Das Struwwelpeter-Manuscript [facsimile]
Text by Heinrich Hoffmann; G. A. E. Bogeng, German,
1881–1960
Frankfurt am Main: Literarische Anstalt Rütten &
Loening, 1925
One photogravure, collotypes. Edition: 104/550
Gift of Molly and Walter Bareiss, 1984.564a–b
Fig. 82

Rudolf Hoflehner, Austrian, 1916–1995
Sisyphos: Hommage à Albert Camus
Stuttgart: Manus Presse, 1965
19 lithographs, some in colors. Edition: 15/90
Gift of Molly and Walter Bareiss, 1984.565

Rudolf Hoflehner (see also listing under HAP Grieshaber)

Alexander Hollweg, British, born 1936
Brick Wall
London: Bernard Jacobson Limited, 1973
Photomechanical reproductions, with die cuts
Gift of Molly and Walter Bareiss, 1984.566

Jenny Holzer, American, born 1950; **Peter Nadin,**
American (born Great Britain), born 1954
Eating through Living
Texts by Jenny Holzer; Peter Nadin
New York: Tanam Press, 1981
Photomechanical reproductions
Gift of Molly and Walter Bareiss, 1984.567

Lorenzo Homar, Puerto Rican, born 1913
*Los Renegados (Narracion Inspirada en un Cuento Popular
Puertorriqueño)*
Text by Ricardo E. Alegría, Puerto Rican, born 1921
San Juan: Instituto de Cultura Puertorriqueña, 1962
5 woodcuts, plus a suite of 5 woodcuts. Edition: 36/50
Gift of Molly and Walter Bareiss, 1984.1346, 1984.1347
(without suite)

*Los Renegados (Narracion Inspirada en un Cuento Popular
Puertorriqueño)*
Text by Ricardo E. Alegría, Puerto Rican, born 1921
San Juan: Instituto de Cultura Puertorriqueña, [after 1962]
(1st ed. 1962)
Photomechanical reproductions
Gift of Molly and Walter Bareiss, 1984.1348

Warja Honegger-Lavater, French (born Switzerland),
born 1913
Die Grille und die Ameise
Text by Jean de La Fontaine, French, 1621–1695; translation
by N. O. Scarpi, 1888–1980
Basel: Basilius Presse, 1962
Lithographs
Gift of Molly and Walter Bareiss, 1984.569

Match
Basel: Basilius Presse, 1962
Lithographs
Gift of Molly and Walter Bareiss, 1984.570

Die Party
Basel: Basilius Presse, 1962
Lithographs
Gift of Molly and Walter Bareiss, 1984.571

La promenade en ville
Basel: Basilius Presse, 1962
Color lithographs
Gift of Molly and Walter Bareiss, 1984.572

William Tell
New York: Junior Council, The Museum of Modern
Art, 1962

Photomechanical reproductions. Edition: unnumbered/
2,000
Gift of Molly and Walter Bareiss, 1984.568

Ausser…ordentlicher Lemuel…reist noch immer
Basel: Basilius Presse, 1963
Lithographs with added color. Edition: unnumbered/500
Gift of Molly and Walter Bareiss, 1984.573

Homo sapiens?
Basel: Basilius Presse, 1965
Color lithographs
Gift of Molly and Walter Bareiss, 1984.574
Fig. 103

*Le petit chaperon rouge, une imagerie d'après un conte de
Perrault*
Paris: Maeght éditeur (Adrien Maeght), 1965
Color lithographs
Gift of Molly and Walter Bareiss, 1984.575

*Le Non-Obéissant: Une imagerie; Der Ungehorsame:
Ein Imagerie*
Text by Warja Honegger-Lavater
Basel: Basilius Presse, in conjunction with New York:
Wittenborn and Company, 1968
Color lithographs
Gift of Molly and Walter Bareiss, 1984.576

Snow White
Paris: Maeght éditeur (Adrien Maeght), 1974 (special edition for The Museum of Modern Art, New York)
Color lithographs
Gift of Molly and Walter Bareiss, 1984.577

Blanche Neige, une imagerie d'après le conte
Paris: Maeght éditeur (Adrien Maeght), 1974
Color lithographs
Gift of Molly and Walter Bareiss, 1984.578

Kazuo Hosaka, Japanese
Kyoki no hana
Text by Ralph Günther Mohnnau, German, born 1937
Frankfurt am Main: Alpha-Presse, 1989
Hand-drawn Japanese brush characters with added paint
and collage elements. Edition: 2/20
Gift of Molly and Walter Bareiss, 1989.126

Georges Hugnet, French, 1906–1974; **Marcel Duchamp,**
American (born France), 1887–1968
La septième face du dé
Text by Georges Hugnet
Paris: Éditions Jeanne Bucher, 1936
One paper collage (Hugnet), embossed photomechanical
reproduction of Duchamp readymade (cover), photome-
chanical reproductions. Edition: G/X
Gift of Molly and Walter Bareiss, 1984.431
Ref.: Symmes cat. 26

Masuo Ikeda, Japanese, active United States, 1934–1997
Gli angeli mi disturbano
Text by Roberto Sanesi, Italian, born 1930
Milano: Edizioni d'Arte Grafica Uno (Giorgio Upiglio),
1969
9 mixed color etchings, one color lithograph (cover).
Edition: 54/99
Gift of Molly and Walter Bareiss, 1984.579
Fig. 118

Jörg Immendorff, German, born 1945
Brandenburger Tor Weltfrage
Texts by Jörg Immendorff; A. R. Penck, German,
born 1939
New York: The Museum of Modern Art, 1982
Photomechanical reproductions
Molly and Walter Bareiss Art Fund and Printed Matter
Matching Gift Fund for Libraries, 1987.54

Grüsse von der Nordfront
Text by A. R. Penck, German, born 1939
München: Fred Jahn, 1982
2 color linoleum cuts (from the same block), photomechanical reproductions. Edition: 2/30

Gift of Molly and Walter Bareiss, 1984.581a–b
Fig. 138

Naht
Text by A. R. Penck, German, born 1939
[S.l.: s.n., 1982?]
6 color linoleum cuts, one lithograph (cover).
Edition: 18/100
Gift of Molly and Walter Bareiss, 1984.582

Jörg Immendorff; A. R. Penck, German, born 1939
Immendorff besucht Y
Text by Jörg Immendorff
München: Rogner & Bernhard, 1979
Photomechanical reproductions
Gift of Molly and Walter Bareiss, 1984.583

Jörg Immendorff (see also listing under A. R. Penck)

Robert Indiana, American, born 1928
Numbers
Text by Robert Creeley, American, born 1926
Stuttgart: Edition Domberger; Düsseldorf: Galerie
Schmela, 1968 (1st ed. 1968, large format)
10 color screen prints. Edition: unnumbered/2,500
Gift of Molly and Walter Bareiss, 1984.584
Ref.: Castleman p. 211

Eugène Ionesco, French (born Romania), 1912–1994
Le blanc et le noir
Text by Eugène Ionesco
St. Gallen, Schweiz: Erker-Presse (Franz Larese, Jürg
Janett), 1981
15 lithographs. Edition: 76/150
Gift of Molly and Walter Bareiss, 1984.585

Yvonne Jacquette, American, born 1934
Aerial: A Collection of Poetry
Texts by various authors; edited by Edwin Denby,
American, 1903–1983
New York: Eyelight Press, 1981
Photomechanical reproductions. Edition: D/unknown
Gift of Molly and Walter Bareiss, 1984.586

Fast Lanes
Text by Jayne Anne Phillips, American, born 1952
New York: Vehicle Editions and Brooke Alexander, Inc.,
1984
Photomechanical reproductions. Edition: unnumbered/
2,000
Gift of Molly and Walter Bareiss, 1985.80

Bernhard Jäger (see listing under Thomas Bayrle)

Marcel Janco (see listing under Jean (Hans) Arp)

Horst Janssen, German, 1929–1996
Horst Janssen
Text by Wieland Schmied, German, born 1929
Hannover: Kestner-Gesellschaft, 1965
One graphite drawing, photomechanical reproductions,
line block reproductions
Gift of Molly and Walter Bareiss, 1984.587

*Petty faüer: 20 guten Morgen + hast die gut geschlafen
Gedichte*
Text by Horst Janssen
Hamburg: Galerie Brockstedt, 1970
Photomechanical reproductions. Edition: unnumbered/
3,000
Gift of Molly and Walter Bareiss, 1984.588

Alfred Jarry (see listing under Pierre Bonnard)

Charles-Édouard Jeanneret-Gris (see Le Corbusier)

Paul Jenkins, American, born 1923
Seeing Voice, Welsh Heart
Text by Cyril Hodges, Welsh, born 1915
Paris: Éditions de la Galerie Karl Flinker, 1965
7 color lithographs. Edition: 144/265
Gift of Molly and Walter Bareiss, 1984.589

The Sun in Scorpio
Text by Joyce Wittenborn, British, active United States

Venezia: Alfieri, 1969
Photomechanical reproductions
Gift of Molly and Walter Bareiss, 1984.590

Jasper Johns, American, born 1930
Jasper Johns: Das graphische Werk, 1960–1970
Texts by Jasper Johns; Johannes Cladders, German,
born 1924; Carlo Huber, German, born 1931
Mönchengladbach, Deutschland: Städtisches Museum
Abteiberg (Johannes Cladders), [1971]
Molded plastic rose, photomechanical reproductions.
Edition: 120/550
Gift of Molly and Walter Bareiss, 1984.591
Fig. 124

Technics and Creativity: Gemini G. E. L.
Text by Riva Castleman, American, born 1930
New York: The Museum of Modern Art, 1971
Multiple: photomechanical reproduction, dry watercolor
pads and paintbrush (box), photomechanical reproductions
of work by various artists. Edition: unnumbered/22,500
Gift of Molly and Walter Bareiss, 1984.592

Poems
Text by Wallace Stevens, American, 1879–1955
San Francisco: Arion Press (Andrew Hoyem), 1985
One etching. Edition: 159/300
Gift of Molly and Walter Bareiss, 1985.128
Ref.: Johnson cat. 164
Fig. 140

Jasper Johns (see also listing under Additional Books)

Edward Powis Jones, American, born 1919
The Confidence Man
[S.l.: s.n., 1960?]
13 etchings with aquatint. Edition: 1/10
Gift of Molly and Walter Bareiss, 1984.593a–m

The Stations of the Cross
New York: E. Powis Jones, 1960
16 mixed etchings, most with aquatint. Edition: 1/10
Gift of Molly and Walter Bareiss, 1984.594a–p

Asger Jorn, Danish, active France, 1914–1973
*Friedhof der Maulwürfe (talpa europaea), oder,
Geländergänge in Tagesläufen: Ein Roman*
Text by C. Caspari
[München]: Edition Galerie van de Loo, 1959
8 etchings with aquatint and drypoint, plus a suite of
8 etchings. Edition: XIII/XXX
Gift of Molly and Walter Bareiss, 1984.595a–i

Siegfried Kaden, German, born 1945
Hannibal: Pähl in Bayern im Sommer 1987 [facsimile]
Text by Siegfried Kaden
Berlin: Rainer (Rainer Pretzell), 1988
Photomechanical reproductions. Edition: 23/1,000
Gift of Molly and Walter Bareiss, 1988.105

Auferstehung
Texts by Helmut A. Müller, German, born 1949; Ivo
Kranzfelder, German, born 1958; Walter Eller, German,
born 1948
Sulgen, Schweiz: Niggli AG, 1993
One ink drawing, photomechanical reproductions
Gift of Molly and Walter Bareiss, 1994.61

Lynda Kalman (see listing under Vivian Alper)

Wassily Kandinsky, French (born Russia), 1866–1944
Über das Geistige in der Kunst, Insbesondere in der Malerei
Text by Wassily Kandinsky
München: R. Piper & Co., 1912
10 woodcut decorations, photomechanical reproductions of
work by various artists, line block reproduction
(Kandinsky, wrappers)
Gift of Molly and Walter Bareiss, 1984.596
Ref.: Garvey cat. 137

Klänge
Text by Wassily Kandinsky
München: R. Piper & Co., [1913]

56 woodcuts, some in colors. Edition: 131/300
Gift of Molly and Walter Bareiss, 1984.599
Ref.: Castleman pp. 144–45, Garvey cat. 138, Hogben cat. 31, Johnson cat. 18, Symmes cat. 32, Wheeler p. 103
Fig. 30

Kandinsky: carnet de dessins, 1941 [facsimile]
Text by Gaëtan Picon, 1915–1976
Paris: Karl Flinker, 1972
Line block reproductions. Edition: 664/900
Gift of Molly and Walter Bareiss, 1984.598

Wassily Kandinsky; August Macke, German, 1887–1914
Kandinsky and His Friends
Text by Hans Konrad Röthel, 1909–1982
London: Marlborough Fine Art (privately printed), 1968
Photomechanical reproduction (Macke), line block reproduction (Kandinsky, wrappers). Edition: 448/500
Gift of Molly and Walter Bareiss, 1984.597

Wassily Kandinsky (see also listings under Jean (Hans) Arp; Various Artists, *Der Blaue Reiter*)

Alex Katz, American, born 1927
Face of the Poet
Texts by various authors
New York: Brooke Alexander, Inc., Marlborough Graphics, Inc., 1978
14 color aquatints. Edition: 7/25
Gift of Molly and Walter Bareiss, 1984.600

Babette Katz, American, born 1932
Getting There
Text by Babette Katz
New York: Visual Studies Workshop Press, 1992
Photomechanical reproductions. Edition: unnumbered/1,000
Molly and Walter Bareiss Art Fund, 1992.44

Yarn
New York: Visual Studies Workshop Press, 1992
Photomechanical reproductions. Edition: unnumbered/1,000
Molly and Walter Bareiss Art Fund, 1992.43

Wilhelm Kaufmann, Austrian, 1895–1975
City of the Rivers
Winnipeg: Bureau of Travel and Publicity, Department of Industry and Commerce, [1956?]
Photomechanical reproductions; one lithograph by Kaufmann laid in (not part of the book)
Gift of Molly and Walter Bareiss, 1984.601

Ines von Ketelhodt, German, born 1961
Konzept II
Offenbach am Main: Unica T, 1989
Photocopies on transparent paper, and on Plexiglas (cover). Edition: 8/30
Gift of Molly and Walter Bareiss, 1990.87
Fig. 146

Anselm Kiefer, German, born 1945
Brünhilde schläft
[S.l.: Anselm Kiefer, 1980]
Photographs with added acrylic emulsion, paint, graphite, chalk (unique book)
Gift of Molly and Walter Bareiss, 1984.602
Ref.: Symmes cat. 33
Fig. 131

Hoffmann von Fallersleben auf Helgoland
Groningen: Groninger Museum, 1980
Photomechanical reproductions. Edition: unnumbered/500
Gift of Molly and Walter Bareiss, 1984.603

Frederick Kiesler, American (born Romania), 1890–1965
Frederick Kiesler: Zwölf Fotografien bei Galerie Pabst
München: Galerie Pabst, 1978
12 photographs. Edition: 2/30
Gift of Molly and Walter Bareiss, 1984.604a–l

Rudyard Kipling, British (born India), 1865–1936
Just So Stories
Text by Rudyard Kipling

Garden City, NY: Doubleday, Doran & Company, [1907?]
(1st ed. 1902)
Line block reproductions
Gift of Molly and Walter Bareiss, 1984.605

Martin Kippenberger, German, 1953–1997
Hotel-Hotel
Köln: Verlag der Buchhandlung Walther König, 1992
Photomechanical reproductions. Edition: 238/950
Gift of Molly and Walter Bareiss, 1992.85
Fig. 13

Ernst Ludwig Kirchner, German, 1880–1938
Das Stiftsfräulein und der Tod [portfolio]
[Berlin]: A. R. Meyer (Alfred Richard Meyer), [1913]
5 woodcuts
Gift of Molly and Walter Bareiss, 1984.608
Ref.: Garvey cat. 141, Symmes cat. 34, Wheeler p. 104

Umbra vitae: nachgelassene Gedichte
Text by Georg Heym, German, 1887–1912
München: Kurt Wolff, 1924
50 woodcuts, some in colors. Edition: 201/510
Gift of Molly and Walter Bareiss, 1984.606
Ref.: Castleman p. 229, Garvey cat. 142, Johnson cat. 46, Symmes cat. 35, Wheeler p. 104
Fig. 83

Das Werk Ernst Ludwig Kirchners
Text by Will Grohmann, German, 1887–1968
München: Kurt Wolff, [1926]
6 color woodcuts, 100 collotypes, line block reproductions. Edition: 297/800
Gift of Molly and Walter Bareiss, 1984.607
Ref.: Hogben cat. 75

Per Kirkeby, Danish, born 1938
Prototyper
Copenhagen: Niels Borch Jensen & Susanne Ottesen, 1983
18 etchings with drypoint and aquatint. Edition: 11/19
Gift of Molly and Walter Bareiss, 1987.284

Bravura
Text by Per Kirkeby
Bern: Gachnang & Springer, 1984
6 drypoints and lift-ground aquatint, one color lithograph (wrappers). Edition: 40/50
Gift of Molly and Walter Bareiss, 1985.81

Per Kirkeby (see also listing under A. R. Penck)

Dietrich Kirsch, Austrian, born 1924
Fischeimer: 15 Materialdrucke
Stierstadt im Taunus, Deutschland: Eremiten-Presse, 1962–63 (© 1962)
16 collagraphs?, some in colors. Edition: 16/120
Gift of Molly and Walter Bareiss, 1984.609

R. B. Kitaj, American, active Great Britain, born 1932
A Day Book
Text by Robert Creeley, American, born 1926
Berlin: Graphis, 1972
10 color screen prints, 4 etchings (some in blind) with added color screen printing, one lithograph. Edition: 98/200
Gift of Molly and Walter Bareiss, 1984.610
Ref.: Hogben cat. 150, Johnson cat. 158

Paul Klee, Swiss, active Germany, 1879–1940
The Prints of Paul Klee
Text by James Thrall Soby, American, 1906–1979
New York: The Museum of Modern Art, 1947 (1st ed. 1945)
40 collotypes, including 8 with added pochoir color, line block reproductions. Edition: unnumbered/2,000
Gift of Molly and Walter Bareiss, 1984.611

Paul Klee; André Masson, French, 1896–1987
The Novices of Sais; Die Lehrlinge zu Sais
Text by Novalis, German, 1772–1801
New York: Curt Valentin, 1949
Line block reproductions
Gift of Molly and Walter Bareiss, 1984.612

Gustav Klimt, Austrian, 1862–1918
Die Hetaerengespraeche des Lukian
Text by Lucian, Greek, ca. 120–180 C.E.; translation by Franz Blei, 1871–1942
Leipzig: Julius Zeitler, 1907
15 collotypes. Edition: 28/50
Gift of Molly and Walter Bareiss, 1984.613
Ref.: Hogben cat. 23

Alfred Klinkan, Austrian, 1950–1994
Hirsch-Malbuch
Wien: Galerie Ariadne, [1979]
One ink drawing, 2 paper collages with added ink and crayon, photomechanical reproductions. Edition: 53/70
Gift of Molly and Walter Bareiss, 1984.615

Annalies Klophaus, German, born 1940
Mot-couleur-roman; Farb-Wort-Roman
Text by Annalies Klophaus
Paris: Éditions Agentzia, 1970
Photomechanical reproductions
Gift of Molly and Walter Bareiss, 1984.616

Rest 1, Annalies; Rest 2, Klophaus
Text by Annalies Klophaus
Grünwald, Deutschland: Engelhornstiftung zur Pflege + Förderung der Kunst GmbH, [1971]
Photomechanical reproductions. Edition: 66/500
Gift of Molly and Walter Bareiss, 1984.617

W. (Wolf) Knoebel, German, born 1940
W. Knoebel
Düsseldorf: Städtische Kunsthalle, 1975
Photomechanical reproductions
Gift of Molly and Walter Bareiss, 1984.618

Gert (Gerhard) Köhler (see listing under HAP Grieshaber)

Oskar Kokoschka, British (born Austria), 1886–1980
Oskar Kokoschka: Zwanzig Zeichnungen
Berlin: Der Sturm, [1913?]
Line block reproductions
Gift of Molly and Walter Bareiss, 1984.621

The Turn of the Screw. The Aspern Papers
Text by Henry James, American, 1843–1916
London: J. M. Dent & Sons, [1935?]
One collage with ink and color pencil drawing, plastic tissue, foil (artist's inscription)
Gift of Molly and Walter Bareiss, 1984.620

Irische Legende: Text zu einer Oper
Text by Werner Egk, German, 1901–1983
Freiburg im Breisgau: Verlagsanstalt Klemm (Erich Seemann), [1955]
5 lithographs. Edition: 219/250
Gift of Molly and Walter Bareiss, 1984.619

Jirí Kolár, Czech (born Bohemia), active France, born 1914
Hinauf und hinunter: Tiefengedicht
Uelzen, Deutschland: Bong & Co., 1969
Photomechanical reproductions. Edition: 54/200
Gift of Molly and Walter Bareiss, 1984.622

Edward Koren, American, born 1935
The Frog Prince
Text by David Mamet, American, born 1947
New York: Vincent FitzGerald & Company, 1984
One etching, line block reproductions. Edition: 48/130
Gift of Molly and Walter Bareiss, 1984.623

Bohumil Krátky, Czech, born 1913
Das Urtheil des Paris: Eine scherzhafte Erzählung nach Lucian
Text by Christoph Martin Wieland, German, 1733–1813
Reicheneck, Deutschland: Aldus-Presse, 1983
5 etchings. Edition: 25/50
Gift of Molly and Walter Bareiss, 1984.624

Dieter Krieg, German, born 1937
Dieter Krieg '71
München: Galerie Stangl, 1971

One lithograph, photomechanical reproductions.
Edition: 54/200
Gift of Molly and Walter Bareiss, 1984.625a–b

Per Krohg, Norwegian, active France, 1889–1965
Jérôme: 60° latitude nord
Text by Maurice Bedel, 1884–1954
[Paris]: Librairie Gallimard, 1929
Photomechanical reproductions with added pochoir color,
line block reproduction (wrappers). Edition: 427/625
Gift of Molly and Walter Bareiss, 1984.626
Ref.: Wheeler p. 105

Barbara Kruger, American, born 1945
My Pretty Pony
Text by Stephen King, American, born 1947
New York: Library Fellows of the Whitney Museum of
American Art (May Castleberry), 1988
9 color lithographs (including one with screen printing);
8 screen prints, some in color; digital clock mounted in
stainless steel cover. Edition: unnumbered/250
Molly and Walter Bareiss Art Fund, 1989.109
Ref.: Castleman pp. 72, 216, Phillips cat. 24
Fig. 60

Alfred Kubin, Czech, active Austria, 1877–1959
20 Bilder zur Bibel
München: R. Piper & Co., 1924
20 collotypes
Gift of Molly and Walter Bareiss, 1985.82

Episoden des Untergangs
Text by Robert R. Schmidt, German, 1892–1948
Heidelberg: Merlin-Verlag, [1926?]
Line block reproductions
Gift of Molly and Walter Bareiss, 1984.632

Magie
Text by Max Roden, 1881–1968
Wien: Neue Galerie, Verlag der Johannes-Presse, 1929
5 lithographs. Edition: unnumbered/500
Gift of Molly and Walter Bareiss, 1984.628

Alfred Kubin
Text by Alfred Kubin
Wien: Neue Galerie, 1931
11 lithographs. Edition: 5/15
Gift of Molly and Walter Bareiss, 1984.629

Tschandala
Text by August Strindberg, Swedish, 1849–1912
Wien: Johannes-Presse, 1937
14 lithographs, line block reproductions. Edition:
unnumbered/90
Gift of Molly and Walter Bareiss, 1984.630

Spiegelungen
Text by Max Roden, American (born Austria), 1881–1968
Wien: Neue Galerie, Johannes-Presse, 1951
Line block reproduction. Edition: unnumbered/200
Gift of Molly and Walter Bareiss, 1984.631

Frank (František) Kupka, Czech, active France, 1871–1957
Quatre histoires de blanc et noir
Text by Frank (František) Kupka
Paris: [Frank Kupka], 1926
29 woodcuts. Edition: 158/300
Gift of Molly and Walter Bareiss, 1984.633
Ref.: Castleman p. 134, Hogben cat. 76, Johnson cat. 50,
Symmes cat. 36

Nicolai Kupreianov (Kupryanov), Russian, 1894–1933
[*Gosplan Literatury. Literaturnyi Tsentr Konstruktivistov.
Stat'i stikhi*]
Text by various authors
Moscow: Krug, [1924?]
Photomechanical reproduction. Edition:
unnumbered/3,000
Molly and Walter Bareiss Art Fund, 1993.67

Alain de La Bourdonnaye, French, born 1930
Les cantiques spirituels de Saint Jean de la Croix
Text by Saint Jean de la Croix, French, 1542–1591;

translation by R. P. Cyprien
[S.l.]: Alain de La Bourdonnaye, 1956
6 etchings, most with color aquatint. Edition: VII/X
Gift of Molly and Walter Bareiss, 1984.292

Le mariage de Roland
Text by Victor Hugo, French, 1802–1885
Paris: Alain de La Bourdonnaye, 1968
21 paper collages, most cut and pasted from magazines.
Edition: 3/40
Gift of Molly and Walter Bareiss, 1984.293

Roger de La Fresnaye, French, 1885–1925
Les illuminations
Text by Arthur Rimbaud, French, 1854–1891
Paris: H. Matarasso, 1949
25 wood-engravings after La Fresnaye, plus a suite of 22
wood-engravings and a suite of 23 wood-engravings
(including 2 with added color). Edition: C/D
Gift of Molly and Walter Bareiss, 1984.642

Oeuvre complète de Roger de La Fresnaye
Texts by Raymond Cogniat, French, 1896–19??; Waldemar
George, French, 1893–19??
Paris: Éditions Rivarol, 1950 (© 1949)
Photomechanical reproductions, plus a suite of 11 collo-
types (including 7 with added pochoir color). Edition:
803/3,500
Gift of Molly and Walter Bareiss, 1984.643

Jean-Émile Laboureur, French, 1877–1943
Petites images de la guerre sur le front britannique
Text by Roger Allard, French, 1885–1942
Paris: L'imprimerie d'A. Vernant, 1917
9 engravings. Edition: 88/120
Gift of Molly and Walter Bareiss, 1984.634
Ref.: Garvey cat. 152
Fig. 74

Chansons madécasses
Text by Évariste Parny, French, 1753–1814
Paris: Éditions de la Nouvelle revue française, 1920
30 color woodcuts. Edition: 86/400
Gift of Molly and Walter Bareiss, 1984.635

Tableau des grands magasins
Text by J. Valmy-Baysse, French, 1874–19??
Paris: Éditions de la Nouvelle revue française, Librairie
Gallimard, 1924
12 engravings. Edition: 64/300
Gift of Molly and Walter Bareiss, 1984.636

Hélène & Touglas, ou les joies de Paris
Text by Jean Giraudoux, French, 1882–1944
Paris: Au sans pareil, 1925
6 engravings, plus a suite of 6 engravings. Edition: 90/120
Gift of Molly and Walter Bareiss, 1984.637

L'envers du music-hall
Text by Colette, French, 1873–1954
Paris: Au sans pareil, 1926
32 engravings. Edition: 395/420
Gift of Molly and Walter Bareiss, 1984.639

Les sonnets du docteur
Text by Georges Camuset, French, 1840–1885
Dijon: Éditions du raisin, 1926 (1st ed. 1887)
8 etchings from 4 plates, decorative letterpress elements.
Edition: 108/305
Gift of Molly and Walter Bareiss, 1984.638

Le portrait de Dorian Gray
Text by Oscar Wilde, Irish, 1854–1900; translation by
Edmond Jaloux, French, 1878–1949, and Félix Frapereau
Paris: Société d'édition "Le livre," 1928
24 engravings. Edition: 137/250
Gift of Molly and Walter Bareiss, 1984.641
Fig. 22

Jean-Émile Laboureur; Jacques Boullaire, French,
1893–1976
À l'ombre des jeunes filles en fleurs
Text by Marcel Proust, French, 1871–1922

Paris: NRF (Nouvelle revue française), Librairie Gallimard,
1948
50 engravings (25 by Laboureur, 25 by Boullaire), plus 4
suites of 25 engravings each. Edition: 26/35
Gift of Molly and Walter Bareiss, 1984.640a–b

Wifredo Lam, Cuban, active France, 1902–1982
La rose et la cétoine; La nacre et le noir
Text by Claude Tarnaud, 1922–1991
[S.l.]: Méconnaissance, 1958
One etching with added color, line block reproduction.
Edition: 6/388
Gift of Molly and Walter Bareiss, 1984.644

Croiseur noir
Text by André Pieyre de Mandiargues, French, 1909–1991
Paris: O.L.V., 1972
6 color etchings, plus a suite of 6 etchings. Edition: 72/125
Gift of Molly and Walter Bareiss, 1984.645

Contre une maison sèche
Text by René Char, French, 1907–1988
[Paris]: Jean Hugues, 1975
9 etchings with aquatint. Edition: 52/135
Gift of Molly and Walter Bareiss, 1984.646
Fig. 128

Octave Landuyt, Belgian, born 1922
Un coin de désert
Text by Harry Torczyner, Belgian, 1911–1998
Courtrai, België: Éditions Vynckier, 1958
Photomechanical reproductions, line block reproduction
(wrappers)
Gift of Molly and Walter Bareiss, 1984.647

Ellen Lanyon, American, born 1926
Transformations II
[S.l.]: Ellen Lanyon, 1982
Photomechanical reproduction (cover), line block
reproductions
Gift of Molly and Walter Bareiss, 1984.648
Ref.: Drucker p. 205

Charles Lapicque, French, 1898–1988
O et M: roman
Text by Charles Estienne, French, 1908–1966?
Paris: Éditions du soleil, Le soleil noir, 1966
Line block reproductions. Edition: 2,105/2,730
Gift of Molly and Walter Bareiss, 1984.649

Marie Laurencin, French, 1885–1956
Eventail
Texts by various authors
Paris: Éditions de la Nouvelle revue française, Librairie
Gallimard, 1922
10 etchings. Edition: 109/300
Gift of Molly and Walter Bareiss, 1984.650
Ref.: Garvey cat. 155

Petit bestiaire
Text by Marie Laurencin
Paris: François Bernouard, 1926
4 lithographs from 2 stones. Edition: P/Z
Gift of Molly and Walter Bareiss, 1984.651

Alice in Wonderland
Text by Lewis Carroll, British, 1832–1898
Paris: Black Sun Press [Le soleil noir] (Caresse Crosby),
1930
6 color lithographs. Edition: 393/420
Gift of Molly and Walter Bareiss, 1984.652

Venus and Adonis
Music by John Blow, British, 1649?–1708
Paris: Éditions de l'oiseau lyre (Louise B. M. Dyer), 1939
8 collotypes with added pochoir color. Edition: XIV/L
Gift of Molly and Walter Bareiss, 1984.653
Fig. 90

Paul-Albert Laurens, French, 1870–1934
Lêda, ou La louange des bienheureuses ténèbres
Text by Pierre Louÿs, French, 1870–1925
Paris: Mercure de France, 1898

10 color collotypes. Edition: 260/600
Gift of Molly and Walter Bareiss, 1984.660

Henri Laurens, French, 1885–1954
Spirales
Text by Paul Dermée, French, 1886–1951
[Paris]: Paul Dermée, 1917
2 etchings, including one with added watercolor. Edition:
III/XXV
Gift of Molly and Walter Bareiss, 1984.654
Ref.: Symmes cat. 38

Les idylles
Text by Theocritus, Greek, ca. 300–260 B.C.E.; translation
by Émile Chambry, French, 1864–19??
Paris: Éditions de la revue Verve (Tériade, Angèle Lamotte),
1945
38 color wood-engravings, one embossing (cover). Edition:
168/200
Gift of Molly and Walter Bareiss, 1984.655
Ref.: Johnson cat. 119, Strachan p. 335
Fig. 36

Entre-temps
Text by Tristan Tzara, French (born Romania), 1896–1963
Paris: Éditions le Point du jour, 1946
One etching, photomechanical reproductions. Edition:
276/300
Gift of Molly and Walter Bareiss, 1984.656

Le bleu de l'aile
Text by Tiggie Ghika, Greek, 1906–1994; translation by
René Char, French, 1907–1988
Paris: Éditions "Cahiers d'art," 1948
3 etchings. Edition: 61/200
Gift of Molly and Walter Bareiss, 1984.657

Dialogues
Text by Lucian, Greek, ca. 120–180 C.E.; translation by
Émile Chambry, French, 1864–19??
Paris: Éditions de la revue Verve (Tériade), [1951]
34 wood-engravings (including table of plates, cover), most
in colors. Edition: 131/250
Gift of Molly and Walter Bareiss, 1984.659
Ref.: Garvey cat. 157, Hogben cat. 125, Strachan p. 336

Contes
Text by William Saroyan, American, 1908–1981; translation
by Anne Green, 1899–19??
[Paris]: Cent bibliophiles de France et d'Amérique, 1953
11 color woodcuts. Edition: "pour Monsieur Claude
Jouglet" 63/100
Gift of Molly and Walter Bareiss, 1984.658
Ref.: Strachan p. 336

Uwe Lausen, German, 1941–1970
Stoffwechsel
München: Gernot von Pape, Edition X (Fred Jahn), 1968
12 screen prints, some in colors. Edition: 57/80
Gift of Molly and Walter Bareiss, 1984.661

Warja Lavater (see Warja Honegger-Lavater)

Louise Lawler, American, born 1947
[Untitled: Mata Hari]
Text by Janelle Reiring, American
New York: Louise Lawler, 1978
Photomechanical reproductions
Molly and Walter Bareiss Art Fund and Printed Matter
Matching Gift Fund for Libraries, 1987.53

Ruth Laxson, American, born 1924
Measure, Cut, Stitch
Atlanta: Press 63+ (Ruth Laxson), 1987
Screen prints, some in colors, with collage and die cuts.
Edition: 29/75
Molly and Walter Bareiss Art Fund, 1988.66

Le Corbusier, French (born Switzerland), 1887–1965
Poème de l'angle droit
Text by Le Corbusier
Paris: Tériade, 1955
138 lithographs, some in colors (18 lithographs are

repeated). Edition: 68/250
Gift of Molly and Walter Bareiss, 1984.662
Ref.: Garvey cat. 162, Johnson cat. 137, Strachan p. 336
Fig. 99

Fernand Léger, French, 1881–1955
La fin du monde filmée par l'ange N.-D.
Text by Blaise Cendrars, French (born Switzerland),
1887–1961
Paris: Éditions de la sirène, 1919
22 color pochoir prints, including one with added hand
color and 6 with line block elements, line block reproductions (wrappers). Edition: 1,115/1,225
Gift of Molly and Walter Bareiss, 1984.663
Ref.: Castleman pp. 170–71, Hogben cat. 54, Johnson cat.
26, Wheeler p. 105
Fig. 80

Die Chapliniade, eine Kinodichtung
Text by Yvan Goll, French, 1891–1950
Dresden: Rudolf Kaemmerer, 1920
Line block reproductions
Gift of Molly and Walter Bareiss, 1984.664

Lunes en papier
Text by André Malraux, French, 1901–1976
Paris: Éditions de la Galerie Simon, André Simon et cie.
(under the direction of Daniel-Henry Kahnweiler), 1921
7 woodcuts. Edition: 66/100
Gift of Molly and Walter Bareiss, 1984.665
Ref.: Garvey cat. 163, Hogben cat. 64, Johnson cat. 34,
Symmes cat. 39, Wheeler p. 105

Broom (vol. 2, no. 4, July 1922)
Texts by various authors
New York: Harold A. Loeb, 1922
One color woodcut (cover), line block reproductions of
work by various artists
Gift of Molly and Walter Bareiss, 1984.1287

Fernand Léger
Text by Efstratios Tériade, French (born Greece), 1897–1983
Paris: Éditions "Cahiers d'art," 1928
One ink and crayon drawing, 88 collotypes, including 5
with added pochoir color, line block reproductions.
Edition: 106/800, unnumbered/800
Gift of Molly and Walter Bareiss, 1984.667, 1984.666
(without drawing)

L'illustre Thomas Wilson
Text by Loys Masson, born West Africa, 1915–1970
Paris: Bordas, 1948 (© 1947)
One color lithograph, line block reproductions.
Edition: 376/500
Gift of Molly and Walter Bareiss, 1984.668

Cirque
Text by Fernand Léger
Paris: Tériade, 1950
83 lithographs, some in colors. Edition: 28/280
Gift of Molly and Walter Bareiss, 1984.669
Ref.: Castleman p. 95, Garvey cat. 164, Hogben cat. 123,
Johnson cat. 131, Strachan pp. 136, 336
Fig. 150

Les cercles magiques
Text by Yvan Goll, French, 1891–1950
Paris: Éditions Falaize, 1951
Photomechanical reproduction with added pochoir color
(cover), line block reproductions
Gift of Molly and Walter Bareiss, 1984.670
Fig. 3

La ville
Paris: Tériade, 1959
29 color lithographs. Edition: 86/180
Gift of Molly and Walter Bareiss, 1984.671

Fernand Léger: mes voyages
Texts by Fernand Léger; Louis Aragon, French, 1897–1982
Paris: Les éditeurs français réunis, 1960
27 lithographs, some in colors. Edition: 40/236
Gift of Molly and Walter Bareiss, 1984.672

Louis Legrand, French, 1863–1951
Cours de danse fin de siècle
Text by [Érastène Ramiro], 1853–19??
Paris: Libraire de la Société des gens de lettres (E. Dentu),
1892
23 color etchings with aquatint (wrappers, 2 states each
of 11 plates, one set with remarques), 47 color wood-engravings. Edition: 30/350
Gift of Molly and Walter Bareiss, 1984.673

Quinze histoires d'Edgar Poë
Text by Edgar Allan Poe, American, 1809–1849; translation
by Charles Baudelaire, French, 1821–1867
Paris: Chamerot et Renouard (for the Société des amis des
livres), 1897
30 aquatints (2 states each of 15 plates), photomechanical
reproductions, line block reproductions. Edition: 114/115
Gift of Molly and Walter Bareiss, 1984.674

Faune parisienne
Text by Erastène Ramiro, 1853–19??
Paris: Gustave Pellet, 1901
20 etchings with aquatint, most in colors, plus a suite of 30
proofs, 50 wood-engravings
Gift of Molly and Walter Bareiss, 1984.675

Cinq contes parisiens
Text by Guy de Maupassant, French, 1850–1893
Paris: Cent bibliophiles, 1905
86 etchings with aquatint, some in colors, line block reproductions (wrappers). Edition: "M. Paul Blondeau" 14/130
Gift of Molly and Walter Bareiss, 1984.676

Georges Lepape, French, 1887–1971
Les choses de Paul Poiret, vues par Georges Lepape
Paris: Paul Poiret, 1911
12 color lithographs with added pochoir color, line block
reproductions. Edition: "exemplaire d'état"
Gift of Molly and Walter Bareiss, 1984.677
Fig. 75

Alfred Leslie, American, born 1927
Permanently
Text by Kenneth Koch, American, 1925–2002
New York: Tiber Press (Tibor de Nagy), 1960
5 color screen prints. Edition: 16/200
Gift of Molly and Walter Bareiss, 1984.1218b
Ref.: Johnson cat. 142

Leo Leuppi (see listing under Jean (Hans) Arp)

John Levee, American, active France, born 1924
A Preface and Four Seasons; A Suite of Five Lithographs
Text by Irwin Shaw, American, 1913–1984
New York: André Emmerich Gallery, 1959
5 color lithographs, line block reproductions. Edition:
11/150
Gift of Molly and Walter Bareiss, 1984.678

Eli Levin, American, born 1938
The Art Fever: Passages Through the Western Art Trade
Text by James Parsons, American, born 1921
Taos, NM: Gallery West, 1981
One ink and wash drawing, photomechanical reproductions, line block reproductions of works by various artists.
Edition: 24/125
Gift of Molly and Walter Bareiss, 1984.679

Sol LeWitt, American, born 1928
*All Double Combinations (Superimposed) of Six Geometric
Figures (Circle, Square, Triangle, Rectangle, Trapezoid, and
Parallelogram)*
New York: Parasol Press, 1977
16 screen prints. Edition: 7/25
Gift of Molly and Walter Bareiss, 1984.680

Ficciones
Text by Jorge Louis Borges, Argentinian, 1899–1986
[New York]: Limited Editions Club, 1984
22 screen prints. Edition: 1,404/1,500
Gift of Molly and Walter Bareiss, 1985.83

Kathleen Lindsley (see listing under Ian Hamilton Finlay)

Leo Lionni, American (born Netherlands), 1910–1999
Suite Lirica: En homenaje a Wallace Stevens
Texts by Wallace Stevens, American, 1879–1955;
José María Martín Triana, Cuban, born 1937
Verona, Italia: Plain Wrapper Press, 1982
5 etchings. Edition: 38/90
Gift of Molly and Walter Bareiss, 1984.1342

El Lissitzky, Russian, 1890–1941
Dlia golosa
Text by Vladimir Mayakovsky, Russian, 1893–1930
Berlin: R. S. F. S. R. Gosiudarstvennoe Izdatel'stvo
(Gosizdat), 1923
14 typographic designs, photomechanical reproduction.
Edition: unnumbered/3,000
Gift of Molly and Walter Bareiss, 1984.681
Ref.: Drucker pp. 54–57, Hogben cat. 68, Johnson cat. 41,
Symmes cat. 40
Fig. 40

George Lockwood, American, 1929–1969
Sixteen Poems in Verse & Wood
Text by Bernard Bockes
Boston: Impressions Workshop, The Cricket Press, 1965
5 color woodcuts; 11 wood-engravings, some in colors; one
blind embossing; one sound recording. Edition: 85/150
Gift of Molly and Walter Bareiss, 1984.682

Anestis Logothetis, Greek, active Austria, born 1921
Anestis Logothetis
Text by John G. Papaioannou, Greek, 1915–2000
Athens: "Ora" Artistic Cultural Centre, 1975
Photomechanical reproductions of visual "polymorphic"
musical notation. Edition: 127/300
Gift of Molly and Walter Bareiss, 1984.683

Richard Long, British, born 1945
*Richard Long Skulptures: England, Germany, Africa, America
1966–1970*
Mönchengladbach, Deutschland: Städtisches Museum
Abteiberg (Johannes Cladders), 1970
Photomechanical reproductions. Edition: 273/330
Gift of Molly and Walter Bareiss, 1984.684

Mud Hand Prints
London: Coracle Press, 1984
2 monoprints made with mud. Edition: unnumbered/100
Molly and Walter Bareiss Art Fund, 1987.19
Ref.: Hogben cat. 167

*Kicking Stones: A 203 Mile Northward Walk in Six Days,
Cork to Sligo, Ireland 1989*
Text by Richard Long
London: Anthony d'Offay Gallery, 1990
Letterpress
Gift of Molly and Walter Bareiss, 2001.7

Joseph Low, American, born 1911
Heads
[Newtown, CT]: Eden Hill Press (Joseph Low), 1960
26 color linoleum cuts, one color woodcut (cover). Edition:
100/450
Gift of Molly and Walter Bareiss, 1984.685
Ref.: Garvey cat. 170

L. J. Lucebert, Dutch, 1924–1994
Lucebert: Gedichte und Zeichnungen
Text by L. J. Lucebert
[Hamburg?]: Heinrich Ellermann, 1962
Photomechanical reproductions
Gift of Molly and Walter Bareiss, 1984.686

Junge Niederländische Lyrik
Texts by various authors; edited by Ludwig Kunz,
1900–19??
Stierstadt im Taunus, Deutschland: Eremiten-Presse, 1965
Line block reproductions. Edition: 22/200
Gift of Molly and Walter Bareiss, 1984.687

Bernhard Luginbühl, Swiss, born 1929
Buminell
Zürich: Galerie Renée Ziegler, 1967
18 color lithographs, photomechanical reproductions.
Edition: 52/200
Gift of Molly and Walter Bareiss, 1984.688

Alexandre Lunois (see listing under Various Artists, *L'effort*)

Markus Lüpertz, German, born 1941
Sieben über ML
München: Edition der Galerie Heiner Friedrich, 1980
Photomechanical reproductions. Edition: unnumbered/
1,000
Gift of Molly and Walter Bareiss, 1984.689

"Und ich, ich spiele…"
Text by Markus Lüpertz
Berlin: Galerie Rudolf Springer, 1981
Line block reproductions, including one with added color.
Edition: 24/30
Gift of Molly and Walter Bareiss, 1984.690

"Ich stand vor der Mauer aus Glas"
Text by Markus Lüpertz
Berlin: Galerie Rudolf Springer, 1982
14 color lithographs (one repeated three times), including
one with overpainting. Edition: 1/30
Gift of Molly and Walter Bareiss, 1984.691
Ref.: Symmes cat. 41

"Die Erschaffung der Welt": Zwölfe Träume
Berlin: Galerie im Körnerpark, 1983
One drypoint with one color linoleum cut printed over the
plate, photomechanical reproductions. Edition: 9/30
Gift of Molly and Walter Bareiss, 1987.282

Tagebuch: New York 1984
Text by Markus Lüpertz
Bern: Gachnang & Springer, 1984
Photomechanical reproductions. Edition: unnumbered/
1,000
Gift of Molly and Walter Bareiss, 1985.84

Markus Lüpertz (see also listing under A. R. Penck)

Jean Lurçat, French, 1892–1966
Corps perdu
Text by Philippe Soupault, French, 1897–1990
Paris: Au sans pareil, 1926
2 drypoints, plus 2 suites of drypoints, line block reproduc-
tions, plus 2 suites of line block reproductions. Edition:
38/990
Gift of Molly and Walter Bareiss, 1984.692

Amédée Lynen, Belgian, 1852–1938
Une messe de minuit
Text by Theodore Hannon, 1851–1916
Bruxelles: Charles Vos, [1888]
13 lithographs, including one in color. Edition: unnum-
bered/150
Gift of Molly and Walter Bareiss, 1984.693

Loren MacIver, American, 1909–1998
Loren MacIver: Recent Paintings 1953–56
New York: Pierre Matisse Gallery, 1956
One color lithograph (wrappers), photomechanical repro-
ductions
Gift of Molly and Walter Bareiss, 1984.695

René Magritte, Belgian, 1898–1967
Les chants de Maldoror
Text by comte de Lautréamont (Isidore Ducasse), French,
1847–1870
Bruxelles: Éditions "La Boëtie," 1948
Line block reproductions. Edition: 443/4,100
Gift of Molly and Walter Bareiss, 1984.696
Ref.: Hogben cat. 117
Fig. 33

*Aube à l'antipode: carnets de bord ténus sous forme de notes
analogiques expéditives*
Text by Alain Jouffroy, French, born 1928
Paris: Éditions du soleil, Le soleil noir, 1966

Photomechanical reproduction (wrappers), line block
reproductions. Edition: 149/1,077
Gift of Molly and Walter Bareiss, 1984.697

Signes de survie aux temps d'amour
Text by Gui Rosey
Paris: Éditions Georges Visat, 1968
3 color etchings, plus a suite of 3 color etchings. Edition:
8/150
Gift of Molly and Walter Bareiss, 1984.698
Fig. 119

Aristide Maillol, French, 1861–1944
Die Eclogen Vergils in der Ursprache und Deutsch
Text by Virgil, Roman, 70–19 b.c.e.; translation by Rudolf
Alexander Schröder, German, 1878–1962
Weimar: Cranach Presse (Harry Kessler); Leipzig: Insel-
Verlag, 1926
47 woodcuts. Edition: 62/250
Gift of Molly and Walter Bareiss, 1984.699
Ref.: Garvey cat. 172, Symmes cat. 42, Wheeler p. 106
Fig. 49

Les pastorales de Longus, ou Daphnis et Chloé
Text by Longus, Greek, active 2nd–3rd centuries c.e.;
translation by Jacques Amyot, French, 1513–1593
(completed by Paul-Louis Courier, French, 1772–1825)
Paris: Les frères Gonin (with Gustave Édouard Gentil), 1937
55 woodcuts, plus a suite of 64 woodcuts. Edition: "H. C.
Maillol" CCXXXI/unknown
Gift of Molly and Walter Bareiss, 1984.700
Ref.: Garvey cat. 174, Strachan pp. 44–45, 76, 337, Symmes
cat. 43, Wheeler p. 106

*Livret de folastries, à janot parisien. Plus, quelques epigrames
grecs: & des dithyrambes chantés au bouc de E. Iodëlle,
poëte tragiq*
Text by Pierre de Ronsard, French, 1524–1585
Paris: Ambroise Vollard, 1938 (printed 1940 by Lucian
Vollard and Martin Fabiani)
43 etchings, wood-engraved table of plates (engraved by
Georges Aubert). Edition: 83/200
Gift of Molly and Walter Bareiss, 1984.702
Ref.: Strachan p. 337, Wheeler p. 106

Concert d'été
Text by Joseph-Sébastien Pons, French, 1866–1962
Paris: Flammarion, 1946
26 woodcuts, plus a suite of 26 woodcuts. Edition: 1/250
Gift of Molly and Walter Bareiss, 1984.703

Dialogues des courtisanes
Text by Lucian, Greek, ca. 120–180 c.e.; translation by
Charles Astruc, born 1916
[Paris]: Henri Creuzevault and Dina Viern, [1948]
35 lithographs after Maillol. Edition: 155/260
Gift of Molly and Walter Bareiss, 1984.704

Les géorgiques, texte latin et version française
Text by Virgil, Roman, 70–19 b.c.e.; translation by Jacques
Delille, French, 1738–1813
Paris: Philippe Gonin, 1937–43 (printed 1950)
122 woodcuts. Edition: 461/750
Gift of Molly and Walter Bareiss, 1984.701a–b
Ref.: Garvey cat. 175, Strachan p. 337

Man Ray, American, active France, 1890–1976
L'ange Heurtebise
Text by Jean Cocteau, French, 1889–1963
Paris: Librairie Stock, 1925
One photogravure of a rayogram. Edition: 73/300
Gift of Molly and Walter Bareiss, 1984.355
Fig. 4

Facile
Text by Paul Éluard, French, 1895–1952
Paris: Éditions G.L.M. (Guy Lévis Mano), 1935
Photomechanical reproductions. Edition: 841/1,020
Molly and Walter Bareiss Art Fund, 1987.9
Ref.: Castleman p. 183, Johnson cat. 108
Fig. 88

Man Ray (see also listing under Georges Braque)

Irva Mandelbaum
I Wanted to Fish off the Penninsula [sic]
Text by Robert Louis Stevenson, Scottish, 1850–1894
Brooklyn, NY: Pratt Adlib Press, 1971 (1st ed. 1967)
Photomechanical reproductions
Gift of Molly and Walter Bareiss, 1984.705

Alfred Manessier, French, 1911–1993
Manessier: 1955–1956, la Hollande
Text by E. de Wilde
[Paris]: Galerie de France, 1956
One color lithograph, photomechanical reproductions.
Edition: 122/2,000
Gift of Molly and Walter Bareiss, 1984.706

Alfred Manessier (see also listing under Various Artists,
XXe siècle)

Édouard Manet, French, 1832–1883
Lettres illustrées de Édouard Manet [facsimile]
Text by Édouard Manet; Jean Guiffrey, French, 1870–19??
Paris: Maurice Legarrec, 1929
22 collotypes with added color. Edition: 165/300
Gift of Molly and Walter Bareiss, 1984.707

The Raven. Le corbeau [facsimile]
Text by Edgar Allan Poe, American, 1809–1849; translation
by Stéphane Mallarmé, French, 1842–1898
New York: Pilgrim Press Corp., 1978 (1st ed. 1875)
Photomechanical reproductions, line block reproductions
Gift of Molly and Walter Bareiss, 1984.708
Ref.: Garvey cat. 178, Hogben cat. 1, Wheeler p. 106

Robert Mangold, American, born 1937
Six Arcs
New York: Lapp Princess Press, 1978
Photomechanical reproductions
Gift of Molly and Walter Bareiss, 1984.709

Sylvia Plimack Mangold, American, born 1938
Inches and Field
Text by Sylvia Plimack Mangold
New York: Lapp Princess Press in association with Printed
Matter, 1978
Photomechanical reproductions
Gift of Molly and Walter Bareiss, 1984.710

Manzi, Italian
Il Sacro Animale
Venezia: Cavallino, 1966
Color screen prints. Edition: 13/400
Gift of Molly and Walter Bareiss, 1984.711

Franz Marc (see listing under Various Artists, *Der Blaue
Reiter*)

André Marchand, French, 1907–1998
Les nourritures terrestres
Text by André Gide, French, 1869–1951
Paris: Les éditions du Grenier à sel, 1948
100 lithographs, plus 136 color lithographed initials.
Edition: 130/195
Gift of Molly and Walter Bareiss, 1984.712
Ref.: Strachan pp. 112, 337

Gerhard Marcks, German, 1889–1981
*Gerhard Marcks: Zeichnungen, Plastik, Holzschnitte von einer
Reise durch Süd Afrika*
Text by Gerhard Marcks
Hamburg: Galerie Rudolf Hoffmann, 1956
Photomechanical reproductions, line block reproductions.
Edition: 283/1,000
Gift of Molly and Walter Bareiss, 1984.713

Louis Marcoussis, Polish, active France, 1883–1941
Planches de salut
Text by Tristan Tzara, French (born Romania), 1896–1963
Paris: Éditions Jeanne Bucher, 1931
13 mixed etchings. Edition: 65/71
Gift of Molly and Walter Bareiss, 1984.714
Ref.: Garvey cat. 186, Strachan p. 337
Fig. 89

Brice Marden, American, born 1938
Thirty-six Poems by Tu Fu
Text by Tu Fu, Chinese, 712–770; translation by Kenneth
Rexroth, American, 1905–1982
New York: Peter Blum Edition (Blumarts Inc.), 1987
One mixed etching, photomechanical reproductions.
Edition: 77/140
Molly and Walter Bareiss Art Fund, 1990.18
Ref.: Johnson cat. 171

Filippo Tommaso Marinetti, Italian, 1876–1944
Les mots en liberté: futuristes
Text by Filippo Tommaso Marinetti
Milano: Edizioni Futuriste di "Poesia," 1919
Typographic designs
Gift of Molly and Walter Bareiss, 1987.185
Ref.: Johnson cat. 31
Fig. 56

Marino Marini, Italian, 1901–1980
Marino Marini
Text by Mario Ramous, Italian, born 1924
Bologna: Edizioni d'Arte Licinio Cappelli, [1951]
One etching, photomechanical reproductions, line block
reproductions. Edition: XXXV/L
Gift of Molly and Walter Bareiss, 1984.715

Marino Marini (see also listing under Various Artists,
XXe siècle)

Albert Marquet, French, 1875–1947
Le Danube: voyage de printemps [facsimile]
Text by Marcelle Marquet, French, 1892–19??
Lausanne: Éditions Mermod, 1954
20 collotypes, some with added pochoir color. Edition:
173/470
Gift of Molly and Walter Bareiss, 1984.716

A.-É. (André Édouard) Marty, French, 1882–1974
Émaux et camées
Text by Théophile Gautier, French, 1811–1872
Paris: Édition d'art H. Piazza, 1943
Line block reproductions with added pochoir color, plus 2
suites of reproductions (one with added pochoir color).
Edition: VII/unknown
Gift of Molly and Walter Bareiss, 1984.718

Le diadème de Flore
Text by Gérard d'Houville, French, 1875–1963
Paris: Société d'édition "Le livre" (Émile Chamontin), 1928
40 color wood-engravings after Marty cut by Georges
Beltrand, plus one suite of 40 wood-engravings, and one
color print for each of the 9 blocks used for the fron-
tispiece. Edition: 45/250
Gift of Molly and Walter Bareiss, 1984.717

Frans Masereel, Belgian, active France, 1889–1972
Hôtel-Dieu: récits d'hôpital en 1915
Text by P. J. (Pierre-Jean) Jouve, French, 1887–1976
Paris: Librairie Ollendorff, 1919 (1st ed. 1918)
25 woodcuts
Gift of Molly and Walter Bareiss, 1984.719

The Glorious Adventures of Tyl Ulenspiegl
Text by Charles de Coster, Belgian, 1827–1879; translation
by Allan Ross Macdougall, 1893–1956
New York: Pantheon Books, 1943
Line block reproductions
Gift of Molly and Walter Bareiss, 1984.720

André Masson, French, 1896–1987
Soleils bas
Text by Georges Limbour, French, 1902–1970
Paris: Éditions de la Galerie, André Simon et cie. (under
the direction of Daniel-Henry Kahnweiler), 1924
4 etchings. Edition: 18/100
Gift of Molly and Walter Bareiss, 1984.721
Ref.: Castleman p. 178, Johnson cat. 51, Wheeler p. 107

Miroir de la tauromachie
Text by Michel Leiris, French, 1901–1990
Paris: G.L.M. (Guy Lévis Mano), 1938

Line block reproductions
Gift of Molly and Walter Bareiss, 1984.722

Syncopes
Text by Alain Bosquet, French, 1919–1998
Brooklyn, NY: Éditions hémisphères (Yvan Goll), 1943
Line block reproductions. Edition: III/X
Gift of Molly and Walter Bareiss, 1984.723

Le serpent dans la galère
Text by Georges Duthuit, French, 1891–1973
New York: Curt Valentin, 1945
One lithograph, 8 collotypes, line block reproductions.
Edition: 39/500
Gift of Molly and Walter Bareiss, 1984.724a–b

L'arme secrète
Text by Philippe Soupault, French, 1897–1990
Paris: Bordas, 1946
One lithograph, line block reproductions. Edition: 166/300
Gift of Molly and Walter Bareiss, 1984.725

Féminaire
Text by André Masson
Paris: Éditions de la Galerie Louise Leiris (under the direction of Daniel-Henry Kahnweiler), 1957
21 color etchings with aquatint, line block reproduction
(wrappers). Edition: 18/50
Gift of Molly and Walter Bareiss, 1984.726

Agonie du Général Krivitski
Text by André Frénaud, French, 1907–1993
Paris: Pierre Jean Oswald, 1960
One color etching with aquatint, line block reproductions.
Edition: 31/60
Gift of Molly and Walter Bareiss, 1984.727

André Masson (see also listing under Paul Klee)

Master of 1515, Italian, active ca. 1500
Der Meister von 1515: Nachbildungen seiner Kupferstiche
Text by Paul Kristeller, German, 1863–1931
Berlin: Bruno Cassirer, 1916
45 collotypes and photo-etchings
Gift of Molly and Walter Bareiss, 1984.728

Henri Matisse, French, 1869–1954
Les jockeys camouflés
Text by Pierre Reverdy, French, 1889–1960
Paris: A la belle édition, 1918
Line block reproductions. Edition: 154/318
Gift of Molly and Walter Bareiss, 1984.729
Ref.: Garvey cat. 195

[*Poésie de Stéphane Mallarmé*] [suite of etchings]
[Lausanne: Albert Skira, 1932]
29 etchings
Gift of Molly and Walter Bareiss, 1984.730a–cc
Ref.: Castleman pp. 92–93, Garvey cat. 196, Hogben cat.
95, Johnson cat. 101, Strachan p. 338, Wheeler p. 107

Pasiphaé, chant de Minos (Les Crétois)
Text by Henri de Montherlant, French, 1896–1972
Paris: Martin Fabiani, 1944
148 linoleum cuts, most in color (including 97 decorative
initials and borders). Edition: "Exemplaire de collabora-
teur."
Gift of Molly and Walter Bareiss, 1984.732
Ref.: Castleman p. 113, Garvey cat. 198, Hogben cat. 112,
Johnson cat. 102, Strachan p. 338, Symmes cat. 44, Wheeler
p. 107

Pierre à feu
Texts by various authors
Paris: Maeght éditeur (Adrien Maeght), 1947
One lithograph, one linoleum cut, 2 color pochoir prints
(wrappers), photomechanical reproductions. Edition:
889/950
Gift of Molly and Walter Bareiss, 1984.733

Jazz [portfolio]
Paris: Tériade, 1947
20 color pochoir prints, line block reproduction.

Edition: 53/100
Gift of Molly and Walter Bareiss, 1985.85
Ref.: Castleman pp. 96–97, Garvey cat. 200, Hogben cat.
114, Johnson cat. 120
Fig. 35

Les Fauves
Text by Georges Duthuit, French, 1891–1973
Genève: Éditions des trois collines (Jean Descoullayes,
François Lachenal), 1949
One color pochoir print (wrappers), photomechanical
reproductions, line block reproductions
Gift of Molly and Walter Bareiss, 1984.734

Poèmes de Charles d'Orléans
Text by Charles d'Orléans, French, 1394–1465
Paris: Éditions de la revue Verve (Tériade), 1950
95 color lithographs. Editon: 1,144/1,200
Gift of Molly and Walter Bareiss, 1984.735
Ref.: Garvey cat. 202

Matisse: His Art and His Public
Texts by Alfred H. Barr, Jr., American, 1902–1981; and
various authors
New York: The Museum of Modern Art, 1951
One lithograph, photomechanical reproductions and line
block reproductions of work by various artists. Edition:
330/495
Gift of Molly and Walter Bareiss, 1984.736

Carnet des dessins [facsimile]
Text by Jean Cassou, French, 1897–1985
Paris: Berggruen & cie. (Huguette Berès), 1955
51 color collotypes, photomechanical reproductions.
Edition: 189/500
Gift of Molly and Walter Bareiss, 1984.739a–b

Portraits
Text by Henri Matisse
Monte Carlo: Éditions du livre (André Sauret), 1955
One lithograph, collotypes (some in colors), photomechan-
ical reproductions, line block reproductions. Edition:
1,568/2,000
Gift of Molly and Walter Bareiss, 1984.738

Henri Matisse: aquarelles, dessins
Text by Henri Matisse
Paris: Galerie Jacques Dubourg, 1962
Photomechanical reproductions
Gift of Molly and Walter Bareiss, 1984.740

Florilège des amours
Text by Pierre de Ronsard, French, 1524–1585
Paris: Éditions L.C.L., 1970 (1st ed. 1948)
Photomechanical reproductions. Edition: 113/3,000
Gift of Molly and Walter Bareiss, 1984.741
Ref.: Garvey cat. 201, Strachan p. 338

Poésies de Stéphane Mallarmé [reduced facsimile]
Text by Stéphane Mallarmé, French, 1842–1898
Genève: Edito-Service, 1976 (1st ed. 1932)
Line block reproductions, plus a suite of reproductions.
Edition: 4,433/unknown
Gift of Molly and Walter Bareiss, 1984.731
Ref.: Castleman pp. 92–93, Garvey cat. 196, Hogben cat.
95, Johnson cat. 101, Strachan p. 338, Wheeler p. 107

*Gravures originales sur le thème de "Chant de Minos (Les
Crétois)". Gravures originales sur le thème de "Pasiphaé"*
Text by Dominique Bozon, French
Paris: [Les héritiers de l'artiste], 1981
90 linoleum cuts, some in color. Edition: 59/100
Gift of Molly and Walter Bareiss, 1984.742a–b
Ref.: Symmes cat. 45

Henri Matisse; Brassaï, Hungarian, active France,
1899–1984; **Leonor Fini,** Italian, 1908–1996
Hommage (n° 2, juin 1944)
Texts by Paul Éluard, French, 1895–1952; André Rouveyre,
French, 1879–1962
Monaco: [s.n.], 1944
One photograph (Brassaï), photomechanical reproductions

(Matisse, Fini). Edition: 181/1,000
Gift of Molly and Walter Bareiss, 1984.1292a–b

Henri Matisse; Henri Cartier-Bresson, French, born 1908
Images à la sauvette: photographies par Henri Cartier-Bresson
Paris: Éditions de la revue Verve (Tériade), 1952
One color pochoir print (Matisse, cover), photomechanical
reproductions
Gift of Molly and Walter Bareiss, 1984.737

Henri Matisse (see also listing under Pierre Bonnard)

Matta (Roberto Sebastian Antonio Matta Echaurren),
Chilean, active France, born 1911
*Les manifestes du Surréalisme suivis de prolégomènes à un
troisième manifeste du Surréalisme ou non*
Text by André Breton, French, 1896–1966
[Paris]: Éditions du sagittaire, 1947 (© 1946)
3 drypoints, line block reproduction of drawing by Breton
(wrappers). Edition: A/C
Gift of Molly and Walter Bareiss, 1984.743

Le ravin de la femme sauvage
Text by Henri Kréa, Algerian, born 1933
Paris: Pierre Jean Oswald, 1959
One color etching with aquatint. Edition: 47/80
Gift of Molly and Walter Bareiss, 1984.745

Come detta Dentro vo Significando
Text by Matta
Lausanne: Éditions Meyer, 1962
22 mixed etchings, most in colors. Edition: 54/100
Gift of Molly and Walter Bareiss, 1984.746
Fig. 101

La fin et la manière
Text by Jean-Pierre Duprey, French, 1930–1959
Paris: Éditions du soleil, Le soleil noir, 1965
Line block reproductions. Edition: 794/2,605
Gift of Molly and Walter Bareiss, 1984.747

Scènes familières
Paris: Le point cardinal, [1965?]
8 color etchings with aquatint. Edition: 17/50
Gift of Molly and Walter Bareiss, 1984.748a–h

Jacques Mauny, French, active United States, 1893–1962
Amica America
Text by Jean Giraudoux, French, 1882–1944
Paris: Éditions Émile-Paul frères, 1928
20 engravings, some with aquatint, plus a suite of 20
engravings. Edition: "H.C."
Gift of Molly and Walter Bareiss, 1984.749

Scott L. McCarney, American, born 1954
Alphabook 3
[Rochester, NY]: Scott L. McCarney, 1986
Die cut letters. Edition: unnumbered/300
Molly and Walter Bareiss Art Fund and Printed Matter
Matching Gift Fund for Libraries, 1987.55a–b

Ann McCoy, American, born 1946
Ann McCoy: The Red Sea and the Night Sea
Text by Ann McCoy
Chicago: Arts Club of Chicago, [1979]
One color lithograph (wrappers), photomechanical repro-
ductions, line block reproductions. Edition: unnumbered/
2,500
Gift of Molly and Walter Bareiss, 1984.694

Christoph Meckel, German, born 1935
Gedichtbilderbuch
Text by Christoph Meckel
Stierstadt im Taunus, Deutschland: Eremiten-Presse, 1964
13 lithographs, 2 woodcuts from the same block (including
one in colors on the wrappers). Edition: 190/250
Gift of Molly and Walter Bareiss, 1984.750

Mathurin Méheut, French, 1882–1958
"Regarde…"
Text by Colette, French, 1873–1954
Paris: J.-G. Deschamps, [1929]
19 line block reproductions with added pochoir colors.

Edition: 164/700
Gift of Molly and Walter Bareiss, 1984.751

Georg Meistermann (see listing under HAP Grieshaber)

Ana Mendieta (see listing under Carl Andre)

Adolph von Menzel, German, 1815–1905
Adolph Menzel: Skizzenbuch 1846 [facsimile]
Berlin: Gebr. Mann, [1936]
Collotypes
Gift of Molly and Walter Bareiss, 1984.752

Mario Merz, Italian, born 1925
Fibonacci 1202: Mario Merz 1970
Torino, Italia: Sperone Editore, 1970
Photomechanical reproductions
Gift of Molly and Walter Bareiss, 1984.753

Willy Meyer, German, born 1934
Willy Meyer Zeichnungen
München: Galerie Stangl, [after 1960?]
Photomechanical reproductions. Edition: 38/100
Gift of Molly and Walter Bareiss, 1984.755

W. Meyer
Text by Carl Linfert, born 1900
Bremen: Böttcherstrasse, 1970
One blind embossing, photomechanical reproductions.
Edition: unnumbered/100
Gift of Molly and Walter Bareiss, 1984.754

Rebecca Michaels, American
The Courtship Patterns of Chairs
Text by Rebecca Michaels
New York: Chicago Books, 1979
Photomechanical reproductions
Gift of Molly and Walter Bareiss, 1984.756

Henri Michaux, French (born Belgium), 1899–1984
Arbres des tropiques
Text by Henri Michaux
[Paris]: Librairie Gallimard, 1942
Line block reproductions. Edition: 4/300
Gift of Molly and Walter Bareiss, 1984.757

Meidosems
Text by Henri Michaux
Paris: Éditions du Point du jour, 1948
13 lithographs, including one in color (wrappers). Edition:
unnumbered/250
Gift of Molly and Walter Bareiss, 1984.758
Ref.: Castleman p. 151

Misérable miracle (La Mescaline)
Text by Henri Michaux
Monaco-Ville: Éditions du Rocher, 1956
48 collotypes. Edition: 117/1,530
Gift of Molly and Walter Bareiss, 1984.759

En appel de visages
Text by Yves Peyré, French, born 1952
Paris: Éditions Verdier, 1983
Photomechanical reproductions. Edition: 66/75
Gift of Molly and Walter Bareiss, 1984.760

Ludwig Mies van der Rohe, German, 1886–1969
*Ludwig Mies van der Rohe: Drawings in the Collection of
The Museum of Modern Art*
Text by Ludwig Glaeser, born 1930
New York: The Museum of Modern Art, 1969
Photomechanical reproductions
Gift of Molly and Walter Bareiss, 1984.761

Manolo Millares, Spanish (born Canary Islands),
1926–1972
Mutilados de paz
Text by Rafael Alberti, Spanish, 1902–1999
Madrid: Artes Graficas Luis Pérez (Gerardo Rueda), 1965
4 color screen prints. Edition: 22/100
Gift of Molly and Walter Bareiss, 1984.762

"Antropofauna"
Barcelona: Gustavo Gili, 1970

5 zinc etchings. Edition: 13/50
Gift of Molly and Walter Bareiss, 1984.763a–e

Zwy Milshtein, Israeli (born Russia), born 1934
Dossier Solange
Text by Zwy Milshtein
Paris: [s.n.], 1967
20 etchings, 2 lithographs (chemise, slipcase). Edition: 31/75
Gift of Molly and Walter Bareiss, 1984.764

Victor Mira, Spanish, born 1949
Estrellas del Infierno
[S.l.: s.n., 197?]
3 etchings. Edition: 3/21
Gift of Molly and Walter Bareiss, 1984.770a–c

Pequeña Serie Roja
[S.l.: s.n., 197?]
5 color etchings. Edition: 2/21
Gift of Molly and Walter Bareiss, 1984.769a–e

Dinámica violada
Text by Victor Mira
Barcelona: Victor Mira, 1977
Collages with printed tickets, receipts, postage stamps, printed newsprint and wrapping paper, with added graphite and colored inks (unique book)
Gift of Molly and Walter Bareiss, 1984.765

Das Buch der drei A
[Barcelona?: Victor Mira?], 1978
15 collages with tissue paper and matchsticks, with added graphite and colored inks (unique book)
Gift of Molly and Walter Bareiss, 1984.768

El Camino del Chino Mira
Barcelona: Victor Mira, 1980
10 color lithographs with painted additions
Gift of Molly and Walter Bareiss, 1984.766

Im Buchstaben liegt das Feuer
München: D. P. Druck-u. Publikations, 1981
Photomechanical reproductions. Edition: unnumbered/300
Gift of Molly and Walter Bareiss, 1984.767

Joan Miró, Spanish, active France, 1893–1983
"Il était une petite pie": 7 chansons et 3 chansons pour Hyacinthe
Text by Lise Hirtz, French, 1898–1980
Paris: Édition Jeanne Bucher, 1928
9 color pochoir prints. Edition: 190/300
Gift of Molly and Walter Bareiss, 1984.771
Ref.: Johnson cat. 98, Symmes cat. 47, Wheeler p. 107

L'arbre des voyageurs
Text by Tristan Tzara, French (born Romania), 1896–1963
Paris: Éditions de la montagne, 1930
4 lithographs. Edition: 11/500
Gift of Molly and Walter Bareiss, 1984.772
Ref.: Garvey cat. 205, Hogben cat. 87, Johnson cat. 97

Parler seul: poème
Text by Tristan Tzara, French (born Romania), 1896–1963
Paris: Maeght éditeur (Adrien Maeght), 1948–50
One collage of color lithograph elements (cover), 72 lithographs, some in colors. Edition: 110/250
Gift of Molly and Walter Bareiss, 1984.773
Ref.: Garvey cat. 206, Johnson cat. 127, Strachan pp. 126, 339, Symmes cat. 48

Anthologie de l'humour noir
Texts by various authors; edited by André Breton, French, 1896–1966
Paris: Éditions du sagittaire, 1950
One color lithograph, photomechanical reproductions
Edition: 22/37
Gift of Molly and Walter Bareiss, 1984.774

Miró: Recent Paintings
Text by James Johnson Sweeney, American, 1900–1986
New York: Pierre Matisse Gallery, 1953
4 lithographs, most in colors, photomechanical reproductions. Edition: "compliments of the publisher"
Gift of Molly and Walter Bareiss, 1984.775

Bagatelles végétales
Text by Michel Leiris, French, 1901–1990
Paris: Jean Aubier, 1956
6 color etchings with aquatint, including 2 with added color fingerprints. Edition: 16/300
Gift of Molly and Walter Bareiss, 1984.778
Ref.: Garvey cat. 207, Johnson cat. 133, Symmes cat. 49

Joan Miró
Texts by Jacques Prévert, French, 1900–1977; Georges Ribemont-Dessaignes, French, 1884–1974
Paris: Maeght éditeur (Adrien Maeght), 1956
One ink drawing, 10 lithographs, most in colors, photomechanical reproductions
Gift of Molly and Walter Bareiss, 1984.776, 1984.777 (without the drawing)

Sculpture in Ceramic by Miró and Artigas
Text by Rosamond Bernier, American, born 1920?
New York: Pierre Matisse Gallery, 1956
6 color lithographs, photomechanical reproductions
Gift of Molly and Walter Bareiss, 1984.779

La bague d'aurore
Text by René Crevel, French, 1900–1935
Paris: Louis Broder, 1957
6 etchings, most in colors. Edition: 102/115
Gift of Molly and Walter Bareiss, 1984.780
Ref.: Symmes cat. 51

Le visage s'invente
Text by Pierre André Benoit, French, 1924–1993
[Alès, France]: PAB (Pierre André Benoit), 1957
2 color drypoints from the same plate. Edition: IX/X
Gift of Molly and Walter Bareiss, 1984.781
Ref.: Symmes cat. 50

À toute épreuve
Text by Paul Éluard, French, 1895–1952
Genève: Gérald Cramer, 1958
80 woodcuts, some with collagraph or collage, most in colors, plus a suite of 80 woodcuts, including one with added gouache. Edition: 25/106
Gift of Molly and Walter Bareiss, 1984.783
Ref.: Castleman pp. 100–101, Garvey cat. 209, Hogben cat. 121, Johnson cat. 139, Strachan p. 168, Symmes cat. 52
Fig. 9

Le tablier blanc
Text by Lise Deharme, French, 1898–1980
Alès, France: PAB (Pierre André Benoit), 1958
One linoleum cut. Edition: 49/50
Gift of Molly and Walter Bareiss, 1984.782

Joan Miró: Drawings and Lithographs in the Collection of Juan de Juanes from Papeles de son Armadans
Text by Camilo José Cela, Spanish, born 1916
Greenwich, CT: New York Graphic Society; Barcelona: Editorial Seix Barral, 1959 (© 1960)
3 color lithographs, photomechanical reproductions. Edition: 150/738
Gift of Molly and Walter Bareiss, 1984.787

The Miró Atmosphere
Text by James Johnson Sweeney, American, 1900–1986
New York: George Wittenborn; Barcelona: Editorial RM, 1959
One color lithograph, photomechanical reproductions, line block reproduction (cover). Edition: 58/160
Gift of Molly and Walter Bareiss, 1984.785

Noël au chemin de fer
Text by André Frénaud, French, 1907–1993
Alès, France: PAB (Pierre André Benoit), 1959
2 color drypoints, 2 découpages with cut paper and ink (wrappers). Edition: 12/35
Gift of Molly and Walter Bareiss, 1984.784

Mavena
Text by Radovan Ivsic, Croatian, active France, born 1921
Paris: Éditions surréalistes, 1960
One color lithograph. Edition: 52/75
Gift of Molly and Walter Bareiss, 1984.786

La rame et la roue
Text by René Cazelles
Paris: Jean Hugues, 1960
3 states of one color lithograph. Edition: 7/25
Gift of Molly and Walter Bareiss, 1984.788

Marrons sculptés pour Miró
Text by Michel Leiris, French, 1901–1990
[Genève]: Edwin Engelberts, 1961
One color lithograph (wrappers). Edition: 42/100
Gift of Molly and Walter Bareiss, 1984.790

Anti-Platon
Text by Yves Bonnefoy, French, born 1923
Paris: Maeght éditeur (Adrien Maeght), 1962
8 etchings with aquatint, most in colors. Edition: 55/125
Gift of Molly and Walter Bareiss, 1984.791

Création Miró 1961
Text by Yvon Taillandier, French, born 1926
Barcelona: Editorial RM, 1962
2 states of one etching with aquatint, including one in colors, photomechanical reproductions. Edition: 9-IX/15-XV
Gift of Molly and Walter Bareiss, 1984.794

La lumière de la lame
Text by André du Bouchet, French, born 1924
Paris: Maeght éditeur (Adrien Maeght), 1962
8 etchings with aquatint, most in colors. Edition: 55/125
Gift of Molly and Walter Bareiss, 1984.792

Saccades
Text by Jacques Dupin, French, born 1927
Paris: Maeght éditeur (Adrien Maeght), 1962
8 etchings with aquatint, most in colors. Edition: 55/125
Gift of Molly and Walter Bareiss, 1984.793

Derrière le miroir: Miró, Artigas (nos 139–140, juin juillet 1963)
Text by André Pieyre de Mandiargues, French, 1909–1991
Paris: Maeght éditeur (Aimé Maeght), 1963
8 color lithographs, photomechanical reproductions, line block reproductions
Gift of Molly and Walter Bareiss, 1984.1238

Tracé sur l'eau
Paris: Maeght éditeur (Adrien Maeght), 1963
One lithograph (wrappers), 14 color collotypes, line block reproductions. Edition: unnumbered/1,000
Gift of Molly and Walter Bareiss, 1984.795

Derrière le miroir: Miró: Cartons (nos 151–52, mai 1965)
Text by Jacques Dupin, French, born 1927
Paris: Maeght éditeur (Aimé Maeght), 1965
Lithographs with added collotype, some in colors
Gift of Molly and Walter Bareiss, 1984.1233

Miró: "Cartones" 1959–1965
Text by Pierre Schneider, French (born Germany), born 1925
New York: Pierre Matisse Gallery, 1965
2 lithographs, including one in colors, 26 collotypes, some with added pochoir color. Edition: 229/1,200
Gift of Molly and Walter Bareiss, 1984.796

Joan Miró
Text by Roland Penrose, British, 1900–1984
London: Marlborough Fine Art, 1966
Photomechanical reproductions
Gift of Molly and Walter Bareiss, 1984.797

Miró: Oiseau solaire, oiseau lunaire, étincelles
New York: Pierre Matisse Gallery, 1967
46 collotypes, some with added pochoir color (including wrappers and die-cut jacket). Edition: 106/1,200
Gift of Molly and Walter Bareiss, 1984.798
Fig. 106

Joan Miró: Oeuvre gravé et lithographié
Genève: Galerie Gérald Cramer, 1969
One lithograph (jacket), photomechanical reproductions. Edition: 723/1,650
Gift of Molly and Walter Bareiss, 1984.799

Derrière le miroir: Miró: peintures sur papier - dessins (nos 193–94, octobre–novembre 1971)

Text by Pierre Alechinsky, Belgian, born 1927; Jacques
Dupin, French, born 1927
Paris: Maeght éditeur (Aimé Maeght), 1971
3 color lithographs, photomechanical reproductions
Gift of Molly and Walter Bareiss, 1984.1235

Le lézard aux plumes d'or [exhibition announcement]
Paris: Berggruen Gallery, 1971
One color lithograph (cover), photomechanical
reproductions
Gift of Molly and Walter Bareiss, 1984.802

Le lézard aux plumes d'or
Text by Joan Miró
[Paris]: Louis Broder, 1971
16 lithographs, most in colors, plus a suite of 13 litho-
graphs, line block reproductions. Edition: 35/150
Gift of Molly and Walter Bareiss, 1984.801a–n

Liberté des libertés
Text by Alain Jouffroy, French, born 1928
Paris: Éditions du soleil, Le soleil noir, 1971
Photomechanical reproductions. Edition: 346/1,800
Gift of Molly and Walter Bareiss, 1984.803

Le vent parmi les roseaux
Text by William Butler Yeats, Irish, 1865–1939; translation
by André Pieyre de Mandiargues, French, 1909–1991
Paris: OLV Collection Paroles Peintes, 1971
3 color etchings with drypoint and aquatint (including
wrappers), plus a suite of 2 etchings. Edition: 76/115
Gift of Molly and Walter Bareiss, 1984.800a–c

Miró sobre papel
Text by Pierre Schneider, French (born Germany),
born 1925
New York: Pierre Matisse Gallery, 1972
One color lithograph, photomechanical reproductions
Gift of Molly and Walter Bareiss, 1984.804

Miró: Paintings, Gouaches, Sobreteixims, Sculpture, Etchings
Texts by various authors
New York: Pierre Matisse Gallery, 1973
One lithograph (wrappers), photomechanical reproductions
Gift of Molly and Walter Bareiss, 1984.805

Le courtisan grotesque
Text by Adrien de Montluc (compte de Cramail), French,
1589–1646
Paris: Le degré quarante et un (Iliazd), 1974
16 mixed etchings, some in colors. Edition: 39/95
Gift of Molly and Walter Bareiss, 1984.806
Fig. 55

Joan Miró; Antoni Tàpies, Spanish, born 1923
Poemes civils
Barcelona: Editorial RM, 1961
One color etching with aquatint (Miró), 2 color screen
prints (Tàpies, cover). Edition: 31/90
Gift of Molly and Walter Bareiss, 1984.789

Joan Miró (see also listings under Henri Cartier-Bresson;
Max Ernst; Various Artists, *XXe siècle*)

Joan Mitchell, American, active France, 1926–1992
The Poems
Text by John Ashbery, American, born 1927
New York: Tiber Press (Tibor de Nagy), 1960
5 color screen prints. Edition: 16/200
Gift of Molly and Walter Bareiss, 1984.1218d
Ref.: Castleman p. 207, Johnson cat. 142

H. (Manuel Hernandez) Mompó, Spanish, born 1927
H. Mompó
Paris: Galerie Claude Bernard, 1966
2 color screen prints, photomechanical reproductions, line
block reproductions. Edition: unnumbered/1,000
Gift of Molly and Walter Bareiss, 1984.807

Monlyn
Images nocturnes
[S.l.]: Monlyn, 1965
10 drypoints with added color. Edition: 4/30
Gift of Molly and Walter Bareiss, 1984.808a–j

Claire Moore, American, 1912–1988
Rubbings, Grids
[S.l.: Claire Moore, 197?]
Photocopies of graphite rubbings
Gift of Molly and Walter Bareiss, 1984.811

Napoleon Is a Brother, Is a Sister
[New York: Chicago Books], 1982
Photomechanical reproductions
Gift of Molly and Walter Bareiss, 1984.809

Half and Half
Text by Claire Moore
[New York: Chicago Books], 1983
Photomechanical reproductions
Gift of Molly and Walter Bareiss, 1984.810

Berthe Morisot, French, 1841–1895
Croquis de ma mère Berthe Morisot [facsimile]
[S.l.: s.n., 1956?]
Hand-colored collotypes
Gift of Molly and Walter Bareiss, 1984.812

Richard Mortensen, Danish, active France, 1910–1993
Richard Mortensen
Köln: Galerie der Spiegel, 1960
4 color screen prints, photomechanical reproductions.
Edition: unnumbered/250
Gift of Molly and Walter Bareiss, 1984.814

Robert Motherwell, American, 1915–1991
Robert Motherwell, Selected Prints: 1961–1974
New York: Brooke Alexander, 1974
One lithograph with collage (wrappers), photomechanical
reproductions. Edition: unnumbered/4,000
Gift of Molly and Walter Bareiss, 1984.815

El Negro
Text by Rafael Alberti, Spanish, 1902–1999; translation
by Vicente Lleó Cañal
Bedford Village, NY: Tyler Graphics, 1983
17 lithographs, some in colors. Edition: 39/51
Gift of Molly and Walter Bareiss, 1984.816
Ref.: Hogben cat. 164, Johnson cat. 170, Phillips cat. 35,
Symmes cat. 53
Fig. 136

Robert Motherwell; Renate Ponsold, American
(born Germany), born 1935
Apropos, Robinson Jeffers
Text by Robinson Jeffers, American, 1887–1962
Long Beach, CA: Art Museum and Galleries, California
State University, 1981
One lithograph (Motherwell), photomechanical
reproductions. Edition: 94/100
Gift of Molly and Walter Bareiss, 1984.1288

Seong Moy, American (born China), born 1921
Seong Moy
Text by Una Johnson, American, 1905–1997
New York: Rio Grande Graphics (Ted Gotthelf), 1952
5 color woodcuts, photomechanical reproduction.
Edition: 58/225
Gift of Molly and Walter Bareiss, 1984.817a–e

Rudolf Mumprecht, Swiss, active France, born 1918
Der Kaiser, der Maler und der Hahn
Bern: [privately published], 1955
4 aquatints, one color relief print. Edition: V/X
Gift of Molly and Walter Bareiss, 1984.818

Shiko Munakata, Japanese, 1903–1975
The "Way" of the Woodcut
Text by Shiko Munakata
Brooklyn, NY: Pratt Adlib Press, 1961
4 woodcuts, including one in color (cover).
Edition: 132/300
Gift of Molly and Walter Bareiss, 1984.819

Bruno Munari, Italian, 1907–1998
"Libro Illeggibile" n. 20
New York: "Italian Book & Craft Inc."
(Bruno Munari), 1953

Book object: torn and cut paper, colored thread.
Edition: 8/11
Gift of Molly and Walter Bareiss, 1984.820
Ref.: Symmes cat. 54

In the Dark of the Night
Text by Bruno Munari
New York: George Wittenborn, [1956]
Book object: color pochoir prints, die cuts, relief prints,
and collage
Gift of Molly and Walter Bareiss, 1984.821

Nella Notte Buia
Text by Bruno Munari
Milano: Muggiani Editore, 1956
Book object: color pochoir prints, die cuts, relief prints,
and collage
Gift of Molly and Walter Bareiss, 1984.822

Bruno Munari's ABC
Cleveland: World Publishing Co., 1960
Photomechanical reproductions
Gift of Molly and Walter Bareiss, 1984.823

Discovery of the Square
Text by Bruno Munari
New York: George Wittenborn, 1962
Photomechanical reproductions. Edition: unnumbered/
1,000
Gift of Molly and Walter Bareiss, 1984.824

Good Design
Text by Bruno Munari
Milano: All'Insegna del Pesce d'Oro (Vanni Scheiwiller),
1963
Photomechanical reproductions. Edition: unnumbered/
2,000
Gift of Molly and Walter Bareiss, 1984.825

Supplemento al Dizionario Italiano
Text by Bruno Munari
Milano: Muggiani Editore, 1963 (1st ed. 1958)
Photomechanical reproductions
Gift of Molly and Walter Bareiss, 1984.826

Libro Illeggibile 1966
Roma: Galleria dell'Obelisco, [1966]
Book object: line block reproductions on glassine
Gift of Molly and Walter Bareiss, 1984.827

Libro Illeggibile N.Y. 1
New York: The Museum of Modern Art, 1967
Book object: die-cut pages with pochoir color, stamping,
thread. Edition: 1,291/unknown
Gift of Molly and Walter Bareiss, 1984.828
Ref.: Castleman p. 224
Fig. 113

Celia Alvarez Muñoz, American, born 1937
Enlightenment #1
Text by Celia Alvarez Muñoz
Arlington, TX: Enlightenment Press, 1982–87
4 photographs, book matches, and scorching, plus one
blind embossing (folder). Edition: 3/10
Molly and Walter Bareiss Art Fund, 1988.37
Fig. 144

Agnes Murray, American
Letters
Text by Jalaluddin Mohammad Rumi, Persian, 1207–1273;
translation by Zahra Partovi
New York: Vincent FitzGerald & Company, 1986
5 color lithographs. Edition: 2/75
Molly and Walter Bareiss Art Fund, 1987.18

Peter Nadin (see listing under Jenny Holzer)

Eriko Nagai, born 1947
Schmuck
Graz, Österreich: Droschl, 1981
Photomechanical reproductions. Edition: unnumbered/300
Gift of Molly and Walter Bareiss, 1984.829

Peter Nagel, German, born 1941
Peter Nagel: Bilder, Graphik
München: Galerie van de Loo, [1971?]
One etching with added color, photomechanical reproductions. Edition: 41/50
Gift of Molly and Walter Bareiss, 1984.830a–b

Ernst Wilhelm Nay, German, 1902–1968
E. W. Nay
Köln: Galerie der Spiegel, 1957
One lithograph, photomechanical reproductions, line block reproductions. Edition: unnumbered/150
Gift of Molly and Walter Bareiss, 1984.831

Portrait des Artisten
Text by Ulrich Serbser
Köln: Galerie der Spiegel, [1957]
One color aquatint. Edition: 10/300
Gift of Molly and Walter Bareiss, 1984.832

Renée Nele, German, active Switzerland, born 1932
Obszönität und das Gesetz der Reflexion
Text by Henry Miller, American, 1891–1980
Köln: Galerie der Spiegel, 1960
10 etchings with aquatint and embossing, some in colors.
Edition: X (artist's proof)
Gift of Molly and Walter Bareiss, 1984.833

Rolf Nesch, Norwegian (born Germany), 1893–1975
[1960 calendar]
Stuttgart: Chr. Belser, 1960
One relief print (cover), photomechanical reproductions
Gift of Molly and Walter Bareiss, 1984.834

Ernst Neukamp, German, born 1937
Ernst Neukamp '73: Wiesenstücke
München: Galerie Stangl, 1973
One color screen print, photomechanical reproductions.
Edition: 12/120
Gift of Molly and Walter Bareiss, 1984.835a–b

John Newman, American, born 1952
John Newman. Zeichnungen
Text by Prudence Carlson
München: Fred Jahn (Jens Jahn), 1990
One linoleum cut with added graphite drawing, photomechanical reproductions. Edition: 16/18
Gift of Molly and Walter Bareiss, 1990.85a–b

Jim Nichols, American, born 1928
Juggernaut
Text by Kirby Congdon, American, born 1924
New York: Interim Books, 1966
Photomechanical reproductions. Edition: 361/500
Gift of Molly and Walter Bareiss, 1984.836

Hermann Nitsch, Austrian, born 1938
Die Eroberung von Jerusalem
Text by Hermann Nitsch
Tübingen: Edition Matala von Ernst-Jürgen Wasmuth, 1973
Photomechanical reproductions. Edition: 75/75
Gift of Molly and Walter Bareiss, 1984.837

Die Eroberung von Jerusalem
Text by Hermann Nitsch
Napoli: Edition Morra; Berlin: Die Drossel, [1973 or after?]
Photomechanical reproductions. Edition: unnumbered/1,000
Gift of Molly and Walter Bareiss, 1984.838

Das O. M. Theater: Objekte, Fotos, Konzepte
Text by Hermann Nitsch
Tübingen: Edition Matala von Ernst-Jürgen Wasmuth, 1973
8 collaged and painted panels, 8 photographs, one color lithograph, photomechanical reproductions. Edition: 30/75
Gift of Molly and Walter Bareiss, 1987.287a–r

Die Arkitektur des Orgien Mysterien Theaters: Mappe I
München: Fred Jahn, 1987
One etching reworked with tusche, tint, and stamping, 35 color lithographs, some with etching. Edition: 23/35

Molly and Walter Bareiss Art Fund, 1988.65a–jj
Fig. 145

Das Orgien Mysterien Theater 80. Aktion: Aufgeführt vom Sonnenaufgang des 27. bis zum Sonnenaufgang des 30. Juli 1984
Text by Hermann Nitsch
München: Fred Jahn, 1988
Photomechanical reproductions. Edition: 181/200
Molly and Walter Bareiss Art Fund, 1989.113

Isamu Noguchi, American, 1904–1988
Secret Haiku
Text by Charles Henri Ford, American, born 1913
New York: Red Ozier Press (Ken Botnick, Steve Miller), 1982
Line block reproductions. Edition: 49/155
Molly and Walter Bareiss Art Fund, 1987.190

Gastone Novelli, Italian, 1925–1968
Scritto sul Muro
Text by Gastone Novelli
Roma: Edizioni "L'Esperienza Moderna" (Pino Rocchi), 1958
30 lithographs, most in colors. Edition: 178/200
Gift of Molly and Walter Bareiss, 1984.839

Viaggio in Grecia
Text by Gastone Novelli
Roma: Edizioni Arco d'Alibert, 1966
6 etchings with aquatint, line block reproductions.
Edition: 34/45
Gift of Molly and Walter Bareiss, 1984.841

Josef Oberberger, German, 1905–1994
O Maria Hilf! und zwar sofort: damit's ein (r)echter Bayer wird!
Text by Kurt Wilhelm, German, born 1923
Rosenheim, Deutschland: Verlagshaus Alfred Förg, 1978
One ink drawing, photomechanical reproductions
Gift of Molly and Walter Bareiss, 1984.842

Thom O'Connor, American, born 1937
Wizards & Cabalists & Mystics & Magicians
Text by Arthur Plotnik, American, born 1937
New York: Associated American Artists, 1966
10 etchings, some with aquatint. Edition: 17/100
Gift of Molly and Walter Bareiss, 1984.843

Claes Oldenburg, American (born Sweden), born 1929
Notes in Hand [facsimile]
Text by Claes Oldenburg
New York: E. P. Dutton & Co. in association with Petersburg Press, 1971
Photomechanical reproductions
Gift of Molly and Walter Bareiss, 1984.844

Luigi Ontani, Italian, born 1943
Acervus
Tübingen, Deutschland: Edition DACIC', 1978
Photomechanical reproductions. Edition: unnumbered/2,500
Molly and Walter Bareiss Art Fund and Printed Matter Matching Gift Fund for Libraries, 1987.56

Kevin Osborn, American, born 1951
Tropos
Arlington, VA: Osbornbook, 1988
Photomechanical reproductions, with die cut.
Edition: unnumbered/1,600
Gift of Molly and Walter Bareiss, 2000.45
Ref.: Drucker pp. 135–36

Mimmo Paladino, Italian, born 1948
Bosforo
Torino: Mello e Noire Editori, Edizioni Tivoli (Franco Mello and Marco Noire), 1983
6 woodcuts, some with added collage or pochoir color
Gift of Molly and Walter Bareiss, 1984.845

Blinky Palermo, German, 1943–1977
[Untitled]
[S.l.: s.n., 1970?]

12 lithographs. Edition: 5/50
Gift of Molly and Walter Bareiss, 1984.848

Palermo: Suite mit vier Farbsiebdrucken auf Packpapier
München: Edition der Galerie Heiner Friedrich (Fred Jahn), 1971
5 screen prints, including title page element, some in colors. Edition: 32/60
Gift of Molly and Walter Bareiss, 1984.846a–d

Heinz Gappmayr: Visuelle Gedichte; Palermo: Fünf Miniaturen
Text by Heinz Gappmayr, Austrian, born 1925
Duisberg, Deutschland: Guido Hildebrandt, 1972
5 color relief prints. Edition: unnumbered/100
Gift of Molly and Walter Bareiss, 1984.847

Giulio Paolini, Italian, born 1940
Ennesima: Appunti per la descizione de sei disegni datati 1975
Torino: Galleria Notizie; Milano: Studio Marconi (Yvonne Lambert), 1975
Line block reproductions. Edition: unnumbered/1,000
Gift of Molly and Walter Bareiss, 1984.849

Eduardo Paolozzi, British, born 1924
As Is When: A Series of Screenprints Based on the Life and Writings of Ludwig Wittgenstein
Text by Eduardo Paolozzi
London: Editions Alecto, 1965
14 color screen prints. Edition: 63/65
Gift of Molly and Walter Bareiss, 1984.852a–p

Moonstrips Empire News, vol. 1
London: Editions Alecto, 1967
100 screen prints, some in colors. Edition: 355/500
Gift of Molly and Walter Bareiss, 1984.850

Eduardo Paolozzi: Plastik und Graphik
Düsseldorf: Städtische Kunsthalle (Karl Ruhrberg), 1968
One color screen print, photomechanical reproductions, line block reproduction
Gift of Molly and Walter Bareiss, 1984.851

Jules Pascin, American (born Bulgaria), active France, 1885–1930
Aus den Memoiren des Herrn von Schnabelewopski
Text by Heinrich Heine, German, 1797–1856
Berlin: Paul Cassirer, 1910
36 transfer lithographs, including 5 with added pochoir color. Edition: 84/250
Gift of Molly and Walter Bareiss, 1984.853
Ref.: Garvey cat. 219, Wheeler p. 108
Fig. 72

Aus den Memoiren des Herrn von Schnabelewopski
Text by Heinrich Heine, German, 1797–1856
Berlin: Paul Cassirer, 1920 (2nd ed., reduced size)
Photomechanical reproductions, including one with added pochoir color (cover)
Gift of Molly and Walter Bareiss, 1984.854
Ref.: Garvey cat. 219, Wheeler p. 108

Cendrillon
Text by Charles Perrault, French, 1628–1703
Paris: Éditions M. P. Trémois, [1929]
6 mixed soft-ground etchings, most in colors, including 5 with added pochoir color; plus a suite of 5 soft-ground etchings; line block reproductions. Edition: 24/66
Gift of Molly and Walter Bareiss, 1984.857a–b
Ref.: Garvey cat. 220, Wheeler p. 108

Tombeau de Pascin
Text by Pierre MacOrlan, French, 1882–1970
[Paris]: Insita Cruce Cor Floret, 1944
4 soft-ground etchings, 2 drypoints, one mezzotint, one wood-engraving. Edition: "pour Madame Daragnès"
Gift of Molly and Walter Bareiss, 1984.855

Pascin: carnet de dessins, Berlin-Tunis 1908 [facsimile]
Text by Claude Roger-Marx, French, 1888–1977
Paris: Berggruen, 1968
Collotypes, some with added pochoir color. Edition: "pour Mr. and Mrs. Walter Bareiss"
Gift of Molly and Walter Bareiss, 1984.856a–b

George Passmore (see Gilbert and George)

Guy Peellaert, Belgian, born 1934
Rock Dreams
Text by Nik Cohn, British, born 1946
New York: Popular Library, 1973
Photomechanical reproductions
Gift of Molly and Walter Bareiss, 1984.858

Rock Dreams: Under the Boardwalk
Text by Nik Cohn, British, born 1946
München: Walter H. Schünemann, 1973
Photomechanical reproductions
Gift of Molly and Walter Bareiss, 1984.859

A. R. Penck, German, born 1939
Standarts
München: Galerie Michael Werner, 1970
Photomechanical reproductions. Edition: unnumbered/
1,000
Gift of Molly and Walter Bareiss, 1981.136
Ref.: Castleman p. 165

"Europäische Sonette"
Text by A. R. Penck
Antwerp: Galerie Wide White Space (Anny de Decker),
1973
Photomechanical reproductions. Edition: unnumbered/500
Gift of Molly and Walter Bareiss, 1984.860

Sanfte Theorie über Arsch, Asche und Vegetation
Text by A. R. Penck
Groningen: Groninger Museum, 1979
Photomechanical reproductions. Edition: unnumbered/500
Gift of Molly and Walter Bareiss, 1984.861

*Hinter der Wüste sterben die Gespenster: Jazz Rock / Afrika
Paranoia: Archaik-Fri-Jazz* [sound recordings]
[S.l.]: Weltmelodie, 1980
Photomechanical reproductions (album cover)
Gift of Molly and Walter Bareiss, 1984.864

Ende im Osten [sketchbook facsimile]
Berlin: Rainer (Rainer Pretzell), 1981
Photomechanical reproductions. Edition: unnumbered/
1,000
Gift of Molly and Walter Bareiss, 1984.862

A. R. Penck: 45 Zeichnungen, Bewusstseinsschichten
Basel: Kunstmuseum, 1982
Photomechanical reproductions
Gift of Molly and Walter Bareiss, 1984.866

4 mm: Westkeller / Endstation [sound recordings]
[S.l.]: Weltmelodie, 1983
Photomechanical reproductions (album cover)
Gift of Molly and Walter Bareiss, 1984.865
Fig. 139

Wolokolamsker Chaussee IV und V
Text by Heiner Müller, German, born 1929
München: Maximilian (Sascha Anderson, Sabine Knust),
1988
36 lithographs. Edition: 20/75
Gift of Molly and Walter Bareiss, 1988.135

Lyrik
Text by Sarah Kirsch, born 1935
Berlin: Edition Malerbücher, [1982]
Color screen prints. Edition: 57/100
Gift of Molly and Walter Bareiss, 1987.279
Ref.: Johnson cat. 176

A. R. Penck as **Ralf Winkler**
Skizzen von 1968 überarbeitet 1979
Text by Ralf Winkler
[Berlin?]: EP Galerie and Edition Jürgen
Schweinebraden, 1979
20 screen prints. Edition: 32/200
Gift of Molly and Walter Bareiss, 1987.280a–t

Kneipen und Kneipentexte
Dresden: Obergrabenpresse, 1980
12 etchings. Edition: 41/50
Gift of Molly and Walter Bareiss, 1987.278a–l

A. R. Penck; various artists
Krater und Wolke Nr. 1–5
Edited by Ralf Winkler
Köln: Michael Werner, 1982–85
Nr. 1 (dedicated to Georg Baselitz): one woodcut (Jörg
Immendorff), two linoleum cuts, one mixed etching
(Markus Lüpertz), photomechanical reproductions, line
block reproductions
Nr. 2. (dedicated to Jörg Immendorff): 2 lithographs
(Georg Baselitz, Penck), one screen print (Immendorff), 3
linoleum cuts (2 by Per Kirkeby), some in colors; photome-
chanical reproductions; one sound recording
Nr. 3 (dedicated to Markus Lüpertz): 3 screen prints (one
by Immendorff, one by Lüpertz?), 2 linoleum cuts
(Baselitz, Penck), photomechanical reproductions, one
sound recording
Nr. 4 (dedicated to Per Kirkeby): photomechanical reproductions
Nr. 5 (dedicated to James Lee Byars): photomechanical
reproductions
Gift of Molly and Walter Bareiss, 1984.863, 1984.1187,
1984.1188, 1986.94, 1986.95

A. R. Penck (see also listing under Jörg Immendorff)

Valentine Penrose (see listing under Pablo Picasso)

Achille Perilli, Italian, born 1927
Le centodue parole
Text by Carla Vasio
[Roma]: L'Esperienza Moderna, 1962
6 color lithographs. Edition: 10/50
Gift of Molly and Walter Bareiss, 1984.867

Gabor Peterdi, Hungarian, active United States, 1915–2001
Peterdi
Text by William S. Lieberman, American, born 1924
New York: Rio Grande Graphics (Ted Gotthelf), 1952
5 mixed etchings, some in color. Edition: 11/200
Gift of Molly and Walter Bareiss, 1984.868a–e

Of Earth and Water
New York: Grace Borgenicht Gallery, 1955
12 mixed etchings, some in color. Edition: 16/25
Gift of Molly and Walter Bareiss, 1984.869a–l

Werner Pfeiffer, American (born Germany), born 1937
Liber Mobile: An Experimental Book
Brooklyn, NY: Pratt Adlib Press, 1967
12 typographic designs with die cuts, some in colors.
Edition: 101/130
Gift of Molly and Walter Bareiss, 1984.870
Fig. 112

1968 [calendar]
Brooklyn, NY: Pratt Adlib Press, 1968
Typographic designs from wood type. Edition:
unnumbered/300
Gift of Molly and Walter Bareiss, 1984.1289

Erwin Pfrang, German, born 1951
Dubliner
Text by James Joyce, Irish, 1882–1941; translation by
Harald Beck, German, born 1964
Leipzig: Reclam-Verlag, 1994
Photomechanical reproductions
Gift of Molly and Walter Bareiss, 1994.62

Tom Phillips, British, born 1937
A Humument, v. 1
London: Tetrad Press, 1970
10 color screen prints. Edition: 57/100
Gift of Molly and Walter Bareiss, 1984.871
Ref.: Drucker pp. 109–10

A Humument: A Treated Victorian Novel
London: Thames and Hudson, 1980
Photomechanical reproductions
Molly and Walter Bareiss Art Fund and Printed Matter
Matching Gift Fund for Libraries, 1987.42
Ref.: Drucker pp. 109–10
Fig. 11

Francis Picabia, French, 1879–1953
Sept manifestes dada
Text by Tristan Tzara, French (born Romania), 1896–1963
Paris: Jean Budry & Co., Éditions du diorama, 1924
Line block reproductions
Gift of Molly and Walter Bareiss, 1984.872

Francis Picabia (see also listing under Jean (Hans) Arp)

Pablo Picasso, Spanish, active France, 1881–1973
21 dessins de Picasso gravés sur bois
[S.l: s.n., 19?? (before 1980)]
21 wood-engravings after Picasso. Edition: 100/250
Gift of Molly and Walter Bareiss in honor of Barbara K.
Sutherland, 1984.947

Saint Matorel
Text by Max Jacob, French, 1876–1944
Paris: [Daniel-]Henry Kahnweiler, 1911
4 etchings, including one with drypoint. Edition: 69/100
Gift of Molly and Walter Bareiss in honor of Barbara K.
Sutherland, 1984.873
Ref.: Castleman p. 91, Garvey cat. 222, Johnson cat. 16,
Strachan p. 46, Symmes cat. 55, Wheeler p. 108
Fig. 46

*Le siège de Jérusalem: grande tentation céleste de Saint
Matorel*
Text by Max Jacob, French, 1876–1944
Paris: [Daniel-]Henry Kahnweiler, 1914
One etching, 2 drypoints (including one with etching).
Edition: 69/100
Gift of Molly and Walter Bareiss in honor of Barbara K.
Sutherland, 1984.874
Ref.: Garvey cat. 223, Johnson cat. 17, Strachan p. 339,
Symmes cat. 56, Wheeler p. 108

Cock and Harlequin: Notes Concerning Music
Text by Jean Cocteau, French, 1889–1963
London: Egoist Press, 1921
Photomechanical reproduction, line block reproductions
Gift of Molly and Walter Bareiss in honor of Barbara K.
Sutherland, 1984.875

Cravates de chanvre
Text by Pierre Reverdy, French, 1889–1960
Paris: Éditions nord-sud, 1922
One etching. Edition: 40/120
Gift of Molly and Walter Bareiss in honor of Barbara K.
Sutherland, 1984.876
Ref.: Johnson cat. 45, Strachan p. 339, Wheeler p. 109

Clair de terre
Text by André Breton, French, 1896–1966
Paris: [André Breton], 1923
One drypoint. Edition: XXXVI/XXXVIII
Gift of Molly and Walter Bareiss in honor of Barbara K.
Sutherland, 1984.877
Ref.: Johnson cat. 44

Les joues en feu: poèmes anciens et poèmes inédits
Texts by Raymond Radiguet, French, 1903–1923;
Max Jacob, French, 1876–1944
Paris: Bernard Grasset, 1925
2 collotypes. Edition: CCXV/CCLXX
Gift of Molly and Walter Bareiss in honor of Barbara K.
Sutherland, 1984.878

Picasso dessins
Text by Waldemar George, 1893–19??
Paris: Éditions des quatre chemins, 1926
15 collotypes, photomechanical reproductions. Edition:
unnumbered/100
Gift of Molly and Walter Bareiss in honor of Barbara K.
Sutherland, 1984.879

Picasso
Text by André Level, French, 1863–1946
Paris: Éditions G. Crès & cie. (George Besson), 1928
One lithograph, photomechanical reproductions. Edition:
192/200
Gift of Molly and Walter Bareiss in honor of Barbara K.
Sutherland, 1984.880
Ref.: Johnson cat. 55

Les métamorphoses
Text by Ovid, Roman, 43 B.C.E.–17 C.E.; translation by
Georges Lafaye, 1854–19??
Lausanne: Albert Skira, 1931
30 etchings, plus a suite of 27 etchings. Edition: "maquette"
Gift of Molly and Walter Bareiss in honor of Barbara K.
Sutherland, 1984.881
Ref.: Castleman p. 111, Garvey cat. 224, Hogben cat. 91,
Johnson cat. 56, Strachan pp. 60–61, 340, Symmes cat. 57,
Wheeler p. 109
Fig. 16

Six Signed Proofs of Original Etchings by Pablo Picasso
Made to Illustrate an Edition of Aristophanes' "Lysistrata"
Published by the Limited Editions Club
New York: Print Club, 1934
6 etchings, including one with aquatint. Edition: 64/150
Gift of Molly and Walter Bareiss in honor of Barbara K.
Sutherland, 1984.882a–f
Ref.: Garvey cat. 226, Strachan p. 340, Symmes cat. 58

La barre d'appui
Text by Paul Éluard, French, 1895–1952
Paris: Éditions "Cahiers d'art," 1936
3 mixed etchings. Edition: 9/40
Molly and Walter Bareiss Art Fund in honor of Barbara K.
Sutherland and Mrs. George W. Stevens Fund, 1985.129
Ref.: Castleman p. 185, Garvey cat. 227, Johnson cat. 62

Les yeux fertiles
Text by Paul Éluard, French, 1895–1952
Paris: G.L.M. (Guy Lévis Mano), 1936
Photomechanical reproduction, line block reproductions.
Edition: 702/1,300
Gift of Molly and Walter Bareiss in honor of Barbara K.
Sutherland, 1984.883
Ref.: Johnson cat. 61

Sueño y mentira de Franco
Text by Pablo Picasso
[Paris: Pablo Picasso, 1937]
2 etchings with aquatint. Edition: 32/150
Gift of Molly and Walter Bareiss in honor of Barbara K.
Sutherland, 1984.884a–c
Ref.: Castleman pp. 126–27, Garvey cat. 228, Hogben
cat. 106, Johnson cat. 63, Symmes cat. 59

Afat: soixante-seize sonnets
Text by Iliazd, Russian, active France, 1894–1975
[Paris]: Le degré quarante et un (Iliazd), 1940
2 aquatints, 4 engravings. Edition: 5/50
Gift of Molly and Walter Bareiss in honor of Barbara K.
Sutherland, 1984.885
Ref.: Garvey cat. 229, Johnson cat. 65, Symmes cat. 60

Pablo Picasso
Text by Georges Hugnet, French, 1906–1974
Paris: Georges Hugnet, 1941
6 lithographs from zinc plates, including 3 with added
engraving. Edition: unnumbered/200
Gift of Molly and Walter Bareiss in honor of Barbara K.
Sutherland, 1984.886

Eaux-fortes originales pour des Textes de Buffon
Text by Georges Louis Leclerc, comte de Buffon, French,
1707–1788
Paris: Martin Fabiani, 1942
31 lift-ground aquatints, etchings, and drypoints.
Edition: 94/226
Gift of Molly and Walter Bareiss in honor of Barbara K.
Sutherland, 1984.887
Ref.: Garvey cat. 231, Symmes cat. 62

La chèvre-feuille
Text by Georges Hugnet, French, 1906–1974
Paris: Robert-J. Godet, 1943
One etching, photomechanical reproductions, plus 3 suites
of reproductions. Editions: 13/525 and 158/525
Gift of Molly and Walter Bareiss in honor of Barbara K.
Sutherland, 1984.888, 1984.890 (without etching or suites)
Ref.: Johnson cat. 66, Symmes cat. 63

Contrée
Text by Robert Desnos, French, 1900–1945
Paris: Robert-J. Godet, 1944
One etching, line block reproductions. Edition: 25/200
Gift of Molly and Walter Bareiss in honor of Barbara K.
Sutherland, 1984.891

Cinq sonnets de Pétrarque
Text by Francesco Petrarca (Petrarch), Italian, 1304–1374;
translated anonymously by Louis Aragon, French, 1897–1982
[Paris]: À la Fontaine de Vaucluse, 1947
One etching with aquatint and burin. Edition: H/J
Gift of Molly and Walter Bareiss in honor of Barbara K.
Sutherland, 1984.894

Deux contes: Le centaure picador, Le crépuscule d'un faune
Text by Ramón Reventós, Spanish, 1881–1924, translation
by Jaume Canyameres, Spanish
Paris: Editorial Albor (Henri Jonquières), 1947
4 drypoints, plus a suite of 4 drypoints. Edition: 2/250
Gift of Molly and Walter Bareiss in honor of Barbara K.
Sutherland, 1984.893
Ref.: Garvey cat. 232, Strachan p. 340

Dos Contes: El Centaure Picador, El Capvespre d'un Faune
Text by Ramón Reventós, Spanish, 1881–1924
Paris and Barcelona: Editorial Albor (Henri Jonquières),
1947
4 engravings. Edition: 26/250
Gift of Molly and Walter Bareiss in honor of Barbara K.
Sutherland, 1984.892
Ref.: Garvey cat. 232, Strachan p. 340

[Escrito (Pismo)]
Text by Iliazd, Russian, active France, 1894–1975
Paris: Latitud Cuarenta y Uno [Le degré quarante et un]
(Iliazd), 1948
5 engravings, 2 etchings. Edition: 18/50
Gift of Molly and Walter Bareiss in honor of Barbara K.
Sutherland, 1984.895
Ref.: Castleman p. 220, Johnson cat. 69

Vingt poëmes de Gongora
Text by Luis de Góngora y Argote, Spanish, 1561–1627;
translation by Z. Milner
[Paris]: [s.n.], 1948
26 lift-ground aquatints, 14 drypoints, one engraving,
20 plates of etched text. Edition: 118/250
Gift of Molly and Walter Bareiss in honor of Barbara K.
Sutherland, 1984.896
Ref.: Johnson cat. 71

Carmen
Text by Prosper Mérimée, French, 1803–1870
Paris: La bibliothèque française, 1949
38 engravings, including decorative initials. Edition: 28/289
Gift of Molly and Walter Bareiss in honor of Barbara K.
Sutherland, 1984.897

Élégie d'Ihpétonga suivie de Masques de cendre
Text by Yvan Goll, French, 1891–1950
Paris: Éditions hémisphères, 1949
4 transfer lithographs. Edition: 43/200
Gift of Molly and Walter Bareiss in honor of Barbara K.
Sutherland, 1984.898
Ref.: Garvey cat. 236

Corps perdu
Text by Aimé Césaire, French (born Martinique), born 1913
Paris: Éditions fragrance, 1950
20 engravings, 10 lift-ground aquatints, one drypoint, and
one etching (wrappers). Edition: 108/207
Gift of Molly and Walter Bareiss in honor of Barbara K.
Sutherland, 1984.899
Ref.: Garvey cat. 233

De mémoire d'homme
Text by Tristan Tzara, French (born Romania), 1896–1963
Paris: Bordas éditeur, 1950
9 lithographs. Edition: 268/330
Gift of Molly and Walter Bareiss in honor of Barbara K.
Sutherland, 1984.900
Ref.: Garvey cat. 234

Le visage de la paix
Text by Paul Éluard, French, 1895–1952
Paris: Éditions cercle d'art, 1951
Line block reproductions. Edition: 845/2,100
Gift of Molly and Walter Bareiss in honor of Barbara K.
Sutherland, 1984.903

La maigre
Text by Guillaume de Vaux (Adrien de Montluc, comte de
Cramail), French, 1589–1646
Paris: Le degré quarante et un (Iliazd), 1952
11 drypoints. Edition: 13/52
Gift of Molly and Walter Bareiss in honor of Barbara K.
Sutherland, 1984.904
Ref.: Johnson cat. 73, Strachan p. 340
Fig. 54

Six contes fantasques
Text by Maurice Toesca, French, born 1904
Paris: Flammarion, 1953
6 drypoints, 6 wood-engraved initial letters by Pierre
Bouchet, plus a suite of 6 drypoints and 6 wood-engraved
letters. Edition: 18/200
Gift of Molly and Walter Bareiss in honor of Barbara K.
Sutherland, 1984.905
Ref.: Hogben cat. 128

[Poèmes et lithographies]
Text by Pablo Picasso
[Paris: Galerie Louise Leiris (under the direction of Daniel-
Henry Kahnweiler)], 1954
14 lithographs. Edition: 4/50
Gift of Molly and Walter Bareiss in honor of Barbara K.
Sutherland, 1984.906a–n
Ref.: Garvey cat. 235, Johnson cat. 74, Strachan p. 340

À haute flamme
Text by Tristan Tzara, French (born Romania), 1896–1963
Paris: Raymond Jaquet, 1955
6 celluloid drypoints. Edition: 11/70
Gift of Molly and Walter Bareiss in honor of Barbara K.
Sutherland, 1984.908

Chevaux de minuit: épopée
Text by Roch Grey, French, died 1950
Paris: Le degré quarante et un (Iliazd), 1956
12 engravings, one drypoint (cover). Edition: 36/52
Gift of Molly and Walter Bareiss in honor of Barbara K.
Sutherland, 1984.909
Ref.: Garvey cat. 237, Johnson cat. 75, Symmes cat. 64

Chroniques des temps héroïques
Text by Max Jacob, French, 1876–1944
Paris: Louis Broder, 1956
3 drypoints, 3 transfer lithographs, including 2 in colors
(cover, slipcase), one proof of slipcase lithograph, 24
wood-engravings after Picasso cut by Georges Aubert.
Edition: 73/150
Gift of Molly and Walter Bareiss in honor of Barbara K.
Sutherland, 1984.912
Ref.: Garvey cat. 238

Picasso: dessins d'un demi-siècle
Paris: Berggruen & cie., 1956
One color transfer lithograph (wrappers), 22 collotypes,
some with added pochoir color. Edition: unnumbered/
1,000
Gift of Molly and Walter Bareiss in honor of Barbara K.
Sutherland, 1984.910

Suite Vollard
Text by Hans Bolliger, Swiss, born 1915
Teufen, Schweiz: Éditions Arthur Niggli; Paris: Éditions
parallèles, 1956
Photomechanical reproductions, line block reproduction
(cover)
Gift of Molly and Walter Bareiss in honor of Barbara K.
Sutherland, 1984.911

40 dessins de Picasso en marge du Buffon
Paris: Berggruen & cie., 1957
One linoleum cut, 41 collotypes. Edition: 3/2,226
Gift of Molly and Walter Bareiss in honor of Barbara K.
Sutherland, 1984.914
Ref.: Johnson cat. 77

balzacs en bas de casse & picassos sans majuscule
Text by Michel Leiris, French, 1901–1990
Paris: Galerie Louise Leiris (under the direction of Daniel-Henry Kahnweiler), 1957
8 transfer lithographs, line block reproduction. Edition: 35/100
Gift of Molly and Walter Bareiss in honor of Barbara K.
Sutherland, 1984.915
Ref.: Johnson cat. 76

Dans l'atelier de Picasso
Text by Jaime Sabartés, Spanish, 1881–1968; translation by J. E. de Lago
Paris: Fernand Mourlot, 1957
6 transfer lithographs, plus a suite of 13 transfer lithographs; collotypes, some with added pochoir color, photomechanical reproductions. Edition: 6/250
Gift of Molly and Walter Bareiss in honor of Barbara K.
Sutherland, 1984.913
Ref.: Garvey cat. 240, Johnson cat. 79

Carnet catalan [facsimile]
Paris: Berggruen & cie., 1958
Collotypes. Edition: "pour Walter Bareiss"
Gift of Molly and Walter Bareiss in honor of Barbara K.
Sutherland, 1984.917a–b

L'escalier de Flore
Text by René Char, French, 1907–1988
Alès, France: PAB (Pierre André Benoit), 1958
2 celluloid drypoints, including one in color, one collage with string and die cut (cover). Edition: 7/36
Gift of Molly and Walter Bareiss in honor of Barbara K.
Sutherland, 1984.920
Ref.: Garvey cat. 241, Johnson cat. 81
Fig. 42

Les Ménines et la vie
Text by Jaime Sabartés, Spanish, 1881–1968; translation by Alfred Rosset
Paris: Éditions cercle d'art (Charles Feld), 1958
One drypoint engraving, photomechanical reproductions.
Edition: 45/100
Gift of Molly and Walter Bareiss in honor of Barbara K.
Sutherland, 1984.918

"Mes dessins d'Antibes"
Paris: Au pont des arts; New York: Galerie Chalette, 1958
17 collotypes, including one with added pochoir in white.
Edition in red: 15/100
Gift of Molly and Walter Bareiss in honor of Barbara K.
Sutherland, 1984.916

Pierres
Text by Pierre André Benoit, French, 1924–1993
Alès, France: PAB (Pierre André Benoit), 1958
One celluloid drypoint. Edition: 22/36
Gift of Molly and Walter Bareiss in honor of Barbara K.
Sutherland, 1984.921
Ref.: Johnson cat. 83, Symmes cat. 65

Sillage intangible
Text by Lucien Scheler, French, 1902–1999
Paris: Le degré quarante et un (Iliazd), 1958
One drypoint. Edition: 39/50
Gift of Molly and Walter Bareiss in honor of Barbara K.
Sutherland, 1984.919
Ref.: Garvey cat. 242, Symmes cat. 67

Carnet de la Californie [facsimile]
Text by Georges Boudaille, born 1925
Paris: Éditions cercle d'art (Charles Feld), 1959 (2nd ed. 1960)
One transfer lithograph, 39 collotypes, plus a suite of 39 collotypes, photomechanical reproductions (cover).

Editions: unnumbered/1,500 and D275/D500
Gift of Molly and Walter Bareiss in honor of Barbara K.
Sutherland, 1984.923 (1st ed.), 1984.925 (2nd ed., without lithograph or suite)

Le frère mendiant, ó libro del conocimiento
Texts by various authors; edited by Iliazd, Russian, active France, 1894–1975
Paris: Latitud Cuarenta y Uno [Le degré quarante et un] (Iliazd), 1959
17 drypoints. Edition: 35/54
Gift of Molly and Walter Bareiss in honor of Barbara K.
Sutherland, 1984.922
Ref.: Garvey cat. 243

Souvenirs d'un collectionneur
Text by André Level, French, 1863–1946
Paris: Alain C. Mazo, 1959
One lithograph. Edition: 492/2,100
Gift of Molly and Walter Bareiss in honor of Barbara K.
Sutherland, 1984.924

La Tauromaquia, ó Arte de Torear
Text by José Delgado y Gálvez (Pepe-Illo), Spanish, 1754–1801
Barcelona: Editorial Gustavo Gili, 1959
26 lift-ground aquatints, one drypoint (wrappers). Edition: 61/250
Gift of Molly and Walter Bareiss in honor of Barbara K.
Sutherland, 1984.926
Ref.: Garvey cat. 244, Johnson cat. 82, Symmes cat. 68

Meurs
Text by Pierre André Benoit, French, 1924–1993
Alès, France: PAB (Pierre André Benoit), 1960
One celluloid drypoint. Edition: 34/40
Gift of Molly and Walter Bareiss in honor of Barbara K.
Sutherland, 1984.928
Ref.: Symmes cat. 69

Température
Text by Jacqueline Roque, French, 1926–1986
Alès, France: PAB (Pierre André Benoit), 1960
4 celluloid drypoints (including wrappers). Edition: 12/28
Gift of Molly and Walter Bareiss in honor of Barbara K.
Sutherland, 1984.931
Ref.: Garvey cat. 245, Johnson cat. 84, Symmes cat. 70

Toros: 15 lavis inédits
Text by Pablo Neruda, Chilean, 1904–1973
Paris: Au vent d'Arles, 1960
15 collotypes. Edition: 231/500
Gift of Molly and Walter Bareiss in honor of Barbara K.
Sutherland, 1984.927

Toute la vie
Text by Pierre André Benoit, French, 1924–1993
Alès, France: PAB (Pierre André Benoit), 1960
One celluloid drypoint. Edition: 26/44
Gift of Molly and Walter Bareiss in honor of Barbara K.
Sutherland, 1984.930
Ref.: Johnson cat. 87, Symmes cat. 71

Vers où l'on voit
Text by Pierre André Benoit, French, 1924–1993
Alès, France: PAB (Pierre André Benoit), 1960
One celluloid drypoint. Edition: 22/33
Gift of Molly and Walter Bareiss in honor of Barbara K.
Sutherland, 1984.929

"A los Toros" avec Picasso
Text by Jaime Sabartés, Spanish, 1881–1968; translation by George Franck
Monte Carlo: André Sauret, 1961
4 transfer lithographs, including one in colors, photomechanical reproductions, line block reproduction (cover)
Gift of Molly and Walter Bareiss in honor of Barbara K.
Sutherland, 1984.933

Toros y Toreros
Texts by Luis Miguel Domínguín, Spanish, born 1926;
Georges Boudaille, French, born 1925
[Paris]: Éditions cercle d'art (Charles Feld), 1961

One transfer lithograph, photomechanical reproductions, plus a suite of 16 photomechanical reproductions, line block reproductions. Edition: 29/125
Gift of Molly and Walter Bareiss in honor of Barbara K.
Sutherland, 1984.932

Les déjeuners
Text by Douglas Cooper, British, 1911–1984
Paris: Éditions cercle d'art (Charles Feld), 1962
Photomechanical reproductions, line block reproductions (variations on Édouard Manet's painting *Le déjeuner sur l'herbe*). Edition: unnumbered/14,000
Gift of Molly and Walter Bareiss in honor of Barbara K.
Sutherland, 1984.935

El Carnet de "La Tauromaquia" de Pepe Illo [facsimile]
Texts by Gustavo Gili, Spanish; Bernhard Geiser, died 1967
Barcelona: Editorial Gustavo Gili, 1963
Collotypes. Edition: 264/840
Gift of Molly and Walter Bareiss in honor of Barbara K.
Sutherland, 1984.937a–b

Le Carmen des Carmen
Text by Prosper Mérimée, French, 1803–1870
Paris: Éditeurs français réunis, 1964
3 aquatints, one drypoint, one color transfer lithograph; collotypes, some with added pochoir color. Edition: 179/245
Gift of Molly and Walter Bareiss in honor of Barbara K.
Sutherland, 1984.938

Le Picasso de poche [facsimile]
Text by Marcel Duhamel, French, 1900–1977
Paris: Aux dépens d'un amateur (David Jacomet), 1964
Collotypes, including one in colors (envelope). Edition: 182/375
Gift of Molly and Walter Bareiss in honor of Barbara K.
Sutherland, 1984.939a–b

Shakespeare
Text by Louis Aragon, French, 1897–1982
Paris: Éditions cercle d'art (Charles Feld), 1965
Photomechanical reproductions, line block reproductions of lettering by Aragon. Edition: 644/2,000
Gift of Molly and Walter Bareiss in honor of Barbara K.
Sutherland, 1984.940

Notre Dame de Vie
Text by Hélène Parmelin, French, 1916–1998
Paris: Éditions cercle d'art (Charles Feld), 1966
Photomechanical reproductions, line block reproductions.
Edition: unnumbered/14,000
Gift of Molly and Walter Bareiss in honor of Barbara K.
Sutherland, 1984.942

Sable mouvant
Text by Pierre Reverdy, French, 1889–1960
Paris: Louis Broder, 1966
10 aquatints, some with drypoint and scraper. Edition: 51/220
Gift of Molly and Walter Bareiss in honor of Barbara K.
Sutherland, 1984.941
Ref.: Johnson cat. 88
Fig. 105

Le cocu magnifique: pièce en trois actes
Text by Fernand Crommelynck, Belgian, 1886–1970
Paris: Éditions de l'atelier Crommelynck, 1968
12 etchings (4 with aquatint, one with aquatint and drypoint). Edition: 129/180
Gift of Molly and Walter Bareiss in honor of Barbara K.
Sutherland, 1984.943
Ref.: Johnson cat. 91, Symmes cat. 72

La Célestine
Text by Fernando de Rojas, Spanish, 1465–1541; translation by Pierre Heugas
Paris: Éditions de l'atelier Crommelynk, 1971
66 etchings and aquatints. Edition: 262/350
Gift of Molly and Walter Bareiss in honor of Barbara K.
Sutherland, 1984.944
Ref.: Johnson cat. 93

Pirosmanachvili 1914
Text by Iliazd, Russian, active France, 1894–1975;
translation by Andrée Robel and André du Bouchet,
French, born 1924
Paris: Le degré quarante et un (Iliazd), 1972
One drypoint. Edition: 13/78
Gift of Molly and Walter Bareiss in honor of Barbara K.
Sutherland, 1984.945
Ref.: Johnson cat. 94
Fig. 51

*Pablo Picasso: pour Eugenia; une suite de 24 dessins inédits
exécutés en 1918*
Text by Douglas Cooper, British, 1911–1984
Paris: Berggruen, 1976
Photomechanical reproductions. Edition: "pour Mr. and
Mrs. Walter Bareiss"
Gift of Molly and Walter Bareiss in honor of Barbara K.
Sutherland, 1984.946

Pablo Picasso; Valentine Penrose, British, 1898–1978
Dons des féminines
Text by Valentine Penrose
Paris: Librairie "Les pas perdus" (Valentine Penrose,
Marcel Zerbib), 1951
3 impressions of an etching, including one from the
canceled plate, one canceled copperplate (Picasso); line
block reproductions (Penrose). Edition: 42/400
Gift of Molly and Walter Bareiss in honor of Barbara K.
Sutherland, 1984.901

Dons des féminines
Text by Valentine Penrose
Paris: Librairie "Les pas perdus" (Valentine Penrose, Marcel
Zerbib), 1951
2 impressions of an etching from the canceled plate
(Picasso), line block reproductions (Penrose). Edition:
303/400
Gift of Molly and Walter Bareiss in honor of Barbara K.
Sutherland, 1984.902

Pablo Picasso; André Villers, French, born 1930
Diurnes: découpages et photographies
Text by Jacques Prévert, French, 1900–1977
Paris: Berggruen, 1962
Pochoir prints after Picasso (cover and box), photomechan-
ical reproductions. Edition: 447/1,000
Gift of Molly and Walter Bareiss in honor of Barbara K.
Sutherland, 1984.934

Pablo Picasso (see also listing under Additional Books)

Walter Pichler, Austrian, born 1936
Walter Pichler: Projects
New York: The Museum of Modern Art, 1975
Photomechanical reproductions
Gift of Molly and Walter Bareiss, 1984.964

Steve Poleskie (see listing under Clayton Pond)

Serge Poliakoff, French (born Russia), 1906–1969
Enluminures
Text by Serge Poliakoff
St. Gallen, Schweiz: Erker-Verlag (Franz Larese, Jürg
Janett), 1972
Photomechanical reproductions
Gift of Molly and Walter Bareiss, 1984.966

Cahier I [facsimile]
St. Gallen, Schweiz: Erker-Verlag (Franz Larese, Jürg
Janett), 1973
Photomechanical reproductions
Gift of Molly and Walter Bareiss, 1984.967

Sigmar Polke, Polish, active Germany, born 1941
Sigmar Polke
Mönchengladbach, Deutschland: Städtisches Museum
Abteiberg, 1983
Photomechanical reproductions
Gift of Molly and Walter Bareiss, 1984.968

Süddeutsche Zeitung No. 46 (Nov. 1995)
München: Magazin Verlagsgesellschaft Süddeutsche

Zeitung, 1995
Photomechanical reproductions
Gift of Molly and Walter Bareiss, 1996.5

Reginald Pollack, American, born 1924
The Magician and the Child
Text by Reginald Pollack
New York: Atheneum, 1971
Photomechanical reproductions
Gift of Molly and Walter Bareiss, 1984.969

Clayton Pond, American, born 1941; **Steve Poleskie,**
American, born 1938
Artist's Proof: The Annual of Prints and Printmaking
Texts by various authors; edited by Fritz Eichenberg,
American (born Germany), 1901–1990
New York: Pratt Graphics Center
v. VI (1966): one color screen print (Pond), photomechani-
cal reproductions of work by various artists
v. VIII (1968): one color screen print (Poleskie), photome-
chanical reproductions of work by various artists
Gift of Molly and Walter Bareiss, 1984.970, 1984.965

Renate Ponsold (see listing under Robert Motherwell)

José Guadalupe Posada, Mexican, 1852–1913
José Guadalupe Posada: 50 aniversario de su muerte
Texts by Paul Westheim, German, 1886–1963; Justino
Fernández, Mexican, 1904–1972; José Julio Rodríguez,
Mexican
[Mexico City]: Instituto Nacional de Bellas Artes, Museo
Nacional de Arte Moderno, 1963
Photomechanical reproductions, line block reproductions
Gift of Molly and Walter Bareiss, 1984.971

Macha Poynder, Russian, active France, born 1962
La punaise
Text by Vladimir Mayakovsky (Maïakovski), Russian,
1893–1930
Paris: Éditions ILM, 1985
Photomechanical reproductions
Gift of Molly and Walter Bareiss, 1997.300

#19E
Text by Marc Dachy, Dutch, born 1952
New York: Marc Dachy and Macha Poynder, 1991
Lithographs. Edition: 13/19
Gift of Molly and Walter Bareiss, 1997.299

Rudy Pozzatti, American, born 1925
Bugs
Los Angeles: Tamarind Lithography Workshop, 1963
10 lithographs. Edition: 12/20
Gift of Molly and Walter Bareiss, 1984.972

Lucio Pozzi, American, born 1935
Unwritten
Text by David Shapiro, American, born 1947
New York: Lapp Princess Press in association with
Printed Matter, 1977
Photomechanical reproduction
Gift of Molly and Walter Bareiss, 1984.973

Emil Preetorius, German, 1883–1973
*Des Luftschiffers Giannozzo Seebuch: Almanach für Matrosen
wie sie sein sollten*
Text by Jean Paul, German, 1763–1825
Leipzig: Insel-Verlag, 1912
16 collotypes, line block reproductions
Gift of Molly and Walter Bareiss, 1984.974

Die wunderbaren Abenteuer des Tartarin von Tarascon
Text by Alphonse Daudet, French, 1840–1897
Dachau: Der Gelbe Verlag Mundt und Blumtritt, 1913
Line block reproductions. Edition: 154/unknown
Gift of Molly and Walter Bareiss, 1984.975

Emil Preetorius; various artists
Das Gelbbuch der Münchener Mappe
Texts by various authors
München: Hyperion, 1921
2 color pochoir prints (cover), photomechanical

reproductions of work by various artists. Edition: 296/500
Gift of Molly and Walter Bareiss, 1984.627

Vojtech Preissig, Czech, 1873–1944
Aucassin and Nicolete
Text by Andrew Lang, Scottish, 1844–1912
New York: Limited Editions Club, 1931
98 color wood-engravings. Edition: 471/1,500
Gift of Molly and Walter Bareiss, 1984.976

Maurice Prendergast, American (born Canada),
1859–1924
Maurice Prendergast, Water-color Sketchbook: 1899 [facsimile]
Text by Peter A. Wick, American, born 1920
Boston: Museum of Fine Arts; Cambridge: Harvard
University Press, 1960
Photomechanical reproductions
Gift of Molly and Walter Bareiss, 1984.977

Ken Price, American, born 1935
The Plain of Smokes
Text by Harvey Mudd, American, born 1940
Santa Barbara: Arabesque Books, 1981
20 screen prints, some in colors. Edition: 51/150
Gift of Molly and Walter Bareiss, 1984.978

Richard Prince, American, born 1949
Wall of Fire / Red Top
[Unpublished], 1976
10 drawings, some with color pencil, some with ink,
some with pencil and ink, some with added collage, one
photomechanical reproduction with added ink drawing,
5 photographs (unique book)
Gift of Molly and Walter Bareiss, 1984.979

Patrick Procktor, Irish, born 1936
One Window
Venezia: Cavallino, 1974
Photomechanical reproductions. 117/200
Gift of Molly and Walter Bareiss, 1984.980

The Rime of the Ancient Mariner
Text by Samuel Taylor Coleridge, British, 1772–1834
London: Editions Alecto, 1976
12 aquatints, some in colors, plus a suite of 4 aquatints,
line block reproduction. Edition: X/XXV
Gift of Molly and Walter Bareiss, 1984.981

Gilbert Proesch (see Gilbert and George)

Ivar Radowitz (see listing under HAP Grieshaber)

Markus Raetz, Swiss, born 1941
Die Buecher [facsimile]
Zürich: Galerie und Edition Staehli, 1975
One lithograph (slipcase), 2 etchings, one color woodcut,
photomechanical reproductions. Edition: 43/600
Molly and Walter Bareiss Art Fund, 1988.72a–c

Markus Raetz: Notizen
Berlin: Rainer, Berliner Künstlerprogramm des Deutschen
Akademischen Austauschdienstes, 1982
Photomechanical reproductions. Edition: unnumbered/
1,200
Molly and Walter Bareiss Art Fund, 1987.44

J.-F. Raffaëlli, French, 1850–1924
Les soeurs Vatard
Text by Joris-Karl Huysmans, French, 1848–1907
Paris: Librairie des amateurs (F. Ferroud), 1909
28 etchings with drypoint, some in colors. Edition: 224/250
Gift of Molly and Walter Bareiss, 1984.983
Fig. 71

J.-F. Raffaëlli (see also listing under Jean-Louis Forain)

Arnulf Rainer, Austrian, born 1929
Gilgamesch: Eine Erzählung aus dem alten Orient
Unna, Deutschland: Ceresit-Werke (Christian Leopold
Heppe), [after 1960]
Photomechanical reproductions. Edition: 185/1,000
Gift of Molly and Walter Bareiss, 1984.987
Fig. 20

Wahnhall [?]
[S.l.]: Arnulf Rainer, 1967
21 lithographs. Edition: 51/96
Gift of Molly and Walter Bareiss, 1984.984

Arnulf Rainer: Selbstdarstellungen (Fotoübermalungen 1968–72)
Text by Arnulf Rainer
München: Galerie van de Loo, [1972?]
One photograph, photomechanical reproductions. Edition: unnumbered/50
Gift of Molly and Walter Bareiss, 1984.988

Leonardo-Überzeichnungen
Text by Arnulf Rainer
Wien: Löcker & Wögenstein, 1977
Photomechanical reproductions. Edition: unnumbered/600
Gift of Molly and Walter Bareiss, 1984.985

Körpersprache
München: Van de Loo und Prelinger, 1980
One photogravure overprinted with drypoint; photo-mechanical reproductions. Edition: 110/1,000
Gift of Molly and Walter Bareiss, 1984.986
Fig. 134

Gunter Rambow, German, born 1938
La Promenade de König Immerlustik
Frankfurt: Kohlkunstpresse, 1968
Photomechanical reproductions. Edition: 744/1,000
Gift of Molly and Walter Bareiss, 1984.989

David Rathman, American, born 1958
Adventures in the Burning Bush
Text by David Rathman
Minneapolis: Vermillion Editions Limited (David Rathman), 1987
11 linoleum cuts. Edition: 32/35
Molly and Walter Bareiss Art Fund, 1987.189a–k

Abraham Rattner, American, 1895–1978
Scenario (A Film with Sound)
Text by Henry Miller, American, 1891–1980
Paris: Obelisk Press, 1937
One linoleum cut. Edition: 8/200
Gift of Molly and Walter Bareiss, 1984.990

Robert Rauschenberg, American, born 1925
Traces suspectes en surface
Text by Alain Robbe-Grillet, French, born 1922
West Islip, NY: Universal Limited Art Editions (Tatyana Grosman), [1978]
36 color lithographs printed on 31 sheets. Edition: 20/36
Gift of Molly and Walter Bareiss, 1984.950
Ref.: Hogben cat. 151, Johnson cat. 163, Phillips cat. 40, Symmes cat. 73
Fig. 132

Photos In + Out City Limits New York C.
Text by Colta (Feller) Ives, American, born 1943
West Islip, NY: Universal Limited Art Editions (Tatyana Grosman), 1982
Photomechanical reproductions. Edition: 39/375
Gift of Molly and Walter Bareiss, 1984.991

Robert Rauschenberg (see also listing under Edwin Schlossberg)

Ray, Man (see Man Ray)

Martial Raysse, French, born 1936
Piano Cono, Piano Sano, Loco Bello
Text by Martial Raysse
Paris: Éditions Karl Flinker, 1976
Photomechanical reproductions
Gift of Molly and Walter Bareiss, 1984.992

Odilon Redon, French, 1840–1916
La damnation de l'artiste
Text by Iwan Gilkin, Belgian, 1858–1924
Bruxelles: Edmond Deman, 1890
One lithograph. Edition: 77/150
Gift of Molly and Walter Bareiss, 1984.993
Ref.: Garvey cat. 254, Johnson cat. 5

Flambeaux noirs
Text by Émile Verhaeren, Belgian, 1855–1916
Bruxelles: Edmond Deman, 1891
One lithograph, line block reproductions (not after Redon). Edition: 42/100
Gift of Molly and Walter Bareiss, 1984.994

La passante
Text by Adrien Remacle, French
Paris: Bibliothèque artistique et littéraire, 1892
One etching. Edition: 144/420
Gift of Molly and Walter Bareiss, 1984.995

La tentation de Saint Antoine
Text by Gustave Flaubert, French, 1821–1880
Paris: Éditions Ambroise Vollard, 1933 (published 1938)
22 lithographs, 16 wood-engravings (including wrappers) and wood-engraved table of plates, cut by Georges Aubert. Edition: 85/210
Gift of Molly and Walter Bareiss, 1984.996
Ref.: Castleman p. 89, Hogben cat. 13, Johnson cat. 6, Wheeler p. 109

Jesse Reichek, American, born 1916
La montée de la nuit
Text by René Char, French, 1907–1988
Alès, France: PAB (Pierre André Benoit), 1961
4 etchings. Edition: 18/50
Gift of Molly and Walter Bareiss, 1984.997

David Reichert (see listing under Josua Reichert)

Josua Reichert, German, born 1937
Hebräisches Konvolut
[S.l.: Josua Reichert?, 196?]
8 color typographic designs
Gift of Molly and Walter Bareiss, 1984.1003

Printer's Island
[S.l.: Josua Reichert?, 196?]
Color typographic designs, photomechanical reproduction
Gift of Molly and Walter Bareiss, 1984.1002

Horst Antes, Gerhard Bogatzki, Josua Reichert, Heinz Schanz, Walter Stöhrer
München: Galerie Friedrich & Dahlem, 1963
Photomechanical reproductions; book design by Reichert
Gift of Molly and Walter Bareiss, 1984.998

Gedichte von Ludwig Greve
Text by Ludwig Greve, German, born 1924
[S.l.]: Josua Reichert, 1964
Color typographic designs. Edition: unnumbered/21
Gift of Molly and Walter Bareiss, 1984.528

Russisches Initialenbuch
[S.l.: Josua Reichert?], 1966
26 typographic designs, most in colors
Gift of Molly and Walter Bareiss, 1984.999

Schriftfest in Sofia
[S.l.: Josua Reichert?], 1969
14 typographic designs, most in colors, photomechanical reproductions. Edition: unnumbered/200
Gift of Molly and Walter Bareiss, 1984.1000

Quellen des Windes
Text by Pierre Reverdy, French, 1889–1960
München: Kösel (Friedhelm Kemp), 1970
2 color typographic designs (cover)
Gift of Molly and Walter Bareiss, 1984.1001

Leidenschaftliche Liebe
[Offenbach/Main, Deutschland: Klingspormuseum], 1982
Color typographic designs, photomechanical reproductions. Edition: unnumbered/3,000
Gift of Molly and Walter Bareiss, 1985.89

Leidenschaftliche Liebe: die Offenbacher Drucke von Josua Reichert 1981
Offenbach/Main, Deutschland: Klingspormuseum, [1982]
2 color typographic designs (cover), photomechanical reproductions. Edition: unnumbered/3,000
Gift of Molly and Walter Bareiss, 1984.1004, 1985.88

Josua Reichert; David Reichert, German
Goethe: Zwei Briefe aus Palermo
Text by Johann Wolfgang von Goethe, German, 1749–1832
[Offenbach/Main, Deutschland: Klingspormuseum], 1982
Photomechanical reproductions. Edition: unnumbered/1,000
Gift of Molly and Walter Bareiss, 1984.1005, 1985.87

Pierre-Auguste Renoir (see listing under Raoul Dufy)

Edda Renouf, American (born Mexico), born 1943
Lines
Milano: Flash Art Edizioni (Françoise and Yvon Lambert), 1974
Photomechanical reproductions. Edition: unnumbered/1,000
Gift of Molly and Walter Bareiss, 1984.1006

Lines and Non-Lines
New York: Lapp Princess Press in association with Printed Matter, 1977
Photomechanical reproductions
Gift of Molly and Walter Bareiss, 1984.1007

David Reynolds (see listing under Leon Golub)

Germaine Richier, French, 1904–1959
Une saison en enfer. Les déserts de l'amour. Les illuminations
Text by Arthur Rimbaud, French, 1854–1891
Lausanne: André Gonin, 1951
24 etchings with aquatint. Edition: 77/118
Gift of Molly and Walter Bareiss, 1984.1008
Ref.: Garvey cat. 260, Strachan p. 341
Fig. 37

Contre Terre
Text by René de Solier, born 1914
Lausanne, Suisse: André and Pierre Gonin, 1958
24 etchings, some with aquatint. Edition: 100/130
Gift of Molly and Walter Bareiss, 1984.1009
Ref.: Strachan p. 341

Gerhard Richter, German, born 1932
Gerhard Richter: Graphik 1965–1970
Essen, Deutschland: Museum Folkwang, 1970
Photomechanical reproductions
Gift of Molly and Walter Bareiss, 1984.1010

Hans Richter (see listing under Jean (Hans) Arp)

Judy Rifka, American, born 1945
Opera of the Worms
Text by Rene Ricard, American, born 1946
New York: Joe Fawbush Editions; Solo Press, 1984
23 lithographs, some in colors, one with embossing. Edition: 6/80
Gift of Molly and Walter Bareiss, 1984.951
Ref.: Symmes cat. 74

Joachim Ringelnatz, German, 1883–1934
Ringelnatz
Text by Joachim Ringelnatz
Berlin: "Ladengalerie" in association with Karl H. Henssel, 1963
Photomechanical reproductions. Edition: unnumbered/5,000
Gift of Molly and Walter Bareiss, 1984.1011

Carla Rippey, American, active Mexico, born 1950
Five Afternoons in the Garden
[S.l.: Carla Rippey, 1995]
Photomechanical reproductions. Edition: 3/10
Molly and Walter Bareiss Art Fund, 1996.2
Fig. 148

Larry Rivers, American, 1923–2002
Stones
Text by Frank O'Hara, American, 1926–1966
West Islip, NY: Universal Limited Art Editions (Tatyana Grosman), 1959
One oil drawing (wrappers), 13 lithographs. Edition: XXII/XXV
Gift of Molly and Walter Bareiss, 1984.952

Ref.: Castleman p. 102, Johnson cat. 143, Phillips cat. 42,
Symmes cat. 75
Fig. 100

Partisan Review, vol. XXXVIII, no. 1
Text by Terry Southern, American, 1924–1995; various
authors
New Brunswick, NJ: Partisan Review, Rutgers University,
1971
Photomechanical reproduction (cover)
Gift of Molly and Walter Bareiss, 1984.1012
Fig. 122

Diana
Text by Kenneth Koch, American, 1925–2002
[West Islip, NY]: Universal Limited Art Editions
(Tatyana Grosman), [1974?]
2 color lithographs, including one with die cuts.
Edition: 12/19
Gift of Molly and Walter Bareiss, 1984.1013

Auguste Rodin, French, 1840–1917
Les cathédrales de France
Text by Auguste Rodin; Charles Morice, French, 1861–1919
Paris: Librairie Armand Colin (H. Floury), [1914]
138 collotypes, some with added pochoir in white.
Edition: 15/250
Gift of Molly and Walter Bareiss, 1984.1014

À la Vénus de Milo
Text by Auguste Rodin
Paris: La jeune Parque, 1945
Photomechanical reproductions, line block reproduction
(cover). Edition: 686/2,500
Gift of Molly and Walter Bareiss, 1984.1015

Douze aquarelles inédites de Rodin
Text by Maurice Aubert, French, 1884–1962
Paris: Librairie des arts décoratifs (A. Calavas), 1949
12 collotypes. 28/600
Gift of Molly and Walter Bareiss, 1984.1016

Kurt Roesch, American (born Germany), 1905–1984
The Sonnets to Orpheus
Text by Rainer Maria Rilke, German, 1875–1926; transla-
tion by M. D. Herter Norton, American, 1894?–1985
New York: Wittenborn and Co., 1944
9 engravings with etching and aquatint. Edition:
XXXI/XXXV
Gift of Molly and Walter Bareiss, 1984.1017
Ref.: Garvey cat. 263, Phillips cat. 43

Franz Roh, German, 1890–1965
*Wer biss mir so sauber den Kopf ab mit den Zähnen b1 und
b2? Metamorphosen des Herrn Miracoloss (1923–50)*
Text by Franz Roh; translation by Michelle Reusch and
Jennifer Macbeth
[Wuppertal, Deutschland]: Galerie Parnass, 1972
Line block reproductions. Edition: 110/500
Gift of Molly and Walter Bareiss, 1984.1018

Gerburg Rohde, German
Klumpen Traurigmann
Text by Heidi Frommann, German, born 1943
Stierstadt im Taunus, Deutschland: Eremiten-Presse, 1964
4 etchings, one color woodcut (cover). Edition: 48/250
Gift of Molly and Walter Bareiss, 1984.1019

Félicien Rops, Belgian, active France, 1833–1898
Félicien Rops
Text by Franz Blei, German, 1871–1942
Berlin: Bard, Marquart & Co., [1906]
Photomechanical reproductions
Gift of Molly and Walter Bareiss, 1984.1020

John Ross, American
The Imaged Word
Text by Rolf Fjelde, American, born 1926
Brooklyn, NY: Pratt Adlib Press, 1962
4 color lithographs (including cover). Edition: 74/350
Gift of Molly and Walter Bareiss, 1984.1021

Adolph Rosenblatt, American, born 1933
N.Y., N.Y.
New York: Peter Deitsch Gallery, 1960
11 lithographs. Edition: 3/6
Gift of Molly and Walter Bareiss, 1984.1022

James Rosenquist, American, born 1933
Drawings while Waiting for an Idea
New York: Lapp Princess Press, 1979
Photomechanical reproductions
Gift of Molly and Walter Bareiss, 1984.1023

Dieter Roth (Diter Rot), German, active Switzerland,
1930–1998
Diter Rot
Chicago: William and Noma Copley Foundation, 1965
Photomechanical reproductions
Gift of Molly and Walter Bareiss, 1984.1024
Fig. 107

*Frische Scheisse, oder: Die Korrumpierung der Germanistik
(Das kommt von Döhl)*
Text by Dieter Roth
[S.l.: s.n., 1972]
One color lithograph (wrappers), one linoleum cut,
line block reproductions. Edition: 169/200
Gift of Molly and Walter Bareiss, 1985.90

Die "Die gesamte Scheisse"
Text by Dieter Roth
Berlin: Rainer (Rainer Pretzell); Stuttgart: Edition
Hansjörg Mayer, 1973 (1st ed. 1968)
Photomechanical reproductions. Edition: 199/400
Gift of Molly and Walter Bareiss, 1984.1025

7 Pokale doloroser Selbstgüte
Mosfellssveit, Ísland: [Dieter Roth], 1978
7 graphite drawings (unique book)
Gift of Molly and Walter Bareiss, 1984.1027

2 Schock schnelle Weichzeichnungen
Berlin: Rainer (Rainer Pretzell), 1983
122 lithographs. Edition: 74/200
Gift of Molly and Walter Bareiss, 1984.1026

Dieter Roth: Gesammelte Werke Band 39: Kleinere Werke
Stuttgart: Edition Hansjörg Mayer, [1985?]
Photomechanical reproductions. Edition: unnumbered/
1,000
Molly and Walter Bareiss Art Fund and Printed Matter
Matching Gift Fund for Libraries, 1987.61

Joel Rothberg, American, born 1943
A Princess of Mars
Text by Edgar Rice Burroughs, American, 1875–1950
[Brooklyn, NY]: Pratt Adlib Press (Fritz Eichenberg), 1965
62 zinc relief prints. Edition: 67/500
Gift of Molly and Walter Bareiss, 1984.1028

Georges Rouault, French, 1871–1958
Georges Rouault
Text by Lionello Venturi, Italian, 1885–1961; translation by
Juliette Bertrand, 1893–19??
New York: E. Weyhe, 1940
One color etching with drypoint and aquatint, photo-
mechanical reproductions. Edition: 24/100
Gift of Molly and Walter Bareiss, 1984.1029

Gaston-Louis Roux, French, 1904–1988
L'avril
Text by André du Bouchet, French, born 1924
Paris: [s.n.], 1963
2 etchings. Edition: 60/60
Gift of Molly and Walter Bareiss, 1984.1030

Pierre Roy, French, 1880–1950
Cent comptines
Paris: Henri Jonquières et cie., 1926
45 color wood-engravings with added pochoir color
(including cover), plus 29 wood-engraved ornaments
with added pochoir color (2 designs repeated 14 times
with varying pochoir colors). Edition: 336/540
Gift of Molly and Walter Bareiss, 1984.1031
Ref.: Wheeler p. 110

Léon Rudnicki (see listing under Various Artists, *L'effort*)

Fritz Ruoff, German, 1906–1988
Fritz Ruoff
Text by Peter Härtling, German, born 1933
Stuttgart: Edition Domberger, [196?]
6 color screen prints. Edition: 24/75
Gift of Molly and Walter Bareiss, 1984.1032

Edward Ruscha, American, born 1937
Every Building on the Sunset Strip
Los Angeles: Edward Ruscha, 1966
Photomechanical reproductions. Edition: unnumbered/
1,000
Gift of Molly and Walter Bareiss, 1984.953, Molly and
Walter Bareiss Art Fund, 1989.30
Ref.: Drucker p. 178

Crackers
Hollywood: Heavy Industry Publications, 1969
Photomechanical reproductions. Edition: unnum-
bered/5,000
Molly and Walter Bareiss Art Fund, 1989.24
Ref.: Drucker pp. 266–67

Real Estate Opportunities
[Los Angeles]: Edward Ruscha, 1970
Photomechanical reproductions. Edition: unnumbered/
4,000
Molly and Walter Bareiss Art Fund, 1989.25

Some Los Angeles Apartments
[Los Angeles]: Edward Ruscha, 1970 (1st ed. 1965)
Photomechanical reproductions. Edition: unnumbered/
3,000
Molly and Walter Bareiss Art Fund, 1989.26

Various Small Fires and Milk
[Los Angeles]: Edward Ruscha, 1970 (1st ed. 1964)
Photomechanical reproductions. Edition: unnumbered/
3,000
Molly and Walter Bareiss Art Fund, 1989.27

Thirtyfour Parking Lots in Los Angeles
[Los Angeles]: Edward Ruscha, [1974] (1st ed. 1967)
Photomechanical reproductions. Edition: unnumbered/
2,000
Gift of Molly and Walter Bareiss, 1984.955, Molly and
Walter Bareiss Art Fund, 1989.23

Nine Swimming Pools and a Broken Glass
[Los Angeles]: Edward Ruscha, 1976 (1st ed. 1968)
Photomechanical reproductions. Edition: unnumbered/
2,000
Gift of Molly and Walter Bareiss, 1984.954, Molly and
Walter Bareiss Art Fund, 1989.28

*The Works of Edward Ruscha (I Don't Want No Retro
Spective)*
Texts by Dave Hickey, American, born 1940; Peter Plagens,
American, born 1941
New York: Hudson Hills Press in association with San
Francisco Museum of Modern Art, 1982
Photomechanical reproductions
Gift of Molly and Walter Bareiss, 1984.1033

Edward Ruscha; Lawrence Weiner, American, born 1942
Hard Light
Los Angeles: Edward Ruscha and Lawrence Weiner, 1978
Photomechanical reproductions. Edition: unnumbered/
3,500
Molly and Walter Bareiss Art Fund, 1989.29

Ursula Rusche-Wolters, German, born 1914; **Michaël
Croissant,** German, born 1928
*Ursula Rusche-Wolters—Munich: tableaux, gouaches, dessins;
Michaël Croissant—Francfort: sculptures*
Paris: Goethe-Institut, Centre Cultural Allemand, 1967
Photomechanical reproductions; one relief print by
Rusche-Wolters laid in (not part of the book)
Gift of Molly and Walter Bareiss, 1984.1034

Théo van Rysselberghe, Belgian, 1862–1926
Almanach: cahier de vers d'Émile Verhaeren
Text by Émile Verhaeren, Belgian, 1855–1916

Paris: Dietrich & Co., 1895
4 wood-engravings; plus wood-engraved ornaments,
some in color
Gift of Molly and Walter Bareiss, 1984.1035

Niki de Saint Phalle, French, 1930–2002
My Love
Text by Niki de Saint Phalle
Malmö, Sverige: Skåneoffset, [196?]
Photomechanical reproductions
Gift of Molly and Walter Bareiss, 1984.1036

AIDS: You Can't Catch It Holding Hands
Text by Niki de Saint Phalle
San Francisco: Lapis Press, 1987
Photomechanical reproductions
Gift of Molly and Walter Bareiss, 1987.267

Fred Sandback, American, born 1943
Fred Sandback: 16 Variationen von 2 diagonalen Linien 1972
München: Edition der Galerie Heiner Friedrich; Erik A.
Mosel, 1973
Photomechanical reproductions. Edition: unnumbered/550
Gift of Molly and Walter Bareiss, 1984.1037

Fred Sandback: 16 Variationen von 2 horizontalen Linien 1973
München: Edition der Galerie Heiner Friedrich; Erik A.
Mosel, 1973
Photomechanical reproductions. Edition: unnumbered/550
Gift of Molly and Walter Bareiss, 1984.1038

Fred Sandback
Text by Hermann Kern, 1941–1985; translation by Malcolm
G. Leybourne and Fred Sandback
München: Kunstraum, 1975
Photomechanical reproductions. Edition: unnumbered/500
Gift of Molly and Walter Bareiss, 1984.1039

Mappe mit 10 Umkehrlithographien, braun
[S.l.: s.n., 1977?]
10 transfer lithographs. Edition: 12/30
Gift of Molly and Walter Bareiss, 1987.275a–j

Ten Isometric Drawings for Ten Vertical Constructions
New York: Lapp Princess Press in association with Printed
Matter, 1977
Photomechanical reproductions
Gift of Molly and Walter Bareiss, 1984.1040

Armin Sandig, German, born 1929
Roman
Text by Helmut Heissenbüttel, German, 1921–1996
Hannover: Der Galerie Dieter Brusberg, 1962
23 color lithographs, including folder and slipcase.
Edition: 22/30
Gift of Molly and Walter Bareiss, 1984.1041

Giuseppe Santomaso, Italian, 1907–1990
An Angle
Text by Ezra Pound, American, 1885–1972
St. Gallen, Schweiz: Erker-Presse (Franz Larese, Jürg
Janett), 1972
7 color lithographs, one sound recording. Edition: 90/200
Gift of Molly and Walter Bareiss, 1984.1042

An Angle [reduced facsimile]
Text by Ezra Pound, American, 1885–1972
St. Gallen, Schweiz: Erker-Presse, [1975?] (1st ed. 1972)
Photomechanical reproductions
Gift of Molly and Walter Bareiss, 1984.1043

Santomaso Basel 1975: Legni, Holz, Wood, Bois
Venezia: Galleria il Capricorna, 1975
One ink drawing, photomechanical reproductions
Gift of Molly and Walter Bareiss, 1984.1044

António Saura, Spanish, active France, 1930–1998
Diversaurio
Text by José Ayllon, Spanish, 1902–1982
[Madrid: António Saura], 1962
11 color screen prints (including cover). Edition: 59/85
Gift of Molly and Walter Bareiss, 1984.1045

António Saura (see also listing under Various Artists,
KWY)

Sylvain Sauvage, French, 1888–1948
Trente-deux poèmes d'amour
Text by Paul Reboux, French, 1877–1963
Paris: G. Crès & cie., 1923
35 etchings (including cover). Edition: 639/1,000
Gift of Molly and Walter Bareiss, 1984.1046

Daphnis & Chloé
Text by Longus, Greek, active 2nd–3rd centuries C.E.;
translation by Jacques Amyot, French, 1513–1593 (translation completed by Paul-Louis Courier, French, 1772–1825)
Paris: Pierre Bouchet, 1925
40 color woodcuts (including cover). Edition: 113/130
Gift of Molly and Walter Bareiss, 1984.1047

Une aventure de Casanova
Text by [Giacomo Casanova], Italian, 1725–1798
Paris: [s.n.], 1926
32 etchings after Sauvage, etched in collaboration with
E. Feltesse. Edition: 445/450
Gift of Molly and Walter Bareiss, 1984.1048

Emilio Scanavino, Italian, 1922–1986
Forse No
Venezia: Cavallino, 1964
Photomechanical reproductions. Edition: 35/200
Gift of Molly and Walter Bareiss, 1984.1049

Josef Scharl, German, active United States, 1896–1954
Josef Scharl
Text by Alfred Neumeyer, American (born Germany),
1901–1973
New York: Nierendorf Editions, 1945
Photomechanical reproductions, line block reproductions.
Edition: unnumbered/1,000
Gift of Molly and Walter Bareiss, 1984.1050

Requiem-Zyklus
Text by Aloys Greither, German, 1913–1986
München: Galerie Günther Franke, 1971
Photomechanical reproductions
Gift of Molly and Walter Bareiss, 1984.1051

Hans Leonhard Schäuffelein (see listing under Albrecht
Dürer)

Ali Schindehütte, German, born 1939
Lakonische Reden
Text by Beat Brechbühl, Swiss, born 1939
Stierstadt im Taunus, Deutschland: Eremiten-Presse, 1965
5 woodcuts (including cover). Edition: 117/150
Gift of Molly and Walter Bareiss, 1984.1052

Oskar Schlemmer, German, 1888–1943
Oskar Schlemmer: Handzeichnung
Text by Will Grohmann, German, 1887–1968
Stuttgart: Württembergischer Kunstverein, 1959
Line block reproductions
Gift of Molly and Walter Bareiss, 1984.1053

Edwin Schlossberg, American, born 1945;
Robert Rauschenberg, American, born 1925
Wordswordswords
Text by Edwin Schlossberg
West Islip, NY: Universal Limited Art Editions
(Tatyana Grosman), 1968
4 blind embossings, 5 lithographs, 12 letterpress prints, one
etching; one etching with embossing (Rauschenberg).
Edition: 25/25
Gift of Molly and Walter Bareiss, 1984.956
Ref.: Phillips cat. 47, Symmes cat. 76
Fig. 115

Wolfgang Schmidt, German, born 1929
Wolfgang Schmidt: Vielfarbengedicht
Frankfurt am Main: Typos, 1962
Photomechanical reproductions. Edition: 76/200
Gift of Molly and Walter Bareiss, 1984.1054

François-Louis Schmied, Swiss, 1873–1941
Le tapis de prières
Text by Lucien Graux, French, 1878–1944
[Paris]: Pour les amis du Docteur Lucien-Graux, 1938

12 color wood-engravings, most with added pochoir color
(including cover, colophon) after François-Louis Schmied,
engraved by Théo Schmied. Edition: 83/125
Gift of Molly and Walter Bareiss, 1984.1055

Rudolf Schoofs, German, born 1932
Schatten eines Manns
Text by Karl Krolow, German, 1915–1999
[Kassel]: Schoofs/Heiderhoff, 1959
6 etchings with aquatint and embossing, one blind emboss-
ing (cover). Edition: 22/25
Gift of Molly and Walter Bareiss, 1984.1056

Gedichte
Text by Günter Eich, German, 1907–1972
Kassel: Schoofs/Heiderhoff, 1960
4 etchings with aquatint and embossing, one blind emboss-
ing (cover). Edition: 10/32
Gift of Molly and Walter Bareiss, 1984.1057
Ref.: Garvey cat. 276

Jugend in einer österreichischen Stadt
Text by Ingeborg Bachmann, Austrian, 1926–1973
Wülfrath, Deutschland: Horst Heiderhoff, 1961
4 color etchings with aquatint and embossing. Edition: 33/55
Gift of Molly and Walter Bareiss, 1984.1058

Rudolf Schoofs: Gravuren
Texts by Harald Seiler; Will Grohman, German, 1887–1968
Wuppertal-Barmen, Deutschland: August Jung & Söhne,
1962
One color engraving with aquatint, photomechanical
reproductions. Edition: 26/50
Gift of Molly and Walter Bareiss, 1984.1059

Karl Schrag, American (born Germany), 1912–1995
The Suicide Club
Text by Robert Louis Stevenson, Scottish, 1850–1894
New York: Pierre Berès, 1941
18 etchings with aquatint and drypoint. Edition: 70/100
Gift of Molly and Walter Bareiss, 1984.1060
Fig. 92

Werner Schreib, German, born 1925
Die makabren Zeichnungen des merkwürdigen Herrn Schreib
Texts by various authors
Stierstadt im Taunus, Deutschland: Eremiten-Presse, 1958
Line block reproductions
Gift of Molly and Walter Bareiss, 1984.1061

Punzen mit Schnatterings
Stierstadt im Taunus, Deutschland: Eremiten-Presse, 1960
12 relief prints (including cover), some in colors. Edition:
unnumbered/130
Gift of Molly and Walter Bareiss, 1984.1062

Otto Schubert, German, 1892–1972
Ganymed: Blätter der Marées Gesellschaft (Zweiter Band)
Text by Julius Meier-Graefe, German (born Hungary),
1867–1935
München: R. Piper & Co., 1920
4 etchings with drypoint (Schubert), 39 collotypes of
work by various artists. Edition: LXIX/C
Gift of Molly and Walter Bareiss, 1984.1063

W. Emil Schult, German, born 1948
A Book of Man: Connected Drawings
[S.l.: s.n., after 1960] (2nd ed.)
Photomechanical reproductions. Edition: 80/100
Gift of Molly and Walter Bareiss, 1984.1065

Das War mal ein Gästebuch!
München: Fred Jahn, 1969
Photomechanical reproductions
Gift of Molly and Walter Bareiss, 1984.1064

Bernhard Schultze, German (born Poland), born 1915
Im Stande der Unschuld
Text by Christian Ludwig Liscov, 1701–1760
Stierstadt im Taunus, Deutschland: Eremiten-Presse
(Dieter Hülsmanns), 1967
8 lithographs. Edition: 63/350
Gift of Molly and Walter Bareiss, 1984.1066

Alfred Otto Wolfgang Schulze (see Wols)

Carloz Schwabe (see listing under Various Artists, *L'effort*)

Aubrey Schwartz, American, born 1928
Predatory Birds
Text by Anthony Hecht, American, born 1923
Northampton, MA: Gehenna Press (Leonard Baskin), 1958
10 lithographs, one wood-engraving (Baskin's publisher device). Edition: 6/25
Gift of Molly and Walter Bareiss, 1984.1069
Ref.: Garvey cat. 277

The Midget & the Dwarf
Northampton, MA: Gehenna Press (Leonard Baskin), 1960
10 lithographs. Edition: 2/20
Gift of Molly and Walter Bareiss, 1984.1070

Ronald Schwerin, American
Mime: The Art of Étienne Decroux
Text by Étienne Decroux, French, 1898–1991; from notes by Fritz Eichenberg, American (born Germany), 1901–1990
Brooklyn, NY: Pratt Adlib Press, 1965
11 relief etchings, some in colors (including cover and box).
Edition: 853/1,000
Gift of Molly and Walter Bareiss, 1984.1071

Kurt Schwitters, German, 1887–1948
Die Kathedrale
Hannover: Paul Steegemann, 1920
8 transfer lithographs, including one with collage (cover)
Gift of Molly and Walter Bareiss, 1984.1072
Ref.: Castleman p. 158, Garvey cat. 278, Johnson cat. 32, Symmes cat. 77

Die Blume Anna; Die neue Anna Blume: eine Gedichtsammlung aus den Jahren 1918–1922
Text by Kurt Schwitters
Berlin: Verlag der Sturm, [1922]
One relief print (cover)
Gift of Molly and Walter Bareiss, 1984.1073

Die Märchen vom Paradies. Band 1
Texts by Kurt Schwitters; Käte Steinitz, German, 1889–1975
Hannover: Apossverlag, 1924
Photomechanical reproductions, line block reproductions
Gift of Molly and Walter Bareiss, 1984.1074

Sekunde durch Hirn: Ein unheimlich schnell rotierender Roman
Text by Melchior Vischer, German, 1895–1975
Berlin: Petersen Press, 1964 (1st ed. 1920)
Line block reproduction (cover). Edition: 85/800
Gift of Molly and Walter Bareiss, 1984.1075

Memoiren Anna Blumes in Bleie: Eine leichtfassliche Methode zur Erlernung des Wahnsinns für Jedermann
Text by Kurt Schwitters
Berlin: Petersen Press, 1964 (1st ed. 1922)
Photomechanical reproductions, line block reproduction (cover). Edition: 182/200
Gift of Molly and Walter Bareiss, 1984.1076

Kurt Schwitters (see also listing under Additional Books)

William Scott, British, 1913–1989
A Girl Surveyed
Text by Edward Lucie-Smith, British, born 1933
London: Hannover Gallery, 1971
Photomechanical reproductions
Gift of Molly and Walter Bareiss, 1984.1077

Leonard Seastone, American, born 1950
Good Movies: A Film Noir in Book Form
[Tannersville, PA]: Tideline Press, 1988
Photomechanical reproductions. Edition: 19/30
Molly and Walter Bareiss Art Fund, 1990.94

Arthur Segal (see listing under Jean (Hans) Arp)

Segonzac, André Dunoyer de (see Dunoyer de Segonzac, André)

Roger Selden, American, born 1945
The River

Text by Paul Zweig, American, 1935–1984
Verona: Plain Wrapper Press, 1981
2 color etchings, including cover. Edition: "Walter Bareiss" 38/120
Gift of Molly and Walter Bareiss, 1984.1081

Kurt Séligmann, American (born Switzerland), 1900–1962
Flaques: poèmes
Text by Jean Paul Collet
Paris: Les écrivains réunis, 1935
3 mixed etchings. Edition: 74/140
Gift of Molly and Walter Bareiss, 1984.1082

Kurt Séligmann (see also listing under Additional Books)

Eusebio Sempere, Spanish, active France, 1924–1985
Nayar
Text by Julio Campal, Spanish (born Uruguay), 1933–1968
Madrid: Galeria Juana Mordo, 1967
4 color screen prints. Edition: 18/50
Gift of Molly and Walter Bareiss, 1984.1083

Alexandre Séon (see listing under Various Artists, *L'effort*)

Georges Seurat, French, 1859–1891
Les dessins de Georges Seurat
Text by Gustave Kahn, French, 1859–1936
Paris: Bernheim-Jeune, 1928
Collotypes
Gift of Molly and Walter Bareiss, 1984.1084a–b

Ben Shahn, American (born Lithuania), 1898–1969
Kay-Kay Comes Home: A Fable of Enthusiasm
Text by Nicholas Samstag, 1903–1968
New York: Curt Valentin, 1952
Photomechanical reproductions
Gift of Molly and Walter Bareiss, 1984.1085

The Alphabet of Creation: An Ancient Legend from the Zohar
New York: Pantheon, 1954
Line block reproductions. Edition: 503/550
Gift of Molly and Walter Bareiss, 1984.1086
Ref.: Castleman p. 109

Love and Joy about Letters
Text by Ben Shahn
New York: Grossman Publishers, 1963
Photomechanical reproductions
Gift of Molly and Walter Bareiss, 1984.1087

A Partridge in a Pear Tree
New York: The Museum of Modern Art, 1963 (1st ed. 1949)
Photomechanical reproductions
Gift of Molly and Walter Bareiss, 1984.1088

Love Sonnets
Texts by various authors; edited by Louis Untermeyer, American, 1885–1977
New York: Odyssey Press, 1964
Photomechanical reproductions
Gift of Molly and Walter Bareiss, 1984.1089

The Cherry Tree Legend
New York: The Museum of Modern Art, 1967
Photomechanical reproductions
Gift of Molly and Walter Bareiss, 1984.1090

Charles Sheeler, American, 1883–1965
Charles Sheeler: A Retrospective Exhibition
Texts by Bartlett H. Hayes, Jr., American, 1904–1988; Frederick S. Wight, American, 1902–1986
Los Angeles: The Art Galleries, University of California, 1954
One color screen print, photomechanical reproductions.
Edition: 10/100
Gift of Molly and Walter Bareiss, 1984.1091
Fig. 96

Laurie Simmons, American, born 1949
In and around the House: Photographs 1976–1979
Buffalo, NY: CEPA, 1983
Photomechanical reproductions
Molly and Walter Bareiss Art Fund and Printed Matter Matching Gift Fund for Libraries, 1987.48

G. Simoes da Fonseca (see listing under Henri Fantin-Latour)

[Simon d'Orléans], French, active 1305–1310
Die Falkenjagd: Bilder aus dem Falkenbuch Kaiser Friedrichs II
Text by Carl A. Willemsen, 1902–1986
Leipzig: Insel-Verlag, 1943
Photomechanical reproductions
Gift of Molly and Walter Bareiss, 1984.506

Gustave Singier (see listing under Various Artists, *XXe siècle*)

Renée Sintenis, German, 1888–1965; **Emil Rudolf Weiss,** German, 1875–1942
[Sappho]
Text by Sappho, Greek, ca. 610–ca. 580 B.C.E
[München: Verlag der Marées-Gesellschaft]; Piper & Co., 1921
12 engravings after Sintenis, engraved by Weiss, 22 engraved poems (Weiss). Edition: 79/185
Gift of Molly and Walter Bareiss, 1984.1092
Ref.: Garvey cat. 286

Guillain Siroux, French
Bestiaire
Paris: Guillain Siroux, 1966
16 mixed etchings, some in colors, with collage. Edition: 34/120
Gift of Molly and Walter Bareiss, 1984.1093

Max Slevogt, German, 1868–1932
Lederstrumpf-Erzählungen
Text by James Fenimore Cooper, American, 1789–1851; translation by Karl Federn, 1868–1942
Berlin: Paul Cassirer, 1909
298 lithographs, plus a suite of 52 lithographs. Edition: 32/60
Gift of Molly and Walter Bareiss, 1984.1094a–b
Ref.: Garvey cat. 288

Scherz und Laune: Max Slevogt und Seine Gelegenheitsarbeiten
Text by Johannes Guthmann, German, 1876–1956
Berlin: Paul Cassirer, 1920
10 color collotypes, line block reproductions. Edition: 289/320
Gift of Molly and Walter Bareiss, 1984.1095

Don Juan: heiteres Drama in zwei Akten
Text by Lorenzo Da Ponte, Italian, 1749–1838
Berlin: Fritz Gurlitt, 1921
20 wood-engravings after Slevogt, engraved by Reinhold Hoberg. Edition: 121/250
Gift of Molly and Walter Bareiss, 1984.1096

Die Inseln Wak Wak: eine Erzählung aus 1001 Nacht
Text by Richard Francis Burton, British, 1821–1890; translation by Felix Paul Greve, German, 1879–1948
Berlin: Bruno Cassirer, [1921]
54 lithographs, one color collotype (cover). Edition: 171/360
Gift of Molly and Walter Bareiss, 1984.1100
Ref.: Garvey cat. 289, Wheeler p. 110

Mozart's Don Giovanni: Bühnen-Entwürfe für die Dresdener Staats Oper
[Berlin]: Bruno Cassirer, 1924
9 lithographs. Edition: 18/100
Gift of Molly and Walter Bareiss, 1984.1097

Goethes Faust, zweiter Teil
Text by Johann Wolfgang von Goethe, German, 1749–1832
Berlin: Bruno Cassirer, 1927
510 lithographs (including borders), 11 etchings. Editions: 130/250 and 8/50
Gift of Molly and Walter Bareiss, 1984.1098; 1984.1099
(portfolio of 428 lithographs, 11 etchings)

Nicholas Sloan (see listing under Ian Hamilton Finlay)

Gerda Smith
Never Get Out!
Text by John Galsworthy, British, 1867–1933

Gaylordsville, CT: Slide Mountain Press, 1931
Line block reproductions. Edition: 77/77
Gift of Molly and Walter Bareiss, 1984.1101

Kiki Smith, American (born Germany), born 1954
RE
[Isla Vista, CA]: Turkey Press, 1994
Photomechanical reproductions. Edition: 68/100
Molly and Walter Bareiss Art Fund, 1995.18

Endocrinology
Text by Mei-mei Berssenbrugge, American (born China),
born 1947
[West Islip, NY]: Universal Limited Art Editions, 1997
Color monoprints, 2 photographs (cover). Edition: 8/40
Molly and Walter Bareiss Art Fund, 1998.1
Fig. 68

Tony Smith, American, 1912–1980
Tanaquil or the Hardest Thing of All
Text by Donald Windham, American, born 1920
Verona: [s.n.], 1972
One lithograph (wrappers). Edition: 42/250
Gift of Molly and Walter Bareiss, 1984.1102

Art Spiegelman, American, born 1948
Maus: A Survivor's Tale I
Text by Art Spiegelman
New York: Pantheon Books, 1986
Photomechanical reproductions
Gift of Molly and Walter Bareiss, 1993.38

Maus: A Survivor's Tale II: And Here My Troubles Began
Text by Art Spiegelman
New York: Pantheon Books, 1991
Photomechanical reproductions
Gift of Molly and Walter Bareiss, 1993.39

Eugen Sporer, German, born 1920
Eugen Sporer: Holzschnitte
Text by Hans Adolf Halbey, German, born 1922
München: Prestel, 1964
73 woodcuts and wood-engravings, some in colors
Gift of Molly and Walter Bareiss, 1984.1103

Klaus Staeck, German, born 1938
Dreizehn Gedichte
Text by Werner Dürrson, German, born 1932
Stierstadt im Taunus, Deutschland: Eremiten-Presse, 1965
5 color woodcuts, including cover. Edition: 126/160
Gift of Molly and Walter Bareiss, 1984.1104

Nicolas de Staël, French (born Russia), 1914–1955
Arrière-histoire du "Poème pulvérisé"
Text by René Char, French, 1907–1988
Paris: Jean Hugues, 1953
One color lithograph. Edition: 42/100
Gift of Molly and Walter Bareiss, 1984.1106

Maximes
Text by Pierre Lecuire, French, born 1922
Paris: Pierre Lecuire, 1955
One color lithograph (wrappers). Edition: 83/200
Gift of Molly and Walter Bareiss, 1984.1107
Ref.: Garvey cat. 291, Strachan p. 342

Arrière-histoire du "Poème pulvérisé"
Text by René Char, French, 1907–1988
Paris: Jean Hugues, 1972 (1st ed. 1953)
Line block reproduction. Edition: 783/1,000
Gift of Molly and Walter Bareiss, 1984.1105

Nicolas de Staël (see also listing under Additional Books)

[Anna] Staritsky, Russian, active Belgium, France,
1908–1981
[*Brigadnii*]/ *Un de la brigade*
Text by Iliazd, Russian, active France, 1894–1975; transla-
tion by Eugène Guillevic, French, born 1907, and André
Marcowicz
[Paris]: Hélène Iliazd, 1982
7 color etchings with aquatint. Edition: XVI/XXV
Gift of Molly and Walter Bareiss, 1984.580

Walter Stein, American, born 1924
Chidiock Tichborne Elegy, 1586
Text by [Isaac D'Israeli], British, 1766–1848
New York: Walter Stein, [1967]
Photomechanical reproductions. Edition: unnumbered/102
Gift of Molly and Walter Bareiss, 1984.1108

Saul Steinberg, American (born Romania), 1914–1999
Steinberg: The Labyrinth
New York: Harper and Brothers, [1960]
Photomechanical reproductions
Gift of Molly and Walter Bareiss, 1984.1109

Théophile Alexandre Steinlen, Swiss, active France,
1859–1923
Des chats: images sans paroles
Paris: Ernest Flammarion, [1898]
One color lithograph (cover), line block reproductions
Gift of Molly and Walter Bareiss, 1984.1110
Ref.: Garvey cat. 293

Pat Steir, American, born 1940
[Line Poem]
Chicago: Landfall Press, 1976
5 drypoints. Edition: 5/10
Gift of Molly and Walter Bareiss, 1984.957a–e
Ref.: Symmes cat. 78

Annet Stirling (see listing under Ian Hamilton Finlay)

Telfer Stokes, British, born 1940; **Helen Douglas,** British
MIM
Deuchar Mill, Yarrow, Scotland: Weproductions, 1986
Photomechanical reproductions
Molly and Walter Bareiss Art Fund and Printed Matter
Matching Gift Fund for Libraries, 1987.43

Jeff Strayer, American
Decisions
Text by Jeff Strayer
[New York: Chicago Books], 1981
Photomechanical reproductions
Gift of Molly and Walter Bareiss, 1984.1112

Intentions
Text by Jeff Strayer
[New York: Chicago Books], 1981
Photomechanical reproduction
Gift of Molly and Walter Bareiss, 1984.1111

Portrait of an Unknown Lady
Text by Jeff Strayer
[New York: Chicago Books], 1982
Photomechanical reproduction on celluloid, attached
objects
Gift of Molly and Walter Bareiss, 1984.1113

*Still Life with Fruit, Wine, Audiotape and Projections (from
Subjects and Objects)*
Text by Jeff Strayer
[New York: Chicago Books], 1982
Photomechanical reproductions (including one on cellu-
loid), attached objects
Gift of Molly and Walter Bareiss, 1984.1114

Untitled No. 5
Text by Jeff Strayer
[New York: Chicago Books], 1982
Photomechanical reproductions, attached objects
Gift of Molly and Walter Bareiss, 1984.1115

Donald Sultan, American, born 1951
Warm and Cold
Text by David Mamet, American, born 1947
New York: Fawbush Editions and Solo Press, 1985
9 lithographs with added color, 2 color photographs.
Edition: 15/100
Gift of Molly and Walter Bareiss, 1985.91
Ref.: Phillips cat. 50

Margaret Sunday, American, born 1957
Manhattan: An Elegy, and Other Poems
Text by Amy Clampitt, American, 1920–1994
Iowa City: University of Iowa Center for the Book, 1990
Color woodcuts. Edition: 56/130
Gift of Molly and Walter Bareiss, 1991.59

Alan Frederick Sundberg, American, born 1948
*Alan Frederick Sundberg: Aquarelle, Gouachen, Collagen
und Zeichnungen*
München: Galerie Thomas, 1981
One color etching with drypoint, photomechanical repro-
ductions. Edition: 22/50
Gift of Molly and Walter Bareiss, 1984.1116

Graham Sutherland, British, 1903–1980
Storia con Sutherland
Text by Giorgio Soavi, Italian, born 1923
Milano: All'Insegna del Pesce d'Oro, 1968
Photomechanical reproductions, line block reproduction
(cover). Edition: 603/1,000
Gift of Molly and Walter Bareiss, 1984.1117

Karin Székessy (see listings under Jan Voss, Paul
Wunderlich)

Michel Tabanou, French, born 1953
Dixain
Text by Henri-Désiré Landru, French, 1869–1922
Paris: Éditions du Fourneau, 1980
10 color woodcuts, one color relief print (cover).
Edition: 4/150
Gift of Molly and Walter Bareiss, 1984.1118

Emilio Tadini, Italian, born 1927
*La Donna con la Bocca Aperta. The Woman with Her
Mouth Open*
Text by Luigi Santucci, Italian, born 1918
Verona: Plain Wrapper Press, 1980
One color screen print. Edition: "Walter Bareiss" 38/110
Gift of Molly and Walter Bareiss, 1984.1119

Sophie Taeuber-Arp (see listings under Jean (Hans) Arp;
Various Artists, *XXe siècle*)

Pierre Tal-Coat, French, 1905–1985
Sur le pas
Text by André du Bouchet, French, born 1924
Paris: Maeght éditeur (Aimé Maeght), 1959
15 aquatints, some in colors. Edition: 64/200
Gift of Molly and Walter Bareiss, 1984.958

Derrière le miroir: Tal-Coat, Dessins d'Aix 1947–1950 (n° 120)
Text by Pierre Schneider, French (born Germany),
born 1925
Paris: Maeght éditeur (Aimé Maeght), 1960
5 lithographs (including cover), photomechanical reproductions
Gift of Molly and Walter Bareiss, 1984.1240

Derrière le miroir: Tal-Coat (n° 131, mai 1962)
Text by Charles Estienne, French, 1908–1966?
Paris: Maeght éditeur (Aimé Maeght), 1962
8 lithographs (including cover), some in colors, photo-
mechanical reproductions, line block reproductions
Gift of Molly and Walter Bareiss, 1984.1239

Derrière le miroir: Tal-Coat (n° 153, juin 1965)
Text by Henri Maldiney, born 1912
Paris: Maeght éditeur (Aimé Maeght), 1965
8 color lithographs (including cover)
Gift of Molly and Walter Bareiss, 1984.1234

Derrière le miroir: Tal-Coat (n° 199, octobre 1972)
Text by Pierre Tal-Coat
Paris: Maeght éditeur (Aimé Maeght), 1972
11 lithographs, some in colors, photomechanical
reproductions
Gift of Molly and Walter Bareiss, 1984.1229

Rufino Tamayo, Mexican, 1899–1991
Rufino Tamayo
Text by Robert Goldwater, American, 1907–1973

New York: Quadrangle Press, 1947
2 etchings with aquatint from the same plate, 80 collotypes, photomechanical reproductions. Edition: 32/75
Gift of Molly and Walter Bareiss, 1984.1120

Yves Tanguy, American (born France), 1900–1955
Feu central
Text by Benjamin Péret, French, 1899–1959
Paris: K éditeur, 1947
4 collotypes. Edition: 303/1,000
Gift of Molly and Walter Bareiss, 1984.1121

Le grand passage
Text by Jean Laude, French, born 1922
Paris: Les presses littéraires de France (Max Clarac-Sérou), 1954
One paper collage, 3 etchings with monotype color, line block reproductions. Edition: G/J
Gift of Molly and Walter Bareiss, 1984.1122
Fig. 97

Yves Tanguy (see also listing under Max Ernst)

Dorothea Tanning (see listing under Additional Books)

Antoni Tàpies, Spanish, born 1923
Air
Text by André du Bouchet, French, born 1924
Paris: Maeght éditeur (Adrien Maeght), 1971
9 mixed etchings (including outer wrappers), some in colors, 7 lithographs (including inner wrappers), most in colors. Edition: 78/150
Gift of Molly and Walter Bareiss, 1984.959
Ref.: Johnson cat. 154
Fig. 12

Derrière le miroir: Tàpies, Objets et grands formats (n° 200, novembre 1972)
Text by Jacques Dupin, French, born 1927
Paris: Maeght éditeur (Aimé Maeght), 1972
4 color lithographs, photomechanical reproductions
Gift of Molly and Walter Bareiss, 1984.1230

La Clau del Foc
Text by Père Gimferrer, Spanish, born 1945
Barcelona: Edicions Polígrafa, 1973
17 color lithographs, including one with collage elements (cover). Edition: 241/500
Gift of Molly and Walter Bareiss, 1984.1123
Ref.: Hogben cat. 153

Jean Daive, Antoni Tàpies
Text by Jean Daive, French, born 1941
Paris: Maeght éditeur (Adrien Maeght), 1975
3 color mixed etchings, 2 blind collagraphs, line block reproductions (some printed over the etchings and collagraphs). Edition: 62/120
Gift of Molly and Walter Bareiss, 1984.1124

Sinnieren über Schmutz
Text by Alexander Mitscherlich, German, 1908–1982
St. Gallen, Schweiz: Erker-Presse, 1976
10 lithographs, some in colors, some with collage elements. Edition: 18/200
Gift of Molly and Walter Bareiss, 1984.1125

La nourriture du bourreau
Text by André Frénaud, French, 1907–1993
[Veilhes, Lavaur]: Gaston Puel (Thierry Bouchard), 1983 (© 1982)
One color etching with drypoint. Edition: 37/100
Gift of Molly and Walter Bareiss, 1984.1126

Antoni Tàpies (see also listing under Joan Miró)

Johannes Constantinides Taxidakis
Inhalt
[S.l.: Johannes Constantinides Taxidakis], 1974
Photocopies of drawings. Edition: 12/15
Gift of Molly and Walter Bareiss, 1984.1128

Johannes Constantinides: Das Kinderbuch für unsere Kinder und unsere Eltern
Text by Johannes Constantinides Taxidakis

[S.l.]: Schumacher und Handburg, 1974
Photocopies of drawings, some with added color. Edition: 13/20
Gift of Molly and Walter Bareiss, 1984.1129

Edgar Dorsey Taylor, American, 1904–1978
The Gulf of California
Falmouth, MA: R. H. Simmons, 1959
10 woodcuts. Edition: 6/25
Gift of Molly and Walter Bareiss, 1984.1127

Giovanni Domenico Tiepolo, Italian, 1727–1804
Picturesque Ideas on the "Flight into Egypt"
Text by Colta Feller Ives, American, born 1943
New York: Metropolitan Museum of Art, 1972
Photomechanical reproductions
Gift of Molly and Walter Bareiss, 1984.1130

Joe Tilson, British, born 1928
Circhi & Cene. Circuses and Suppers
Text by Andrea Zanzotto, Italian, born 1921
Verona: Plain Wrapper Press, 1979
2 color etchings with aquatint. Edition: "Walter Bareiss" 38/150
Gift of Molly and Walter Bareiss, 1984.1131

Walasse Ting, Chinese, born 1929
Hot and Sour Soup
Text by Walasse Ting
[San Francisco?]: Sam Francis Foundation, 1969
22 color lithographs, photomechanical reproduction (cover). Edition: 75/1,050
Gift of Molly and Walter Bareiss, 1984.1132

Walasse Ting (see also listing under Various Artists, *1¢ Life*)

Jean Tinguely, Swiss, 1925–1991
"Méta"
Text by Karl Gunnar Pontus Hultén, born 1924
Paris: Pierre Horay, 1973 (1st ed. 1972)
One painting executed by Tinguely's machine "Meta-matic no. 6," photomechanical reproductions, one sound recording
Gift of Molly and Walter Bareiss, 1984.1133
Fig. 126

Romain de Tirtoff (see Erté)

Mark Tobey (see listing under Various Artists, *XXe siècle*)

Robert Tomlinson, American
Exiles
Text by Robert Tomlinson
Brooklyn, NY: Pratt Adlib Press, 1962
6 woodcuts, including 2 in colors. Edition: 256/300
Gift of Molly and Walter Bareiss, 1984.1134

Henri de Toulouse-Lautrec, French, 1864–1901
Yvette Guilbert
Text by Gustave Geffroy, French, 1856–1926
Paris: L'estampe originale, 1894
17 lithographs (including cover). Edition: 15/100
Gift of Molly and Walter Bareiss, 1984.1135
Ref.: Castleman pp. 84–85, Garvey cat. 301, Hogben cat. 10, Symmes cat. 80

Catalogue d'affiches artistiques, français [et] étrangère, estampes
Paris: Imprimerie Henon (A. Arnould), 1896
One color lithograph (cover), photomechanical reproductions of work by various artists
Gift of Molly and Walter Bareiss, 1984.1136
Fig. 70

Hors les lois: comédie en un acte en vers
Text by Louis Marsolleau, French, 1864–1935; Arthur Byl
Paris: P.-V. Stock (Ancienne librairie Tresse & Stock), 1898
One lithograph (wrappers)
Gift of Molly and Walter Bareiss, 1984.1137

Histoires naturelles
Text by Jules Renard, French, 1864–1910
Paris: H. Floury, 1899
23 lithographs, including cover. Edition: 95/100

Gift of Molly and Walter Bareiss, 1984.1138
Ref.: Castleman p. 118, Garvey cat. 304, Johnson cat. 9, Symmes cat. 81, Wheeler p. 111

A Sketch Book by Toulouse-Lautrec [facsimile]
Text by Carl O. Schniewind, American, 1900–1957
New York: Curt Valentin, 1952
Collotypes. Edition: unnumbered/1,200
Gift of Molly and Walter Bareiss, 1984.1139a–b

Tomonori Toyofuku, Japanese, active Italy, born 1925
Segni e Vibrazioni
Venezia: Cavallino, 1964
Color lithographs. Edition: 34/120
Gift of Molly and Walter Bareiss, 1984.1140

David Tremlett, British, born 1945
Some Places to Visit
London: Nigel Greenwood Inc. Books, 1974 (© 1975)
Photomechanical reproductions
Gift of Molly and Walter Bareiss, 1984.1141

Hann Trier, German, 1915–1999
Lob de Hand
Text by Henri Focillon, French, 1881–1943
Köln: Galerie der Spiegel, 1962
One lithograph, 12 etchings with aquatint, including some with drypoint, some in colors. Edition: 13/65
Gift of Molly and Walter Bareiss, 1984.1142

Heinz Trökes, German, 1913–1997
Contre-Espace
Text by Iaroslav Serpan, French (born Czechoslovakia), 1922–1976
Angers, France: J. Boutin, 1951
6 lithographs. Edition: 60/100
Gift of Molly and Walter Bareiss, 1984.1143

Heinz Trökes
Köln: Galerie der Spiegel (Ulrich Serbser), 1958
One etching, one lithograph, one relief print (jacket), line block reproductions. Edition: unnumbered/150
Gift of Molly and Walter Bareiss, 1984.1144

Tage Nacht Buch
Köln: Galerie der Spiegel, 1963
Photomechanical reproductions. Edition: 94/199
Gift of Molly and Walter Bareiss, 1984.1145

Eldorado: Ein Bilderbuch von Amerika
Köln: Galerie der Spiegel, 1965
One color ink drawing, 38 screen prints, photomechanical reproductions, some with added screen-printed color.
Edition: 18/25
Gift of Molly and Walter Bareiss, 1984.1146

Reflexionen Lehrsätze Imaginationen
Text by Leonardo da Vinci, Italian, 1452–1519
Berlin: Rainer (Rainer Pretzell, Friedemann Siebrasse), 1966
8 etchings, photomechanical reproductions. Edition: 22/100
Gift of Molly and Walter Bareiss, 1984.1147

Augenreise
Berlin: Rembrandt Verlag, 1968
12 screen prints, some in colors. Edition: 83/200
Gift of Molly and Walter Bareiss, 1984.1148

Fata Morgana
Berlin: Rembrandt Verlag, 1972
12 color screen prints. Edition: 89/120
Gift of Molly and Walter Bareiss, 1984.1149

Ernest Trova, American, born 1927
Fable of the Bees
Texts by Bernard Mandeville, Dutch, 1670–1733; Michael Scriven, British, born 1947
New York: Pace Editions (2:30 Productions), [1973?]
10 screen prints, some in colors. Edition: 20/150
Gift of Molly and Walter Bareiss, 1984.1150

Richard Tuttle, American, born 1941
Book
Lausanne: Paul Bianchini Books, Éditions de Masson,

in collaboration with Yvon Lambert, 1974
Letterpress
Gift of Molly and Walter Bareiss, 1984.1151

Interlude: Kinesthetic Drawings
[New York]: Brooke Alexander, 1974
12 lithographs with color china-marker additions.
Edition: AP 23/24
Gift of Molly and Walter Bareiss, 1984.1152

Geschichtete Farbzeichnungen, 1971
München: Editions der Galerie Heiner Friedrich, 1975
Photomechanical reproductions. Edition: 93/100
Gift of Molly and Walter Bareiss, 1984.1153

Hiddenness
Text by Mei-mei Berssenbrugge, American (born China),
born 1947
New York: Library Fellows of the Whitney Museum of
American Art (May Castleberry), 1987
Color lithographs, color screen prints, color hand stamps.
Edition: unnumbered/120
Molly and Walter Bareiss Art Fund, 1988.34
Fig. 65

Cy Twombly, American, active Italy, born 1929
Fifty Days at Iliam: A Painting in Ten Parts
[Berlin]: Propyläen, 1979
Photomechanical reproductions
Gift of Molly and Walter Bareiss, 1984.1154

Raoul Ubac, Belgian, active France, 1910–1985
Derrière le miroir: Ubac (n° 142, mars 1964)
Text by Yves Bonnefoy, French, born 1923
Paris: Maeght éditeur (Aimé Maeght), 1964
8 color lithographs (including cover), photomechanical
reproductions, line block reproductions
Gift of Molly and Walter Bareiss, 1984.1236

Derrière le miroir (n° 195, décembre 1971)
Texts by various authors
Paris: Maeght éditeur (Aimé Maeght), 1971
One color lithograph (Ubac), collotypes and photomechan-
ical reproductions of work by various artists
Gift of Molly and Walter Bareiss, 1984.1224

Derrière le miroir: Ubac (n° 196, mars 1972)
Texts by Gaëtan Picon, 1915–1976; Claude Esteban, French,
born 1935
Paris: Maeght éditeur (Aimé Maeght), 1972
10 lithographs, some in colors (including cover)
Gift of Molly and Walter Bareiss, 1984.1225

Hans Uhlmann, German, 1900–1975
Uhlmann
Text by Will Grohmann, German, 1887–1968; Ernst
Wilhelm Nay, German, 1902–1968
Köln: Galerie der Spiegel, 1956
3 lithographs, photomechanical reproduction (cover).
Edition: unnumbered/100
Gift of Molly and Walter Bareiss, 1984.1155a

Unknown artist
The Christmas Tobacco
Text by Christopher Morley, British, 1890–1957
[New York: George Arents], 1960
Photomechanical reproduction. Edition: unnumbered/300
Gift of Molly and Walter Bareiss, 1984.813

Minchiate di Firenze [Tarot cards]
Venezia: Legatoria Piazzesi, [197?]
Line block reproductions. Edition: 33/450
Gift of Molly and Walter Bareiss, 1984.1252

Le Panama ou Les aventures de mes sept oncles: poème
Text by Blaise Cendrars, French (born Switzerland),
1887–1961
Paris: Éditions de la sirène, 1918
Line block reproductions, including maps and advertise-
ments. Edition: 42/554
Gift of Molly and Walter Bareiss, 1984.337

Picasso
Text by Vicente Aleixandre, Spanish, 1898–1984

Milano: All'Insegna del Pesce d'Oro (Vanni Scheiwiller),
1962
Photomechanical reproduction, line block reproductions of
Nerja cave drawings. Edition: 166/1,000
Gift of Molly and Walter Bareiss in honor of Barbara K.
Sutherland, 1984.936

[Tarot cards]
Venezia: Legatoria Piazzesi, [1975?]
Line block reproductions. Edition: 220/220
Gift of Molly and Walter Bareiss, 1984.1251

Marjorie Van Dyke (see listing under Susan Weil)

Various Artists
1¢ Life
Text by Walasse Ting, Chinese, born 1929; edited by Sam
Francis, American, 1923–1994
Bern: E. W. Kornfeld, 1964
62 lithographs, most in colors, photomechanical reproduc-
tions. Edition: 1,417/2,000
Gift of Molly and Walter Bareiss, 1984.963
Ref.: Castleman pp. 208–9, Hogben cat. 135, Johnson cat.
155, Phillips cat. 55, Symmes cat. 87
Fig. 104

11 Pop Artists
[New York: Original Editions, 1965?]
18 color screen prints, including 2 with collage, 4 color
lithographs. Edition: 129/200
Gift of Molly and Walter Bareiss, 1984.1220a–v

*XIV. Ausstellung der Vereinigung Bildender Künstler Österre-
ichs Secession Wien: Klinger, Beethoven*
[Wien: Die Vereinigung, 1902]
16 woodcuts, plus decorative elements, line block
reproductions
Gift of Molly and Walter Bareiss, 1984.1308

*15 Litografías de Artistas Españoles en la XXXIII Bienal de
Venecia*
Text by Luis González Robles, Spanish
Macerata, Italia: Foglio Editrice (Giorgio Cegna, Silvio
Craia), [1966?]
15 lithographs, one color screen print (cover), photo-
mechanical reproductions. Edition: 196/250
Gift of Molly and Walter Bareiss, 1984.1329

XXe siècle (Nouvelle série)
Texts by various authors; edited by Gualtieri di San
Lazzaro, born 1908
[Paris: Chroniques du jour]
n° 1 (1951), *Nouveaux destins de l'art:* 4 color lithographs,
photomechanical reproductions
n° 2 (1952), *Nouvelles conceptions de l'espace:* 3 color lithographs, one etching, photomechanical reproductions.
Edition: 24/25
n° 3 (1953), *Art et poésie depuis Apollinaire:* 4 color lithographs, photomechanical reproductions
n° 4 (1954), *Rapport sur l'art figuratif:* 2 color lithographs
(Alfred Manessier, Victor Vasarély), 2 woodcuts (Jean
(Hans) Arp), photomechanical reproductions
n° 5 (1955), *La matière et le temps dans les arts plastiques:* 4
color lithographs (Mark Tobey, Marino Marini, Gustave
Singier), photomechanical reproductions
n° 6 (1956), *Le papier collé du cubisme à nos jours:* one
pochoir print (Jean (Hans) Arp), 6 collotypes with added
pochoir color, photomechanical reproductions
n° 7 (1956), *Dix années d'art contemporain (1945–1955):*
2 pochoir prints (Sophie Taeuber-Arp, Sonia Delaunay),
4 collotypes with added pochoir color, photomechanical
reproductions, line block reproductions
n° 8 (1957), *Art et humour au XXe siècle:* 2 pochoir prints
(after Jean (Hans) Arp, Jean Dubuffet), one lithograph
(Joan Miró), 2 collotypes with added pochoir color, photomechanical reproductions, line block reproduction
n° 9 (1957), *Vrai et faux réalisme dans l'art contemporain:*
2 color lithographs, including one with relief element,
2 pochoir prints, 2 collotypes with added pochoir color,
photomechanical reproductions
n° 10 (1958), *L'écriture plastique:* 5 lithographs, 2 pochoir

prints, 2 collotypes with added pochoir color, photomechanical reproductions
n° 11 (1958), *Les nouveaux rapports de l'art et de la nature:*
2 color lithographs, 2 pochoir prints, 2 collotypes with
added pochoir color, photomechanical reproductions
n° 12 (1959), *Psychologie de la technique:* 2 color lithographs,
one pochoir print, 2 collotypes with added pochoir color,
photomechanical reproductions
n° 26 (1966), *Quatre thèmes:* 2 color lithographs (Marc
Chagall, Maria Helena Vieira da Silva), photomechanical
reproductions
Gift of Molly and Walter Bareiss, 1984.1273, 1984.1274,
1984.1275, 1984.1276, 1984.1277, 1984.1278, 1984.1279,
1984.1280, 1984.1281, 1984.1282 (2nd copy n° 9), 1984.1283,
1984.1284, 1984.1285, 1984.1271, 1984.1272 (2nd copy n° 26)

50. Ausstellung: Bilder und Plastiken aus 5 Jahren
Hannover: Galerie Brusberg, 1964
3 lithographs, one screen print, 3 etchings, one aquatint,
some in colors, photomechanical reproductions. Edition:
37/100
Gift of Molly and Walter Bareiss, 1984.1314a–b

Actualité d'un bilan
Text by Yvon Lambert, French
Paris: [Galerie Yvon Lambert?], 1972
Photomechanical reproductions
Gift of Molly and Walter Bareiss, 1984.1298

Adlib
Texts by various authors
Brooklyn, NY: Pratt Adlib Press
No. 8 (1960), *Illustration:* 17 woodcuts (including cover), 2
wood-engravings, one linoleum cut, one zinc etching, some
in colors. Edition: 232/250
No. 9 (1961), *On Brooklyn:* one linoleum cut, 5 relief etchings, 9 woodcuts (including cover), some in colors.
Edition: 267/300
No. 10 (1962), *Mythology and Science:* 3 woodcuts, 5 wood-
engravings, one blind embossing, 11 zinc relief etchings,
photomechanical reproduction (cover). Edition: 127/300
No. 11 (1963), *The Human Drama:* 11 woodcuts, 5 wood-
engravings, 2 linoleum cuts, 11 zinc relief etchings (including cover), some in colors
No. 12 (1964): woodcuts, linoleum cuts, wood-engravings,
zinc etchings, one lithograph, some in colors, photomechanical reproductions
No. 13 (1966), *American Mime Theater:* 6 typographic
designs, 2 linoleum cuts, 11 woodcuts (including cover),
7 relief etchings, 5 lithographs, some in colors
No. 14 (1966): 11 zinc relief etchings, 3 linoleum cuts,
2 screen prints, 4 woodcuts, 2 wood-engravings, some in
colors
No. 15 (1967), *Circles [1]. Circles [2]. Masks. Dreams. Letters:*
5 woodcuts, book object with typographic designs and die
cuts, 2 screen prints, 2 zinc relief etchings, book object with
relief etchings and die cuts, linoleum cuts with typographic
designs, some in colors, photomechanical reproductions
No. 16 (1968), *Theater Graphics:* one photograph, photomechanical reproductions
Gift of Molly and Walter Bareiss, 1984.1249, 1984.1248,
1984.1247, 1984.1246, 1984.1245, 1984.1244, 1984.1243,
1984.1242, 1984.1241

[*Affiches d'expositions*]
Texts by various authors
Paris: Fernand Mourlot
No. I (1955): photomechanical reproductions. Edition:
"Pour Monsieur Walter Bareiss"
No. 2 (1956): one color lithograph (Jean Cocteau), photo-
mechanical reproductions. Edition: "Exemplaire de
Monsieur Walter Bareiss"
No. III (1959): one color lithograph (Maurice Brianchon),
photomechanical reproductions. Edition: "Pour M. Walter
Bareiss"
No. 4 (1960): one color lithograph (Marc Chagall), photo-
mechanical reproductions. Edition: "Exemplaire Walter
Bareiss"
No. [5] (1963): 4 color lithographs (Joan Miró), photo-

mechanical reproductions. Edition: 60/125
No. VI (1965): one lithograph (Bernard Buffet),
photomechanical reproductions. Edition: 40/125
Gift of Molly and Walter Bareiss, 1984.1335a–ss,
1984.1332a–mm, 1984.1334a–xx, 1984.1336a–zz,
1984.1333a–ddd, 1984.1331a–ddd

L'Albero Poeta
Text by Guido Ballo, Italian, born 1914
Milano: Galleria Schwarz, 1966
10 mixed etchings, some in colors. Edition: 23/100
Gift of Molly and Walter Bareiss, 1984.1304

Der Anbruch: Zweiter Jahrgang 1919/1920 [portfolio]
Texts by various authors; edited by Otto Schneider;
J. B. Neumann, German, 1887–1961
Berlin: J. B. Neumann, [1921?]
Photomechanical reproductions
Gift of Molly and Walter Bareiss, 1984.1303a–j
Ref.: Symmes cat. 88
Fig. 8

Der Anbruch: IV. Jahrgang (Nr. 2-9, 1921/1922)
Texts by various authors; edited by Otto Schneider;
J. B. Neumann, German, 1887–1961
Berlin: Erich Reiss, 1921–22
Photomechanical reproductions
Gift of Molly and Walter Bareiss, 1984.1303k–p

Antologia del Possibile
Texts by various authors; edited by Gaston Novelli, Italian,
1925–1968
Milano: All'Insegna del Pesce d'Oro (Vanni Scheiwiller,
Piero Draghi), 1962
Photomechanical reproductions. Edition: 674/1,000
Gift of Molly and Walter Bareiss, 1984.840

Artists & Writers Protest against the War in Viet Nam
Texts by various authors
[New York]: Artists & Writers Protest, 1967
9 screen prints (including one with die cut and one with
punched holes), most in colors, 6 lithographs (including
one with embossing), most in colors, one soft-ground etching. Edition: 17/100
Gift of Molly and Walter Bareiss, 1984.1222

*L'Avanguardia Internazionale / L'avant-garde internationale /
The International Avant-garde*
Edited by Tristan Sauvage, Italian (born Egypt), 1924
Milano: Galleria Schwarz, 1962–64
Vol. 1: 14 etchings (some with aquatint, some with drypoint), 2 soft-ground etchings, 2 drypoints (with aquatint
or lift-ground aquatint), one blind embossing, one mezzotint. Edition: 14/60
Vol. 2: 15 mixed etchings, 2 soft-ground etchings, 3 drypoints (including one with soft-ground etching). Edition:
14/60
Vol. 3: 14 etchings (some mixed), 5 soft-ground etchings,
one lift-ground aquatint
Vol. 4: 15 etchings (some mixed), 2 soft-ground etchings
(including one with aquatint), one drypoint, one collotype,
one color linoleum cut. Edition: 24/60
Vol. 5: 12 etchings (including one with aquatint and one
with soft-ground etching), 4 soft-ground etchings (including one with pencil additions and one with drypoint), 3
photogravures (including 2 with etching or soft-ground
etching), photomechanical reproduction with embossing.
Edition: 14/60
Gift of Molly and Walter Bareiss, 1984.1259, 1984.1260,
1984.1261, 1984.1262, 1984.1263

Die Biene
Frankfurt am Main: Galerie für Grafik-Freunde, 1966
9 lithographs, some in color. Edition: 23/50
Gift of Molly and Walter Bareiss, 1984.1330

Der Bildermann (Nr. 1-18, Apr.–Dez., 1916)
Texts by various authors
Berlin: Paul Cassirer, 1916
Lithographs
Gift of Molly and Walter Bareiss, 1984.1299a–r

Der Blaue Reiter
Texts by various authors; edited by Wassily Kandinsky,
Russian, active France, 1866–1944; Franz Marc, German,
1880–1916
München: R. Piper & Co., 1914 (1st ed. 1912)
Photomechanical reproductions, line block reproductions.
Edition: unnumbered/1,000
Gift of Molly and Walter Bareiss, 1984.1321
Ref.: Garvey cat. 139, Johnson cat. 20

Calderara, Fruhtrunk, Girke, Jochims, Prantl
Text by Umbro Apollonio, Italian, born 1911
[München: Galerie Stangl], 1969
5 color screen prints, photomechanical reproductions,
line block reproduction
Gift of Molly and Walter Bareiss, 1984.1326a–f

*Carl Andre, Robert Barry, Douglas Huebler, Joseph Kosuth,
Sol Lewitt, Robert Morris, Lawrence Weiner*
New York: Siegelaub/Wendler, 1968
Photocopies. Edition: unnumbered/1,000
Gift of Molly and Walter Bareiss, 1984.1305
Ref.: Castleman p. 163, Drucker pp. 321–22

*L'effort: La madone. L'antéchrist. L'immortalité. La fin
du monde*
Texts by Edmond Haraucourt, 1856–1941
Paris: Les sociétaires de l'Académie des beaux livres,
Bibliophiles contemporains, 1894
Cover, half title, *justification du tirage*, title page: line block
reproductions with added pochoir color (after Léon
Rudnicki)
La madone: 18 color lithographs (Alexandre Lunois)
L'antéchrist: line block reproductions with added color
(after Eugène Courboin)
L'immortalité: 33 etchings, including 21 with added pochoir
color (after Carlos Schwabe, etched by Auguste Massé)
La fin du monde: line block reproductions (after Alexandre
Séon)
Edition: 97/180
Gift of Molly and Walter Bareiss, 1984.1068a–d
Fig. 149

Das Experimentelle Photo in Deutschland 1918–1940
Text by Emilio Bertonati, Italian, born 1934
München: Galleria del Levante, 1978
Photomechanical reproductions
Gift of Molly and Walter Bareiss, 1984.1344

Farbiges Alphabet: In die Maschine gemalt
Stierstadt im Taunus, Deutschland: Eremiten-Presse, 1963
71 color collagraphs?, photomechanical reproductions.
Edition: 40/174
Gift of Molly and Walter Bareiss, 1984.1309

Formen der Farbe
Text by Dieter Honisch, German, born 1932
Stuttgart: Württembergischer Kunstverein, 1967
Photomechanical reproductions, line block reproductions
Gift of Molly and Walter Bareiss, 1984.1325

Freibord (Erstes Extra)
[Vienna: Edition Freibord, 1984]
3 ink drawings (including one with wash), one graphite
drawing, one relief print, one photograph, 2 lithographs
(including one in colors). Edition: 7/20
Gift of Molly and Walter Bareiss, 1987.281a–g

Geflecht: Antiobjekte (Nr. 2, Juli 1965–April 1966)
Texts by various authors
[München: Gruppe Geflecht, 1965?]
Photomechanical reproductions. Edition: unnumbered/
2,000
Gift of Molly and Walter Bareiss, 1987.1286, 1984.1297

*Grafik des Kapitalistischen Realismus: KP Brehmer, Hödicke,
Lueg, Polke, Richter, Vostell*
Text by René Block, German, born 1942
Berlin: René Block, 1971
One etching, 3 screen prints, 2 offset lithographs, some in
colors, photomechanical reproductions. Edition: 103/120
Gift of Molly and Walter Bareiss, 1987.1316a–g

*Die Graphik Der Neuzeit, vom Anfang des XIX. Jahrhunderts
bis zur Gegenwart*
Text by Curt Glaser, German, 1879–1943
Berlin: Bruno Cassirer, 1922
4 etchings, one lithograph, one wood-engraving,
photomechanical reproductions. Edition: 127/150
Gift of Molly and Walter Bareiss, 1987.1327

*A Graphic Experiment: Clad, D'Vorzan, Goya-Lukich,
Momiyama, Rabinowitz, Stiles, Trakis*
New York: Martin Levitt, [1959]
17 lithographs. Edition: 10/250
Gift of Molly and Walter Bareiss, 1987.1217

Hommage à Roger Lacourière
Texts by Iliazd, Russian, active France, 1894–1975;
Pablo Picasso, Spanish, active France, 1881–1973
Paris: Le degré quarante et un (Iliazd), 1968
10 mixed etchings, one aquatint with soft-ground etching,
2 drypoints. Edition: 38/50
Gift of Molly and Walter Bareiss, 1987.1313
Ref.: Johnson cat. 89

Hommage (n° 1, décembre 1943)
Text by Pierre Emmanuel, French, 1916–1984; edited by
[Robert Lang]
Monaco: [s.n.], 1943
Photomechanical reproductions. Edition: 719/1,000
Gift of Molly and Walter Bareiss, 1987.1291

In Memory of My Feelings
Text by Frank O'Hara, American, 1926–1966
New York: The Museum of Modern Art, 1967
Photomechanical reproductions. Edition: 161/2,500
Gift of Molly and Walter Bareiss, 1987.1221
Ref.: Hogben cat. 138

Interfunktionen 2
Texts by various authors; edited by Friedrich Wolfram
Heubach, born 1944
Köln-Wiedenspech: Interfunktionen (Friedrich Wolfram
Heubach), 1968
Photomechanical reproductions
Molly and Walter Bareiss Art Fund, 1988.146a

*Interfunktionen. Zeitschrift für neue Arbeiten und
Vorstellungen* (Nr. 11, 12)
Texts by various authors
Köln: B. H. D. Buchloh, 1974–75
Photomechanical reproductions
Molly and Walter Bareiss Art Fund, 1988.146b–c; Gift of
Molly and Walter Bareiss, 1984.1324 (2nd copy Nr. 11)

J. B. Neumanns Bilderhefte [Nr. 1, 4]
Berlin: Graphisches Kabinett Jsrael [Israel] Ber
Neumann, 1920
Photomechanical reproductions
Gift of Molly and Walter Bareiss, 1984.1301, 1984.1302

*Kochbuch für Feiertage: Blütenlese von Bildern, Rezepten
und Poesien*
Texts by various authors; edited by Vauo Stomps,
1897–1970
Stierstadt im Taunus, Deutschland: Eremiten-Presse, 1964
6 woodcuts, 3 linoleum cuts, 2 montages, 13 collagraphs?
(including cover), 3 lithographs, one "smudging"
("Originalverwischung"), one wood cutout, one screen
print, some in colors. Edition: 182/400
Gift of Molly and Walter Bareiss, 1984.1311

KWY
Texts by various authors
Paris: Lourdes Castro, Christo, Jan Voss, René Bertholo,
1961–63
n° 6 (June 1960): 4 screen prints (José Escada, António
Saura), some in colors, photomechanical reproductions
n° 8 (autumn 1961): 18 screen prints, some in colors,
embossed foil (cover), collage elements, photomechanical
reproductions
n° 9 (spring 1962): 12 screen prints (including cover),
some in colors, photomechanical reproductions
n° 10 (autumn 1962): 16 screen prints (including cover),

some in colors, one découpage
n° 11 (spring 1963): screen prints, some in colors, photomechanical reproductions
n° 12 (winter 1963): screen prints, some in colors, photomechanical reproductions
Edition: unnumbered/300
Gift of Molly and Walter Bareiss, 1984.1265, 1984.1266, 1984.1267, 1984.1268, 1984.1269, 1984.1270

Mitten ins Fleisch: Farbiges Alphabet 1966
Stierstadt im Taunus, Deutschland: Eremiten-Presse (Friedolin Reske), 1966
65 collagraphs? (including cover), most in colors. Edition: 85/330
Gift of Molly and Walter Bareiss, 1984.1345

Oberdeutsche Federzeichnungen aus der Jahren 1457 und 1483
Text by Otto Fischer, 1886–1948
München: O. C. Recht (Otto Fischer), 1923
Collotypes, some with added pochoir
Gift of Molly and Walter Bareiss, 1984.1300a–r

Poésie de mots inconnus
Texts by various authors; edited by Iliazd, Russian, active France, 1894–1975
Paris: Le degré quarante et un (Iliazd), 1949
6 etchings, 3 drypoints, 2 aquatints, 6 lithographs, 7 woodcuts, 2 engravings, one linoleum cut, some in colors, line block reproduction (cover). Edition: "compagnon XXXVI Paul Éluard"
Gift of Molly and Walter Bareiss, 1984.962
Ref.: Castleman p. 98, Garvey cat. 305, Symmes cat. 86
Fig. 53

Pour Daniel-Henry Kahnweiler
Texts by various authors; edited by Werner Spies, German, born 1937
Stuttgart: Gerd Hatje, 1965
9 lithographs, some in colors, photomechanical reproductions
Gift of Molly and Walter Bareiss, 1984.1310

I Precursori dell'Avanguardia: Futuristi, Abstrattisti, Dadaisti / Les précurseurs de l'Avant-garde: Futuristes, Abstraits, Dadaïstes / The Forerunners of the Avant-Garde: Futurists, Abstractionists, Dadaists
Edited by Tristan Sauvage, Italian (born Egypt), born 1924
Milano: Galleria Schwarz, 1962
20 etchings, some mixed, including one in color. Edition: 14/60
Gift of Molly and Walter Bareiss, 1984.1264

Press-Art (National-Zeitung)
[Basel: National-Zeitung, 1973?]
Line block reproductions
Molly and Walter Bareiss Art Fund, 1988.38

Les revendications: Apoèmes. Les armes de justice. Evolution de la révolution
Text by Henri Pichette, French, born 1924
Paris: Mercure de France, 1958
Photomechanical reproductions
Gift of Molly and Walter Bareiss, 1984.1318

Rezepte gegen Notstände: Kalender der Eremiten-Presse 1968
Text by Felix Rexhausen, German, born 1932
Stierstadt im Taunus, Deutschland: Eremiten-Presse, [1967?]
13 color relief prints, including cover
Gift of Molly and Walter Bareiss, 1984.1340

Royal Garden Blues
Text by Jean Jacques Lévêque, French, born 1931
Paris: Michel Cassé, 1964
10 color lithographs. Edition: 32/100
Gift of Molly and Walter Bareiss, 1984.1322

Self Portrait in a Convex Mirror
Text by John Ashbery, American, born 1927
San Francisco: Arion Press (Andrew Hoyem), 1984
4 lithographs, one woodcut, one soft-ground etching with aquatint, one "etching reproduced by photogravure" with added color, photomechanical reproductions, one sound

recording. Edition: 75/150
Gift of Molly and Walter Bareiss, 1984.1337
Ref.: Johnson cat. 173
Fig. 133

The Smile at the Foot of the Ladder
Text by Henry Miller, American, 1891–1980
New York: Duell, Sloan and Pearce, 1948
Photomechanical reproductions
Gift of Molly and Walter Bareiss, 1984.1216

S.M.S. (No. 1, February 1968)
Edited by [Cply], American, 1919–1996
New York: Letter Edged in Black Press, 1968
Multiples: photomechanical reproductions, some with die cuts
Gift of Molly and Walter Bareiss, 1984.1315
Fig. 116

SPUR WIR
Texts by various authors
[München?]: SPUR WIR, 1965
25 linoleum cuts, some in colors. Edition: unnumbered/1,500
Gift of Molly and Walter Bareiss, 1984.1296
Fig. 110

Stadtplan Stattplan
Frankfurt am Main: Typos (Adam Seide), 1964
5 lithographs, some in colors, one color woodcut, one blind embossing, one paper collage, one screen print, one etching with collage element. Edition: 35/40
Gift of Molly and Walter Bareiss, 1984.246

Stierstadter Gesangbuch: Böse Lieder
Texts by various authors
Stierstadt im Taunus, Deutschland: Eremiten-Presse (Friedolin Reske), 1968
2 color woodcuts, 2 color collagraphs?, 17 transfer lithographs, most in colors
Gift of Molly and Walter Bareiss, 1984.1343

Les temps Situationnistes (n° 6, Édition parisienne)
Edited by Jacqueline de Jong
Paris: Jacqueline de Jong, 1967
33 lithographs, some in colors
Gift of Molly and Walter Bareiss, 1984.1306

Un poème dans chaque livre
Text by Paul Éluard, French, 1895–1952
Paris: Louis Broder, 1956
6 mixed etchings, 3 drypoints, one engraving, 2 woodcuts, one lithograph, 3 aquatints, some in colors. Edition: 55/100
Gift of Molly and Walter Bareiss, 1984.1312

Verve: revue artistique et littéraire
Texts by various authors
Paris: Éditions de la revue Verve (Tériade)
Vol. 1, n° 1–4 (1937–39; English edition): 17 color lithographs, 2 linoleum cuts, photomechanical reproductions
Vol. 2, n° 5–8 (1939–40; English edition): 10 color lithographs, photomechanical reproductions
Vol. IV, n° 13 (1945): photomechanical reproductions, line block reproductions (after Henri Matisse)
Vol. IV, n° 16 (1946), *Livre des Tournois du Roi René*: photomechanical reproductions of works by unknown medieval artist
Vol. VIII, n° 33–34 (1956), *Bible*: 30 lithographs (Marc Chagall), some in colors, photomechanical reproductions (after Chagall)
Vol. X, n° 37–38 (1960), *Dessins pour la Bible*: 25 color lithographs (Marc Chagall), photomechanical reproductions (after Chagall)
Gift of Molly and Walter Bareiss, 1984.1253, 1984.1254, 1984.1258, 1984.1257, 1984.1256, 1984.1255
Fig. 102 (Vol. X)

Zeichen für Zeichen: 14 original Graphiken
Text by Umbro Apollonio, Italian, born 1911
[Frankfurt am Main]: Typos, 1963
6 lithographs, some in colors, one color screen print, 2 color etchings, 5 typographic designs with color line

block elements, one color woodcut. Edition: 21/40
Gift of Molly and Walter Bareiss, 1984.1223

Die Zeitschrift SPUR (B. 1, Nr. 1–7 [1960–61])
Texts by various authors
München: Gruppe SPUR, 1962
One color screen print (cover), 32 lithographs, some in colors, photomechanical reproductions
Gift of Molly and Walter Bareiss, 1984.1295, 1984.1294 (2nd copy of Nr. 4)

Victor Vasarély, Hungarian, active France, 1908–1997
Victor Vasarély
Text by Michel Seuphor, French (born Belgium), 1901–1999
Köln: Galerie der Spiegel, 1961
One blind embossing (cover); 4 screen prints (including 2 with embossing), some in colors; line block reproductions, some with embossing and die cuts
Gift of Molly and Walter Bareiss, 1984.1159

Naissances
Text by Victor Vasarély
Köln: Galerie der Spiegel, 1963
2 screen prints, photomechanical reproductions.
Edition: 126/450
Gift of Molly and Walter Bareiss, 1984.1160

Victor Vasarély (see also listing under Various Artists, *XXe siècle*)

Henry van de Velde, Belgian, 1863–1957
Salutations, dont d'angéliques
Text by Max Elskamp, Belgian, 1862–1931
Bruxelles: Paul Lacomblez, 1893
2 color relief prints (cover). Edition: 120/200
Gift of Molly and Walter Bareiss, 1984.1157
Fig. 27

Bram van Velde, Dutch, active France, 1895–1981
Bram van Velde
Genève: Galerie Krugier, 1962
7 lithographs, including cover, some in colors
Gift of Molly and Walter Bareiss, 1984.1158

La folie du jour
Text by Maurice Blanchot, French, born 1907
[Montpellier]: Éditions Fata Morgana, 1973
6 color lithographs. Edition: 33/75
Gift of Molly and Walter Bareiss, 1986.33

Johannes Vennekamp, German (born Turkey), born 1935
Der Sperling und andere Vögel
Text by Günter Bruno Fuchs, German, 1928–1977
Stierstadt im Taunus, Deutschland: Eremiten-Presse, 1964
28 color relief prints, including cover. Edition: 119/500
Gift of Molly and Walter Bareiss, 1984.1161

Ulmer Brettspiele
Text by Peter O. Chotjewitz, German, born 1934
Stierstadt im Taunus, Deutschland: Eremiten-Presse, 1965
21 color relief prints, including cover. Edition: 99/250
Gift of Molly and Walter Bareiss, 1984.1162

Johannes Vennekamp: Reklame für mich
[Heidelberg]: Merlin, 1971
One color engraving, photomechanical reproductions.
Edition: 33/100
Gift of Molly and Walter Bareiss, 1984.1164

Schraeffeeren
Berlin: Rainer (Rainer Pretzell), 1977
One etching, photomechanical reproductions.
Edition: 53/500
Gift of Molly and Walter Bareiss, 1984.1163

André Verdet, French, born 1913
Formes et Paroles
Venezia: Cavallino, 1965
Lithographs, some in colors. Edition: 60/120
Gift of Molly and Walter Bareiss, 1984.1165

Marcel Vertès, French (born Hungary), 1895–1961
Chéri

Text by Colette, French, 1873–1954
Paris: Éditions de la Roseraie (Édouard Chimot), 1929
48 drypoints. Edition: 47/100
Gift of Molly and Walter Bareiss, 1984.1166

Maria Helena Vieira da Silva, French (born Portugal),
1908–1992
Kô et Kô, les deux Eskimaux
Text by Pierre Guéguen, French, 1889–1965
Paris: Éditions Jeanne Bucher, 1933
13 color pochoir prints, including cover. Edition:
unnumbered/300
Gift of Molly and Walter Bareiss, 1984.1167

Le banquet
Text by Plato, Greek, 428–347 B.C.E.; translation by Pierre
Boutang, French, born 1916
Paris: Hermann, 1972
Photomechanical reproductions. Edition: unnumbered/30
Gift of Molly and Walter Bareiss, 1984.1168

Maria Helena Vieira da Silva (see also listing under
Various Artists, *XXe siècle*)

Daniel Vierge, Spanish, active France, 1851–1904
Le cabaret des trois vertus
Text by Saint-Juirs, French, 1848–1890
Paris: L. Baschet, 1895
4 graphite drawings, including 2 with wash, 66 wood-
engravings after Vierge, cut by Clément Bellenger, plus a
suite of 57 etchings. Edition: 3/50
Gift of Molly and Walter Bareiss, 1984.1169

Joan Vilacasas, Spanish, born 1920
Vilacasas
Text by Rafael Santos Torroella, Spanish, born 1914
Barcelona: [s.n.], 1961
One etching, photomechanical reproductions. Edition: 3/50
Gift of Molly and Walter Bareiss, 1984.1170

Eduardo Vilches, Chilean, born 1932
Diez Xilografías Originales
Rosario, Argentina: Ediciones Ellena, 1965
10 woodcuts. Edition: 11/50
Gift of Molly and Walter Bareiss, 1984.1171

André Villers (see listing under Pablo Picasso)

Jacques Villon, French, 1875–1963
Cantique spirituel
Text by Jean Racine, French, 1639–1699
Paris: Raoul Mortier, 1945
5 etchings. Edition: 62/225
Gift of Molly and Walter Bareiss, 1984.1172
Ref.: Garvey cat. 312, Strachan p. 344

Laus veneris
Text by Algernon Charles Swinburne, British, 1837–1909
[Paris]: Manuel Bruker, [1956]
11 etchings with aquatint (including cover), some in
colors, plus 2 suites of 10 etchings each. Edition: 8/150
Gift of Molly and Walter Bareiss, 1984.1173

Alfredo de Vincenzo, Argentinian, born 1921
Seis Xilografías Originales
Rosario, Argentina: Ediciones Ellena, 1963
6 woodcuts. Edition: 22/50
Gift of Molly and Walter Bareiss, 1984.1174

Bernd Völkle, German, born 1940
Die Geschichte der Aubergine
Text by Ulrich Hartmann, born 1930
Stuttgart: Manus Presse, 1970
Photomechanical reproductions. Edition: unnumbered/
1,000
Gift of Molly and Walter Bareiss, 1984.1175

Jan Voss, German, active France, born 1945
Das Kanalisationsproblem (gelöst): jetzt effektvoll
[S.l.: s.n.], 1969
Photomechanical reproductions. Edition: 72/150
Gift of Molly and Walter Bareiss, 1984.1177

Jan Voss; Karin Székessy, German, born 1939
Porträt Nr. 7
Hannover: Dieter Brusberg, 1969
3 screen prints, including one in colors; 3 color lithographs.
Edition: 45/60
Gift of Molly and Walter Bareiss, 1984.1176
Fig. 117

Édouard Vuillard, French, 1868–1940
Nouvelles passionnés
Text by Maurice Beaubourg, 1866–19??
Paris: Éditions de la Revue blanche, 1893
One color lithograph. Edition: unnumbered/350
Gift of Molly and Walter Bareiss, 1984.1178
Ref.: Garvey cat. 316

Cahier de dessins [facsimile]
Text by Annette Vaillant
Paris: Quatre chemins, 1950
Color collotypes. Edition: 374/500
Gift of Molly and Walter Bareiss, 1984.1179a–b

Bernd Otto Wallmann, German, born 1942
Fahrplan: Gedichte
Text by Guntram Vesper, German, born 1941
Stierstadt im Taunus, Deutschland: Eremiten-Presse, 1964
5 color relief prints, including cover. Edition: 113/150
Gift of Molly and Walter Bareiss, 1984.1180

Andy Warhol, American, 1928–1987
Andy Warhol's Index (Book)
New York: Random House, 1967
Photomechanical reproductions with collage and pop-up
elements, one sound recording
Gift of Molly and Walter Bareiss, 1984.960
Ref.: Drucker p. 154, Symmes cat. 82
Fig. 61

Max Weber, American (born Poland), 1881–1961
Woodcuts and Linoleum Blocks
New York: E. Weyhe, 1956
34 woodcuts and linoleum cuts. Edition: 148/200
Gift of Molly and Walter Bareiss, 1984.1181

Things
Text by Max Weber
Brooklyn, NY: Pratt Adlib Press (Arnold Bank,
Igal Roodenko), 1960
One woodcut. Edition: 85/300
Gift of Molly and Walter Bareiss, 1984.1182

Carl-Heinz Wegert, German, born 1926
Der Verurteilte
Text by Horst Bienek, German (born Poland), born 1930
München: Edition Günter Stöberlein, 1972
12 drypoints, some with aquatint, some in colors; wire box
with hinged lid and clasp. Edition: 7/27 (Edition A)
Gift of Molly and Walter Bareiss, 1984.961
Ref.: Symmes cat. 83
Fig. 123

Susan Weil, American, born 1930
The Reed
Text by Jalaluddin Mohammad Rumi (Maulana Jalal
al-Din Rumi), Persian, 1207–1273; translation by Zahra
Partovi
New York: Vincent FitzGerald & Company, 1989
Watercolor drawings, line etchings, color mezzotints with
added color, cut paper and collage. Edition: 3/50
Molly and Walter Bareiss Art Fund, 1989.31

Susan Weil; Marjorie Van Dyke, American, born 1956
The Epiphanies
Text by James Joyce, Irish, 1882–1941
New York: Vincent FitzGerald & Company, 1987
Etchings and lithographs with added collage, embossing,
hand coloring, and die cuts. Edition: 8/50
Molly and Walter Bareiss Art Fund, 1988.50
Ref.: Phillips cat. 62

Lawrence Weiner (see listing under Edward Ruscha)

Seth Weinhardt, American
Unreasonable Simulacrum / Interrogation Point
Text by Seth Weinhardt
New York: Chicago Books, 1985
Photomechanical reproductions
Molly and Walter Bareiss Art Fund and Printed Matter
Matching Gift Fund for Libraries, 1987.45

Emile Rudolf Weiss, German, 1875–1942
Bei Sinkendem Licht: Dialoge
Text by Hans Bethge, German, 1876–1946
Leipzig: H. Seemann, 1903
5 woodcuts. Edition: 2/15
Gift of Molly and Walter Bareiss, 1984.1183

Emile Rudolf Weiss (see also listing under Renée Sintenis)

Neil Welliver, American, born 1929
Henrik Ibsen: Poems
Text by Henrik Ibsen, Norwegian, 1828–1906; translation
by Michael Feingold, American, born 1945
New York: Vincent FitzGerald & Company, 1987
5 color etchings, one color lithograph, handwoven cloth
design (cover, by Sara Dochow). Edition: 3/75
Molly and Walter Bareiss Art Fund, 1988.10

Hunting Stories
Text by William Faulkner, American, 1897–1962
[New York]: Limited Editions Club, 1988
2 color etchings with aquatint. Edition: "This is one
of 50 presentation copies, out of series"
Molly and Walter Bareiss Art Fund, 1993.16

William T. Wiley, American, born 1937
A Suite of Daze
[Chicago]: Landfall Press, 1977
11 mixed etchings; 3 lift-ground aquatints, including one
in colors; 2 blind embossings; line block reproductions.
Edition: 21/50
Gift of Molly and Walter Bareiss, 1984.1184
Ref.: Johnson cat. 167

Emmett Williams, American, born 1925
Faustzeichnungen
Berlin: Rainer (Rainer Pretzell), 1983
Photomechanical reproductions. Edition: 99/130
Gift of Molly and Walter Bareiss, 1984.1185
Fig. 135

Robert Wilson, American, born 1941
Alcestis
Austin, TX: University of Texas, Department of Art,
Guest Artist in Printmaking, [1987?]
9 lithographs. Edition: 6/20
Molly and Walter Bareiss Art Fund, 1990.53a–i

James Wines, American, born 1932
18 Lithographs Illustrating the Text of "Candide" by Voltaire
Text by François Marie Arouet de Voltaire, French,
1694–1778
Roma: Roberto Bulla, 1959
18 lithographs. Edition: 12/50
Gift of Molly and Walter Bareiss, 1984.1186

Michael Winkler, American, born 1952
Word Art / Art Words
[Swarthmore, PA]: Michael Winkler, 1985
Photomechanical reproductions
Molly and Walter Bareiss Art Fund and Printed Matter
Matching Gift Fund for Libraries, 1987.49

Ralf Winkler (see listing under A. R. Penck)

Fritz Winter, German, 1905–1976
[Fritz Winter]
Text by Will Grohmann, German, 1887–1968
Köln: Galerie der Spiegel, 1955
2 lithographs, photomechanical reproductions
Gift of Molly and Walter Bareiss, 1984.1155b

Fritz Winter: Acht Zeichnungen 1939–1944
München: Studio Bruckmann, 1975

Photo-etchings. Edition: 45/120
Gift of Molly and Walter Bareiss, 1984.1189

Terry Winters, American, born 1949
Terry Winters: Fourteen Drawings, Fourteen Etchings
Text by David Shapiro, American, born 1947
München: Fred Jahn (Jens Jahn), 1990
One aquatint, photomechanical reproductions.
Edition: 6/20
Gift of Molly and Walter Bareiss, 1990.86a–b

R. (Rainer) Wittenborn, German, born 1941
Destination: New York
Köln: Edition Hake, [197?]
8 screen prints. Edition: 28/30
Gift of Molly and Walter Bareiss, 1984.1190

Jürgen Wölbing, German, born 1942
Die Leute von Turakarki
Text by Kurt Neuburger, German, 1902–1996
Stierstadt im Taunus: Eremiten-Presse, 1966
7 color transfer lithographs, including cover. Edition:
53/180
Gift of Molly and Walter Bareiss, 1984.1191

Wols, German, active France, 1913–1951
Le berger d'Écosse. La pierre philosophale. Les passagers
Text by Jean Paulhan, French, 1884–1968
Paris: Livre français, 1948
5 drypoints. Edition: 20/115
Gift of Molly and Walter Bareiss, 1984.1192

Visages, précédé de Portraits officiels
Text by Jean-Paul Sartre, French, 1905–1980
Paris: Pierre Seghers, 1948
4 drypoints. Edition: 657/916
Gift of Molly and Walter Bareiss, 1984.1193
Ref.: Castleman p. 188, Hogben cat. 118, Symmes cat. 84

Troels Wörsel, Danish, active Germany, born 1950
Tegninger i Mørket
Text by Niels Vørsel, Danish, born 1953
Copenhagen: Ivan Edeling, 1977
30 lithographs. Edition: 77/90
Gift of Molly and Walter Bareiss, 1984.1194

*19 Radierungen zu Gottlob Frege "Die Grundlagen
der Arithmetik"*
Text by Gottlob Frege, German, 1848–1925
München: Fred Jahn, 1980
19 etchings. Edition: 1/25
Gift of Molly and Walter Bareiss, 1984.1195

[Notes Come and Go]
Texts by Troels Wörsel; Niels Vørsel, Danish, born 1953
München: Fred Jahn, [1986?]
v. 1: *Troels Wörsel,* photomechanical reproduction (cover)
v. 2: *Notes for Shapes Come and Go,* photomechanical reproductions, line block reproduction (cover)
v. 3: *Notes on Painting: A Philosophical Negative,* line block
reproduction (cover)
Gift of Molly and Walter Bareiss 1986.70, 1986.68, 1986.69

Fritz Wotruba, Austrian, 1907–1975
Wotruba: Zeichnungen, Druckgraphiken, Ölbilder, Bronzen
Wien: Graphische Sammlung Albertina, 1965
Photomechanical reproductions
Gift of Molly and Walter Bareiss, 1984.1196

Hommage à Fritz Wotruba
Text by Eugène Ionesco, French (born Romania),
1912–1994
St. Gallen, Schweiz: Erker-Presse, 1975
One etching with drypoint. Edition: 77/100
Gift of Molly and Walter Bareiss, 1984.1198

Discours d'ouverture du Festival de Strasbourg, 1972
[reduced facsimile]
Text by Eugène Ionesco, French (born Romania),
1912–1994
St. Gallen, Schweiz: Erker-Presse, 1976 (1st ed. 1974)
Photomechanical reproductions
Gift of Molly and Walter Bareiss, 1984.1197

Paul Wunderlich, German, born 1927
Altweibersommer: Roman
Text by Karl Mickinn, born 1926
Bremen: Carl Schünemann (Walther H. Schünemann),
1967
One color lithograph (wrappers). Edition: 193/400
Gift of Molly and Walter Bareiss, 1984.1199

Skizzen 1966–1974
Text by Max Bense, German, 1910–1990
Offenbach am Main: Volker Huber, 1974
One color lithograph, photomechanical reproductions.
Edition: 248/625
Gift of Molly and Walter Bareiss, 1984.1200

Paul Wunderlich; Karin Székessy, German, active France,
born 1939
Modelle
Hannover: Dieter Brusberg, [19??]
2 lithographs (Wunderlich), one photograph (Székessy),
8 collotypes. Edition: 33/90
Gift of Molly and Walter Bareiss, 1984.1201

Phyllis Yampolsky (see listing under Peter Forakis)

Adja Yunkers, American (born Latvia), 1900–1983
Adja Yunkers
Text by John Palmer-Leeper
New York: Rio Grande Graphics (Ted Gotthelf), 1952
5 color woodcuts. Edition: 38/225
Gift of Molly and Walter Bareiss, 1984.1203

Enrique Zañartu, Chilean (born France), born 1921
Mythologie du vent
Text by Jacques Charpier
Paris: Presses littéraires de France (Max Clarac-Sérou), 1955
6 etchings, some with aquatint or drypoint, including one
with added color (wrappers), plus a suite of 5 color etch-
ings. Edition: 2/400
Gift of Molly and Walter Bareiss, 1984.1205
Ref.: Symmes cat. 85

Zañartu
Paris: Galerie du dragon (Max Clarac-Sérou), 1955
Photomechanical reproductions, line block reproductions.
Edition: unnumbered/1,000
Gift of Molly and Walter Bareiss, 1984.1204

Les Indes: poème de l'une et l'autre terre
Text by Édouard Glissant, West Indian (born Martinique),
born 1928
Paris: Falaize (Georges Fall), 1956
6 mixed etchings. Edition: 36/56
Gift of Molly and Walter Bareiss, 1984.1206

Rencontre
Text by Michel Butor, French, born 1926
Paris: Éditions du dragon; Stockholm: Herman Igell, 1962
5 mixed etchings with aquatint, most in colors
Gift of Molly and Walter Bareiss, 1984.1207

Hommage et profanations
Text by Octavio Paz, Mexican, 1914–1998; translation by
Carmen Figueroa
Paris: Jean Hugues, 1963
3 etchings with drypoint and aquatint, plus a suite of
3 color etchings. Edition: 13/75
Gift of Molly and Walter Bareiss, 1984.1208

Histoire des rechutes
Text by Michel Deguy, French, born 1930
Poitiers, France: Éditions promesse, 1968
4 soft-ground etchings with engraving, 2 engravings,
2 blind embossings (cover), plus a suite of 8 color etchings
and engravings. Edition: "H.C. graveur"
Gift of Molly and Walter Bareiss, 1984.1209

La rose séparée
Text by Pablo Neruda, Chilean, 1904–1973; translation by
Max Clarac-Sérou, French
Paris: Éditions du dragon, 1972
6 color soft-ground etchings, including 5 with engraving;
2 blind embossings. Edition: 33/90
Gift of Molly and Walter Bareiss, 1984.1210

Le rêve du déménagement (2ème partie)
Text by Michel Butor, French, born 1926; Roger Méyère
Braine-Le-Comte, België: Éditions Lettera Amorosa, 1974
One color etching, photomechanical reproduction.
Edition: 14/64
Gift of Molly and Walter Bareiss, 1984.1211

Georges de Zayas, Mexican (active United States),
1880–1961
*Caricatures par Georges de Zayas: Huit peintres, deux
sculpteurs, et un musicien très moderne*
Text by Curnonsky, French, 1872–1956
Paris: [s.n.], 1919
11 lithographs. Edition: 88/160
Gift of Molly and Walter Bareiss, 1984.1212

Kirill [Cyrille] Zdanevich, Russian, 1892–1969
[*Uchites' khudogi: stikhi*] (*Learn, Artists!: Poems*)
Text by A. (Aleksei) Kruchenykh, Russian, 1886–1969?
Paris: Galerie Darial, 1973 (1st ed. 1917)
Photomechanical reproductions. Edition: 170/200
Gift of Molly and Walter Bareiss, 1984.1213
Ref.: Johnson cat. 22

Amy Zerner, American, born 1951
Essays on Asian Music and Theater
Texts by William P. Malm, American, born 1928; Alan
C. Heyman; David Ming-Yüeh Liang, Chinese, born 1941
[New York]: Performing Arts Program of the Asia Society,
[1971?]
One woodcut, photomechanical reproductions.
Edition: 834/900
Gift of Molly and Walter Bareiss, 1984.1307a–c

Walter Zimbrich, German, born 1933
Es funktioniert
Text by W. E. Richartz, German, born 1927
Stierstadt im Taunus, Deutschland: Eremiten-Presse, 1964
4 color collagraphs?, line block reproduction (cover).
Edition: 37/200
Gift of Molly and Walter Bareiss, 1984.1214

Philip Zimmermann, American, born 1951
Civil Defense
Barrytown, NY: Space Heater Multiples, 1984
Photomechanical reproductions
Molly and Walter Bareiss Art Fund and Printed Matter
Matching Gift Fund for Libraries, 1987.57

Janet Zweig, American, born 1950
Heinz and Judy: A Play
[S.l.]: Janet Zweig, 1985
Photomechanical reproductions
Molly and Walter Bareiss Art Fund and Printed Matter
Matching Gift Fund for Libraries, 1987.47
Ref.: Drucker pp. 314–15
Fig. 152, jacket front

Books with No Artist, Listed by Title
Les épiphanies
Text by Henri Pichette, French, born 1924
[Paris]: K éditeur, 1948
Letterpress, printer's ornaments. Edition: unnumbered/215
Gift of Molly and Walter Bareiss, 1984.744

Mon salon; augmenté d'une dédicace et d'un appendice
Text by Émile Zola, French, 1840–1902
Paris: Librairie centrale, 1866
Letterpress
Gift of Molly and Walter Bareiss, 1984.492

L'ours et la lune: farce pour un théatre de marionnettes
Text by Paul Claudel, French, 1868–1955; music by Darius
Milhaud, French, 1892–1974
Paris: Éditions de la Nouvelle revue française, 1919
Letterpress. Edition: unnumbered/125
Gift of Molly and Walter Bareiss, 1984.351a–c

Rubáiyát of Omar Khayyám of Naishápúr
Text by Omar Khayyám, Persian, 1048–1131; translation
by Edward Fitzgerald, British, 1809–1883
München: Verlag der Münchner Drucke, 1923

Letterpress. Edition: 73/200
Gift of Molly and Walter Bareiss, 1984.614

Six Poems by Ungaretti
Text by Giuseppe Ungaretti, Italian, 1888–1970
Verona: Plain Wrapper Press, 1980
Letterpress. Edition: unnumbered/120
Gift of Molly and Walter Bareiss, 1984.1156

Wooings: Five Poems by Brendan Gill
Text by Brendan Gill, American, 1914–1997
Verona: Plain Wrapper Press, 1980
Letterpress. Edition: "Walter Bareiss"
Gift of Molly and Walter Bareiss, 1984.521

Additional Books

The following books were already in the collection of the Toledo Museum of Art when the Bareiss Collection was donated. Duplicates of these titles were returned to the collector.

Jean (Hans) Arp, French (born Alsace), 1887–1966
Élémente
Text by Jean (Hans) Arp
Zürich: [Karl Schmid?], 1950
10 woodcuts, some in color. Edition: 36/200
Museum Purchase, 1979.15

Dreams and Projects
Text by Jean (Hans) Arp; translation by Ralph Mannheim
New York: Curt Valentin, [1952]
28 woodcuts, plus a suite of 28 woodcuts. Edition: 5/320
Museum Purchase, 1979.14
Ref.: Garvey cat. 4, Phillips cat. 2

Leonard Baskin, American, 1922–2000
A Little Book of Natural History
Worcester, MA: Gehenna Press (Leonard Baskin), 1951
25 linoleum cuts, some in color; 3 wood-engravings, including press device; one woodcut; one color linoleum engraving (title label, cover). Edition: 40/50
Museum Purchase, 1979.16a–ee
Ref.: Garvey cat. 11

Alexander Calder, American, 1898–1976
Fables of Aesop, According to Sir Roger L'Estrange
Text by Aesop, Greek, 620!–560! B.C.E.; translation by Roger L'Estrange, British, 1616–1704
Paris: Harrison of Paris; New York: Minton, Balch and Co., [1931]
Line block reproductions. Edition: 519/595
Museum Purchase, 1979.18
Ref.: Castleman p. 120, Garvey cat. 47, Johnson cat. 100, Wheeler p. 99

Three Young Rats and Other Rhymes
Texts by unknown authors; edited by James Johnson Sweeney, American, 1900–1986
New York: Curt Valentin, 1944
Line block reproductions. Edition: unnumbered/700
Museum Purchase, 1979.110
Ref.: Phillips cat. 9, Wheeler p. 99

Max Ernst, French (born Germany), 1891–1976
La brebis galante
Text by Benjamin Péret, French, 1899–1959
Paris: Les éditions premières, 1949
3 color etchings; photomechanical reproduction (cover); line block reproductions, some with added pochoir color. Edition: 126/300
Museum Purchase, 1979.21
Ref.: Garvey cat. 100, Johnson cat. 123

Paul Gauguin, French, 1848–1903
Noa Noa [facsimile]
Text by Paul Gauguin
[München: R. Piper & Co., 1926]
Collotypes, some in colors. Edition: unnumbered/400
Museum Purchase, 1979.49
Ref.: Castleman pp. 82–83, Garvey cat. 115, Hogben cat. 15, Wheeler p. 102

David Hockney, British, active United States, born 1937
Six Fairy Tales
Text by the Brothers Grimm: Jakob Grimm, German, 1785–1863; Wilhelm Grimm, German, 1786–1859; translation by Heiner Bastian, German, born 1942
London: Petersburg Press in association with Kasmin Gallery, 1970
39 etchings, some mixed, plus a suite of 6 proofs. Edition: 26/100 (Edition A)
Mrs. George W. Stevens Fund, 1976.46a–g
Ref.: Hogben cat. 146

Jasper Johns, American, born 1930
Foirades / Fizzles
Text by Samuel Beckett, Irish, active France, 1906–1989
[London]. Petersburg Press, 1976
33 mixed etchings (including 2 in colors), 2 color lithographs (lining box). Edition: 167/250
Mrs. George W. Stevens Fund, 1978.12
Ref.: Castleman pp. 214–15, Hogben cat. 156, Johnson cat. 162, Phillips cat. 23
Fig. 63

Pablo Picasso, Spanish, active France, 1881–1973
Le chef-d'oeuvre inconnu
Text by Honoré de Balzac, French, 1799–1850
Paris: Ambroise Vollard, 1931
13 etchings, 68 wood-engravings (including cover). Edition: 301/305
Mrs. George W. Stevens Fund, 1984.24a–n
Ref.: Garvey cat. 225, Hogben cat. 92, Johnson cat. 54, Strachan pp. 60–62, 339, Wheeler p. 109
Fig. 14

Le chant des morts
Text by Pierre Reverdy, French, 1889–1960
Paris: Éditions Verve (Tériade), 1948
125 lithographs (including cover). Edition: 249/250
Museum Purchase, 1979.33
Ref.: Castleman p. 129, Johnson cat. 70, Strachan p. 340

Kurt Schwitters, German, 1887–1948
Anna Blume: Dichtungen
Text by Kurt Schwitters
Hannover: Paul Steegemann, 1919
Photomechanical reproduction (cover). Edition: unnumbered/10,000
Museum Purchase, 1979.103
Ref.: Hogben cat. 52

Kurt Séligmann, American (born Switzerland), 1900–1962
Les vagabondages héraldiques
Text by Pierre Courthion, French (born Switzerland), born 1902
Paris: Éditions des chroniques du jour, 1934
15 etchings with drypoint, some with aquatint. Edition: 74/100
Museum Purchase, 1979.37
Ref.: Hogben cat. 101

Nicolas de Staël, French (born Russia), 1914–1955
Poèmes de René Char
Text by René Char, French, 1907–1988
Paris: "aux dépens de l'artiste" (Jacques Dubourg), 1952
14 wood-engravings, one color lithograph (chemise). Edition: unnumbered/105
Museum Purchase, 1979.40
Ref.: Castleman p. 192, Garvey cat. 290, Hogben cat. 127

Dorothea Tanning, American, born 1913
Accueil
Text by René Crevel, French, 1900–1935
Paris: Jean Hugues, 1958
14 color mixed etchings, including cover. Edition: 25/50
Museum Purchase, 1979.42
Ref.: Garvey cat. 299

Various Artists
Solidarité
Text by Paul Éluard, French, 1895–1952; translation by Brian Coffey, Irish, born 1905
[Paris: Paul Éluard and G.L.M. (Guy Lévis Mano)], 1938
6 etchings, including 2 with aquatint; one engraving with etching. Edition: 113/150
Museum Purchase, 1979.19a–h
Ref.: Johnson cat. 112

Index to the Checklist

This index includes only the names of authors, translators, editors, and publishers cited in the checklist entries. It does not include the names of artists, who are listed alphabetically by last name in the checklist proper.

Index to the Essays

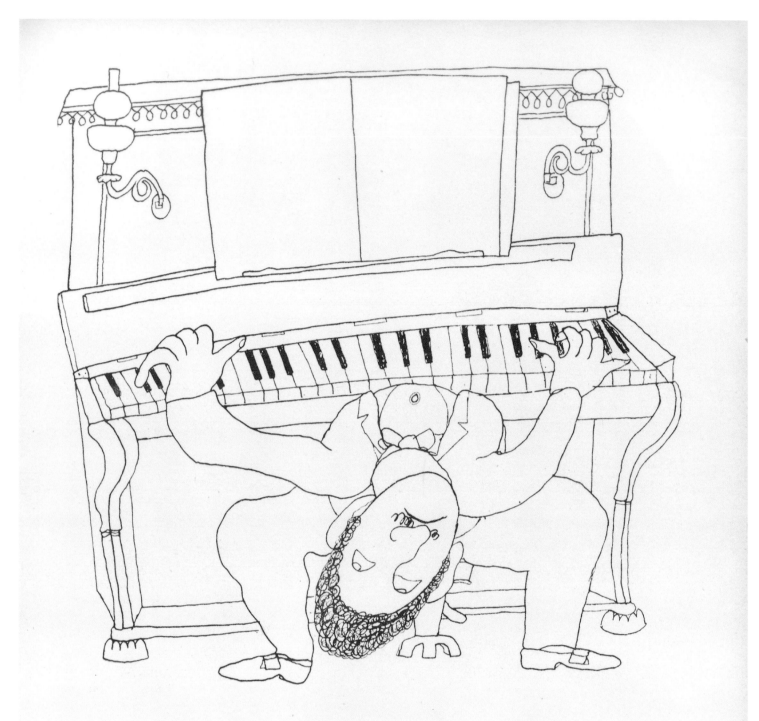

Fig. 151. Jean Cocteau from *Dessins* (Paris: Librairie Stock, Delamain, Boutelleau & cie., 1924). Line block reproduction.

Selected Bibliography on Molly and Walter Bareiss and the Bareiss Art Collections

Bareiss, Walter. Oral history, transcript. Interview conducted by Sharon Zane. New York: The Museum of Modern Art Oral History Project, 1991.
———. "A Print Collector's View." *Books and Prints, Past and Future: Papers Presented at The Grolier Club Centennial Convocation.* New York: The Grolier Club, 1984.
———. *20th-Century Masters of the Illustrated Book: A Selection.* Greenwich, CT: Friends of the Greenwich Library, 1983.

Baumer, Dorothea. "Die Masken der Moderne: Der Sammler Walter Bareiss liebt radikale Kunst und Skulpturen aus Afrika." *Süddeutsche Zeitung* (April 8, 1988).

Bothmer, Dietrich Felix von. "Aspects of a Collection: Vases of Walter Bareiss." *The Metropolitan Museum of Art Bulletin* 27 (June 1969): 425–41.

Brody, Jacqueline. "Focus on Collecting: Walter Bareiss." *Print Collector's Newsletter* 25, no. 2 (May–June 1994): 50–56.

Burke, Susan M., and Pollitt, Jerome J. *Greek Vases at Yale.* New Haven: Yale University Art Gallery, 1975.

Canaday, John. "Greek Vases [review]." *The New York Times* (June 14, 1969): 29.

Chazen, Lois. *African Art: Selections from the Collection of Molly and Walter Bareiss.* Bennington, VT: Bennington College, 1986.

Classically Modern: Classical Texts with Modern Prints from the Bareiss Collection of Modern Illustrated Books. Essay by Andrew Szegedy-Maszak. Toledo: Toledo Museum of Art, 2000.

Corpus Vasorum Antiquorum, The J. Paul Getty Museum, Molly and Walter Bareiss Collection (Malibu, CA: The J. Paul Getty Museum, 1988–98), fasc. 1 Andrew J. Clark (1988), fasc. 2 Andrew J. Clark (1990), fasc. 5 Marit R. Jentoft-Nilsen in collaboration with A. D. Trendall (1994), fasc. 7 Richard T. Neer (1997), fasc. 8 Mary B. Moore (1998).

Cotter, Holland. "Revelation and Mystery in African Sculpture." *The New York Times* (December 17, 1999): 48.

Cummings, Paul. "Interview: Walter Bareiss Talks with Paul Cummings." *Drawing* 6, no. 4 (November–December 1984): 84–86.

Don't Feed the Books: Birds, Bugs, and Bestiaries Featuring the Molly and Walter Bareiss Collection of Modern Illustrated Books. Essay by Teresa K. Nevins. Toledo: Toledo Museum of Art, 2001.

50 Selections from the Collection of Mr. and Mrs. Walter Bareiss. New York: Junior Council of The Museum of Modern Art, 1958.

German and Austrian Contemporary Art from the Bareiss Collection. New Haven: Yale University Art Gallery, 1989.

German Expressionist Prints: From the Walter Bareiss 1940s Collection. New Haven: Yale University Art Gallery, 1966.

Goldschmidt, Lucien. "Notes on the Collecting of the Modern Illustrated Book." *Print Quarterly* 3, no. 3 (September 1986): 240–41.

Greek Vases: Molly and Walter Bareiss Collection. Malibu, CA: The J. Paul Getty Museum, 1983.

"In Brief." *Fine Print* 12, no. 4 (October 1986): 188.

Knüttel, Brigitte. *Sammlung Walter Bareiss: Handzeichnungen, Aquarelle, und Collagen.* Stuttgart: Staatsgalerie Stuttgart Graphische Sammlung, 1965.

Mellby, Julie. "The Molly and Walter Bareiss Collection of Modern Illustrated Books." *FABS* (Friends of American Book Societies) *newsletter* (autumn 2000): 9–10.

Metzger, Henri. "The J. Paul Getty Museum, Malibu…Molly and Walter Bareiss Collection." *Revue Archéologique* (1993): 131–32.

Moore, M. B. "Neck-Amphora in the Collection of Walter Bareiss." *American Journal of Archaeology* 76 (January 1972): 1–11.

"Neue Mitglieder: Bayerisch Akademie waehlt." *Süddeutsche Zeitung* (June 27, 1998).

Paintings, Drawings, and Sculpture Collected by Yale Alumni. New Haven: Yale University Art Gallery, 1960.

Raynor, Vivien. "Yale Samples the Contemporary German and Austrian Art from the Bareiss Collection." *The New York Times* (February 19, 1989): 26.

Roy, Christopher D. "African Art from the Bareiss Collection." *African Arts* 32, no. 2 (summer 1999): 52–69.
———. *Kilengi: afrikanische Kunst aus der Sammlung Bareiss.* Hannover: Kestner Gesellschaft, 1997.
———. *Kilengi: African Art from the Bareiss Family Collection.* Hannover: Kestner Gesellschaft; Seattle: University of Washington Press, 1999.

Sammlung Walter Bareiss [Katalog der Ausstellung in der] Neue Staatsgalerie München. München: Bayerische Staatsgemäldesammlungen, 1965.

Symmes, Marilyn F. *The Bareiss Collection of Modern Illustrated Books from Toulouse-Lautrec to Kiefer.* Toledo: The Toledo Museum of Art, 1985.
———. "The Bareiss Collection of Modern Illustrated Books Acquired by The Toledo Museum of Art." *Print Council Newsletter* (1985).
———. *Bonnard to Kiefer: 20th-Century Artist-Illustrated Books from the Bareiss Collection at the Toledo Museum of Art.* Purchase, NY: Neuberger Museum of Art, 1988.
———. "Illustrated Books at the Toledo Museum of Art." *Journal of Decorative and Propaganda Arts* 7 (winter 1988): 52–71.
———. *Picasso as an Illustrator.* Toledo: The Toledo Museum of Art, 1988.

Thaw, Eugene Victor. "Forum: Degas's Femme Debout." *Drawing* 7, no. 3 (September–October 1985): 60.

Victor, Steve. "The Yale Medal Recognizes Outstanding Contributions of Service to Yale." *Yale Alumni Magazine* (February 2000).

Zimmer, William. "Dramatic Neuberger Show of Artist-Illustrated Books." *The New York Times* (October 9, 1988)

Selected Bibliography on Modern Illustrated Books

Adriani, Götz, ed. *The Books of Anselm Kiefer, 1969–1990*. New York: George Braziller, 1991.

Agusti, Anna. *Tàpies, The Complete Works, 1976–1981*. New York: Rizzoli, 1994.

Albert Skira: The Man and His Work. New York: Hallmark Gallery, 1966.

Alfred Jarry: De Los Nabis a la Patafisica. Valencia: IVAM Centre Julio González, 2000.

Anthonioz, Michel. *L'album Verve*. Paris: Flammarion, 1987.

Arntz, Wilhelm F. *Hans Arp, Das graphische Werk, 1912–1966*. Haag, Deutschland: Verlag Gertrud Arntz, 1980.

L'art et le livre. Morlanwelz, Belgique: Musée royal de Maiemont, 1988.

The Arts of the Book: A Project Devoted to an Appreciation of 20th-Century Book Arts. Philadelphia: University of the Arts, 1988.

Ayrton, Michael. "Chagall as a Book Illustrator." *Signature* (London), n.s., no. 2 (November 1946): 31–46.

Bolliger, Hans. *Tériade éditeur: revue Verve*. Bern: Klipstein & Kornfeld, 1960.

Books Illustrated by Painters and Sculptors. Chicago: The Arts Club of Chicago, 1980.

The Books of Antonio Frasconi. New York: Grolier Club, 1996.

Bury, Stephen. *Artists' Books: The Book as a Work of Art, 1963–1995*. Brookfield, VT.: Scolar Press, 1995.

Castleman, Riva. *A Century of Artists Books*. New York: The Museum of Modern Art, 1994.
———. *Modern Artists as Illustrators*. New York: The Museum of Modern Art, 1981.

Catalogue complet des Éditions Ambroise Vollard. Paris: Portique, 1930.

A Catalogue of the Gifts of Lessing J. Rosenwald to the Library of Congress, 1943 to 1975. Washington, D.C.: Library of Congress, 1977.

Cate, Phillip Dennis. *Prints Abound: Paris in the 1890s*. Washington, D.C.: National Gallery of Art, 2000.

Chapon, Françoise. *Le peintre et le livre: l'âge d'or du livre illustré en France, 1870–1970*. Paris: Flammarion, 1987.

Compton, Susan P. *Russian Avant-Garde Books, 1917–34*. Cambridge, MA: MIT Press, 1993.

Coron, Antoine, ed. *Les Éditions GLM, 1923–1974: bibliographie*. Paris: Bibliothèque nationale, 1981.
———. *Le livre et l'artiste: tendances du livre illustré français, 1967–1976*. Paris: Bibliothèque nationale, 1977.

Courtney, Cathy. *Speaking of Book Art*. Los Altos Hills, CA: Anderson-Lovelace, 1999.

Cramer, Patrick, ed. *Joan Miró, The Illustrated Books: Catalogue Raisonné*. Genève: Patrick Cramer, 1989.
———. *Marc Chagall, The Illustrated Books: Catalogue Raisonné*. Genève: Patrick Cramer, 1995.

Crispolti, Enrico, ed. *The Catalogue Raisonné for Baj's Complete Works*. Torino: G. Bolaffi Publishing House, 1973.

Daniel-Henry Kahnweiler: Marchand, éditeur, écrivain. Paris: Centre Georges Pompidou, 1984.

Debbaut, Jan, and Mariëlle Soons, eds. *El Lissitzky, 1890–1941*. New York: Thames and Hudson, 1990.

D'Oench, Ellen G., and Jean E. Feinberg. *Jim Dine Prints, 1977–1985*. New York: Harper & Row, 1986.

Drake, Christopher. *Ambroise Vollard, Éditeur*. London: Agnew's, 1991.

Drucker, Johanna. *The Century of Artists' Books*. New York: Granary Books, 1995.

Dube-Heynig, Annemarie, and Wolf-Dieter Dube. *E. L. Kirchner: Das graphische Werk*. München: Prestel, 1980.

Duthuit, Claude. *Henri Matisse: Catalogue raisonné des ouvrages illustrés*. Paris: Claude Duthuit, 1988 (© 1987).

Eisenstadt, Eve. *The Making of a "Livre de Lux" and Artists' Books in America 1960 to 1982*. Ann Arbor, MI: University Microfilms International, 1985.

Engberg, Siri. *Edward Ruscha, Editions 1959–1999, Catalogue Raisonné*. Minneapolis: Walker Art Center, 1999.

Field, Richard S. *The Prints of Jasper Johns 1960–1993, A Catalogue Raisonné*. New York: Universal Limited Art Editions, 1994.

French Livres d'artiste in Oxford University Collections. Oxford: Bodleian Library, 1996.

Furst, Margo, ed. *Grieshaber, das Werk: Hommage zum 80. Geburtstag*. Stuttgart: Hatje, 1989.

Garvey, Eleanor M. *The Artist & the Book, 1860–1960 in Western Europe and the United States*. Boston: Museum of Fine Arts; Cambridge: Houghton Library, 1961.

Glasmeier, Michael. *Die Bücher der Künstler*. Stuttgart: Institut für Auslandsbeziehungen, 1994.

Goeppert, Sebastian, Herma Goeppert-Frank, and Patrick Cramer. *Pablo Picasso: The Illustrated Books: Catalogue Raisonné*. Genève: Patrick Cramer, 1983.

Graham, Lanier. "The Rise of the *Livre d'artiste* in America." *The Tamarind Papers* 13 (1990): 35–41.

Guérin, Marcel. *Catalogue raisonné de l'oeuvre gravé et lithographié d'Aristide Maillol*. Genève: Pierre Cailler, 1965–67.

Hogben, Carol, and Rowan Watson, eds. *From Manet to Hockney: Modern Artists' Illustrated Books*. London: Victoria & Albert Museum, 1985.

Horodisch, Abraham. *Picasso as a Book Artist*. Expanded ed. London: Faber and Faber, 1962.

Isselbacher, Audrey. *Iliazd and the Illustrated Book*. New York: The Museum of Modern Art, 1987.

Ives, Colta, Helen Giambruni, and Sasha M. Newman. *Pierre Bonnard: The Graphic Art*. New York: The Metropolitan Museum of Art, 1989.

Jahn, Fred. *Baselitz: peintre-graveur: Werkverzeichnis der Druckgrafik, 1963–1982*. Bern: Gachnang & Springer, 1983–87.

Jentsch, Ralph. *The Artist and the Book in Twentieth-Century Italy*. Torino: Umberto Allemandi, 1992.

Johnson, Robert Flynn. *Artists' Books in the Modern Era 1870–2000*. San Francisco: Fine Arts Museums of San Francisco, 2001.

Johnson, Una E. *Ambroise Vollard, Éditeur, 1867–1939*. New York: Wittenborn, 1944.
———. *Ambroise Vollard, Éditeur, Prints, Books, Bronzes*. New York: The Museum of Modern Art, 1977.

Kaeser, Hans-Peter. *Partnerschaft, Literatur, Kunst: Bibliophile Bücher der Erker-Presse*. St. Gallen, Schweiz: Kunstverein St. Gallen, 1979.

Klima, Stefan. *Artists Books, A Critical Survey of the Literature*. New York: Granary Books, 1998.

Koelen, Martin van der. *Eduardo Chillida, Catálogo Completo de la Obra Gráfica*. Mainz: Chorus, 1996–97.

Laboureur, Sylvain. *Catalogue complet de l'oeuvre de Jean-Émile Laboureur*. Neuchâtel, Suisse: Ides et Calendes, 1989–91.

Lang, Lothar. *Expressionist Book Illustration in Germany, 1907–1927*. Boston: New York Graphic Society, 1976.
———. *Impressionismus und Buchkunst in Frankreich und Deutschland*. Leipzig: Edition Leipzig, 1998.
———. *Konstruktivismus und Buchkunst*. Leipzig: Edition Leipzig, 1990.
———. *Surrealismus und Buchkunst*. Leipzig: Edition Leipzig, 1992.

Lauf, Cornelia, and Clive Phillpot. *Artist / Author: Contemporary Artists' Books*. New York: American Federation of Arts, 1998.

Le Gris-Bergmann, Françoise. *Iliazd, maître d'oeuvre du livre moderne*. Montréal: L'Université du Québec, 1984.

Levarie, Norma. *The Art & History of Books.* New Castle, DE: Oak Knoll Press, 1995.

Lissitzky-Küppers, Sophie. *El Lissitzky: Life, Letters, Texts.* Greenwich, CT: New York Graphic Society, 1968.

Lust, Herbert C. *Giacometti: The Complete Graphics.* Rev. and suppl. ed. San Francisco: Alan Wofsy Fine Arts, 1991.

Lyons, Joan, ed. *Artists' Books: A Critical Anthology and Sourcebook.* Rochester, NY: Visual Studies Workshop Press, 1985.

Miles, Rosemary. *Complete Prints of Eduardo Paolozzi, Prints, Drawings, Collages, 1944–77.* London: Victoria & Albert Museum, 1977.

Milet, Solange. *Louis Marcoussis: catalogue raisonné de l'oeuvre gravé.* København: Forlaget Cordelia, 1991.

Minkoff, George Robert. *A Bibliography of the Black Sun Press.* Great Neck, NY: G. R. Minkoff, 1970.

Moeglin-Delcroix, Anne. *Esthétique du livre d'artiste, 1960/1980.* Paris: Bibliothèque nationale de France, 1997.

Moldehn, Dominique. *Buchwerke: Künstlerbücher und Buchobjekte 1960–1994.* Nürnberg: Verlag für Moderne Kunst, 1996.

P A B: éditeur, auteur, illustrateur, collectionneur. Paris: Loudmer, 1994.

Pantus, Willem Jan. *Jugendstil in Wort und Bild: illustrierte Dichtkunst um 1900.* Köln: Letter Stiftung, 2000.

Penck, A. R., and Erik Mosel. *A. R. Penck: Graphik, Ost/West.* Braunschweig: Kunstverein Braunschweig, 1986.

Phillips, Elizabeth, and Tony Zwicker. *The American, Livre de Peinture.* New York: Grolier Club, 1993.

Pick up the Book, Turn the Page, and Enter the System: Books by Sol LeWitt. Minneapolis: Minnesota Center for Book Arts, 1988.

Prat, Jean-Louis. *Peintres-illustrateurs du XXe siècle: Aimé Maeght bibliophile.* Saint-Paul de Vence: Fondation Maeght, 1986.

———. *Collection de la Fondation Maeght: un choix de 150 oeuvres.* Saint-Paul de Vence: Fondation Maeght, 1993.

Puig, Arnau. *Tàpies und die Bücher.* Frankfurt am Main: Schirn Kunsthalle, 1991.

Rainwater, Robert, ed. *Max Ernst: Beyond Surrealism: A Retrospective of the Artist's Books and Prints.* New York: New York Public Library; Oxford: Oxford University Press, 1986.

———, and Robert M. Murdock. *Richard Tuttle, Books & Prints.* New York: New York Public Library, 1997.

Ramiro, E. *Louis Legrand peintre-graveur.* Paris: H. Floury, 1896.

Ray, Gordon N. *The Art of the French Illustrated Book, 1700 to 1914.* New York: Pierpont Morgan Library; Ithaca, NY: Cornell University Press, 1982.

Reed, Orrel P. *German Expressionist Art: The Robert Gore Rifkin Collection.* Los Angeles: Frederick S. Wight Art Gallery, 1977.

Reinhardt, Georg, ed. *Georg Baselitz, Druckgraphik 1963–1988: Radierungen, Holzschnitte, Linolschnitte.* Leverkusen, Deutschland: Museum Morsbroich, 1989.

Rewald, John. "Maillol illustrateur." *Portique* 1 (1945): 27–38.

Rivière, Yves, ed. *Pierre Alechinsky, les estampes de 1946 à 1972.* Paris: R. Rivière, 1973

Rolo, Jane, and Ian Hunt, eds. *Book Works: A Partial History and Sourcebook.* London: Book Works, 1996.

Das rote Tuch, der Mensch das unappetitlichste Vieh, Hermann Nitsch, das Orgien Mysterien Theater im Spiegel der Presse, 1960–1988. Wien: Freibord, 1988.

Ruhé, Harry. *Multiples, etcetera.* Amsterdam: Tuja Books, 1991.

Saphire, Lawrence. *Léger: The Complete Graphic Work.* New York: Blue Moon, 1978.

Schellmann, Jörg, ed. *Joseph Beuys, The Multiples: Catalogue Raisonné of Multiples and Prints.* 8th ed. Munich and New York: Edition Schellmann, 1997.

Schwarz, Arturo. *The Complete Works of Marcel Duchamp.* Rev. and exp. ed. London: Thames & Hudson, 1997.

Sievers, Johannes, and Emil Waldmann. *Max Slevogt, das druckgraphische Werk.* San Francisco: Alan Wofsy Fine Arts, 1991.

Skira, Albert. *Anthologie du livre illustré par les peintres et sculpteurs de l'école de Paris.* Genève: Skira, 1946.

Sorlier, Charles. *Marc Chagall: The Illustrated Books.* Paris: Éditions André Sauret and Éditions Michèle Trinckvel, 1990.

Stein, Donna. *Cubist Prints/Cubist Books.* New York: Franklin Furnace, 1983.

Strachan, W. J. *The Artist and the Book in France: The 20th Century Livre d'artiste.* New York: Wittenborn, 1969.

Terrasse, Antoine. *Pierre Bonnard Illustrator: A Catalog Raisonné.* London: Thames and Hudson, 1989.

Themes & Variations: The Publications of Vincent Fitz Gerald & Company 1980–2000. New York: Columbia University, 2000.

Tiessen, Wolfgang, ed. *Die Buchillustration in Deutschland, Österreich, und der Schweiz seit 1945.* Neu-Isenburg, Deutschland: Verlag der Buchhandlung Wolfgang Tiessen, 1968–89.

Unica T: zehn Jahre Künstlerbücher. [Offenbach am Main]: Unica T, 1996.

Vallier, Dora. *Braque, The Complete Graphics: Catalogue Raisonné.* New York: Alpine Fine Arts Collection, 1988.

Vieillard, Roger. *Georges Braque: Grands livres illustrés.* Paris: Adrien Maeght, 1958.

Watson, Rowan. "Bing, Art Nouveau and the Book in the Late Nineteenth Century." *Apollo* 151, no. 459 (winter 2000): 32–40.

Webel, Sophie. *L'oeuvre gravé et les livres illustrés par Jean Dubuffet, Catalogue raisonné.* Paris: B. Lebon, 1991.

Weitenkampe, Frank. *Illustrated Books of the Past Four Centuries.* New York: New York Public Library, 1920.

Werner, Michael. *Marcel Broodthaers: Catalogue des livres . . . 1957–1975.* Köln: Galerie Michael Werner, 1982.

Werth, Léon. "Pierre Bonnard illustrateur." *Portique* 7 (1950): 9–20.

Wheeler, Monroe. *Modern Painters and Sculptors as Illustrators.* New York: The Museum of Modern Art, 1946.

Wick, Peter A. *Toulouse-Lautrec: Book Covers & Brochures.* Cambridge: Houghton Library, 1972.

Woimant, Françoise, Marie-Cécile Miessner, and Anne Moeglin-Delcroix. *De Bonnard à Baselitz, estampes et livres d'artistes.* Paris: Bibliothèque nationale, 1992.

Wolff, Geoffrey. *Black Sun: The Brief Transit and Violent Eclipse of Harry Crosby.* New York: Random House, 1976.

Wye, Deborah. *The Russian Avant-garde Book, 1910–1934.* New York: The Museum of Modern Art, 2002.

———. *Thinking Print: Books to Billboards, 1980–95.* New York: The Museum of Modern Art, 1996.

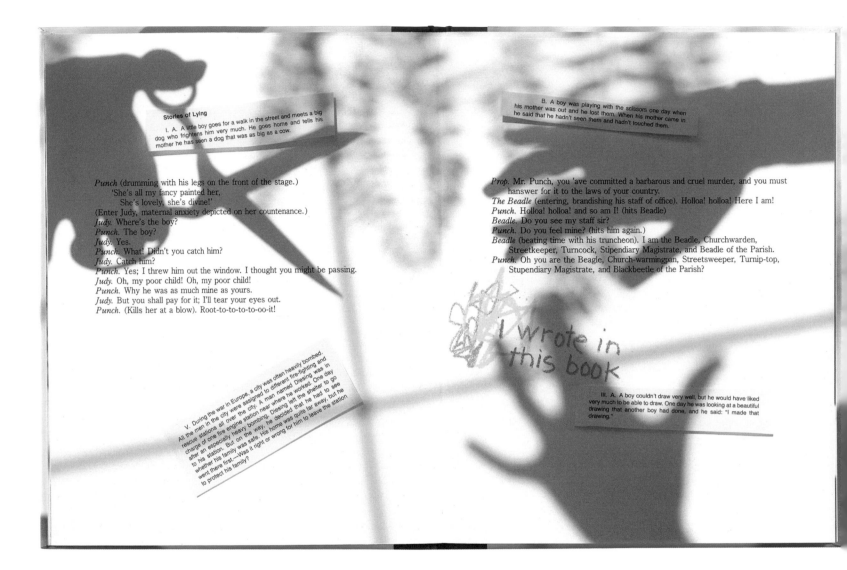

Fig. 152. Janet Zweig from *Heinz and Judy: A Play* ([S.l.]: Janet Zweig, 1985). Photomechanical reproduction.

List of Contributors

Walter Bareiss, Art Collector, Stamford, Connecticut, and Munich. President of COBAR Management, Inc. Member of the Visiting Committee for 20th-Century Art at The Metropolitan Museum of Art, New York; member of the Governing Board of the Yale University Art Gallery, New Haven; member of the Committee for Prints and Illustrated Books at The Museum of Modern Art, New York; member of the Münchner Galerie-Verein; and member of various other art institutions. Collections assembled with his wife, Molly Bareiss, include African art, Greek vases, Modern paintings, Japanese ceramics, Modern illustrated books, and Italian majolica.

Mei-mei Berssenbrugge, Poet, New York City and Abiquiu, New Mexico. Publications include *Random Possession* (1979); *The Heat Bird* (1983); *Hiddenness,* with Richard Tuttle (1987); *Empathy* (1989); *Sphericity,* with Richard Tuttle (1993); *Endocrinology,* with Kiki Smith (1997); *Four Year Old Girl* (1998); and *Nest* (2002).

May Castleberry, Editor of Library Council Publications, The Museum of Modern Art, New York. Formerly Editor of the Artists and Writers Series and Librarian at the Whitney Museum of American Art, New York. Publications and exhibitions include *My Pretty Pony,* images by Barbara Kruger, words by Stephen King (1989); *Fables, Fantasies, and Everyday Things* (1994); *On the Music of the Spheres,* photographs by Linda Connor and poetry by Charles Simic (1996); *Perpetual Mirage* (1996); *Rockwell Kent by Night* (1997); and *Notes on a Room,* essays by Gini Alhadeff and Brendan Gill, poetry by Daniel Halpern, images by Richard Artschwager, Louise Lawler, and Sol LeWitt (1998).

Riva Castleman, Chief Curator Emerita, Department of Prints and Illustrated Books, and former Deputy Director, The Museum of Modern Art, New York. Publications and exhibitions include *Prints of the Twentieth Century: A History* (1976); *American Impressions: Prints since Pollock* (1985); *Prints from Blocks: Gauguin to Now* (1985); *Jasper Johns: A Print Retrospective* (1986); *The Prints of Andy Warhol* (1990); *Seven Master Printmakers* (1991); *A Century of Artists Books* (1994); and *Toulouse-Lautrec: Posters and Prints from the Collection of Irene and Howard Stein* (1998).

Johanna Drucker, Robertson Professor of Media Studies, University of Virginia, Charlottesville. Independent Book Artist. Publications and exhibitions include *The Word Made Flesh* (1989); *Simulant Portrait* (1990); *Luminous Volumes: Granary's New Vision of the Book* (1993); *The Alphabetic Labyrinth: The Letters in History and Imagination* (1995); *The Century of Artists' Books* (1995); *The Corona Palimpsest: Present Tensions of the Book* (1995); *The Dual Muse: The Writer as Artist, the Artist as Writer,* with William H. Gass (1997); *Figuring the Word: Essays on Books, Writing and Visual Poetics* (1998); *The Next Word: Text and/as Image and/as Design and/as Meaning* (1998); and *Night Crawlers on the Web* (2000).

Eleanor M. Garvey, Philip Hofer Curator Emerita, Department of Printing and Graphic Arts, Houghton Library of the Harvard College Library, Cambridge, Massachusetts. Publications and exhibitions include *The Artist & the Book, 1860–1960, in Western Europe and the United States* (1961); *The Arts of the French Book, 1900–1965, Illustrated Books of the School of Paris,* with Peter A. Wick (1967); *The Turn of a Century, 1885–1910,* with Anne B. Smith and Peter A. Wick (1970); *The Philip Hofer Bequest* (1988); *Artist Books of the Kaldewey Press* (1988); and *An Exhibition of Limited Edition Books by Angela Lorenz* (1994).

Michael Semff, Director, Staatliche Graphische Sammlung, Munich. Publications and exhibitions include *Willi Baumeister: Zeichnungen* (1996); *Brice Marden: Work Books, 1964–1995* (1997); *Von Baselitz bis Winters: Vermächtnis Bernd Mittelsten Scheid* (1998); *Charles Despiau: Zeichnungen* (1998); *Giorgio Morandi: die letzten Zeichnungen* (1999); *Sigmar Polke: Arbeiten auf Papier 1963–1974* (1999); and *Édouard Vuillard, les tasses noires: Arbeiten auf Papier 1903–1928* (2001).

Kiki Smith, Independent Visual Artist, New York City. Recent exhibitions and catalogues include *Kiki Smith, Silent Work* (1992); *The Fourth Day Destruction of Birds* (1997); *Kiki Smith: Convergence* (1997); *Kiki Smith's Dowry Book* (1997); *Kiki Smith,* text by Helaine Posner (1998); *Werke, 1988–1996* (1998); *Kiki Smith: All Creatures Great and Small,* text by Carsten Ahrens (1999); *My Nature: Works with Paper by Kiki Smith,* text by Olivia Lahs-Gonzales (1999); and *Kiki Smith: Telling Tales,* text by Helaine Posner (2001).

PHOTOGRAPHY CREDITS

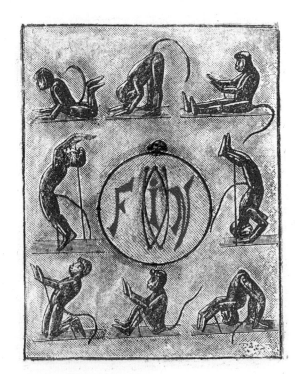